STUDIES IN MODERN BRITISH RELIGIOUS HISTORY

Volume 24

SYON ABBEY AND ITS BOOKS
READING, WRITING AND RELIGION,
c.1400–1700

STUDIES IN MODERN BRITISH RELIGIOUS HISTORY

ISSN: 1464–6625

General editors

Stephen Taylor
Arthur Burns
Kenneth Fincham

This series aims to differentiate 'religious history' from the narrow confines of church history, investigating not only the social and cultural history of religion, but also theological, political and institutional themes, while remaining sensitive to the wider historical context; it thus advances an understanding of the importance of religion for the history of modern Britain, covering all periods of British history since the Reformation.

Previously published volumes in this series are listed at the back of this volume.

SYON ABBEY AND ITS BOOKS

READING, WRITING AND RELIGION,

c.1400–1700

Edited by E. A. Jones and Alexandra Walsham

THE BOYDELL PRESS

First published 2010
The Boydell Press, Woodbridge

ISBN 978–1–84383–547–9

The Boydell Press is an imprint of Boydell & Brewer Ltd
PO Box 9, Woodbridge, Suffolk IP12 3DF, UK
and of Boydell & Brewer Inc.
668 Mt Hope Avenue, Rochester, NY 14620, USA
website: www.boydellandbrewer.com

A CIP catalogue record for this book is available
from the British Library

The publisher has no responsibility for the continued existence or accuracy of
URLs for external or third-party internet websites referred to in this book,
and does not guarantee that any content on such websites is, or will remain,
accurate or appropriate.

This publication is printed on acid-free paper

Printed in Great Britain by
CPI Antony Rowe, Chippenham and Eastbourne

CONTENTS

IV History and Memory

ILLUSTRATIONS

Figure 1.1: Thomas Robinson, *The anatomie of the English nunnery at Lisbon in Portugall: dissected and laid open by one that was sometime a yonger brother of the covent* (London, 1630), title page. © The British Library Board. All rights reserved. British Library shelfmark RB23.a.9192.

Figure 1.2: William Bonde, *Here begynneth a deuout treatyse in Englysshe, called the Pylgrimage of perfection very p[ro]fitable for all christen people to rede: and in especiall, to all relygious p[er]sons moche necessary* (London, 1526), sig. A6v. © The British Library Board. All rights reserved. British Library shelfmark G.11740.

Figure 1.3: *Here begynneth the orcharde of Syon in the whiche is conteyned the reuelacyons of seynt [sic] Katheryne of Sene, with ghostly fruytes [and] precyous plantes for the helthe of mannes soule* (London, [1519]), sig. A1v. © The British Library Board. All rights reserved.

Figure 4.1: *Here begynneth the orcharde of Syon in the whiche is conteyned the reuelacyons of seynt [sic] Katheryne of Sene, with ghostly fruytes [and] precyous plantes for the helthe of mannes soule* (London, [1519]), title page, sig. A1r. © The British Library Board. All rights reserved. British Library shelfmark C.11.b.6.

Figure 4.2: William Bonde, *Here begynneth a deuout treatyse in Englysshe, called the Pylgrimage of perfection very p[ro]fitable for all christen people to rede: and in especiall, to all relygious p[er]sons moche necessary* (London, 1526), sig. A1v. © The British Library Board. All rights reserved. British Library shelfmark G.11740.

Figure 4.3: *Here after folowith the boke callyd the myrroure of Oure Lady very necessary for all relygyous persones* (London, 1530), sig. A1r. © The British Library Board. All rights reserved. British Library shelfmark C.11.b.8.

Figure 6.1: N. Caussin, *The holy court fourth tome* (Rouen, 1638). Exeter University Library shelfmark Syon Abbey 1638/CAU/X. By permission of the Abbess of Syon Abbey, South Brent, Devon.

Figure 6.2: Exeter University Library, Syon Abbey unnumbered MS: 'English Saintes of Kinges & Bishopps in the primitive times of the Catholique Church when our Countrie of England was governed by Heptarchie of seaven Kinges translated out of Surius Carthusianus his eight tomes of the lifes of Saintes by revrd Father Brother Bibianus alias John Bibian moncke of the holy order of St Birgitt our Holy Mother. Revived by the helpe & industrie of P Frey Estevan of the conception Moncke of the same order on the 41 year of his profession being 69 yeares of age, borne in 1593 the yeare before this monasterie removed to Lisbon 1594', title page of vol. 2. By permission of the Abbess of Syon Abbey, South Brent, Devon.

Figure 7.1: The Syon Martiloge: British Library, MS Additional 22, 285, fol. 55v: (Septembris). © The British Library Board. All rights reserved.

ACKNOWLEDGEMENTS

This volume arose out of a conference on 'Syon Abbey and its Books' held at the University of Exeter in October 2005 to mark the deposit for safe-keeping in the University's library of medieval and early modern manuscripts from Syon Abbey. It also commemorates the further deposit of some 150 manuscripts dating from the sixteenth through to the twentieth century, which took place in March 2009.

We are indebted to the British Academy for its generous support of the conference. The editors are grateful to all who attended, offered papers, and participated in the lively discussions that followed the sessions. We thank the contributors to the volume for responding to the invitation to contribute to the collection and for tolerating considerable delays. We also wish to thank Jessica Gardner, Special Collections Librarian at the University of Exeter, and Charlotte Berry and Christine Faunch, Archivists, for their support and assistance over many years. At Boydell & Brewer, we are indebted to Caroline Palmer for her interest in the project at the outset and for the exemplary patience she has demonstrated in the intervening years.

Chapter 3 is reprinted by permission of the University of Notre Dame, from *Religion and Literature*, 37.2 (Summer 2005).

We dedicate this collection to the Abbess and nuns of Syon Abbey. We thank them for entrusting the care of their precious books and manuscripts to the library of the University of Exeter.

E. A. Jones and Alexandra Walsham
(University of Exeter)

NOTES ON CONTRIBUTORS

Virginia R. Bainbridge is Editor of the Victoria County History of Wiltshire at the University of the West of England, Bristol. Her research focuses on the Reformation. She has developed a detailed knowledge of the effects of social and religious change of that era from studying local institutions. Her doctoral work was published as *Gilds in the Medieval Countryside c. 1350–1558* (1996). Since then her main research interest has been the history of Syon Abbey, c.1415–1600. She has published a number of articles on this subject and is preparing further publications.

Caroline Bowden is Research Fellow and Project Manager of the 'Who were the Nuns?' project funded by the AHRC at Queen Mary University of London, which examines the membership of the English convents in exile 1600–1800 and their supporting networks (http://wwtn.history.qmul.ac.uk). In 2001 she established the research network 'History of Women Religious of Britain and Ireland' with Dr Carmen Mangion. She has published a number of papers on women's education and learning both inside and outside the convents, including 'The Library of Mildred Cooke Cecil' in *The Library* (2005) and 'Women in Educational Spaces' in Laura Knoppers (ed.), *The Cambridge Companion to Early Modern Women's Writing* (2009).

Peter Cunich is Associate Professor in History at the University of Hong Kong. His previous publications have been in the areas of Tudor state finance, late medieval English monasticism (especially the Benedictines and Carthusians), and the dissolution of the monasteries, and include an essay on the experiences of the ex-religious in James G. Clark (ed.), *The Religious Orders in Pre-Reformation England* (2002). He is director of the University of Hong Kong's Monastic Database Project.

Claes Gejrot is the editor-in-chief of the national Swedish medieval charters series, *Diplomatarium Suecanum*, at the National Archives in Stockholm. He is also attached to Stockholm University as an associate professor of Latin. His research has centred upon editing medieval Latin texts, with a special focus on Birgittine studies. At present he is working on a first edition of the Syon Abbey *Martiloge* (with biographical texts by Virginia Bainbridge). Among his publications are *Diarium Vadstenense* (1988 and 1996), *Diplomata Novevallensia*

(1994), *Poetry for the Occasion* (1999). *The Fifteen Oes* (in *The Medieval Translator* 7, 2000) and *Diplomatarium Suecanum* (1991–2009).

Vincent Gillespie is J.R.R. Tolkien Professor of English Literature and Language at the University of Oxford, and a Fellow of Lady Margaret Hall. He works on catechetical, devotional and contemplative texts produced in England in the Middle Ages. He is also interested in medieval literary theory, translation, and the psychology of literary response. Much of his work has focused on the Birgittine house of Syon Abbey, and in particular on the books and spirituality of the brethren. His edition of the brethren's library *registrum* was published in 2001 as part of the *Corpus of British Medieval Library Catalogues*. More recently he has been exploring the orthodox reform movement in fifteenth-century England. A selection of his articles will be published in 2010 as *Looking in Holy Books: Essays on Late-Medieval Religious Writing in England*, as will his co-edited *Cambridge Companion to Medieval English Mysticism*.

C. Annette Grisé is Associate Professor of English and Cultural Studies at McMaster University. Her main areas of research interest are the cult of continental female mystics in late medieval England, and Middle English devotional manuscripts and early printed books associated with religious women. She is co-editing a collection of essays on devotional reading in late-medieval England, and has written recent essays on topics such as devotional manuscripts associated with Syon Abbey and fifteenth-century women's poetry. She is completing a chapter on Catherine of Siena for volume one of the History of British Women's Writing series by Palgrave.

Ann M. Hutchison is currently Chair of the English Department of Glendon College, York University, Toronto, and an Associate Fellow of the Pontifical Institute of Mediaeval Studies. Her research on women's literacy and late medieval spirituality led her to St Birgitta and the English house of her order, Syon Abbey. In 'What the Nun's Read: Literary Evidence from the English Bridgettine House, Syon Abbey' (*Mediaeval Studies*, 57 (1995), 205–22), she noted that a number of the Choir Sisters read Latin as well as vernacular texts. Later, her edition of the Life of Marie Champney, a post-Dissolution nun, sparked her interest in the history of Syon Abbey up to the present time.

E. A. Jones is Senior Lecturer in English Medieval Literature and Culture at the University of Exeter. He works on late-medieval religious culture, with particular interests in hermits, anchorites, and followers of other non-regular vocations, and mystical and devotional literature. He has edited *The 'Exhortacion' from Disce Mori*, Middle English Texts 36 (2006) and *The Medieval Mystical Tradition in England*, Exeter Symposium VII (2004). A long-term commitment is the revision of Rotha Mary Clay's *Hermits and Anchorites of England*. He is currently working on a book on hermits in late-medieval England and planning the eighth Exeter Symposium.

Claire Walker is Senior Lecturer in early modern European history at the University of Adelaide. She has worked extensively on the exiled female religious cloisters in France and the southern Netherlands in the seventeenth century. Her publications include *Gender and Politics in Early Modern Europe: English Convents in France and the Low Countries* (2003) and, most recently, she co-edited with David Lemmings, *Moral Panics, the Press and the Law in Early Modern England* (2009).

Alexandra Walsham is Professor of Reformation History at the University of Exeter. Her research interests centre on the religious and cultural history of early modern Britain and she has published widely in this field. She is the author of *Church Papists: Catholicism, Conformity and Confessional Polemic in Early Modern England* (1993); *Providence in Early Modern England* (1999); *Charitable Hatred: Tolerance and Intolerance in England 1500–1700* (2006); and *The Reformation of the Landscape: Religion, Identity and Memory in Early Modern Britain and Ireland* (forthcoming). She is also the editor (with Julia Crick) of *The Uses of Script and Print 1300–1700* (2004) and (with Peter Marshall) of *Angels in the Early Modern World* (2006).

ABBREVIATIONS

ARCR	A. F. Allison and D. M. Rogers, *The Contemporary Printed Literature of the English Counter-Reformation between 1558 and 1640: An Annotated Catalogue,* 2 vols (Aldershot, 1989–94)
BL	British Library, London
CRS	Catholic Record Society
De Hamel, *Syon Abbey*	Christopher de Hamel, *Syon Abbey: The Library of the Bridgettine Nuns and their Peregrinations after the Reformation*, Roxburghe Club (Otley, 1991)
EETS	Early English Text Society
EHR	*English Historical Review*
Eklund (ed.), *Regula Salvatoris*	Sten Eklund (ed.), *Sancta Birgitta: opera minora. I, Regula Salvatoris*, Samlingar utgivna av Svenska fornskriftsallskapet, Andra serien, Latinska skrifter, Band 8 (Lund, 1975)
Emden, *BRUO to 1500*	B. Emden, *A Biographical Register of the University of Oxford to A.D. 1500*, 3 vols. (Oxford, 1957)
Emden, *BRUO 1501–1540*	B. Emden, *A Biographical Register of the University of Oxford A.D. 1501–1540* (Oxford, 1974)
Emden, *BRUC*	A. B. Emden, *Biographical Register of the University of Cambridge* (Cambridge, 1963)
Gillespie, *Syon Abbey Catalogue*	Vincent Gillespie (ed.), *Syon Abbey*, with *The Libraries of the Carthusians*, ed. A. I. Doyle, Corpus of British Medieval Library Catalogues 9 (London, 2001)
Hogg (ed.), *Rewyll*	James Hogg (ed.), *The Rewyll of Seynt Sauioure and Other Middle English Brigittine Legislative Texts*, vols 2–4, Salzburger Studien zur Anglistik und Amerikanistik (Salzburg, 1978–80), vol. 2
Hogg (ed.), *Laybrothers' Additions*	James Hogg (ed.), *The Rewyll of Seynt Sauioure and Other Middle English Brigittine Legislative Texts*, vols 2–4, Salzburger Studien zur Anglistik und Amerikanistik (Salzburg, 1978–80), vol. 3

Hogg (ed.), *Sisters' Additions*	James Hogg (ed.), *The Rewyll of Seynt Sauioure and Other Middle English Brigittine Legislative Texts*, vols 2–4, Salzburger Studien zur Anglistik und Amerikanistik (Salzburg, 1978–80), vol. 4
JEH	*Journal of Ecclesiastical History*
LP	*Calendar of Letters and Papers, Foreign and Domestic, of the Reign of Henry VIII* (London, 1864–1932)
ODNB	*Oxford Dictionary of National Biography*, online edition (Oxford, 2004–) [http://www.oxforddnb.com]
STC	A. W. Pollard and G. R. Redgrave, *A Short-Title Catalogue of Books Printed in England, Scotland and Ireland and of English Books Printed Abroad 1475–1640*, 2nd edn, rev. and enlarged by W. A. Jackson, F. S. Ferguson and K. F. Pantzer, 3 vols (London and Oxford, 1976–91)
TNA	The National Archives, Kew, London

SYON ABBEY: AN OUTLINE CHRONOLOGY

1391	Canonization of St Bridget of Sweden
1406	Henry Lord Fitzhugh visits Vadstena
1415	Foundation of Syon Abbey at Twickenham (3 March)
1420	First professions at Syon (21 April)
1425	Papal bull grants *vincula* indulgence to pilgrims visiting Syon
1425	*Mare Anglicanum*, papal bull asserting the rights and privileges of Syon, and establishing its independence within the Order
1431	Community moves to new site in Isleworth and is re-enclosed
1481	Thomas Betson, Syon librarian, resigns as rector of Wimbish prior to entering the monastery
1488	Consecration of abbey church
1500	Betson's *Profitable treatise* printed by De Worde
1533	Syon named in the trial of Elizabeth Barton, the 'Holy Maid of Kent'
1535	Execution of Richard Reynolds
1539	Act for the Dissolution of the Greater Monasteries; expulsion of community and granting of pensions
1545–1563	Sessions of the Council of Trent
1557	Marian restoration under Abbess Katherine Palmer
1559	Community begins its exile in the Low Countries
1576	Death of Abbess Katherine Palmer
1580	After Sack of Mechelen, community moves to France and sets up in Rouen
1584	Profession of Seth Foster, and his election as Confessor General
1594	Having fled France, community lands at Lisbon on 20 May, initially staying with nuns of Esperança
1597	Syon taken under direct protection of Holy See
1599	Community established in their own premises at Sitio de Mocambo
1623	Petition of the Bridgettines in Lisbon to Philip III against the backdrop of the negotiations for a match between Prince Charles and the Infanta Maria
1640	Portugal declares independence from Spain
1651	Convent (and most of the sisters' papers) destroyed by fire
1695	Death of George Griffin, Confessor General and the last brother of Syon

1755	Lisbon earthquake destroys monastery
1791	Catholic Relief Act permitted Catholic worship in England
1809	Failed attempt at return to England under Abbess Dorothy Halford
1840	Publication of Aungier's *History and Antiquities of Syon Monastery*
1861	Return of community to England, initially at recently vacated convent at Spettisbury (Dorset)
1886	Beatification of Richard Reynolds
1887	Community moves to Chudleigh
1925	Community moves to Marley House, South Brent
1970	Canonization of Richard Reynolds
1990	Community moves to specially-designed accommodation in converted stables of Marley House
	Syon's collection of pre-1850 books is deposited with University of Exeter Special Collections
2004	The community's medieval and some early-modern manuscripts are deposited with University of Exeter Special Collections
2009	A further 180 manuscripts, sixteenth- to twentieth-century, are deposited with University of Exeter Special Collections

INTRODUCTION

Syon Abbey and its Books:
Origins, Influences and Transitions

E. A. JONES AND ALEXANDRA WALSHAM

Remembrynge þat god is there present and seeth what ye do Lete none
see you from the seruyce of god or vnoccupyed. In redynge of
prophetes epystles, gospelles, sayntes lyues, & other dedes of vertue
doynge, hauynge euer bokes in your handes, studyenge or wrytynge,
þat people seynge you may saye. Beholde here the seruaunt of god, &
the lanternes of the worlde.

So wrote Thomas Betson, deacon, librarian and author of Syon Abbey in his
Ryght Profytable Treatyse published by Wynkyn de Worde in 1500.[1] A devotional compilation incorporating basic catechetical material alongside supplications and exhortations to the cloistered sisters of the Bridgettine house he
served,[2] Betson's advice was taken to heart by a long succession of nuns of
this contemplative order, as well as by a wider constituency of devout lay
people who sought to mimic their piety. Reading and prayer were intricately
linked in the religious lives of the women and men who entered this double
monastery in the pre-Reformation period. Books remained central to the
community during its travails in exile after the dissolution of the monasteries
and the Protestant Reformation, as the library they lovingly preserved and
carried back with them to England in the nineteenth century reveals. Among
its many treasures is a tiny worn leather-bound book filled with meditations
for each day of the week written by the Tridentine archbishop of Milan,
Charles Borromeo, together with *The contract and testament of the soule*

---

[1]   Thomas Betson, *Here begynneth a ryght profytable treatyse co[m]pendiously drawen out of
many [and] dyuers wrytynges of holy men, to dyspose men to be vertuously occupied in theyr
myndes [and] prayers* ([Westminster, 1500]), sig. C4v.
[2]   Throughout, we have preferred the fully anglicised 'Bridget' and 'Bridgettine' over 'Birgit'
and 'Birgittine'.

1

(1638) which he invited each Christian to enter into for his or her spiritual health. The Syon copy is a poignant living artefact, bearing the signature of a certain Sister Mary, and incorporating, in the blank pages bound at the end, a series of three handwritten 'Exercises or Prayers to be devoutly said before the most Blessed Sacrament for the continual performance of your three most solemn Vows' of poverty, obedience and chastity, together with a further supplication in French. It allows us an intimate glimpse of an expatriate community whose adversities were tempered by an earnest conviction that God would eventually restore Catholicism in their native land.[3]

Together, Betson's exhortation and Borromeo's testament provide a convenient point of entry to the theme of this collection of essays: the interconnections between late medieval and post-Reformation monastic history and the rapidly evolving world of communication, learning, reading and books. Taking Syon Abbey as its focus, the volume represents the convergence of two scholarly trends. It builds on a burgeoning literature illuminating the vibrancy of religious culture and institutions on the eve of the Reformation and an equally substantial body of research on manifestations of early modern Catholic renewal in England and Europe. Simultaneously, it both reflects and extends a surge of scholarly interest in the implications of the spread of literacy and the gradual and uneven transition from manuscript to print between the fourteenth and the seventeenth centuries. Transcending traditional disciplinary boundaries, the book brings together historians and literary scholars to trace the fortunes of the Bridgettines over this critical period and to examine the various ways in which reading and writing shaped its identity and defined its experience. In the process, it seeks to raise and address larger questions about the processes and consequences of religious, intellectual and cultural change in late medieval and early modern England. This introduction explores the origins of the community, situates Syon Abbey in its wider historical environment, and sketches the scholarly frameworks within and against which the following essays should be read.

St Bridget of Sweden and the Origins of Syon Abbey

Settled today at South Brent in Devon, Syon Abbey is the only English religious house that can trace its history in an unbroken line from the Middle Ages to the present. It was one of the few English monasteries to survive the Dissolution with some form of community intact, and one of a mere handful

---

3   Charles Borromeo, *The contract and testament of the soule* (St Omer, 1638), Exeter University Library shelfmark Syon Abbey 1638/CON.

2

to be restored briefly under Mary I. Even before it attained that unlooked-for distinction, however, Syon was exceptional, as the only English foundation of the Birgittine or Bridgettine order.

The origins of the idea for an English Bridgettine house can be located quite precisely.[4] In October 1406, Philippa, daughter of Henry IV, married Eric of Pomerania, king of Sweden, at Lund. Among her entourage was Henry FitzHugh, lord of Ravensworth, a committed supporter of Henry IV and subsequently chamberlain to Henry V. He was also a man of piety, who would later go on crusade in Prussia and the Levant and attend the Council of Constance.[5] In November 1406, he accompanied Philippa on a visit to Vadstena, the mother-house of the Order of the Most Holy Saviour.

The order was the creation of St Bridget of Sweden, a noble, married laywoman and mother, and prophet and visionary, who died in 1373 and was canonised in 1391.[6] It was a double order, whose monasteries housed both women and men, though Bridget described it as being 'first and foremost for women'. This is reflected in her specifications for the make-up of a fully populated Bridgettine monastery: sixty nuns, thirteen priests, four deacons and eight lay brothers. The numbers were symbolic: the priests represented the twelve apostles and Paul and the deacons the four Doctors of the Church; the total of eighty-five recalled the thirteen apostles plus the seventy-two disciples commissioned by Christ in Luke 10. The community was under the spiritual guidance of one of the priests, the Confessor General, but final authority was reserved to the Abbess. Nuns and brothers lived in separate courts under strict enclosure. Although they shared a single abbey church, separation was maintained by a unique 'double-decker' arrangement, the brothers sitting in the lower choir, and the sisters in an upper storey, 'vndir the rofe'. The order technically followed the Rule of St Augustine, but most details of its observance came from the *Regula Salvatoris*, a rule revealed to Bridget by Christ himself in a sequence of visions.[7] The nuns were to dedicate

---

[4]   This outline of the foundation of Syon Abbey is based on the following principal sources: G. J. Aungier, *The History and Antiquities of Syon Monastery, the Parish of Isleworth, and the Chapelry of Hounslow* (London, 1840); Margaret Deanesly, *The Incendium Amoris of Richard Rolle of Hampole* (Manchester, 1915), pp. 91–131; J. R. Fletcher, *The Story of the English Bridgettines of Syon Abbey* (Bristol, 1933); F. R. Johnston, 'Syon Abbey', in *The Victoria History of the County of Middlesex*, vol. 1 (Oxford, 1911), pp. 182–91. They in turn are primarily dependent on London, British Library, MS Add. 22285, the *Syon Martiloge*, for which see further Claes Gejrot's essay below.

[5]   See the entry by A. C. Reeves in *ODNB*.

[6]   The chief source for this summary is Bridget Morris, *St Birgitta of Sweden* (Woodbridge, 1999).

[7]   The standard edition is Eklund (ed.), *Regula Salvatoris*. See also the facsimile editions of

themselves entirely to meditation and contemplation, with a special devotion to the Virgin Mary; the brothers provided for their spiritual needs, but combined this with a more outward-facing role that included regular public preaching. Papal approval for the order was first given in 1378, though controversy persisted (especially over the question of double monasteries) for another fifty years, and final and unequivocal approval did not come until 1435.[8]

Vadstena, a former royal palace, had been granted to Bridget for the establishing of a monastery in 1346, soon after the death of her husband, though building work began only in 1369.[9] The abbey was formally consecrated in 1384.[10] At the time of FitzHugh's visit, Vadstena was mother-house of an order that had already spread through Scandinavia and north-east Europe, and had also become established in Italy.[11] Evidently inspired by what he saw, FitzHugh declared his intention of founding a Bridgettine house in England, promising his manor of Cherry Hinton (Cambridgeshire) towards its endowment.[12] At his request Vadstena sent two brothers to England to help with the foundation. But the project stalled. It met with warm words from Henry IV, who stated his desire to be 'the special friend and protector of the order', but nothing more tangible.[13] In 1409 a scheme was floated for the Bridgettines to take over the struggling St Nicholas's Hospital in York, but this failed to take off.[14]

With the accession of Henry V in 1413, however, the project received

the Latin *Regula* and its Middle English translation by Hogg (ed.), *Rewyll*. Specifications for the numbers of nuns and brothers are given in chapter 10. Quotations from the *Rewyll* will usually be from the Middle English text. Abbreviations are expanded silently, and modern word-division is imposed. This quotation: *ibid.*, p. 33. There are two important studies of the Bridgettine legislation: Roger Ellis, *Syon Abbey: The Spirituality of the English Bridgettines*, Analecta Cartusiana 68:2 (Salzburg, 1984), and M. B. Tait, 'The Brigittine Monastery of Syon (Middlesex) with Special Reference to its Monastic Usages' (unpublished Oxford DPhil thesis, 1975).

[8] Morris, *St Birgitta*, pp. 161–2; Hans Cnattingius, *Studies in the Order of St. Bridget of Sweden I: The Crisis in the 1420s* (Stockholm, 1963); and Peter Cunich's essay, below, pp. 55–6.

[9] Morris, *St Birgitta*, p. 86.

[10] *Ibid.*, p. 168.

[11] Tore Nyberg, 'The Development of the Order of St Birgitta', in *Birgitta: Una santa svedese* (Rome, 1974), pp. 135–79.

[12] Claes Gejrot (ed.), *Diarium Vadstenense: The Memorial Book of Vadstena Abbey* (Stockholm, 1988), pp. 150–1; Deanesly, *Incendium Amoris*, pp. 97–9.

[13] Henry's letter to Vadstena of 1408, promising to be the order's *fundator et tutor spiritualis* in England, is printed by Elin Andersson, 'Birgittines in Contact: Early Correspondence Between England and Vadstena', *Eranos*, 102 (2004), 1–29 (pp. 12–13).

[14] Eric Graff, 'A Neglected Episode in the Prehistory of Syon Abbey: The Letter of Katillus Thornberni in Uppsala University Library Pappersbrev 1410–1420', *Mediaeval Studies*, 63

decisive new impetus. Henry incorporated the idea of a Bridgettine foundation into his ambitious plans for a complex of monasteries surrounding the
refurbished royal palace at Sheen – 'almost an Escorial', as Jeremy Catto
describes it.[15] The old notion, given currency by Shakespeare, that these
monastic foundations were made in expiation for the death of Richard II (or,
alternatively, of Archbishop Scrope) has no firm evidence behind it, but there
are nevertheless grounds for seeing them as part of a strategy for legitimising
the Lancastrian regime. Founding a house of the Bridgettine order was in
keeping with Henry's personal piety and his sense of sacral kingship, his
interest in monastic reform and zeal against heresy, combined with what
seems to have been a deep and genuine devotion to Bridget herself. The will
he drew up in 1415 as he prepared for the great battle at Agincourt appealed
directly to the saint by name. It is by no means irrelevant that her visions
appeared to vindicate his claim to the French throne.[16] Henry laid the foundation stone in person at Twickenham (Middlesex) on 22 February 1415, and
issued the foundation charter for 'The Monastery of St Saviour and St Bridget
of Syon' on 3 March.[17] The endowment was large, and the lands widely
dispersed: there were holdings in most counties of southern England, from
Kent to St Michael's Mount off the Cornish coast, and as far north as
Lincolnshire and Lancashire. Many had been the property of the alien prio-
ries, dissolved by Parliament in 1414.[18] Henry underwrote the revenues in the
sum of 1,000 marks per annum, any shortfall to be made up from the Exche-
quer. Syon became the richest nunnery in England and, with the exception

---

(2001), 323–36. The projected monastery may, however, already have been known by the
name 'Syon'; see p. 327.

[15] Jeremy Catto, 'Religious Change under Henry V', in G. L. Harriss (ed.), *Henry V: The Practice of Kingship* (Oxford, 1985), pp. 97–115, at p. 110. Syon was to be complemented by houses
of the Carthusian and Celestine orders, though in the event the latter was never built. Sheen
Charterhouse, however, maintained a close relationship with Syon up until the Dissolution.

[16] Henry's motives are explored by Neil Beckett, 'St. Bridget, Henry V and Syon Abbey', in
James Hogg (ed.), *Studies in St Birgitta and the Birgittine Order*, 2 vols (Salzburg, 1993),
ii.125–50. See also Nancy Bradley Warren, 'Kings, Saints and Nuns: Gender, Religion and
Authority in the Reign of Henry V', *Viator*, 30 (1999), 307–22. For Shakespeare's 'Two chan-
tries where the sad and solemn priests / Sing still for Richard's soul', see *Henry V*, IV.i.307–8,
in J. H. Walter (ed.), *King Henry V*, Arden Shakespeare (London, 1954).

[17] It is printed in William Dugdale *et al.*, *Monasticon Anglicanum*, 6 vols (London, 1817–30),
vi.542–3.

[18] For the community's subsequent uneasiness on this point, see Beckett, 'St. Bridget, Henry V
and Syon Abbey', p. 133. In fact, as Robert Dunning notes, 'Many of these estates had already
been granted to farm for terms of years or for life, so that the grants to Syon were, in effect,
reversions', and the abbey only gradually came into full possession of them. 'The Muniments
of Syon Abbey: Their Administration and Migration in the Fifteenth and Sixteenth Centuries',
Bulletin of the Institute of Historical Research, 37 (1964), 103–11 (p. 103).

only of the long established Benedictine houses, the wealthiest monastery for either women or men.

At Henry's request, Vadstena sent a party of nuns, postulants and brothers to England to help set up the new monastery. The pope confirmed the foundation in 1418, building work commenced, and the *Syon Additions* to the Bridgettine Rule, designed to adapt the usage of the order to the new foundation's particular circumstances, began to be drafted.[19] But it was not until five years after the foundation, on 21 April 1420, that the first professions were made, bringing to an end a period of gestation that had sometimes been stressful. The interim administration of Matilda Newton and William Alnwick was replaced, Joan North becoming Abbess and Thomas Fishbourne Confessor General, and they presided over an initial community comprising twenty-seven nuns, five priests, two deacons and three lay brothers.

A key date in Syon's early history is 1425. In this year, Pope Martin V issued the bull *Mare Anglicanum*. This was in part a confirmation for the recently-founded English house's benefit of the bull *Mare Magnum* which had, in 1413, detailed the rights and privileges of the Bridgettine order. But it also gave Syon independence from Vadstena as mother-house, and released it from obedience to the general chapter of the order.[20] In a separate bull, the pope also extended to Syon the grant previously made to Bridget herself and her order of the *Vincula* indulgence – that is, the plenary remission otherwise available only to pilgrims to the Church of St Peter ad Vincula (Peter in Chains) at Rome. The indulgence was available on the feast of St Peter in Chains (1 August, Lammas) and during its octave. Plenary remission could also be obtained by visiting Syon on Mid-Lent Sunday, and remission for a third of all sins could be received by pilgrims visiting the monastery on any day of the year. Three hundred days of pardon could be obtained by hearing a sermon delivered by one of the brothers.[21] The poet John Awdelay celebrated Syon and its pardons early in its history and Margery Kempe was there for Lammas 1434.[22]

---

[19] Bridget had specified that such 'additions' should be drawn up for each new foundation. See Eklund (ed.), *Regula Salvatoris*, ch. 23. The additions for the sisters have been edited by Hogg (Hogg (ed.), *Sisters' Additions*); those for the lay brothers are in Hogg (ed.), *Laybrothers' Additions*. Only a fragment of the additions for the brothers survives; this is included in Hogg (ed.), *Rewyll*.

[20] See Cnattingius, *Studies*, pp. 148–55. Notwithstanding, relations with Vadstena seem to have continued cordially throughout the period.

[21] For a list of indulgences available at Syon, see Aungier, *History and Antiquities of Syon Monastery*, pp. 421–6. A Syon sermon on the general topic of indulgences, and including a list of those available at the monastery, is discussed by R. N. Swanson, *Indulgences in Late Medieval England* (Oxford, 2007), pp. 336–45.

[22] See Hutchison, below, p. 229.

In 1426 the growing community (which numbered fifty-four by 1428) took the decision to move from their original site in Twickenham, which had proved unhealthily marshy and was becoming cramped, to a spot a little further down river at Isleworth, more or less directly opposite Sheen Charterhouse.[23] Work began in February, and in November 1431 the community was translated and re-enclosed at its new location. Building continued for the rest of the century; the abbey church was consecrated in 1488, but further work – in brick and timber as well as Caen and other stone – was being done for another thirty years.[24] The scale and ambition of the project, evident from the surviving accounts, is also now being revealed by archaeological investigations at Syon Park: a church 'of astonishing size' that was 'one of the greatest buildings in late medieval England, and one of the highlights of the royal Thames in the Lancastrian, Yorkist and early Tudor periods'.[25]

But by the 1550s it was gone, partly reworked but mostly razed and replaced by the Protector Somerset's private residence, Syon House. The story of Syon's suppression – of the ailing Fewterer, the yielding Copynger, the principled Whitford, and the heroic Reynolds – is recounted in Peter Cunich's chapter. The abbey was never formally surrendered but it fell under a praemunire. In November 1539, the community (numbering fifty-six women and seventeen men) dispersed, but did not disband, many of them spending the next years in a number of smaller, household groupings.[26] In 1553, a group came together under Katherine Palmer, now Abbess, at the Bridgettine convent of Maria Troon, Termonde (Dendermonde) in the Netherlands, and resumed conventual life.[27] For the brief restoration under Mary in 1557, twenty sisters were re-enclosed along with Palmer, though the number of men had dwindled to two priests and a lay brother.

Within two years, the abbey was suppressed again. This time, the community remained together as they entered their long and arduous exile. Sharing a boat provided by Philip II of Spain with the nuns of Dartford, they sailed to

---

[23] Membership of the community in 1428 was recorded at the election of Robert Bell as Confessor General. See Tait, 'Brigittine Monastery of Syon', ii.241–51.

[24] R. W. Dunning, 'The Building of Syon Abbey', *Transactions of the Ancient Monument Society*, NS, 25 (1981), 16–26. We note without comment Bridget's stipulation that 'no monastery is to be inhabited until fully built'. Eklund (ed.), *Regula Salvatoris*, p. 164.

[25] Jonathan Foyle, 'Syon Park: Rediscovering Medieval England's Only Bridgettine monastery', *Current Archaeology*, 192 (2004), 550–5, quotations from pp. 554, 555.

[26] This period is also discussed in detail in Cunich's essay (Chapter 1). For the impact of the Dissolution on nunneries more generally, see Kathleen Cooke, 'The English Nuns and the Dissolution', in John Blair (ed.), *The Cloister and the World: Essays on Medieval History in Honour of Barbara Harvey* (Oxford, 1996), pp. 287–301.

[27] See, in addition to his essay here, Peter Cunich's life of Palmer in *ODNB*.

Antwerp, before travelling on to Termonde where they spent five years again as guests of the Bridgettines of Maria Troon.[28] Thus began the 'wanderings of Syon' – nearly forty years in which the community traversed a Netherlands and France in the grip of religious wars, setting up temporary home in various abandoned monasteries and townhouses, dogged by unhealthy conditions and harried by anti-monastic mobs. This period is discussed in detail in the chapters by Peter Cunich, Claire Walker and Ann Hutchison. When Rouen, where they had been since 1580, fell to Henry IV in 1592, the community decided to leave for Spain. Twenty-two nuns and eight brothers landed at Lisbon on 20 May 1594, and here they remained in relative stability (notwithstanding Portugal's declaration of independence in 1640, and the Lisbon earthquake of 1755) for the next two centuries. Although this period saw the death of the last Syon brother, the Confessor General George Griffin, in 1695, it also allowed the community to regroup and to resume many of those activities and observances that had characterised their pre-Reformation existence. The Bridgettine Rule and Syon Additions were revised to take into account the post-Tridentine monastic dispensation, not to mention a very different, southern climate;[29] and, as Caroline Bowden shows in her chapter, the convent set about acquiring, copying and reading books in earnest once again.

With the passing of the Catholic Relief Act in 1791, a return to England started to become a realistic prospect.[30] In 1809, at the height of the Napoleonic Wars, the greater part of the community under Abbess Dorothy Halford left Lisbon for England, taking valuables, relics and books with them. But within a few years this group had broken up and died out, its possessions (books included) being dispersed.[31] The four sisters and three lay sisters who had decided not to travel with the others formed the basis of the community that remained in Lisbon until 1861. When they did return to England they initially took over a recently vacated convent at Spettisbury (Dorset), before moving to Chudleigh (Devon) in 1887. In 1925 they were able to purchase from the Carew family Marley House, near South Brent, a little under twenty miles south-west of Chudleigh. Here they remain, although in 1990 the community moved out of the main house and into specially-designed

---

[28] Paul Lee, *Nunneries, Learning and Spirituality in Late Medieval English Society* (York, 2001), p. 128.

[29] These revisions are discussed in Ellis, *Spirituality of the English Bridgettines*, pp. 124–43.

[30] The best accounts of this period of Syon's history are Fletcher, *Story of the English Bridgettines*, pp. 141–64; and de Hamel, *Syon Abbey*, pp. 130–3. There is ample material, in the Fletcher Manuscripts and the abbey's archive, for a new history of Syon's return to England.

[31] The books lost to the community at this time included the *Syon Martiloge*, sold to the Earl of Shrewsbury, from whose estate it passed to the British Library. See Claes Gejrot's essay, Chapter 7, below.

accommodation in a converted group of farm buildings. At the time of writing, the community of Syon Abbey consists of the Lady Abbess and two sisters.

The Bridgettines of Syon and Transformations in Religious Life

In the historiography of the Dissolution of the monasteries, and of the English Reformation in general, Syon has figured as the exception that proves the rule. It has invariably been excluded from an enduringly influential narrative about the terminal decline of these religious institutions which finds its taproot in sixteenth-century Protestant polemic – a narrative that characterises late medieval monasticism as stagnant, corrupt and moribund, desperately out of touch with the spiritual needs of the wider populace surrounding it. The tradition of Syon's singularity goes back to the earliest sources. It is implied in the chronicler Charles Wriothesley's melancholic observation that the recently suppressed abbey had been 'the vertues howse of religion that was in England'.[32] Its echoes can be detected four centuries later in the elegiac third volume of Knowles's monumental *Religious Orders in England*. For Knowles, the English Bridgettines were, with the Carthusians and Observant Franciscans, one of 'the three families of religious that stood apart from the rest'; 'something unique in Tudor England', 'a group without parallel'. The Syon brothers (he is more or less entirely silent on the sisters) 'by their books, by their direction of a fervent and aristocratic nunnery, and by their influence as counsellors and confessors of leading laymen, were a power to be reckoned with in a religious world which contained all too few centres of enlightened piety'.[33] For A. G. Dickens too, the Bridgettines were one of the few beacons of hope in a landscape otherwise bedimmed by darkness and disillusionment: they stood apart from the lamentable 'spectacle of an uninspired and lukewarm establishment'.[34] G. R. Elton likewise classed Syon with the Carthusians and Observants as 'the most austere religious houses in the realm' against 'their laxer brethren'; Syon in particular 'commanded genuine

---

32 Charles Wriothesley, *A Chronicle of England during the Reigns of the Tudors from AD 1485 to 1559*, ed. W. D. Hamilton, Camden Society 1 (London, 1875), p. 109.
33 David Knowles, *The Religious Orders in England*, vol. 3, *The Tudor Age* (Cambridge, 1959), pp. 160, 215, 213. The Bridgettines were grouped with the Carthusians and Observants in the letter of the Black Monks to Wolsey of 1522: *ibid.*, pp. 159–60. For the substantial neglect of women religious in Knowles's work, see Joan Greatrex, 'After Knowles: Recent Perspectives in Monastic History', in James G. Clark (ed.), *The Religious Orders in Pre-Reformation England* (Woodbridge, 2002), pp. 35–47, at p. 45.
34 A. G. Dickens, *The English Reformation* (London, 1967 edn; first pub. 1964), p. 87.

regard even from Cromwell'.[35] And in her recent survey of Tudor England, Susan Brigden excepts the same three groups from the general declension and secularisation that for her characterise late medieval monasticism: 'Few truly religious houses remained', but Syon 'manifested a spirit of renewal'.[36]

Even on the other side of what has become, over the last twenty years, a major historiographical divide, Syon has tended to be valued more for the unusual extent of its connections with lay and para-monastic piety than for its place among the other religious houses of pre-Reformation England. For Christopher Harper-Bill its nuns broke out of the mould of those in other houses, which were generally 'the repository of young ladies surplus to the marriage-market whose conduct and demeanour often left much to be desired'. It sheltered a rare spiritual elite, which from the seclusion of the cloister, provided sympathetic inspiration for devout people outside it. Christopher Haigh, meanwhile, begins the first part of his *English Reformations*, polemically entitled 'A Church unchallenged', with an account of the publications of Richard Whitford, Syon brother, opponent of the Royal Supremacy, and author of a number of books that spoke to the spiritual aspirations of the pious laity in the 1530s.[37] That other architect of revisionism, Eamon Duffy, similarly concentrates on those literary initiatives issuing from Syon that looked towards an audience beyond the monastery's walls.[38] These foundational attempts to rediscover the vigour and viability of the old religion in the period of Reformation tended to do so by focusing almost exclusively on the parish: the place where ordinary believers practised and displayed their devotion to the Catholic faith. The religious orders in general were missing from these projects, and their absence could be read as a tacit acknowledgement of the reformers' charges.

The work of revising the revisionists on this point is now well underway. Detailed studies of particular religious houses, such as the Dominican priory of Dartford and the many small convents of the diocese of Norwich, have

---

[35] G. R. Elton, *Reform and Reformation: England, 1509–1558* (London, 1977), p. 187. 'Carthusians' in this context invariably seems to mean Sheen, the royal foundation contemporaneous with Syon, with perhaps the addition of the London Charterhouse (which, like the other two houses, could claim a martyr). The spirituality of the seven other English charterhouses in this period is rarely considered.

[36] Susan Brigden, *New Worlds, Lost Worlds: The Rule of the Tudors 1485–1603* (Harmondsworth, 2000), pp. 80–1.

[37] Christopher Harper-Bill, *The Pre-Reformation Church in England 1400–1530* (London and New York, 1989), pp. 42–3; Christopher Haigh, *English Reformations: Religion, Politics, and Society under the Tudors* (Oxford, 1993), pp. 25–8.

[38] Eamon Duffy, *The Stripping of the Altars: Traditional Religion in England c.1400–1580* (New Haven and London, 1991), pp. 62, 118, 295.

begun to paint a much more positive picture of their contribution to late medieval ecclesiastical and intellectual life. In his monograph on the Benedictine community at St Albans, James Clark even speaks of a 'monastic renaissance' in the century before the Reformation.[39] The turning of the tide of interpretation was emphatically signalled by Clark's landmark collection of essays re-appraising *The Religious Orders in Pre-Reformation England*, which appeared in 2002.[40] Since then, research by Martin Heale and others has further refined settled assumptions about the marginal relevance of England's many lesser monasteries to the laity by demonstrating the key role they played in sustaining the flourishing cult of saints and pilgrimage. A volume edited by Janet Burton and Karen Stöber published in 2008 depicts 'a rich and vibrant monastic culture which was different from that of earlier centuries, but far from in decline'. Far from teetering on the brink of self-destruction even before the Dissolution, religious houses retained their spiritual importance and remained firmly integrated within a series of social communities and external networks.[41]

The reformed house of Syon Abbey has sometimes sat rather uneasily on the margins of these projects, as a foil against which the vitality of older orders and smaller monasteries must be reasserted against the disparaging claims of Protestant propagandists and old-style historians. It is true that Bridget conceived her order as a remedy against the deficiencies of contemporary monasticism. But there is no reason to read this as anything other than the latest of a series of reforming initiatives which sought to reinvent the movement in the image of the austere religious purity of its initial founders. The *Regula Salvatoris* opens with a vision in which Christ likens himself to a king looking ruefully at his vineyards. Although they had 'brow3t furth ry3t good wyne long tyme', now his servants tell him:

> Syre we haue considered thy vyn3erdes and we fynde in them full fewe brawnches þat bere ony wyne. And that worste sede that ys worth ry3t nou3t but to brenne hath growe vp oute of mesure.

39 See Marilyn Oliva, *The Convent and the Community in Late Medieval England: Female Monasteries in the Diocese of Norwich, 1350–1540* (Woodbridge, 1998); Lee, *Nunneries, Learning and Spirituality*; James Clark, *A Monastic Renaissance at St Albans: Thomas Walsingham and his Circle, c.1350–1440* (Oxford, 2004).
40 Clark, 'The Religious Orders in Pre-Reformation England', in idem (ed.), *Religious Orders in Pre-Reformation England*, pp. 3–33.
41 Martin Heale, 'Training in Superstition? Monasteries and Popular Religion in Late Medieval and Reformation England', *JEH*, 58 (2007), 417–39. Janet Burton and Karen Stöber (eds), *Monasteries and Society in the British Isles in the Later Middle Ages* (Woodbridge, 2008), p. 2.

So the king resolves:

> I shal plante me a newe vyne3erde wher shall be brou3t brawnches.
> and they shal sende down rotys into the grownde. and I myself shal
> put aboute it fatnesse or downg. And it shal be full fyllid with wyne
> aldirbest.

The vision recalls the unfruitful vine of Isaiah 5, but whereas the owner in that
narrative rather peevishly rips up the hedge around his vineyard, breaks down
the wall and generally 'lay[s] it waste' (5:6), Bridget's Christ speaks the
language not of revolution but of regeneration: 'Of this vyne3erde many
vyne3erdys beyng long tyme drye. shal begynne to be renewyd. and do aftyr
the dayes of ther renewyng'.[42] In her vision, houses of the Bridgettine order
would exist, not to point up the failings of the older orders or argue their irre-
versible spiritual bankruptcy, but to assist in their reform. The logical consequence of the growing body of recent research on late medieval monasticism
is to reduce the conventional contrast drawn between the Bridgettines and
their less illustrious religious cousins. It is to present Syon less as an anomaly
than as a particularly shining example of trends and tendencies from which
monastic communities elsewhere were by no means wholly excluded or
immune.

More broadly, the emergence of the Bridgettine order gave expression to
currents of contemporary spirituality that enriched and reinvigorated late
medieval Catholicism as an institution and as a system of piety, even as they
contributed to destabilising it and fragmenting its coherence. Established by a
woman, with a rule dictated to her in a collection of divine revelations, the
Bridgettine order reflected the flowering of late medieval mysticism in four-
teenth- and fifteenth-century Europe. It was one manifestation of an intense
interior quest for union with God which preoccupied many pious men and
women across the Continent in this period, from the Dominicans Meister
Eckhart and Henry Suso and their disciples in Germany, to St Catherine of
Siena in Italy, and Richard Rolle, Walter Hilton and Julian of Norwich in
England. The revelations vouchsafed to such individuals gave them an access
to the divine unmediated by language, tradition or the sacerdotal priesthood
and they were often regarded by the Church with ambivalence, if not suspi-
cion, especially when the recipients were women. In the context of the Great
Schism, prominent clerics like the conciliarist Jean Gerson worried about the
suggestibility of the female sex and learnedly pondered the problem of the
discernment of spirits. The papal endorsement of St Bridget's religious

---

[42] Hogg (ed.), *Rewyll*, pp. 3–4, 5.

project occurred against a backdrop of anxiety about her gender and the status of her ecstatic experiences, and continued to dog it with controversy for several decades to come.[43] But whereas other manifestations of mysticism like the Free Spirits fell foul of the establishment and were pushed beyond the pale of theological orthodoxy into the wilderness of heresy, the Bridgettine brand became more or less successfully absorbed into the ecclesiastical mainstream. Its implantation in England embodied impulses that were also beginning to flourish within the Carthusian order, which underwent a revival and expansion in the half-century preceding 1420. Its ethic of ascetic, eremitical retreat and inner contemplation was highly conducive to mystical piety and the charterhouses at Mount Grace Priory in Yorkshire and Sheen served as a conduit for its diffusion more widely.[44] With Syon itself, they helped to popularise modes of religiosity associated with the *devotio moderna* as practised in the Rhineland and Low Countries and epitomised in Thomas Kempis's *Imitation of Christ*, which circulated in translation within both religious orders in the late fifteenth century.[45]

The personalised, introspective piety that became a hallmark of the Bridgettine outlook converged with developments that were subtly transforming the religion of those on the edges of, and outside, the cloister, notably the emergence of Christocentric devotion to the Holy Name, Five Wounds and Sacred Heart. St Bridget's own connection to such devotions can be seen most immediately in the distinctive habits worn by members of her order. The sisters wore on their heads a crown of white linen onto which were sewn small pieces of red cloth in the shape of 'fyve dropys' in the pattern of a cross; the mantles of the lay brothers were similarly adorned with white crosses and red patches 'for the reuerence of the fyve woundys of crist'; while the brothers bore a red cross over their heart, 'and in myddis of the crosse. a litel rounde of white cloth for mistery of the body of cryst whiche they offre yche day'.[46] The

---

43 See Morris, *St Birgitta*, pp. 152–9; Rosalynn Voaden, *God's Words, Women's Voices: The Discernment of Spirits in the Writing of Late-Medieval Women Visionaries* (York, 1999); Dyan Elliott, 'Seeing Double: John Gerson, the Discernment of Spirits, and Joan of Arc', *American Historical Review*, 107 (2002), 26–54.

44 See Knowles, *Religious Orders*, vol. 2, pp. 129–38.

45 See Roger Lovatt, 'The "Imitation of Christ" in Late Medieval England', *Transactions of the Royal Historical Society*, 5th ser., 18 (1968), 97–121, though this article takes a pessimistic view of the impact and dissemination of the ethos of the *devotio moderna* in England. Recently, Vincent Gillespie has argued that, although the Carthusians were avid collectors of this kind of material, it was chiefly Syon that was interested in its dissemination. See his 'The Haunted Text: Reflections in *The Mirror to Deuout People*', in *Medieval Texts in Context*, ed. Denis Renevey and Graham D. Caie (London, 2008), pp. 136–66.

46 Hogg (ed.), *Rewyll*, pp. 11–12, 35, 34.

iconography of Bridgettine dress was in keeping with an emotional and medi-tative focus on the symbols of the Passion that had indigenous as well as Continental roots. It is probably no coincidence that Henry FitzHugh, respon-sible for the Bridgettine order's introduction into England, owned a copy of Richard Rolle's *Incendium Amoris*.[47] The Syon Confessor General John Fewterer's translation of Ulrich Pinder's *The myrrour or glasse of Christes passion* (1534) was a further reflection of the preoccupation with the sacrifice and physical sufferings of Christ that gathered growing momentum among the devout laity of pre-Reformation England,[48] alongside the cult of his Holy Name, the official feast of which was fixed in the calendar in 1489. Votive masses in its honour proliferated. As Susan Wabuda, Christine Peters, and Robert Lutton have shown, the rise and spread of these devotions was symp-tomatic of internal changes that were taking place within Catholic orthodoxy of which Syon Abbey was in many respects a further straw in the wind. They provide evidence of a complexity and heterogeneity that belies revisionist claims about the fundamentally consensual and unitary character of 'tradi-tional religion'. They sowed the seeds both of receptiveness to evangelical reform and of stubborn resistance to the impending Protestant storm.[49]

Equally Janus-faced in relation to the Reformation was the Christian humanism of Desiderius Erasmus and Thomas More. At the heart of the movement was a desire to streamline popular piety and purge it of supersti-tious and dubious accretions and to refocus devotion on the reading of Scrip-ture and hearing of the preached Word. This functioned in some cases as a bridge to the cause of reform and in others as a stimulus to stand in defiance of it. Such preoccupations were combined with a commitment to a return, *ad fontes*, to original biblical and classical sources and a rigorous brand of textual criticism that decisively altered intellectual life in the universities. Like the friars,[50] Syon Abbey was deeply immersed in the world of the 'New Learning'.[51] Many of those who joined the ranks of the brethren had been

---

[47] De Hamel, *Syon Abbey*, pp. 55–6; Deanesly, *Incendium Amoris*, pp. 96–7.

[48] Ulrich Pinder, *The myrrour or glasse of Christes passion*, trans. John Fewterer (London, 1534).

[49] See Susan Wabuda, *Preaching during the English Reformation* (Cambridge, 2002), p. 9 and ch. 4 *passim*; Christine Peters, *Patterns of Piety: Women, Gender and Religion in Late Medi-eval and Reformation England* (Cambridge, 2003); Robert Lutton, *Lollardy and Orthodox Religion in Pre-Reformation England* (Woodbridge, 2006), conclusion and *passim*. See also Robert Lutton and Elisabeth Salter (eds), *Pieties in Transition: Religious Practices and Experi-ences c.1400–1640* (Aldershot, 2007).

[50] See Richard Rex, 'The Friars in the English Reformation', in Peter Marshall and Alec Ryrie (eds), *The Beginnings of English Protestantism* (Cambridge, 2002), pp. 38–59.

[51] See Richard Rex, *The Theology of John Fisher* (Cambridge, 1991); idem, 'The New Learning', *JEH*, 44 (1993), 26–44.

nurtured in the Oxford and Cambridge colleges where it put down the firmest roots: Richard Terenden had been a fellow of New College, Oxford, before his profession in or soon after 1488; John Fewterer, Syon's Confessor General from 1523 to 1536, had come from Pembroke Hall, Cambridge; Richard Whitford was at Queen's, Cambridge, before joining the Bridgettines around 1512; and Richard Reynolds, reckoned by Cardinal Reginald Pole as 'the only English monk well versed in the three principal languages' of Latin, Greek and Hebrew, had been a fellow at Corpus Christi College, Cambridge.[52] As Vincent Gillespie shows in his essay in this volume, the humanist credentials of Syon's men are attested by the books they donated to the brothers' library. The Bridgettine house consequently became a magnet for native and foreign scholars of distinction and lustre: the Spanish humanist Juan Luis Vives visited the abbey with Katherine of Aragon in January 1524 and both John Fisher and More regularly frequented and corresponded with its members.[53] In her contribution, Virginia R. Bainbridge demonstrates the extent to which the sisters themselves emerged from the same intellectual milieux. They were integrated within the webs of patronage and benefaction that embedded Renaissance learning within the households of the English gentry and aristocracy.

Households of this kind exhibited a conspicuous appetite for forms of quasi-monastic piety inspired in large part by the Bridgettine tradition itself. Noblewomen like Cicely, Duchess of York, were devoted readers of St Bridget's revelations and modelled their daily lives on those of the nuns of Syon; Margaret, Lady Hungerford (d. 1478), recreated the abbey church in her own chapel and adopted elements of the Bridgettine office for use within it; Lady Margaret Beaufort, mother of Henry VII, herself had strong connections with the house and displayed deep sympathy with its ethos. A regular visitor to Syon, the latter had acquired special papal permission to enter monasteries of the Carthusians and other orders of enclosed religious and 'hold salutary conversation with them and eat there', in 1504, and her household accounts reveal regular payments made in support of its incumbents, together with offerings to St Bridget. She also commissioned the printing in 1491 of the *Fifteen Oes*, a favourite compilation of prayers apocryphally linked with the Swedish saint.[54] Well-to-do widows like Alice Beselles,

---

[52] See the entries for these men in *ODNB* and the summary biographies in Gillespie, *Syon Abbey Catalogue*, pp. 576–7, 591–2, 585–6. For Pole's estimation of Reynolds, see *ibid.*, p. lix.
[53] Maria Dowling, *Humanism in the Age of Henry VIII* (London, 1986), p. 145; Rex, *Theology of John Fisher*, p. 149. See also n. 126, below.
[54] See C. A. J. Armstrong, 'The Piety of Cicely, Duchess of York: A Study in Late Mediaeval Culture', in *England, France and Burgundy in the Fifteenth Century* (London, 1983), pp.

Susan Kyngeston, and Dorothy and Susan Fettyplace sought refuge and found new vocations as vowesses or nuns within Syon's walls after their husbands' deaths,[55] while others left bereft reproduced the routine of the Bridgettines within their own homes. Further attestations of the order's influence beyond the confines of the abbey and of a fashionable cult of its foundress that increasingly extended beyond elite circles are provided by the brief vernacular life of St Bridget that circulated in Capgrave's *Nova Legenda Anglie*, the popularity of the sixty-three-bead Bridgettine rosary, the pilgrims who flocked to Syon to obtain its rich indulgences on feast days, and the burgeoning market for the publications that emanated from the pens of its brethren in the early decades of the sixteenth century.[56]

This curious combination of an avant-garde style of introspective devotion with characteristic elements of the traditional religion of saints and pilgrimage makes Syon an emblem of the remarkable vitality of Catholicism on the eve of the Reformation, even as it underlines the vulnerability of late medieval monasticism to savage assault by evangelical reformers animated by anxiety about 'superstition' and 'idolatry'. Its occupants could not close their ears to the stream of polemic against the institutionalised idleness of the monasteries that began to emerge: Richard Whitford's *Pype or tonne of the lyfe of perfection* (1532) acknowledged and reproved some of the abuses to which the religious were prone, but offered a robust defence of the cloistered life against the 'false and subtyll deceites' of its heretical Lutheran detractors.[57] Such efforts reflect the resilience of the order on the eve of its suppression, but they could not prevent its demise. Even before the shadow of the Dissolution fell, the Bridgettines had been implicated in a dangerous protest against Henry VIII's decision to divorce Katherine of Aragon and marry Anne Boleyn, via the *cause célèbre* of Elizabeth Barton, the notorious nun of Kent, whose 'fantasies and counterfeit visions' were said to have resulted from her

135–56; M. A. Hicks, 'The Piety of Margaret, Lady Hungerford (d. 1478)', *JEH*, 38 (1987), 19–38; Susan Powell, 'Syon Abbey and the Mother of King Henry VII: The Relationship of Lady Margaret Beaufort with the English Birgittines', *Birgittiana*, 19 (2005), 211–24, and 'Margaret Pole and Syon Abbey', *Historical Research*, 78 (2005), 563–7.

[55] Mary C. Erler, 'The Books and Lives of Three Tudor Women', in Jean R. Brink (ed.), *Privileging Gender in Early Modern England* (Kirksville, MI, 1993), pp. 5–17, and her *Women, Reading and Piety in Late Medieval England* (Cambridge, 2002), ch. 4.

[56] See F. R. Johnston, 'The English Cult of St Bridget of Sweden', *Analecta Bollandiana*, 103 (1985), 75–93; H. Thurston, 'The So-Called Bridgettine Rosary', *The Month*, 100 (1902), 189–203. See also Ann M. Hutchison, 'Reflections on Aspects of the Spiritual Impact of St Birgitta, the Revelations and the Bridgettine Order in Late Medieval England', in E. A. Jones (ed.), *The Medieval Mystical Tradition*, 7 (Cambridge, 2004), pp. 69–82.

[57] Richard Whitford, *Here begynneth the boke called the pype or tonne of the lyfe of perfection* (London, 1532), fo. ii v, and *passim*.

exposure to the revelations of St Bridget and St Catherine of Siena read to her during various visits to Isleworth.[58] Tainted by the association of several of its senior brethren with the political prophetess executed for treason and by the defiance of Richard Reynolds, martyred alongside the Carthusian monks for denying the Royal Supremacy in 1535, the 'vertues howse' of Syon could hardly have escaped the fate that befell the monastic profession in England as a whole.

The closure of the abbey and the dispersal of its inhabitants represented a violent blow against a religious order that partially anticipated the priorities of the movement for internal renewal of the Church of Rome that was beginning to put forth green shoots across the Continent. Far from a merely defensive reaction to the advent of Protestantism, the Catholic Reformation is now envisaged as a parallel strand of a reforming impulse that transcended the confessional barriers that later became set in stone. The early sixteenth century witnessed the birth of a series of new spiritual communities, including the Oratory of Divine Love in Italy and Ignatius Loyola's Society of Jesus, as well as primitive revivals of older religious orders like the Franciscans in the guise of the Capuchins. Through the commitment of its brothers to preaching and outreach and the pursuit of deep communion with the divine which was central to the lives of the sisters, Syon was infused with a spirituality marked by some of the same initiative and vigour.[59]

It is not therefore surprising that it was one of the first (and few) religious houses to be actively revived after the accession of Mary I in 1553. For too long indicted for manifestly failing to capture the spirit of the Counter Reformation, the reputation of the queen and her chief advisors has been radically rehabilitated in recent years. Where earlier writers dismissed her short-lived

---

[58] See L. E. Whatmore (ed.), 'The Sermon Against the Holy Maid of Kent and Her Adherents, Delivered at Paul's Cross, November the 23rd, 1533, and at Canterbury, December the 7th', *EHR*, 58 (1943), 463–75, (p. 469). See also Diane Watt, 'The Prophet at Home: Elizabeth Barton and the Influence of Bridget of Sweden and Catherine of Siena', in Rosalynn Voaden (ed.), *Prophets Abroad: The Reception of Continental Holy Women in Late Medieval England* (Cambridge, 1996), pp. 161–76; Ethan H. Shagan, *Popular Politics and the English Reformation* (Cambridge, 2003), ch. 2; Andrew Hope, 'Martyrs of the Marsh: Elizabeth Barton, Joan Bocher and Trajectories of Martyrdom in Reformation Kent', in Lutton and Salter (eds), *Pieties in Transition*, pp. 41–55.

[59] It has been suggested that Loyola visited Whitford at Syon in 1530, though this is speculative. See A. M. Peters, 'Richard Whitford and St Ignatius' Visit to England', *Archivum Historicum Societatis Jesu*, 25 (1956), 328–50. For recent overviews of work on the new orders, see Richard L. DeMolen (ed.), *Religious Orders of the Catholic Reformation* (New York, 1994); John Patrick Donnelly, 'New Religious Orders for Men', in R. Po-Chia Hsia (ed.), *The Cambridge History of Christianity*, vol. 6, *Reform and Expansion 1500–1660* (Cambridge, 2007), pp. 162–79.

programme to restore Catholicism as inept, reactionary and flawed, historians now emphasise its forward-looking and pioneering qualities. Overseen by Cardinal Reginald Pole, a churchman immersed in the circles of the Italian *spirituali* and in the vanguard of Tridentine reform, this was an enterprise that made Marian England, according to Eamon Duffy, 'the closest thing in Europe to a laboratory for counter-reformation experimentation', if not the very place of its 'invention'.[60] The role of the restoration of Syon, Sheen and several other religious houses (including the Observant Franciscans at Greenwich and the Dominican convent at Dartford) in this story has so far been rather neglected, but deserves greater attention: it was probably more central to Pole's plans for the spiritual rejuvenation of the nation than sceptical commentators such as David Loades have supposed. Had Mary lived longer, these and other revived monasteries might indeed have become 'powerhouses' of Catholic reform.[61] As it was, her premature death brought Pole's embryonic project to an abrupt halt.

It can also be argued that, having absorbed studied withdrawal from secular society into their rule, the Bridgettine order adopted a reformed model of female monasticism that foreshadowed that which the Council of Trent later sought to enforce across the board. Determined to counteract damaging Protestant claims made about the sexual promiscuity of the ostensibly celibate religious, in its twenty-fifth and final session in 1563 the Council re-enacted the provisions of Boniface VIII's constitution *Periculoso* of 1298 and ordered the compulsory claustration of all professed Catholic women.[62] Reinforced by the 1566 bull, *Circa Pastoralis*, this policy was designed to protect nuns from the evils of the world, preserve their chastity intact, and subject them to tighter surveillance by male confessors and visiting bishops. For many nuns the determination of the Tridentine fathers to separate the holy from the profane represented a significant rupture of settled patterns of social interaction that had characterised medieval conventual life, which it proved very difficult to

---

[60] See Duffy, *Stripping of the Altars*, pp. 524–64; idem, *Fires of Faith: Catholic England under Mary Tudor* (New Haven and London, 2009), p. 8, ch. 9 and *passim*; Eamon Duffy and David Loades (eds), *The Church of Mary Tudor* (Aldershot, 2006); John Edwards and Ronald Truman (eds), *Reforming Catholicism in the England of Mary Tudor* (Aldershot, 2005); William Wiseman, *The Theology and Spirituality of Mary Tudor's Church* (Aldershot, 2006).

[61] Thomas F. Mayer, *Reginald Pole: Prince and Prophet* (Cambridge, 2000), pp. 283–8, though he remains cautious; Loades, 'The Personal Religion of Mary I', in Duffy and Loades (eds), *Church of Mary Tudor*, pp. 23–4. On the potential for the monasteries to operate as 'power-houses' of Catholic reform, see the passing comment of Dickens, *English Reformation*, p. 383.

[62] H. J. Schroeder (ed.), *The Canons and Decrees of the Council of Trent* (Rockford, IL, 1978), pp. 220–1.

enforce strictly. It was often vigorously resisted, if not flagrantly violated: as Mary Laven's memorable study of the *Virgins of Venice* has revealed, the gentlewomen who inhabited the city's many nunneries continued to behave in ways that raised eyebrows and scandalised the ecclesiastical hierarchy. The implementation of clausura did not wholly sever convents from contact with the world or represent their subjugation to repressive masculine authority; they remained spaces and places within which women exercised spiritual and temporal autonomy and agency. The walls of the cloister remained porous and fluid. Nor did the edicts of Trent prevent the emergence of new congregations like the Ursulines, the Daughters of Charity, and the Institute of Mary Ward which sought to carve out a place for a female apostolate of carers, teachers and missionaries: while the former two survived and flourished, albeit in a refined and regulated form, famously the latter fell victim to papal hostility in the 1630s.[63]

The Bridgettines were representative of a more contemplative impulse among the devout women of early modern Europe, which perhaps found fullest and most influential expression inside the reformed (discalced) Carmelite houses founded by Teresa of Avila in the late sixteenth century. Within the circumscribed boundaries of the convent, with its gates and grilles, Teresa and her disciples pursued a goal of intense dialogue between God and the soul that could result in mystical transports that bypassed the mediation of the Church and enabled women tacitly to circumvent the control of those who supervised them.[64] They exemplify the dangers of drawing too sharp a contrast between the dynamic and passive strands of post-Reformation female monasticism[65] and of overlooking the extent to which claustration

---

63 On Catholic reform and female monasticism, see Kathryn Norberg, 'The Counter-Reformation and Women Religious and Lay', in John W. O'Malley (ed.), *Catholicism in Early Modern History: A Guide to Research* (St Louis, MI, 1988), pp. 133–46; Elizabeth Rapley, *The Devotés: Women and the Church in Seventeenth-Century France* (Montreal, 1990); Maria Rosa, 'The Nun', in Rosario Villari, *Baroque Personae*, trans. Lydia G. Cochrane (Chicago and London, 1995), pp. 195–238; R. Po-Chia Hsia (ed.), *The World of Catholic Renewal 1540–1770* (Cambridge, 1998 edn), pp. 33–41; Amy E. Leonard, 'Female Religious Orders', in R. Po-Chia Hsia (ed.), *A Companion to the Reformation World* (Oxford, 2004), pp. 237–54. Mary Laven, *Virgins of Venice: Enclosed Lives and Broken Vows in the Renaissance Convent* (London, 2002); Laurence Lux-Sterritt, *Redefining Female Religious Life: French Ursulines and English Ladies in Seventeenth-Century Catholicism* (Aldershot, 2005). See also Silvia Evangelisti, *Nuns: A History of Convent Life 1450–1700* (Oxford, 2007).
64 On Teresa of Avila there is a vast literature, among which see Alison Weber, *Teresa of Avila and the Rhetoric of Femininity* (Princeton, 1990); G. T. W. Ahlgren, *Teresa of Avila and the Politics of Sanctity* (Ithaca, NY, 1996); J. Bilinkoff, 'Teresa of Jesus and the Carmelite Reform', in DeMolen (ed.), *Religious Orders of the Catholic Reformation*, pp. 165–86.
65 On this theme, see Craig Harline, 'Actives and Contemplatives: The Female Religious of the Low Countries Before and After Trent', *Catholic Historical Review*, 89 (1995), 541–67.

could be a form of spiritual liberation and empowerment rather than a mechanism for patriarchal domination. Some historians have seen the growing number of women who entered Continental convents in this period as a form of social engineering – as a convenient financial solution for families with surplus daughters and a shortage of cash to supply marriage dowries.[66] But this is too dismissive of the possibility that many felt compelled by a genuine calling and vocation to enter a secluded life of private prayer and pious meditation.

It is in this context that the survival of the Bridgettine community in exile and its capacity to attract new recruits must be analysed. Its character and internal constitution were subtly transformed by the challenges it faced in sustaining itself in (successively) two different foreign environments and by the changes to its liturgy it was obliged to accept to comply with the Tridentine drive for standardisation. If the balance of power within the double monastery gradually shifted away from the Abbess over time (in line with the tenor of the Council's decrees and as a consequence of the exigencies of its refugee experience), this was partly counterbalanced by the declining numbers of men who entered as brethren. The last of these died in 1695, whereafter the nuns' spiritual direction was taken over by Benedictine monks. By the beginning of the eighteenth century, the feminine magisterium originally envisaged by St Bridget had been eroded and its retinue of preaching and publishing monks consigned to oblivion.[67]

It is also important to situate the post-Reformation history of the order against the backdrop of the foundation of some twenty-two English contemplative houses in France and the Southern Netherlands, beginning with a Benedictine convent in Brussels in 1598. As Claire Walker has demonstrated in her book on this remarkable revival, the women who entered these nunneries were predominantly the daughters of the recusant aristocracy and gentry. By leaving England to take vows abroad, they believed that they could make a decisive spiritual, practical and even political contribution to relieving it of the burdensome yoke of heresy and restoring it to the obedience of the Mother Church of Rome. They represented significant pockets of spirited confessional resistance to the Protestant regime that persecuted their faith. Geographically dislocated from their relatives at home and linguistically and culturally divided from the host societies that surrounded them, they were

---

[66] See, for example, Christine Klapisch-Zuber, 'The Griselda Complex: Dowry and Marriage Gifts in the Quattrocento', in her *Women, Family and Ritual in Renaissance Italy* (Chicago, 1985), pp. 213–46; Jutta Sperling, *Convents and the Body Politic in Late Renaissance Venice* (Chicago, 1999).

[67] See Cunich's essay, Chapter 1, below.

nevertheless an important part of what John Bossy has described as the English Catholic community. They developed a characteristic *mentalité* honed by their expatriate experience and inventively negotiated the strictures of the cloister in ways that once again highlight the artificiality of opposing the active and contemplative life.[68]

Walker's contribution to this volume presents the post-Reformation Bridgettines as a distinctive variation on these themes. Pioneers of monastic exile, the sisters of Syon continued to hope and work for a return to their homeland: both through the supplications to the Almighty they made in their cells and through the proselytising missions back to England carried out by individuals like Elizabeth Sander (sister of the controversialist Nicholas), whose exploits are examined here in more detail by Ann Hutchison. This was a community politically astute enough to ally itself with the Catholic League and the Spanish crown and to utilise the negotiations for a match between the Infanta Maria and Prince Charles in the early 1620s as an opportunity to secure and shape its future.[69] For all its commitment to mystical solitude and silence, it also became embroiled in the international politics of the Counter Reformation. For this and other reasons, it did not fail to attract hostile Protestant attention: 'anatomised' in a scurrilous pamphlet by Thomas Robinson, the Bridgettines in Lisbon became the focus of an anti-Catholic myth that wove together early Reformation polemical commonplaces about the lasciviousness of the religious and elements of the evolving black legend within the parameters of a story about the author's own narrow escape from the seductive evils of popery. Depicting the convent as a bawdy house filled with 'unholy sisters' seduced abroad by scheming priests and 'silly women' who lived in 'servile obedience' to their male superiors, this text assaulted the community's own self-image of sanctified suffering (Figure I.1).[70] This image of heroic survival with providential aid was constructed in narratives like the 'Wanderings of Syon' (discussed here by Hutchison) and sharpened by a consciousness of its ancient lineage. The Bridgettines in Lisbon looked back to the glory days of the order at the abbey in Isleworth, which they ritually recalled, together with their dead, through daily readings of the 'martiloge', described by Claes Gejrot in Chapter 7. As Gejrot shows, the

---

68 Claire Walker, *Gender and Politics in Early Modern Europe: English Convents in France and the Low Countries* (Basingstoke, 2003). John Bossy, *The English Catholic Community 1570–1850* (London, 1975).

69 The illuminated petition the nuns presented to Philip III, dedicated to the Infanta, is printed and the images reproduced in de Hamel, *Syon Abbey*, pp. 23–47.

70 Thomas Robinson, *The anatomie of the English nunnery at Lisbon in Portugall: dissected and laid open by one that was sometime a yonger brother of the covent* (London, 1623 and 1630), quotations from 1630 edn, at pp. 4, 17.

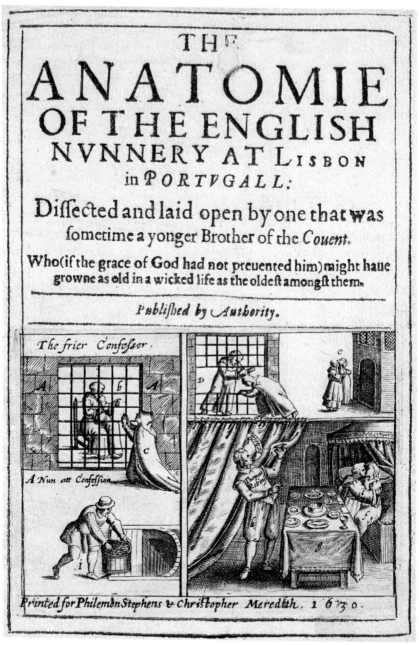

Figure 1.1: The post-Reformation Bridgettines satirised as a bawdy house: Thomas Robinson, *The anatomie of the English nunnery at Lisbon in Portugall: dissected and laid open by one that was sometime a yonger brother of the covent* (London, 1630), title-page. British Library shelfmark RB23.a.9192.

additions made to this manuscript emanated a spirit of militant defiance. They ensured that the sacred memory of its martyrs, benefactors and relics remained alive and transformed the book into a physical link between the present and the community's Lancastrian past. The mental and psychological experience of exile evidently served as a powerful spur to the task of remembering and, indeed, inventing an historical tradition that would be carried on in the twentieth century by Syon's foremost chronicler, Canon John Fletcher.[71]

Reading, Writing and Religion in Late Medieval and Early Modern England

As Virginia Bainbridge comments in her essay in this volume, medieval Syon was 'a house full of books'.[72] St Bridget had envisaged as much in her original *Rule*. This was strict on the provision of liturgical texts, which (in keeping with her wider insistence on merely adequate provision without excess or surplus) were to be supplied 'as many as be necessary to doo dyvyne office and moo in no wyse'. By contrast, she set no limits on the acquisition of works 'in whiche ys to lerne or to studye': 'Thoo bookes they shalt haue as many as they wyll'.[73] The *Additions* to the *Rule* make it clear that the abbey's two communities, brothers and nuns, each had their own library. These were places 'wherin silence is streytly to be kepte', especially 'whyls any suster is there alone in recordyng of her redynge' and during the times when the brothers were dedicated to study.[74] But reading took place, and books were to be found, elsewhere within the double monastery: during the singing and saying of the office in the choir, in the course of the brothers' chapter, and at meal times in the frater. The *Sisters' Additions* specified that this latter task was to be carried out by the legister: 'distynctly and openly, that al may vnsterstonde it', she was to 'rede suche mater, as the abbes or chauntres assigneth, to the edyfyeng of sowles'.[75] The monastic day also ended in this

---

71 See Hutchison's essay, Chapter 8, below.
72 See below, p. 101.
73 Hogg (ed.), *Rewyll*, pp. 49–50. Once a Bridgettine house had secured sufficient endowment, no more gifts were to be accepted and any end-of-year financial surplus was to be distributed to the poor. At Syon, each sister was allowed in her cell 'her necessaryes and no more': Hogg (ed.), *Sisters' Additions*, p. 200.
74 Hogg (ed.), *Sisters' Additions*, p. 72; Hogg (ed.), *Laybrothers' Additions*, p. 45.
75 Hogg (ed.), *Sisters' Additions*, p. 161. Further details of the form to be followed for such reading are promised 'in the laste endynge of thys boke', but the manuscript is defective at the end and this matter is missing. Seven large-format leaves, now Exeter University Library, Syon Fragments, MS 1, contain part of the vernacular *Rewyll of Seynt Sauioure* and *Sisters' Additions*. Their texts have been rubricated for reading aloud, suggesting that they may have come

space with a collation: a 'lytel draught of ale' and a reading.[76] The early fifteenth-century translation of the Bridgettine office and guide to devotional practice, *The Myroure of oure Ladye*, recommended 'some spyrytuall matter of gostly edyfycacion. to helpe to gather to gyther the scaterynges of the mynde. from all oute warde thynges' before the nuns retired to bed, and to keep them 'in inwarde peace and stableness of mynde all the nyghte folowynge'.[77] The regular pattern of Bridgettine religious life thus revolved around direct or indirect contact with written texts of various kinds.

The care of its books was consequently of vital concern to the community. To 'defoyle any boke ... or trete it unhonestly' was an offence, while stealing, destroying or defacing any of the common registers was a 'grievous fault' that would result in severe punishment, if not imprisonment.[78] The books were the responsibility of two monastic officers. The chantress was charged with recording the names of those who entered the convent and took vows and with adding obits to the Martiloge; in addition she was to have oversight of all the books to be used in the church, chapter and frater, 'to se þat they be corrected, and made of one accorde'. She was thus answerable for the textual integrity of the manuscript books that defined the monastery's identity. She shared responsibility for the physical preservation of the volumes that comprised the library with the sacristan (or sexton).[79] Surviving accounts for the years 1506–1536 testify to the constant attention that was paid to the maintenance of the collection, revealing regular payments to bookbinders for mending, cleaning, and copying, together with the purchase of other materials relating to book repair and production.[80] Syon seems also to have had a resident scribe: an ordinance of 1482 records the appointment of Thomas Baillie, keeper of the brother's locutory (or parlour) to this role, a decision prompted by consideration of the 'greete hurtte and notable dayly Enpayremente of oure singler

---

from a volume designed for the purpose. See Laura Saetveit Miles, 'Scribes at Syon: The Communal Usage and Production of Legislative Manuscripts at the English Birgittine House', in C. Gejrot, S. Risberg and M. Åkestam (eds), *Saint Birgitta, Syon and Vadstena: Papers from a Symposium in Stockholm 4–6 October 2007* (forthcoming). See also de Hamel, *Syon Abbey*, pp. 71–2. We thank Laura Miles for allowing us access to her essay in advance of its publication.

[76] Hogg (ed.), *Sisters' Additions*, p. 175.

[77] John Henry Blunt (ed.), *The Myroure of oure Ladye*, EETS, extra ser., 19 (London, 1873), p. 165.

[78] Hogg (ed.), *Sisters' Additions*, pp. 2, 15. See also Hogg (ed.), *Laybrothers' Additions*, pp. 19 and 30.

[79] See Hogg (ed.), *Sisters' Additions*, pp. 147–50, 155 (quotation from p. 149). It is likely that the arrangements on the brothers' side were similar, though no details are extant.

[80] Mary C. Erler, 'Syon Abbey's Care for Books: Its Sacristan's Account Rolls 1506/7–1535/6', *Scriptorium*, 39 (1985), pp. 293–307.

tresour Bokes' and a desire 'to purvey this remedye'.[81] Daily use evidently took a heavy toll and necessitated an ongoing programme of renewal.

Further evidence of the solicitude of the Bridgettine house for its books comes in the guise of the arrival in 1481 of Thomas Betson, a Cambridge graduate, formerly rector of Wimbish in Essex, as its librarian. Betson's catalogue of the brothers' library is a testament to what seems to have been a concerted attempt to reinvigorate and expand it.[82] Consisting of some 1,421 volumes in manuscript and print (all but 200 of them donated by the brethren, the majority upon their profession), it was a decidedly academic and intellectual collection, mostly in Latin, and conspicuously lacking in vernacular religious and mystical literature.[83] The significant and growing presence of humanist editions of the *opera* of Virgil, Plato and Plotinus and other classical texts suggests that had the Dissolution not intervened, it 'might have equalled or eclipsed the richest colleges of the universities as a renaissance palace of culture and religion'.[84]

We know much less about the size and scope of the sisters' library before it was scattered to the winds by the Dissolution, though inferences can be drawn from surviving books and other references. Some fifty-seven texts (forty-six manuscripts and eleven printed books) linked with Syon have been identified. Half of them are liturgical (breviaries, psalters, processionals, etc.) and would not therefore have formed part of the formal library collection itself. Among the rest, devotional authors catch the eye: Richard Rolle, Walter Hilton, and Thomas Kempis, as well as the writings of some of the brethren themselves. There are a number of anonymous treatises and compilations of prayers and meditations of a similar character. The majority (some 67 per cent) of these are in English: indeed Syon's name is connected with one-third of all extant vernacular books associated with the female religious houses of pre-Reformation England.[85] Although the extent to which late medieval nuns

---

81 Robert Jowitt Whitwell, 'An Ordinance for Syon Library, 1482', *EHR*, 25 (1910), pp. 121–3.
82 See the entry in *ODNB* and Gillespie, *Syon Abbey Catalogue*, esp. pp. xlv–xlvi.
83 See Vincent Gillespie, 'Dial M for Mystic: Mystical Texts in the Library of Syon Abbey and the Spirituality of the Syon Brethren', in Marion Glasscoe (ed.), *The Medieval Mystical Tradition in England, Ireland and Wales*, 6 (Cambridge, 1999), pp. 241–68.
84 De Hamel, *Syon Abbey*, p. 48. For humanism in the library, see Gillespie's essay, Chapter 3, below. On the dispersal of monastic libraries, see James P. Carley, 'Monastic Collections and their Dispersal', in John Barnard and D. F. McKenzie, with the assistance of Maureen Bell (eds), *The Cambridge History of the Book in Britain*, vol. 4, *1557–1695* (Cambridge, 2002), pp. 339–47.
85 See David N. Bell, *What Nuns Read: Books and Libraries in Medieval English Nunneries* (Kalamazoo and Spencer, MA, 1995), pp. 175–205, and see his comments on pp. 36–8, 74. See

were literate or partially literate in Latin should not be underestimated, it is clear that most of the Bridgettines' reading was done in the mother tongue.[86]

Insight into how the nuns of Syon were intended to read this material is provided by the treatise that opens the second part of *The Myroure of oure Ladye*. Reading is described here as an integral part of the task of contemplation, that 'causyth moche grace. and comforte to the soulle yf yt be well and dyscretely vsed'. It should take place in a spirit of devotion and receptivity: 'For lyke as in prayer. man spekyth to god; so in redynge god spekyth to man'. Haste was to be avoided and any difficult passages reread until they were fully comprehended. Books fall into two categories: they either instruct the reader in virtuous living and aid the examination of conscience; or they can be designed to 'quyken. & to sturre vp the affeccyons of the soule'. The sisters were to use discernment to choose the kind of reading that best fitted their need and disposition at the time. They were to dwell on each word of the texts they perused and absorb it as a form of spiritual nourishment: 'fede your soulles therwith, for yt is fode of lyfe'.[87]

Aimed at those moments 'when ye rede by your selfe alone',[88] such advice envisaged reading as a solitary pursuit, akin to meditation, which enabled the nun to transcend the temporal world and enter into a higher spiritual realm. Hints of the intimate, personal relationship that some of the medieval sisters had with their books are supplied by the signatures and annotations in them indicating private ownership or use. The flyleaf of a manuscript copy of Hilton's *Eight Chapters* and the *Cloud*-author's *Discretion of Spirits*, for instance, bears the text 'Thys boke is ssuster Anne Colvylle', while a printed edition of Robert Copeland and Michael Fawkes's *Devout Treatyse called the Tree & XII Frutes of the Holy Goost* (1534–5) has the name of 'Mar[gare]t Windesor, domina de Syon', who is listed as prioress in 1518 and 1539. A surviving medieval processional in the Bridgettine library is inscribed 'Dorothe Slyght', one of the nuns listed in the deed of restoration of 1557.[89]

At the same time, it is important to recognise that reading in medieval Syon was an activity that united the nuns as a body dedicated to the service of the Lord. Books forged and cemented bonds between them. As a note on the first

---

also Ann M. Hutchison, 'What the Nuns Read: Literary Evidence from the English Bridgettine House, Syon Abbey', *Mediaeval Studies*, 57 (1995), 205–22.

[86] Bell, *What Nuns Read*, ch. 3; and see the comments of Bainbridge in her essay, Chapter 2, below.

[87] Blunt (ed.), *Myroure of our Ladye*, pp. 65–71, at 65–6, 68–9, 64.

[88] *Ibid.*, p. 67.

[89] Bell, *What Nuns Read*, pp. 190, 183 (items 25 and 14 in the list of extant books relating to Syon). See also pp. 38–9. Exeter University Library, Syon MS 262/1. This item was held in private hands until the nineteenth century and bought back by the Syon community for £40.

folio reveals, two religious incunables printed by Wynkyn de Worde were 'the gyfte of Syster Mary Nevell' to Sister Audrey Dely: 'God reward her in heven for yt'. In other cases, texts functioned as a stimulus to acts of supplication and intercession on behalf of fellow religious: in one pious compilation of prayers, we find the injunction 'Good syster of your charyte I you pray, remember the scrybeler when that ye may, with an Ave Maria or els thys swete word Ihesu'.[90] Reading was thus 'an element in spiritual obligation toward others'.[91] It was often, moreover, a communal and interactive activity: the *Myroure* declared, 'yf ye cannot vnderstonde what ye rede. Aske of other that can teche you. And they that can oughte not to be lothe to teche other.'[92] In this sense Syon was what Brian Stock has called a textual community: a community bound together by oral recitation of its rule, constitutions, custumals and chronicles, but also by verbal discussion of the liturgical and devotional works that its members perused. The textuality of the Bridgettines, to echo a remark of Felicity Riddy, was 'a textuality of the spoken as well as the written word'. This was a world in which women talked avidly about 'the things of God' they encountered in books.[93]

Itself a textual community, Syon was also a member of numerous other textual communities, of varying degrees of formality. One of the larger communities in which the medieval house at Isleworth participated was that of the Bridgettine order. Although *Mare Anglicanum* weakened some of their ties, Syon and Vadstena maintained intercourse throughout the fifteenth century. When Robert Bell and Thomas Stevinton visited the mother-house in 1427, the two parties exchanged gifts of books. The English brothers were given a splendid copy of Bridget's Revelations, and in turn gave their hosts a copy of Hilton's *Scale of Perfection* written by one of their confrères, Clement Maidstone.[94]

Syon also had horizontal textual relationships with other English religious houses. Most notable is the partnership with Sheen. A number of surviving Syon books (including a copy of the Bridgettine Rule) were written by Sheen Carthusians, and the neighbouring houses were a nexus for the collection, copying and transmission of 'mystical' writings from England and the Continent. In 1502, for example, Abbess Elizabeth Gibbs commissioned William

---

90 Bell, *What Nuns Read*, pp. 187, 191–2 (nos. 20, 29).
91 Erler, *Women, Reading and Piety*, p. 28.
92 Blunt (ed.), *Myroure of our Ladye*, p. 67.
93 Brian Stock, *The Implications of Literacy: Written Language and Models of Interpretation in the Eleventh and Twelfth Centuries* (Princeton, 1983), ch. 2; Felicity Riddy, ' "Women Talking about the Things of God": A Late Medieval Sub-Culture', in Carol M. Meale (ed.), *Women and Literature in Britain, 1150–1500* (Cambridge, 1993), pp. 104–27, at p. 111.
94 De Hamel, *Syon Abbey*, p. 57.

Darker of Sheen to copy an English version of Thomas Kempis's *Imitation of Christ*.[95] The two houses also provided the protagonists for the unacceptably intimate textual community that developed between the Carthusian James Grenehalgh and the Bridgettine novice Joanna Sewell. Their story began with reciprocal annotations to a number of books, but ended with him in exile and her in Syon's monastic prison.[96] Yet, if Sheen was Syon's most celebrated partner, there are hints of other connections too. One of the most intriguing comes in a covering letter written by Thomas Betson to accompany some texts sent from the Bridgettine house to an unknown nunnery, with exhortations for their use and further circulation:

> Of such goostly writyngis as oure susturs have with us we sende you part. Consailing and willyng you for encresse of oure mede to lete thies be comoun emong you & yif copy of them to othere of religioun that dwell nygh you.[97]

If books changed hands and created links between Syon and other religious houses, they also enmeshed the nuns within a wider network of literate pious laity, especially women who emulated the monastic life and sometimes entered the convent as widows or vowesses. Mary Erler's work has underlined the permeability of female lay and religious culture in the late medieval period and demonstrated the mutual influence that they exerted upon one another. Again their surviving books bear 'silent witness' to the ties of kinship, friendship, clientage and patronage that bound the Bridgettines with lay people outside the cloister. Traffic occurred in both directions: if wealthy gentlewomen bestowed book gifts on the nuns, nuns in turn used them as tokens of affection, gratitude, and earnest request: the British Library copy of William Bonde's 1526 *Pylgrimage of Perfection* is a presentation copy

---

[95] Michael G. Sargent, 'The Transmission by the English Carthusians of some Late Medieval Spiritual Writings', *JEH*, 27 (1976), 225–40; Veronica Lawrence, 'The Role of the Monasteries of Syon and Sheen in the Production, Ownership and Circulation of Mystical Literature in the Late Middle Ages', in James Hogg (ed.), *The Mystical Tradition and the Carthusians*, vol. 10, Analecta Cartusiana 130 (Salzburg, 1996), pp. 101–15. For Gibbs and Darker, see Hutchison, 'What the Nuns Read', p. 217.

[96] M. G. Sargent, *James Grenehalgh as Textual Critic*, Analecta Cartusiana 85 (Salzburg, 1984), vol. 1, pp. 75–109; and idem, 'James Grenehalgh: The Bibliographical Record', in *Kartäusermystik und –mystiker: Dritter Internationaler Kongress über die Kartäuser-geschichte und –spiritualität, Band 4*, Analecta Cartusiana 55 (Salzburg, 1982), pp. 20–54.

[97] A. I. Doyle, 'A Letter Written by Thomas Betson, Brother of Syon Abbey', in Takami Matsuda, Richard A. Linenthal and John Schahill (eds), *The Medieval Book and A Modern Collector* (Cambridge, 2004), pp. 255–67, at p. 255. Doyle argues that this is a fair copy of a letter that originally accompanied another group of texts than the Latin miscellany that it is now found with, in Durham University Library, Cosin MS V.iii.16.

bearing the inscription 'of your charyte I pray you to pray for dame Iohan Spycer in syon' (Figure I.2).[98] This was a broader phenomenon, of which Marilyn Oliva has found evidence in the smaller nunneries of Norfolk such as Thetford priory, to which the Norwich widow Margaret Purdans bequeathed her copy of the Revelations of St Bridget in 1481.[99] But there can be little doubt that Syon was close to the heart of the dense webs of book exchange that wove together the inhabitants of convents and the wider communities of which they were a constituent part. Nor was this brought to an end by the events of the 1530s: in 1556 the Bridgettine Eleanor Fettyplace gave a recently printed Sarum missal to the parish church of Buckland, Berkshire, near where she now resided, in memory of her sister Elizabeth, a former nun of Amesbury, for whom, together with herself, she implored the prayers of good Christian people.[100]

The fashionable culture of devotional literacy explored by Margaret Aston and others operated as a further ligature between the religiously inclined laity and the Bridgettine order in late medieval England.[101] The desire of the former to participate vicariously in the contemplative life of the sisters of Syon is attested by the widespread diffusion of vernacular translations of its unique liturgy far beyond its walls. This occurred in manuscript even before the advent of print, but it was greatly augmented by the development of the mechanical press, which permitted the mass production of key texts like the *Myroure*, which was published in 1530. Prepared by the brethren for their sisters, the original audience for these printed editions was monastic, but they soon expanded beyond its boundaries to a second readership. As C. Annette Grisé shows in her essay here, such texts encouraged readers to mimic the devout lifestyle of the nuns invoked by their prologues, prefatory letters, title-pages, and woodcuts. Commercial printers quickly recognised their potential to supply a voraciously growing demand for aids to personal piety, which also found expression in the proliferation of books of hours. Although Eamon Duffy has questioned the extent to which the latter index an impulse for 'devotional isolation' and reflect a move towards mysticism, 'reclusive interiority' and individualism,[102] there seems little doubt that the liturgical

---

[98] Erler, *Women, Reading and Piety*, citations at pp. 138, 45 and fig. 4 on p. 46.

[99] See Oliva, *Convent and the Community*, pp. 64–72. See also Riddy, 'Women Talking about the Things of God', pp. 107–11.

[100] Erler, *Women, Reading and Piety*, p. 95.

[101] Margaret Aston, 'Devotional Literacy', repr. in her *Lollards and Reformers: Images and Literacy in Late Medieval England* (London, 1984), pp. 101–33.

[102] Duffy, *Stripping of the Altars*, esp. chs 6–7; idem, *Marking the Hours: English People and Their Prayers 1240–1570* (New Haven and London, 2006), pp. 55–6, 59–64.

Figure 1.2: Gift inscription: 'of your charyte I pray you to pray for dame Iohan Spycer in syon': William Bonde, *Here begynneth a deuout treatyse in Englysshe, called the Pylgrimage of perfection very p[ro]fitable for all christen people to rede: and in especiall, to all relygious p[er]sons moche necessary* (London, 1526), sig. A6v. British Library shelfmark G.11740.

material that emanated from Syon attests to a trend in the direction of greater intimacy.

The Bridgettines also played a critical role in catering for the hunger and thirst of the laity for religious instruction, alongside the Carthusians whose vow of silence obliged them to speak through the surrogate medium of books. By contrast, as observed above, pastoral outreach in the form of public preaching was a specified duty of the brothers of Syon. From early on, they were quick to see the potential of both script and print to fulfil this aspect of their vocation. Vincent Gillespie has suggested that the full extent of their involvement in disseminating vernacular literature in the fifteenth century may have been eclipsed by a self-effacing wish for anonymity.[103] In the prologue to the *Life of Jerome*, which the Syon brother Simon Wynter wrote in the second quarter of the fifteenth century for Margaret, Duchess of Clarence, he expressed the hope that she would not only use it to her own 'goostly profyte' but have it copied for the 'edificacion of other that wolde rede hit or here hit … . For ther is thynge therynne ful needfull to be knowe, and had in mynde of alle folk.'[104] The first Syon text to be printed, by Wynkyn de Worde in 1499, this was followed within a year by Thomas Betson's *Ryght Profytable Treatyse*, which was advertised as being 'in lyke wyse medefull to religyous people as to the laye people'.[105] As Grisé shows, the publication of the *Orcharde of Syon*, a version of the dialogues of St Catherine of Siena, in 1519 (Figure I.3), inaugurated a period of exceptional publishing industry, during which the Bridgettines lost many of their inhibitions about outward visibility. Nowhere is this more apparent than in the case of the monastery's most prolific author, Richard Whitford, at the centre of whose extensive *oeuvre* stands the well-known *Werke for Housholders*. Running through seven editions between 1530 and 1537, this guide to domestic piety for 'them that have the guiding or governaunce of any company' was the bestselling book of the decade. Whitford's ministry of the word focused on teaching 'symple soulles' basic religious belief and providing them with advice about traditional devotional practice: how to behave in church, go to confession, receive the host at communion, prepare for death, and learn the Ave Maria, Paternoster, and Creed.[106]

Filled with lengthy quotations from Scripture, Whitford's works represented the acceptable face of vernacular piety in a context in which the project of making the Bible available to lay people in their own tongue continued to be surrounded by ecclesiastical anxiety and in which, in Shannon McSheffrey's words, the relationship between heterodoxy and orthodoxy was characterised by porosity, plasticity and relativity.[107] Syon itself had had to

---

[103] Vincent Gillespie, 'Hid Divinite: The Spirituality of the English Syon Brethren', in Jones (ed.), *Medieval Mystical Tradition*, pp. 189–206, esp. p. 196. For an effective overview, see J. T. Rhodes, 'Syon Abbey and its Religious Publications in the Sixteenth Century', *JEH*, 44 (1993), 11–25.

[104] E. Gordon Whatley with Anne B. Thompson and Robert K. Upchurch (eds), *Saints' Lives in Middle English Collections* (Kalamazoo, 2004), lines 8–13.

[105] *Ryght Profytable Treatyse*, sig. a ii r.

[106] Richard Whitford, *A werke of preparacion or of ordinauance unto communion or howselyng. The werke for householder with the golden pistle and alphabete or a crosrowe called an A.B.C.* (London, [1530]) (STC 6833–36). See the entry in *ODNB*.

[107] Shannon McSheffrey, 'Heresy, Orthodoxy and English Vernacular Religion 1480–1525', *Past and Present*, 186 (2005), 47–80, (p. 79).

Figure 1.3: A religious community: St Catherine of Siena with twelve nuns:
*Here begynneth the orcharde of Syon in the whiche is conteyned the reuelacyons
of seynt [sic] Katheryne of Sene, with ghostly fruytes [and] precyous plantes for
the helthe of mannes soule* (London, [1519]), sig. A1v. British Library shelfmark
C.11.b.6.

negotiate carefully the restrictions which Arundel's Constitutions of 1409 had placed around reading texts containing translations of biblical material. Written in their shadow, the *Myroure* has been seen as an attempt to preserve the Bridgettines' 'distinctive insular culture of reading' without raising 'the specter of heresy', to strike 'a delicate balance between granting the sisters readerly agency and controlling the ways in which they exercise that agency'.[108] Against the backdrop of the renewed concerns about religious deviance that emerged in the early sixteenth century about both Lollardy and Lutheranism, this was a community that could not remain wholly immune to the worries that continued to surround vernacular theology. Whitford's own works were sometimes bound up with anonymous heretical texts and the nuns' purchase of sixty copies of *The Ymage of Love*, recalled by the authorities as suspect, raised concern about the dangers of exposing the vulnerable female mind to mystical works of this kind.[109] Some Syon publications held the potential to enable their readers to bypass the gatekeeper of the clerical hierarchy and communicate with the divine themselves.[110] Their religious conservatism cannot disguise the potential risks linked with the democratisation of Bridgettine spirituality in the age of print.

The quantity of printed literature produced by the house at Isleworth reminds us that Syon embraced the new technology with alacrity and enthusiasm, as both consumer and producer. Gillespie's essay shows that under the guidance of Betson the brothers' library systematically discarded manuscript copies to replace them with typographical versions.[111] Whitford himself was well aware of the benefits of the new medium over scribal copying, commenting in his *Dayly Exercyse* (1534) that 'I have ben compelled (by the charytable instance and request of dyvers devout persones) to wryte it agayne and agayne. And bycause that wrytynge unto me is very tedyouse: I thought better to put it in print.'[112] The willingness of the Bridgettines (and indeed the Carthusians of Sheen and Mount Grace Priory) to exploit the press to disseminate their writings outside monastic precincts unsettles ingrained assumptions

108 Elizabeth Schirmer, 'Reading Lessons at Syon Abbey: The *Myroure of Oure Ladye* and the Mandates of Vernacular Theology', in Linda Olson and Kathryn Kerby-Fulton (eds), *Voices in Dialogue: Reading Women in the Middle Ages* (Notre Dame, IA, 2006), pp. 345–76, at p. 348.
109 Rhodes, 'Syon Abbey', pp. 15, 17. On *The Ymage of Love*, see Grisé, Chapter 4, below.
110 See also the subtle discussion of Carthusian texts in these terms by Emily Richards in 'Writing and Silence: Transitions between the Contemplative and the Active Life', in Lutton and Salter (eds), *Pieties in Transition*, pp. 163–79, and Alexandra Walsham's comments in the 'Afterword', p. 188.
111 See Gillespie, pp. 109–10, below.
112 Richard Whitford, *A dayly exercyse and experience of dethe* (London, 1537 edn), sig. A1v (STC 251414).

about Catholicism's inherently hostile attitude towards print that have lingered long in scholarly discourse. There is now growing awareness of the extent to which the late medieval Church and its officials utilised printing for both administrative and pastoral purposes, to promote the indulgences attached to pilgrimage shrines, to standardise the liturgy, and to issue episcopal ordinances; while James Clark has demonstrated the readiness with which the Benedictines embraced it, setting up provincial presses inside several of their monasteries, including St Albans and St Augustine's, Canterbury, on the very eve of the Reformation itself.[113] Such work does much to undermine the confessional myth that links Protestantism and the press as agents of progress and instruments of liberation and presumes that Rome must have set its face against this new-fangled and dangerous medium from the very beginning.

The violent caesura of the Dissolution thus fatally disrupted a publishing enterprise at Syon that surely would have flowered further had Catholicism retained its hold on the religious establishment in England. This enterprise needs to be seen as one of the currents that flowed into the substantial river of English Counter Reformation vernacular literature catalogued by the great bibliographers Allison and Rogers.[114] Printed clandestinely at home or on foreign presses abroad, this was a literature in which the original writings of missionary priests and exiled divines coexisted with new editions of older mystical, devotional and liturgical works, including a reprint of a version of Kempis's own *Imitation of Christ* attributed to Whitford and a popular set of godly prayers and petitions adapted from another of his works, which became known as the Jesus Psalter.[115] These were published alongside translations of modern classics produced by Catholic reformers, Tridentine bishops, and the members of new and revived religious orders elsewhere. Embodying at least some of the priorities and tendencies that would come to fullest fruition in the spirituality of the Society of Jesus, the books of the English Bridgettine brothers were an important forerunner of the surge of treatises produced for

---

113 Natalia Nowakowska, 'Catholic Bishops, Liturgical Books and the Printing Press in the Fifteenth Century', *Past and Present* (forthcoming); Swanson, *Indulgences*, pp. 95, 102, 250–3, 475. For the Benedictines, see James G. Clark, 'Print and Pre-Reformation Religion: The Benedictines and the Press, c.1470–c.1550', in Julia Crick and Alexandra Walsham (eds), *The Uses of Script and Print 1300–1700* (Cambridge, 2004), pp. 71–92.

114 *ARCR*. Works in English are listed in vol. 2; works in Latin and other languages are in vol. 1.

115 See *ARCR*, ii. nos. 803–4; 193 and ff. The Kempis translation appeared in two post-Dissolution editions in c.1575, though with the false imprint of an earlier edition: *The folowinge of Chryste* (London, [1556]) (STC 23966), and again in 1585. The Jesus Psalter is adapted from STC 14563.

popular lay consumption by influential figures such as Francis de Sales, Luis de Granada, and Ignatius Loyola. The sheer volume of tracts that emanated from clandestine and Continental presses may be a function of the ambivalence of the Counter Reformation hierarchy about making the Bible available to the laity in their mother tongue, though the need to counteract the appeal of the heretical Scriptures compelled them to produce the Douai New Testament in 1582. Conscious that they could penetrate where priests were now unable to enter, the recusant clergy employed such books as 'domme preachers', though they too could not always control the way they were used. They devoted great effort to making the deluge of texts prepared by their brethren past and present accessible to the English Catholic community, both at home and abroad.[116]

From the outset, these initiatives were frequently inspired by the needs of the exiled religious, as the many dedicatory epistles to the mother superiors of convents in France and the Low Countries reveal. Some reflected the learning of the nuns themselves: a 1632 translation of the rule of St Benedict was presented to Lady Eugenia Poulton, Abbess of the Benedictine nunnery in Ghent, by 'her professed and vowed child', Alexia Gray, and intended to raise 'newe comfort, ioy, and solace' in the minds and hearts of its 'newe Embracers, who vnder your ladyshipps gouerment, happely doe a newe inioy the splendour of that light', as well as to 'spreed her rayes a broade in our English tonge'.[117] Many more were the work of male clerics who had some connection with them. In 1557, the Dominican William Peryn translated Nicholas van Esch's *Exercitia theologiae mysticae* to satisfy the 'verye godly and importune desyre' of Katherine Palmer, leader of the Bridgettine nuns to Termonde, and Dorothy Clement of the Poor Clares for guidance in how to ascend the steps to 'perfeccyon'.[118] The Capuchin Father Benet (William Fitch)'s *Rule of Perfection*, a 'breif and perspicuous abridgement of the wholle spirituall lyfe (to weet) Actiue, Contemplatiue, and Supereminent',

---

[116] See also Alexandra Walsham, ' "Domme Preachers"? Post-Reformation English Catholicism and the Culture of Print', *Past and Present*, 168 (2000), 72–123. On Catholicism and the Bible, see also her 'Unclasping the Book? Post-Reformation English Catholicism and the Vernacular Bible', *Journal of British Studies*, 42 (2003), 141–66, esp. comments at pp. 162–3; and more broadly Dominique Julia, 'Reading and the Counter-Reformation', in Guglielmo Cavallo and Roger Chartier (eds), *A History of Reading in the West*, trans. Lydia G. Cochrane (Cambridge, 1999), pp. 238–68.

[117] *The rule of the most blissed Father Saint Benedict patriarke of all munkes*, trans. Alexia Gray (Ghent, 1632), sigs (2)r–(3)v. (*ARCR*, ii. no. 359; STC 1860).

[118] Nicolaus van Esch, *Spirituall exercises and goostly meditations, and a neare way to come to perfection and lyfe contemplative* (London, 1557), dedicatory epistle (STC 19784). This was reprinted in 1598: *ARCR*, ii. no. 641; STC 19785.

was addressed to the Abbess and Fitch's two professed female cousins in the Bridgettine house in Lisbon and designed to assist them to make 'dayly progresse in all vertue'.[119] The Jesuit Thomas Everard rendered Luca Pinelli's *Mirrour of religious perfection* in English for the benefit of Barbara Wiseman, head of the same 'holy house', and its members, in 1618, in the hope that it would bring 'spirituall light to your soules' and 'Happiness to our afflicted Countrey by your returne to your Ancient SION, now forlorne and desolate by your Absence'.[120] Another 'well willer and true frende in Christ Jesu' to the nuns during their time in Rouen was the staunch recusant George Cotton, who translated Diego de Estella's *The contempte of the world, and the vanitie thereof* in his prison cell in London and smuggled it out to be published in 1584.[121] Such books open a window onto the ties that bound the Bridgettines with their friends, relatives and fellow expatriates dispersed across the Continent or still suffering in England, mitigating the tyranny of distance and the difficulties of living as strangers in a foreign land.

The library that the nuns accumulated in exile is a remarkable testimony to the voluminous literary fruits of what was truly an international movement for Catholic renewal. The handful of volumes it contains dating from before the suppression of the convent are probably the residue of the books which the dissolved community carried into exile across the Channel in 1539 and again after Elizabeth's accession in 1558. Dominated, as at Isleworth, by vernacular works, the library they assembled was a working collection, bearing the physical marks of continual use. As Caroline Bowden shows in her contribution to this volume, reading continued to play a vital role in the devotional and spiritual routine of the community in Lisbon. Like Mary Ward, the nuns seem to have 'spent much time by day and sometimes by night in this employment'.[122] The reading of the Bridgettines, Bowden argues, was not recreational but 'goal oriented', directed at the end of strengthening their faith and devotion

---

119 Benoît de Canfield, *The rule of perfection contayning a breif and perspicuous abridgement of all the wholle spirituall life, reduced to this only point of the (vvill of God.) Diuided into three partes* (Rouen, 1609), dedicatory epistles. (*ARCR*, ii. no. 275, STC 10928). Only the 1609 edition survives, but it is clear that there was an earlier edition c.1599. The former contained a further dedication to the Ursuline nuns at Louvain and the Benedictines at Brussels, 'because I owe yow and your howses the like office'.

120 Luca Pinelli, *The mirrour of religious perfection devided into foure bookes* (n.p., 1618), sig. *4r–v. (*ARCR*, ii. no. 258; STC 19938).

121 Diego de Estella, *The contempte of the world, and the vanitie thereof*, trans. George Cotton (Rouen, 1584), sig A4v. (*ARCR*, ii. 160; STC 10541). Copies of the Canfield, Pinelli and Estella may be found among the Syon Abbey books now held in Exeter University Library.

122 Mary Ward, *A Briefe Relation ... . With Autobiographical Fragments and a Selection of Letters*, ed. Christina Kenworthy-Browne, CRS 81 (Woodbridge, 2008), p. 122.

and enabling them to grow in the contemplative life they had chosen to pursue.

Indeed, it might be suggested that the experience of displacement and isolation created conditions in which devotional literacy flourished anew. Cut off from the temporal world they had abandoned when they took their vows, as well as from their homeland, English Catholic nuns found solace and refuge in books, as well as a sense of identity with their co-religionists. Such convents were also scribal communities which continued to make manuscript copies of spiritual texts: one surviving Syon manuscript, containing 'A looking glace for the religious' (a translation of Louis of Blois's *Speculum Monachorum*), has been copied by a late seventeenth- or early eighteenth-century hand.[123] They were also places from which correspondence flowed back and forth to their co-religionists in England and to patrons and sympathisers, in ways that both literally and psychologically breached clausura.[124] Both letters and books were critical in the circumstances of persecution in which England's Catholics found themselves after 1559. They functioned as a ligature and lifeline between the religious and the faithful elsewhere.

Like their pre-Reformation precursors, many of the texts produced for and read by the Bridgettines in exile were prepared with a double audience in mind. In the first instance they sought to provide spiritual succour to those who had chosen the veil and the cloister, though as before their authors were also conscious that they were likely to find a second audience among pious lay people. The recusant laity read and meditated on devotional books of this kind in deliberate 'imitation of Religious persons'. As John Bossy comments, one place we are sure to find 'a typographical *pietas* practised by silent readers' is among committed Catholics perusing primers, psalters and other illicit publications in their closets, chambers, and, in the case of church papists, also their pews.[125] The desire to emulate the monastic life that had been such a feature of

---

[123] Exeter University Library, MS 262/18. Discussed by Veronica Lawrence, 'Syon MS 18 and the Medieval English Mystical Tradition', in Marion Glasscoe (ed.), *The Medieval Mystical Tradition in England*, 5 (Cambridge, 1992), pp. 145–62. The translation has been attributed to Whitford, but doubt is cast on this by James Hogg in his introduction to the facsimile edition: *Richard Whitford*, vol. 3 *Syon Abbey MS 18: A Looking Glace for the Religious*, Salzburg Studies in English Literature (Salzburg, 1992), pp. v–xviii.

[124] Claire Walker, ' "Doe not Suppose me a Well Mortifyed Nun Dead to the World": Letter-Writing in Early Modern English Convents', in James Daybell (ed.), *Early Modern Women's Letter Writing, 1450–1700* (Basingstoke, 2001), pp. 159–76.

[125] Anthonie Batt, *A Poore Mans Mite. A Letter of a Religious Man of the Order of Saint Benedict, vnto a Sister of his, Concerning the Rosarie or Psalter of our Blessed Ladie, Commonly Called the Beades* ([Douai, 1639]), p. 39. John Bossy, *Christianity in the West 1400–1700* (Oxford, 1985), p. 101.

late medieval piety persisted in the early modern era. The devotions practised by the Bridgettines in their cells in Termonde, Rouen and Lisbon were mimicked by men and women compelled to practise their religion in the secrecy and solitude of their homes and in other private places hidden from the sight of Protestant pursuivants. The tradition of spirituality that Syon Abbey had embodied and exported outside its walls in the fifteenth and early sixteenth centuries thus continued, albeit fundamentally transformed by the traumatic rupture it had suffered. It might be seen as an umbilical cord linking pre- and post-Reformation English Catholicism. Preserved and perused by 'papists waiting for another day', copies of older Bridgettine liturgies and books performed the same function. They served as a symbol of hope that England might once more be reconciled to the faith professed by past generations.[126]

This introduction has sought to provide a substantial backdrop to the eight essays that comprise this volume. Individually and collectively, these add new dimensions to our understanding of Syon Abbey and the survival and evolution of the Bridgettine order between 1400 and 1700, and the transformations which Catholic piety underwent in this period. More broadly, we hope that the collection will serve to stimulate further thinking about the relationship between the history of the book and of reading and the history of religion, especially as practised in monastic institutions, but also outside them. Its wider aim is to foster further attempts to chart continuity and change across the series of divides that have opened up between script and print, England and the Continent, and between medieval and early modern studies.

---

[126] Two important studies appeared after this introduction was written. James G. Clark, 'Humanism and Reform in Pre-Reformation English Monasteries', *Transactions of the Royal Historical Society*, 6th ser., 19 (2009), 57–93, provides essential context for our discussion of Syon and the New Learning (above, pp. 14–15). R. W. Pfaff includes a discussion of Syon's liturgy, with an emphasis on its Englishness, in his monumental *The Liturgy in Medieval England: A History* (Cambridge, 2009), pp. 529–39.

1

The Brothers of Syon, 1420–1695

PETER CUNICH

Past scholarship on Syon Abbey has focused almost entirely on the nuns who formed the larger part of the English Bridgettine community.[1] The nuns, who were more usually referred to as 'sisters' in England, were certainly numerically superior and constitutionally more central to the life of Syon than their male counterparts, but the brothers were nevertheless an indispensable element within the distinctive Bridgettine regular life.[2] The primary role of the brothers was to provide spiritual services to the strictly enclosed female community, but they also had their own choral duties to perform and spent a great deal of their time in study. For this reason Syon attracted men of learning from Oxford, Cambridge and London, and they brought with them their personal collections of books which in time formed one of the largest monastic libraries in late medieval England. This role in amassing such a splendid collection of books would be reason enough to justify a closer examination of the brothers of Syon. Throughout its existence, however, the monastery also drew into its cloisters men of considerable piety and even sanctity, and two of these brothers were to die for their faith during the Henrician reformation. In the words of Dom David Knowles, this was a group of male religious

> ... without parallel in Tudor England; men who combined personal austerity of life with theological or devotional competence, and who

[1] I am grateful to the Lady Abbess of Syon for her continued assistance in answering enquiries over many years. I also acknowledge with gratitude the hospitality and professional assistance of the staff at the University of Exeter Library Special Collections. This essay makes use of data from the University of Hong Kong's Monastic Database Project (Hong Kong Research Grants Council Project No. HKU 7176/97H).
[2] The best account of the spiritual life of the Syon brothers is to be found in Roger Ellis, *Syon Abbey: The Spirituality of the English Bridgettines* (also known under the title of *Viderunt eam Filie Syon: The Spirituality of the English House of a Medieval Contemplative Order from its Beginnings to the Present Day*), Analecta Cartusiana 68:2 (Salzburg, 1984), pp. 50–76.

by their books, by their direction of a fervent and aristocratic nunnery, and by their influence as counsellors and confessors of leading laymen, were a power to be reckoned with in a religious world which contained all too few centres of enlightened piety.[3]

Indeed, Knowles placed the Bridgettines of Syon among the spiritually elite company of the Observant Franciscans and the Carthusians, the only other sections of the regular clergy which he felt were deserving of lamentation after the suppression of the monasteries in the 1530s.[4]

Historians of Syon Abbey are in the fortunate situation of having at their disposal a range of surviving constitutional and customary documents which allows them to reconstruct the distinctive form of religious life led by the English Bridgettines. They also have access to a greater quantity of prosopographic data relating to the sisters and brothers of Syon than is available for almost any other religious order in England at the end of the Middle Ages. Much of this information originates from the *Syon Martiloge*, the obit book kept by the brothers, but this basic data was much supplemented by the detailed research of Canon John Fletcher in the 1920s and 1930s.[5] The library catalogue of Syon offers further information on the brothers who gave books to the abbey from the beginning of the fifteenth century through to the 1520s, and Vincent Gillespie's recent edition of that manuscript includes a large number of biographical notes on the brothers.[6] In recent years a great deal more detailed data on the post-suppression activities of the religious has become available through a closer analysis of the pension records of the Court of Augmentations.[7] The English state papers from the 1530s illuminate some of the otherwise secret spiritual struggles taking place within the monastery during Henry VIII's reformation, and Bridgettine records from other countries help fill other gaps.[8] It is therefore possible for today's historian to

3 David Knowles, *The Religious Orders in England*, vol. 3, *The Tudor Age* (Cambridge, 1959), p. 213.
4 *Ibid.*, pp. 210–11, 466.
5 The *Syon Martiloge* is BL, Add. MS 22,285. Canon Fletcher's notebooks detailing his many years of research are deposited at the University of Exeter Library Special Collections as part of the Syon Collection (hereafter FLE).
6 Gillespie, *Syon Abbey Catalogue*, especially pp. xxxi–xxxvi, 567–94. The catalogue was first edited by Mary Bateson, *Catalogue of the Library of Syon Monastery Isleworth* (Cambridge, 1898).
7 The University of Hong Kong's 'Monastic Database Project for England and Wales in the Sixteenth Century' has attempted to collect in one place the various data on Syon pensioners from several sources including the Augmentations records; see http://147.8.24.253:571/monastic.
8 See especially the 'Vadstena Diary', Claes Gerjot (ed.), *Diarium Vadstenense: The Memorial Book of Vadstena Abbey* (Stockholm, 1988). Likewise, the records of the Bridgettine

reconstruct the lives of the religious at Syon to an extent never imagined by earlier scholars.

This essay will focus on the lives and activities of the brothers of Syon from the earliest years until the dissolution and beyond. Eighty-two choir brothers and forty-seven lay brothers have been identified in the period between the first professions at Syon in 1420 and the suppression of the house in 1539, a total of 129 brothers. During the same period slightly more than two hundred sisters were professed. A further twenty-seven choir brothers and six lay brothers have been identified in the years between 1559 and the death of the last remaining brother, George Griffin, at Lisbon in 1695.[9] The spiritual life of Syon did not therefore cease with its suppression at the hands of Henry VIII in 1539. Indeed, the brothers of Syon contributed to the formation and mainte-nance of small groups of sisters in household-based communities in the years between the dissolution and the full re-establishment of the abbey under Mary Tudor in 1557. The role of the brothers in this singularly successful survival strategy will be examined, as also will their role within the peripatetic Syon community during the first thirty years of its long exile from England after 1559. This was a period during which male and female roles within the Syon community slowly evolved in conformity with the Tridentine decrees, leading to a greater subordination of the sisters to the brothers in several areas of the religious life, but most significantly in temporal matters. The brothers ulti-mately disappeared towards the end of the seventeenth century, however, and this development requires some explanation, as does the means by which the sisters resolved the problem of spiritual guidance during the eighteenth century.

The Vocation of a Bridgettine Brother

That the Bridgettine brothers should have had a secondary role within the Order of the Holy Saviour is not surprising. The prologue to the *Rule of the Holy Saviour* stated unequivocally that the order was principally for women, and elsewhere it was made clear that the abbess was to be the 'head and lady' of the monastery.[10] The occupants of the sisters' side of the double monastery

monastery of Porta Paradiso in Florence have been used extensively in revealing the activities in Rome of the first English Confessor General Thomas Fishbourne; see Hans Cnattingius, *Studies in the Order of St Bridget of Sweden*, 1, *The Crisis of the 1420s*, Stockholm Studies in History, 7 (Stockholm, 1963), pp. 131–55.

[9] See FLE/12, 'Syon's Who's Who', vol. 3, for Canon Fletcher's biographical listings of the brothers.

[10] The English text of the Rule used here is taken from Cambridge University Library MS Ff.6.33 as transcribed by James Hogg (ed.), *The Rewyll of Seynt Sauioure and A Ladder of*

and the liturgical activities that they undertook were emphasised throughout the constitutional documents governing the order. The Rule's twenty-four chapters therefore dealt almost exclusively with the regulation of the sisters and their day-to-day activities, while only two chapters were concerned specifically with the brothers.[11] The brothers and sisters were further regulated by their own customaries, in England consisting of three texts known collectively as the *Syon Additions*. Only a fragment of the Latin *Additions* for the choir brothers survives, but the Middle English *Additions* for the lay brothers reveal a great deal about the daily routine within the brothers' convent.[12] Moreover, the *Additions for the Sisters* provides further information on the role of the priest-brothers.[13] The paucity of surviving regulatory legislation for the choir brothers can be further overcome by reference to the Rule, for St Bridget clearly expected the brothers to follow closely its provisions for the sisters in so far as they could be applied to the male side of the community.[14] The brothers therefore observed a similarly strict level of enclosure and silence, and more importantly they were to strive for the same heights of humility, charity and poverty as the female religious.[15] Even in such important ceremonies as the clothing and profession of the brothers, the rubrics and prayers for the sisters were used.[16] In this sense the Rule treated male and female religious with a remarkable level of equality considering the time at which St Bridget's constitutions were written. Certainly the Bridgettine religious enjoyed far more equality within their double houses

---

Foure Ronges by the which men mowe clyme to Heven, Analecta Cartusiana 183 (Salzburg, 2003) (hereafter *Rewle*), pp. 59–81, at p. 61. The Latin text of the Rule used here is the Σ Text approved by Pope Urban VI on 3 December 1378 which appears to have been the most common exemplar used in fifteenth-century England, taken from Eklund (ed.), *Regula Salvatoris*, pp. 141–73, at p. 161.

[11] These were chapters 11 on the religious habit of the brothers and 13 on the role of the priest-brothers as preachers and confessors; see Eklund (ed.), *Regula Salvatoris*, pp. 159–60, 161–2. The brothers were mentioned in passing at various other points in the Rule, especially in chapters 12, 19 and 22; pp. 161, 168, 169–70.

[12] The fragment of the Latin *Additions* for the choir brothers (priests and deacons) exists in one manuscript only (St John's College Cambridge MS 11) and has been published by Hogg (ed.), *Rewyll*, pp. 103–76. The version of the *Additions for the Lay Brothers* used here was written in Middle English and is taken from St Paul's Cathedral Library MS as transcribed by Hogg (ed.), *Laybrothers' Additions*. Roger Ellis has argued that all three known versions of the *Syon Additions* are likely to have descended from a single exemplar which is now lost; see Ellis, *Syon Abbey*, pp. 134–9.

[13] The *Additions for the Sisters* was also written in Middle English and the version used here is taken from the BL MS Arundel 146 as transcribed by Hogg (ed.), *Sisters' Additions*.

[14] Ellis, *Syon Abbey*, pp. 26, 32.

[15] Eklund (ed.), *Regula Salvatoris*, chs 6, 5, 2, 8 and 1.

[16] *Ibid.*, ch. 9 (pp. 152–9) for the sisters and ch. 11 (pp. 159–60) for the brothers.

than was the case in the native English Gilbertine order in which the female religious were at an early stage subordinated to 'parasitic' yet dominant male superiors.[17]

Fully endowed Bridgettine monasteries consisted of sixty sisters and twenty-five brothers, the entire complement of eighty-five religious representing Christ's thirteen apostles and seventy-two disciples.[18] It probably took the foundation at Syon many years to reach this full number for the complex of monastic buildings to house such a large community and the endowment to support it took some time to establish. Ten brothers and twenty-seven sisters were professed when the community was formally created on 1 April 1420, but by 1428 the number of brothers had increased to fourteen and there were forty-one sisters.[19] Numbers probably increased rapidly after 1431 when the community moved from its original home at Twickenham to the new site at Isleworth, and from the 1480s until just before the suppression in 1539 the house boasted a virtually full complement of brothers and sisters.[20] On the brothers' side, the full community was to consist of thirteen priest-brothers (*sacerdotes*) representing the thirteen apostles and headed by a Confessor General, four deacon-brothers (*dyaconi*) representing the four doctors of the church, and eight lay brothers (*laici/focarii*) who were to assist the priests and deacons in their liturgical duties.[21] During the fifteenth and sixteenth centuries monastic communities consisting of twenty-five male religious were not common in England outside the larger Benedictine and Cistercian establishments. The brothers of Syon were therefore recognised as an important religious community in their own right even though forming only one part of a much larger *conventus*.[22]

The twenty-five brothers in the Syon community lived lives of similarly harsh discipline to the strictly enclosed sisters. They all wore habits of burrel, a coarse woollen fabric which was used for both underclothing and outer

---

[17] Brian Golding, *Gilbert of Sempringham and the Gilbertine Order c.1130–1300* (Oxford, 1995), pp. 133–7.

[18] Eklund (ed.), *Regula Salvatoris*, ch. 10, p. 159.

[19] F. R. Johnston, 'Syon Abbey', *Victoria History of the Counties of England, Middlesex*, vol. 1 (London, 1969), p. 184.

[20] On 2 September 1518 there were fifty-six professed sisters at the election of Constance Brown as abbess (London Guildhall Library, MS 9531/9, Register of Bishop Richard Fitzjames, fols 130v–132). In early 1538 Syon had a full complement of sixty sisters but only nineteen brothers.

[21] Eklund (ed.), *Regula Salvatoris*, 10:152–3, p. 159.

[22] Only a few of the greater Benedictine houses boasted large numbers of monks; Canterbury Cathedral Priory had fifty-eight monks in 1539, while Glastonbury and York St Mary's each had fifty-one. Syon's community of twenty-five was about the same as Abingdon (26) and Whitby (24), or the Cistercian houses at Byland (26) and Jervaulx (25).

habits. Each brother was provided with ankle-length shoes and hose for the summer, and in the winter he had shoes lined with fur and burrel. Their clothing included two sets of undertunics made from white burrel, one tunic or 'regular coat' for everyday wear, a cowl with a hood attached for divine office, and an overmantle, all made from grey burrel. For cold weather each brother could wear under his mantle a pilch of lamb or sheep skin lined with fur.[23] These different elements of the habit were all imbued with symbolic meaning which was explained to the candidate during the ceremony of clothing on the day of profession.[24] Significantly, the clothing service for the brothers used the same prayers as the ceremony for the sisters. The new brother became a 'spouse of Christ' at the hands of the bishop in the same way that a sister did. Even though he did not receive the ring as a sign of espousal (the bishop simply held his hand), the prayer used by the bishop was unambiguous: 'I bless you as a spouse of God, and place you in His everlasting possession.'[25] Nor were the brothers given the veil, but the bishop nevertheless prayed over the brother's newly shaven head using the same words as for a sister's veiling, praying that Christ's wisdom and understanding would lead his soul towards heavenly things. Later in the ceremony at the point where the bishop would normally pin on the sister's distinctive Bridgettine crown, he made the sign of the cross over the brother's head, praying that the new brother would be stable and persevere in the religious life.[26] The fact that the same profession ceremony and virtually the same habit was used for both brothers and sisters made a strong statement about the essential unity of the Bridgettine community despite the strict separation of brothers and sisters in different enclosures on opposite sides of the abbey church. Likewise, in making their obedience to their respective superiors both brothers and sisters were exhorted to seek 'very meekness', 'pure chastity', and 'wilful poverty' as the true callings of all Bridgettine religious.[27]

The vow of humility meant that the brothers all wore the same clothing irrespective of rank or class within the order. The only distinguishing marks were the cloth badges worn on the left breast of their overmantles. For priests, the badge was a red cross with a white circle representing the eucharistic mystery which they celebrated each day. Deacons wore a white circle representing the 'incomprehensible wisdom' of the four doctors of the church with five small tongues of red cloth representing the Holy Spirit who 'inflamed

23 Eklund (ed.), *Regula Salvatoris*, 11:156, p. 159.
24 *Ibid.*, 9:120–30, pp. 155–6.
25 *Ibid.*, 9:117, pp. 154–5; Hogg (ed.), *Rewyll*, p. 110.
26 Eklund (ed.), *Regula Salvatoris*, 9:135–8, p. 157.
27 Hogg (ed.), *Laybrothers' Additions*, ch. 17, pp. 51–2.

them with the excellence of the Godhead, the mystery of the incarnation of Christ, the vanity and contempt of the world, the victory of the righteous, and the pains of the wicked'.[28] The lay brothers wore a white cross for innocence with five small red stains in reverence of the wounds of Christ.[29]

All brothers, whether destined for the choir or lesser duties, were required to be at least twenty-five years of age before they could be admitted to the community. Data on the age of brothers at the time of profession is far from complete, but it appears that a large number of them were in fact well over the minimum age when they entered Syon. John Pinchbeck (professed c.1459), Stephen Saunder (c.1478), William Bonde (c.1509), John Fewterer (c.1517) and Richard Whitford (c.1511) were all at least thirty years of age on entry; Richard Terenden (c.1488) and John Steyke (c.1489) were approximately thirty-five years old; Clement Maidstone (c.1430), William Asplyon (c.1460) and Thomas Betson (c.1481) were in their early forties; and Thomas Westhaw (c.1460) and John Lawsby (c.1476) were both well into their forties. John Bracebridge must have been nearly fifty when he was professed in 1420, an age at which most religious orders would refuse to accept an aspirant.

The greater maturity of the men who entered Syon must have contributed substantially to the extraordinary stability of the monastic community, a feature which was increasingly evident from the 1440s. At a time when most male religious orders were recruiting boys aged between sixteen and eighteen, the community at Syon waited until the boys had grown into men before accepting them. The convent could therefore be fairly certain that aspirants were making well-informed decisions before entering the religious state. Most of the men entering as priest- or deacon-brothers were already ordained and several had been active as parish priests for some time before their religious profession: Thomas Betson was rector of Wimbish, Essex from 1466 and vicar of Lissington in Lincolnshire until 1473, and John Steke was successively rector of St Laurence's Norwich (1480–3) and Blundell, Norfolk (1483–9).[30] Many of the later brothers entered the community straight from university careers at Oxford and Cambridge: John Trowell was a fellow of Merton College (1481–91) and sub-warden at the time of his entry to Syon; Richard Whitford was a fellow of Queens' College Cambridge (1498–1504), but had also spent time at the University of Paris (1498–9) where he met Erasmus, and later acted as chaplain to Bishop Fox of Winchester (1504–7);

[28] Eklund (ed.), *Regula Salvatoris*, 11:157–9, pp. 159–60.
[29] *Ibid.*, 11:160, p. 160.
[30] Emden, *BRUC*, pp. 59, 552–3.

while Richard Reynolds was University Preacher at Cambridge in 1509–10 and became a fellow of Corpus Christi College (1510–13).[31] John Bracebridge may not have been a graduate, but he appears to have had a long career as a schoolmaster in Lincolnshire (c.1390–1420) before being professed in 1420.[32] Thomas Westhaw had experience of both academic and parish life before answering the call to a more austere religious life, being a fellow of Pembroke Hall, Cambridge (1436–46), and rector of All Hallows London (1448–59).[33] The same is true of William Asplyon, Stephen Saunder, John Dodde, and Richard Terenden.[34] Other men in the community had some experience of the religious life already, including most of the original brothers professed in 1420.[35]

It is not possible to determine what any of the lay brothers did before they entered Syon, but the fact that the same minimum age requirement was applied to them reinforces the serious intent of the Bridgettine monastic life for all men who wished to enter. Whatever their social rank, previous experience of the religious life or their seniority in clerical orders, all aspirants to the strictly enclosed life of a Bridgettine brother were required to persevere during a year of testing outside the monastery before being clothed. As described above, the clothing ceremony for the brothers was identical to that for the sisters. For the more mature brothers, many of whom had a great deal of clerical or academic experience already, the ceremony's symbolism must have been a powerful reminder of the strict life to which they were being called. The brothers' ceremony included the processional use of a red martyr's banner with images of their new 'spouse', the crucified Christ, and his mother the Virgin Mary. The new brother was urged to learn patience and poverty from Christ, charity and meekness from the Blessed Virgin.[36] Moreover, during most of the profession Mass the new brother knelt before a portable funeral bier sprinkled with soil, reminding him both of his own mortality and the fact that he was about to die to his old life and take on a very different and difficult calling. Each brother would remain within the enclosure for the rest of his life, and at the end would be buried in the south aisle or

---

[31] Emden, *BRUO to 1500*, p. 1910; 'John Trowell', 'Richard Whitford', 'Richard Reynolds', in *ODNB*.
[32] 'Bracebridge, John', in *ODNB*.
[33] Emden, *BRUC*, pp. 630–1; noting that Westhaw did not enter Sheen Charterhouse in 1459, see Gillespie, *Syon Abbey Catalogue*, p. xlvi.
[34] Emden, *BRUO to 1500*, p. 61; Emden, *BRUC*, p. 507; Emden, *BRUO to 1500*, pp. 580, 1855–6.
[35] David Knowles, *The Religious Orders in England*, vol. 2, *The End of the Middle Ages* (Cambridge, 1955), p. 180; Emden, *BRUC*, p. 466.
[36] Hogg (ed.), *Rewyll,* p. 106.

ambitus fratrum of the abbey church beside his brothers without any distinction being made between lay and choir brothers.[37]

Despite the comparatively large size of the male religious community at Syon, the three classes of Bridgettine brothers were numerically inferior to the sisters and they played a negligible role in the government of the monastery. The abbess and her obedientiaries exercised complete control over the temporal resources of the abbey and there was little legislative provision for the brothers to have any say whatsoever in the disposition of the monastery's goods. They played no part in the election of the abbess. In matters of great importance to the whole community the abbess and Confessor General might call together the most senior and wiser brothers and sisters as a council to advise the abbess, but the abbess was always to have full temporal authority over the house.[38] The Confessor General acted as 'sovereign' over the brothers only, but was given spiritual authority over both communities, acting as 'conservator of the order' and ensuring that the Rule was kept 'in all points' by both brothers and sisters. The abbess was enjoined to assist him in this grave task, and he was to do nothing without the consent of the abbess, except as 'sovereign' of the brothers and in the spiritual 'conservation of the order'.[39] The Confessor General's role in the temporal affairs of the house was therefore minor, but he could leave the enclosure on behalf of the abbess in bringing 'good order' to the monastery.[40] The only occasion on which a Confessor General appears to have been involved in the temporal affairs of the abbey was in the late 1480s and 1490s when he and his 'council' directed some of the building works for the new church.[41]

The abbess and the Confessor General were expected to be mother and father to the 'whole congregation' of sisters and brothers at Syon, and they were both required to be sober, chaste, mild, meek, benign, peaceable and 'dreaders of God'. Together they were to ensure the total enclosure of the religious, a matter of central importance in fostering the spiritual vitality of the house.[42] The Confessor General was to provide careful spiritual direction to the abbess so that 'the worship of religion be saved and kept' within the

---

[37] Only the confessors general were buried separately, presumably in places of honour, but the fifth Confessor General, John Trowel (died 1523), was laid to rest with the other brothers in the *ambitus fratrum*.

[38] Hogg (ed.), *Sisters' Additions*, ch. 58, p. 199.

[39] *Ibid.*, p. 198; Eklund (ed.), *Regula Salvatoris*, 12:161.

[40] Ellis, *Syon Abbey*, p. 33.

[41] The National Archives, Kew: SC6/Addenda/3485/3, account of repairs to the new church (1488–9); SC6/HenVII/1715, account of works (1494–5).

[42] Ellis, *Syon Abbey*, p. 33.

abbey, and he was enjoined by the Rule to warn an errant abbess twice or three times 'with charity and due reverence' before calling upon the bishop to admonish or depose her.[43] These constitutional arrangements were intended to promote exemplary spiritual observance by male and female religious living under one roof, and gave the Bridgettine religious communities a durability and a greater level of internal self-sustainability than almost any other religious order. The numerous checks and balances between female temporal and male spiritual authority which St Bridget wrote into her Rule were directed at creating perfect religious communities, but the central role played by the Confessor General as spiritual 'conservator' could also be an Achilles' heel should the office be occupied by a weak or indisposed superior as was the case at Syon in the 1530s.

The functions of the different classes of brothers at Syon were enumerated in the Rule and the *Additions for the Lay Brothers*. The priest-brothers were to celebrate masses for the sisters and together with the deacon-brothers were to sing the office of the church in their 'nether choir' (*chorus inferior*) according to the local usage of the canons at St Paul's Cathedral in London.[44] The abbey church at Syon was constructed so that the sisters could see the sacrament being celebrated by the brothers on the high altar from the privacy of their raised eastern choir (*chorus superior*) and could hear the office being sung by the brothers in their western choir. The two choirs were to alternate their office so that a continuous prayer would rise up from Syon every day.[45] The choir brothers spent the largest portion of their day in their choir stalls singing the divine office. Seven chapters in the *Additions* dealt with the way in which the lay brothers were to assist at divine office,[46] a further five chapters gave directions for the celebration of mass and other ceremonies in the church,[47] while twelve chapters gave detailed instructions for all the major seasons and feast days during the liturgical year.[48] The lost *Additions* for the choir brothers no doubt dealt with their divine office in far greater detail, but even the *Additions* for the lay brothers was full of provisions to ensure that the divine office and all liturgical ceremonies were performed with reverence and exactness.

As in most other monasteries, a hebdomadarian was appointed each week from among the choir brothers to ensure that the service books were carefully prepared for divine service, and at Syon he no doubt also performed the

---

[43] Hogg (ed.), *Sisters' Additions*, ch. 58, p. 204.
[44] Eklund (ed.), *Regula Salvatoris*, 10:150–1, p. 159; Hogg (ed.), *Rewle*, p. 71.
[45] Ellis, *Syon Abbey*, p. 111; Hogg (ed.), *Rewyll*, vol. 4, ch. 18, p. 102.
[46] Hogg (ed.), *Laybrothers' Additions*, chs 18, 19, 20, 21, 24, 25 and 26.
[47] *Ibid.*, chs 22, 23, 27, 28 and 29.
[48] *Ibid.*, chs 30–41.

various duties listed in the *Ordinacio officiorum chori* of the Vadstena *Liber usuum*.[49] The hebdomadarian's role in the choir and at the high and Lady altars was important in maintaining the dignity of services in the church, but it was the cantor who shouldered most responsibility for the proper performance of the divine office. The office of cantor is hardly mentioned in the lay brothers' *Additions* and that of the succentor not at all, but it seems likely that their duties would have been virtually identical to those described in the Vadstena *Liber usuum*, or those for the chantress and subchantress on the sisters' side at Syon.[50] The only mention of the cantor in the lay brothers' *Additions* prescribed his role as being to organise and discipline the lay brothers in the performance of their liturgical duties – a very small part of his central role in organising the choir.[51] As the male equivalent of the sister-chantress, the cantor was responsible for seeing that everything was done well in choir and that nothing was omitted from the office. The succentor acted as the cantor's deputy and drew up the weekly roster of duties for the brothers' choir.[52]

The Rule was deliberately strict in enjoining the priest-brothers (and presumably, by extension, the deacon-brothers) to attend only to divine office, study and prayer. They were forbidden to have any other temporal duties or offices in the monastery.[53] Within the cloister, however, the Confessor General was assisted by two 'searchers' who helped to maintain the strict discipline of the Rule and oversaw the activities of the other officials.[54] The Confessor General also appointed brothers to special offices to assist him in his spiritual work.[55] Four offices to be held by choir brothers are mentioned in the *Additions for the Lay Brothers*: the hebdomedarian or 'hebdomedar',[56] and the cantor or 'chauntour',[57] whose roles are discussed above; the other two officers were the sacristan,[58] and the reader or 'legister' in the refectory.[59] The sacristan could be either a priest or a deacon but the

---

[49] *Ibid.*, ch. 19, p. 55; Sara Risberg (ed.), *Liber usuum fratrem monasterii Vadstenensis: The Customary of the Vadstena Brothers: A Critical Edition with an Introduction*, Studia Latina Stockholmiensia 50 (Stockholm, 2003), pp. 198–203.

[50] For the duties of the cantor and succentor at Vadstena see Risberg, *Liber usuum*, pp. 204–11. For the chantress and subchantress at Syon see Hogg (ed.), *Rewyll*, vol. 4, ch. 45, pp. 147–50.

[51] Hogg (ed.), *Laybrothers' Additions*, ch. 45, p. 99. For his other duties see Hogg (ed.), *Sisters' Additions*, ch. 45, pp. 147–50.

[52] Hogg (ed.), *Sisters' Additions*, ch. 45, p. 150.

[53] Eklund (ed.), *Regula Salvatoris*, 13:173, p. 161.

[54] Hogg (ed.), *Laybrothers' Additions*, ch. 56, p. 125; ch. 8, p. 38.

[55] *Ibid.*, ch. 13, pp. 43–4.

[56] *Ibid.*, ch. 19, p. 55.

[57] *Ibid.*, ch. 45, p. 99.

[58] *Ibid.*, ch. 48, p. 106.

[59] *Ibid.*, ch. 50, p. 113.

requirements for the other offices are not clearly stated in the surviving *Additions*. Two other offices seem likely to have been held by lay brothers – the 'butler' and the 'keeper of the wheel' – but the *Additions* are silent as to the brothers who were eligible to hold these offices.[60] Another office, the librarian (*custos librorum*), is not mentioned in Syon's extant constitutional documents but we know that the deacon-brother Thomas Betson held the office from the late fifteenth century until the 1520s.[61] All office-bearers were to be men of sobriety, cheerfulness, discretion, peace, wisdom, and circumspection, ensuring at all times that each brother's needs were satisfied with gentleness and understanding.[62]

The only other duties the priest-brothers were allowed to perform were spiritual: preaching in the abbey church each Sunday and on high feast days, and confessing the other brothers and sisters regularly.[63] Preaching was given an unusually important place in the liturgical routine of the monastery, with perhaps one hundred or more sermons preached every year. Syon therefore became a magnet for the pious and intellectually curious alike although the sermons were probably long, dry and far from original in their content.[64] Public sermons were always delivered in English and the preachers were enjoined to preach in such a way that the lay people would be able to profit from hearing their sermons.[65] Brothers who preached were given leave from the choral office for three days so that they could prepare their sermons without distraction, and on the day of the sermon the preacher was allowed to take the first portion from the common meal tray after the president.[66] These privileges were probably also extended to brothers who preached for Syon's popular *ad vincula* indulgence when the public flocked to the abbey in large numbers, including, on one occasion, Margery Kempe.[67] Preaching was therefore recognised and rewarded within the cloister as one of the most important duties of the priest-brothers, and the centrality of preaching in the weekly liturgy certainly helps to explain the existence of such an extraordinarily large library. Collected by the priest-brothers from the foundation of

[60] *Ibid.*
[61] Gillespie, *Syon Abbey Catalogue*, pp. xlvi–li; A. I. Doyle, 'Thomas Betson of Syon Abbey', *The Library*, 115 (1956), 115–18.
[62] Hogg (ed.), *Laybrothers' Additions*, ch. 56, p. 123.
[63] Eklund (ed.), *Regula Salvatoris*, 13:174–8, pp. 161–2.
[64] Susan Powell, *Preaching at Syon Abbey*, Working Papers in Literary and Cultural Studies, 29 (Salford, 1997), pp. 6, 23. Only one identifiable Syon sermon is known to survive in manuscript.
[65] Ellis, *Syon Abbey*, pp. 19, 28.
[66] Hogg (ed.), *Laybrothers' Additions*, chs 55 and 52, pp. 122, 117.
[67] Gillespie, *Syon Abbey Catalogue*, p. xxxii.

the monastery, its main use was to aid in both the preparation of sermons and the spiritual guidance of the sisters.

While a preacher was given three days of leisure to prepare his sermon, much of the normal working day of the other priests was taken up not with study and sermon-writing but with confessing the sisters and the other brothers. All the religious at Syon were required to confess to the Confessor General at least three times each year, unburdening their faults and any difficulties they had in keeping the Rule. Moreover, frequent confession was encouraged by the example of St Bridget who sometimes confessed up to three times a day. The Rule insisted that provision be made for the sisters to confess daily if they wished, and the *Additions* listed failure to confess among the faults which were to be corrected in chapter.[68] The section of the church housing the confessional grilles (or 'windows' as they were known at Syon) was therefore one of the busiest places in the whole monastery, and the fact that the superior of the brethren held the title of 'Confessor General' emphasises the importance placed on the role of the priests as confessors. The priest-brothers also heard the confessions of the laity who flocked to Syon on certain feast days.

The spiritual life of the priest-brothers was therefore dominated by their roles as preachers and confessors. Undoubtedly they also shared in the contemplative spiritual life of the sisters, but this element has left little record in surviving documents. The literary output of the brothers provides evidence of a 'sober, sane and moderate asceticism', but they seem to have had little engagement with mystical literature.[69] Indeed, their spirituality has been described as 'traditional' or 'conventional' even though the daily lections of the brothers' *Martiloge* exhorted them to spiritual self-reflection and contemplation.[70] The spiritual life of a Bridgettine brother was to a large extent 'fuelled by radical humility and self-abnegation' demanded by the Rule of the Holy Saviour, and the very invisibility which their life encouraged makes a full assessment of their distinct spirituality very difficult.[71]

The choir brothers certainly occupied a central place in the spiritual life of

---

68 Ellis, *Syon Abbey*, p. 12; Eklund (ed.), *Regula Salvatoris*, 13:173, 178, pp. 161, 162; Hogg (ed.), *Laybrothers' Additions*, chs 2 and 3, pp. 21, 25; Hogg (ed.), *Sisters' Additions*, chs 2, 3 and 4, pp. 3, 8, 12.

69 Vincent Gillespie, 'Dial M for Mystic: Mystical Texts in the Library of Syon Abbey and the Spirituality of the Syon Brethren', in Marion Glasscoe (ed.), *The Medieval Mystical Tradition*, 6 (Cambridge, 1999), pp. 241–68, at pp. 262, 268.

70 Vincent Gillespie, ' "Hid Diuinite": The Spirituality of the English Syon Brethren', in E. A. Jones (ed.), *The Medieval Mystical Tradition in England*, 7 (Cambridge, 2004), pp. 189–206, at pp. 202–5.

71 *Ibid.*, p. 196.

Syon, but the eight lay brothers also had clearly defined roles to play in the complex Bridgettine liturgy, and controlled domestic arrangements in the brothers' cloister. Their liturgical duties were arranged according to an eight-week rota in which their seniority of profession was strictly observed.[72] The lay brothers served all the masses and other major ceremonies in the abbey church, and during the hours of the divine office they were required to be present in the brothers' choir and follow the actions of the priests and deacons whenever they rose, bowed or sat down.[73] While the lay brothers stood apart from the priests in front of the choir stalls during office and did not sing these services, the literate lay brothers were required to say daily the 'Lady Service' while the illiterate recited instead a prescribed number of Our Fathers and Hail Marys.[74] When serving Mass and moving around the high altar they were to behave 'like angels', and observe silence always.[75] Moreover, the lay brothers literally set the pace of the day at Syon, for they were in charge of ringing the many different bells which called the brothers and sisters to choir and gave structure to their various daily activities.[76]

One of the lay brothers was appointed to be 'minister of the sacristy' in addition to his other liturgical duties, and he had numerous responsibilities to perform under the guidance of the brother-sacristan.[77] Another lay brother was always to be appointed infirmarian. He was required to be a strong man who could lift his ill brethren in and out of bed, but also someone who could treat the sick with reverence and love.[78] It is also likely that a lay brother was 'keeper of the wheel' which allowed limited communication and the passing of various goods and books between the two sides of the monastery.[79] As well as the duties listed above, the lay brothers took care of numerous domestic chores within the brothers' cloister. These duties included making the fires, preparing and serving meals, washing all the clothing, shaving the other brothers once a week, cleaning the cloisters and church, and tending the gardens and orchards. The lay brothers were admonished to 'dig and delve' and 'set and sow' for the common profit of the whole monastery, and the *Additions* reminded them that they were not received into the order to live idle lives, but rather to obey the Confessor General's bidding and minister with humility to the priests and deacons in all their needs, whether in the

---

[72] Hogg (ed.), *Laybrothers' Additions*, ch. 46, pp. 100–2.
[73] *Ibid.*, ch. 18, p. 53.
[74] *Ibid.*, ch. 47, p. 103.
[75] *Ibid.*, p. 104.
[76] *Ibid.*, ch. 49, pp. 109–12.
[77] *Ibid.*, ch. 48, pp. 106–7.
[78] *Ibid.*, ch. 57, pp. 126–7.
[79] *Ibid.*, ch. 16, p. 49; ch. 56, p. 124.

church or cloister.[80] It was also the lay brothers who dug and 'dressed' the burial pits, and who carried their brothers and sisters to the grave.[81] While they had their own chapter which assembled just before that of the priests and deacons, they followed the same 'observances' as their clerical brethren and any serious faults were corrected with the same penalties in the presence of the choir brothers in their chapter.[82] Even in death the choir and lay brothers were buried side by side in order of passing with no distinction between them. In an order which took death so seriously and went to so much effort and expense in planning for the provision of burial spaces for the deceased members of the convent, such equality in death among the three classes of brothers is both completely consistent with the spirituality of the Bridgettines but at the same time rather striking in an age when social stratification was typically reflected in the ordering of monastic communities.[83]

In the community records of Syon the lay brothers were referred to as *focarii* rather than *conversi*, and this perhaps recognised an essential difference in their function within the Bridgettine order as compared with other late medieval religious orders. Their role as 'ministers' to the priests and deacons in the community in both liturgical and claustral settings was continually emphasised and they were clearly not limited to functioning merely as servants or agricultural labourers, a practice which was common in other orders such as the Carthusians and Cistercians. In this sense they were an integral part of the balanced constitution of the Bridgettine monastic community, performing specific duties within Christ's vineyard in the same way that men and women were treated with remarkable equality within the order's constitutional documents. The lay brothers were certainly performing tasks which were probably perceived as being of lesser importance than the chanting of the office by the choir brothers and sisters, but it would be a mistake to make too great a distinction on this point. It is the inclusivity and balance of the Bridgettine Rule which distinguishes it from other medieval monastic rules.[84]

Whatever their duties within the cloister, the lay and choir brothers all lived lives which were strictly confined by the *clausura*, the enclosed space delimited by the iron grilles in the church, the thick walls of their conventual buildings, and the precinct walls which surrounded their orchard and gardens. The

---

[80] *Ibid.*, ch. 47, p. 104.
[81] *Ibid.*, ch. 42, p. 93.
[82] *Ibid.*, ch. 1, p. 12.
[83] Roberta Gilchrist and Barney Sloane, *Requiem: The Medieval Monastic Cemetery in Britain* (London, 2005), pp. 137, 139. Only the abbesses and confessors general were routinely buried apart from the rest of the community in places of honour.
[84] Ellis, *Syon Abbey*, pp. 66–72, however emphasises the inferior status assigned to the lay brothers.

enclosure of the Bridgettine brothers was much stricter than that which restricted the movement of monks in other English monasteries, only excepting the Carthusians with whom the Bridgettines were often compared. The physical space in which the brothers lived and moved was evolving for much of the fifteenth century, with major building works continuing throughout the periods 1461–79 and 1488–1509. The abbey church was not ready for full liturgical use until 1485 at the earliest, finally being consecrated on 20 August 1488.[85] The abbey church was the line of demarcation between the two communities, with the sisters' cloister to the north and the brothers' cloister to the south. Recent archaeological excavations have revealed just how large the abbey church was – wider than Westminster Abbey and nearly as long – and it was here that the brothers had the widest rights of access, with only the sisters' upper choir out of bounds.[86] The sisters were ever present, always to be heard singing their office, but never seen. The brothers could only enter the sisters' enclosure for specific purposes, and even then access was tightly controlled.[87] The sisters never entered the brothers' enclosure, not even the abbess.

Bridgettine brothers were only allowed to venture outside the enclosure on business which was for the good of the monastery or to refute heretics, but this modification of St Bridget's original and much stricter rule of perpetual enclosure for the brothers seems to have been limited in its application at Syon. It would appear that only the Confessor General and an accompanying brother were authorised to venture forth from the monastery.[88] The rules governing egress for brothers at Vadstena were applied much more liberally, and with good reason. Two brothers were sent from Vadstena in 1408 to make preparations for establishing Syon: John Peterson stayed in England until 1416 and Katillus Thorbernus did not return to Vadstena until 1421. Another two brothers accompanied a group of professed sisters and aspirants from Sweden to England in 1415 and one of them returned to Vadstena a year later.[89] This was normal practice within the Bridgettine order and the Vadstena Diary is full of examples of brothers being sent to daughter houses either to form communities or reform abuses.[90] The Vadstena *Liber usuum*

85 R. W. Dunning, 'The Building of Syon Abbey', *Transactions of the Ancient Monuments Society*, NS, 25 (1981), 16–26.

86 For a comparative plan see Jonathan Foyle, 'Syon Park: Rediscovering Medieval England's Only Bridgettine monastery', *Current Archaeology*, 16:12 (no. 192, June 2004), p. 553.

87 Eklund (ed.), *Regula Salvatoris*, 22:252, p. 170.

88 Ellis, *Syon Abbey*, pp. 23–4.

89 Gerjot, *Diarium Vadstenense*, pp. 150, 152, 153, 172, 186; FLE/12, pp. 1–3; FLE/23, pp. 157–8.

90 FLE/23, pp. 54, 68, 79, 81, 84, 85.

limited such visits to no more than two weeks, and the visiting brothers were only allowed to converse with the Confessor General. Syon was given special permission to accept visiting brothers for up to six months, but after the departure of Katillus Thorbernus in 1420 there are no further records of visitors from Vadstena or any other house of the order.[91] Syon brothers are known to have visited Rome in 1423 and Vadstena in 1427, but these were rare examples of egress and there are few other recorded instances of brothers venturing beyond their cloister in the later history of Syon.[92]

The Brothers of Syon in the Fifteenth Century

The mission of the Syon brothers to Rome in 1423, within only three years of the formal enclosure of the foundation community, was in response to disquieting news from the Holy City: on 13 February 1422, Pope Martin V issued a bull ordering the separation of all double monastic houses in Europe. This act seriously threatened the future of the fledgling community at Syon. It had taken seven years for a permanent community to be formed and in the five years between 1415 and 1420 there had been a certain amount of upheaval with the intended abbess and Confessor General both leaving the community before enclosure took place. The wider Bridgettine order was already in a state of turmoil: its privileges were under attack from belligerent ecclesiastical authorities, there was internal division over 'improvements' which had recently been made to the order's original constitutions, and the formation of an all-male Bridgettine community by breakaway Italian brothers had worsened the situation considerably. The Syon community decided to send their Confessor General, Thomas Fishbourne, to Rome to petition the pope directly for a revocation of the bull of separation.[93] Fishbourne was a cousin of Bishop Clifford of London and had been confessor to Henry V before entering Syon, so he was well placed to influence members of the Curia and even the pope himself. Arriving in Rome on 11 August 1423, Fishbourne quickly made contact with other Bridgettine supporters and on 18 August he was admitted to his first audience with Martin V, outlining the ways in which the 1422 bull of separation would spell disaster for the spiritual lives of the sisters of Syon if they were denied the guidance of the brothers.[94] On 21 September the pope accepted a petition drawn up by Fishbourne in Henry VI's name asking that

---

[91] Risberg, *Liber usuum*, pp. 25–6, 102–4.
[92] FLE/12, pp. 14–15.
[93] Cnattingius, *The Crisis of the 1420s*, pp. 128–30; an earlier account of the Syon deputation to Rome can be found in FLE/26, pp. 189–96.
[94] Cnattingius, *The Crisis of the 1420s*, pp. 133–8.

the case be decided by a panel of judges drawn from outside the college of cardinals.[95]

Fishbourne immediately procured the services of two leading canon lawyers, Nicolaus Panormitanus and Domenico da San Gemignano, to write statements of opinion putting the Bridgettine case. Panormitanus argued that the Bridgettine monasteries were not in fact 'double houses' as defined by the 1422 bull of separation, but rather single houses intended primarily for women (*per mulieres primo et principaliter*).[96] Martin V accepted this explanation and recognised that the strict double enclosure of Bridgettine monasteries guarded against any risk of scandal.[97] He therefore issued a new bull on 4 November 1423 revoking the earlier bull of separation with regard to Syon.[98] This represented an extraordinary victory for Fishbourne and the Syon community, but the rest of the order benefited too. Martin V quickly issued a similar bull of revocation for the five northern European Bridgettine houses on 15 December 1423, and extended the same provisions to the single Italian house, Porta Paradiso in Florence, on 13 February 1427.[99] On 2 February 1425 Martin confirmed for Syon Abbey all the traditional Bridgettine privileges contained in the earlier bull *Mare Magnum* by issuing a new bull, the so-called *bulla reformatoria* which later became known as the *Mare Anglicanum*. This document was largely drafted by Fishbourne himself and restated the canonical formula regarding the role of the Bridgettine brothers as suggested by Panormitanus, but it also confirmed the original visitational privileges of the local bishop and insisted that all twenty-five brothers were to live within the enclosure at Syon. Moreover, it gave Syon Abbey independence from both the old mother house at Vadstena and the newer headquarters of the 'conservator general' in Florence, raising Syon in the process to the position of head house of the order in England.[100] *Mare Anglicanum* ensured the independence of Syon for the rest of its existence; the other Bridgettine abbeys returned to a more centralised model in which Vadstena played the role of mother house, with regular general chapters to decide major policy issues for the whole order.

The threat from Martin V's 1422 bull was just one of the difficulties faced by Syon in its early years. The period between the arrival of the small party of Swedish religious from Vadstena in 1415 and the first professions in 1420

---

95 *Ibid.*, p. 135.
96 *Ibid.*, pp. 139–42.
97 *Ibid.*, pp. 142–3, 145–7.
98 *Ibid.*, p. 148.
99 *Ibid.*, pp. 148–9, 155.
100 *Ibid.*, pp. 151–3.

was a time of great uncertainty: few aspirants were attracted to the new monastery, Henry V's nominees as abbess and Confessor General both left the community to return to their previous religious lives, and Henry V died in 1421 leaving a child as heir. The Confessor General's absence in Rome for such a long period of time from mid-1423 until late-1425 may have contributed to further destabilisation of the convent, and perhaps the very strict interpretation of St Bridget's Rule enforced at Syon by Thomas Fishbourne after the promulgation of *Mare Anglicanum* rendered the Bridgettine religious life just too difficult for some of the early English aspirants. By 1427 it was necessary to send two of the brothers to Vadstena in order to resolve pressing questions which had arisen over the implementation of the Rule, and there is even evidence in the *Additions for the Lay Brothers* of a minor revolt over the implementation of *Mare Anglicanum*.[101] Whatever the reasons for the difficulties in the 1420s, there can be no doubt that some of the earliest brothers left the community after they had been professed. It must be noted, however, that these were not cases of apostasy, but applications for transfer *ad ordinem laxiorem*. The fact that no instances of apostasy have been found among the Syon brothers in the period before the 1530s reinforces the impression of extraordinary stability within this monastery.[102] Despite these departures, then, the number of brothers in the community increased marginally from ten in 1420 to fourteen in 1428, and continued to climb in the years that followed.

Although the growth of the brothers' community was slow in the first two decades and a small number of the professed brothers defected, those who were professed during this time were able to lay strong foundations for the future. One aspect of this was the formation and augmentation of the conventual library, a collection which by the end of the Middle Ages was acknowledged as one of the largest and best-organised libraries in England, consisting of more than 1,400 volumes incorporating many thousands of manuscripts and printed texts.[103] The first brothers brought with them to Syon at least 165 volumes to form the core of their library. John Bracebridge was the largest contributor, giving 122 volumes which he had collected over a lifetime of teaching, while Thomas Fishbourne (18 volumes) and William

---

[101] See F. R. Johnston, 'Joan North, First Abbess of Syon, 1420–33: qui celestia simul et terrena moderaris', *Birgittiana*, 1 (Naples, 1996), pp. 47–65; Ellis, *Syon Abbey*, pp. 74–5.

[102] See F. Donald Logan, *Runaway Religious in Medieval England, c.1240–1540* (Cambridge, 1996), p. 45. Logan was not able to find any evidence of apostasy at Syon: see pp. 184–256.

[103] The best description of the brothers' library at Syon is Christopher de Hamel, *Syon Abbey: The Library of the Bridgettine Nuns and their Peregrinations after the Reformation* (London, 1991), pp. 48–109.

Fitzthomas (12 volumes) deposited smaller personal collections of books.[104] From the early 1420s until the late 1450s there seems to have been a lull in donations from brothers entering the monastery. During this forty-year period newly-professed brothers added approximately seventy volumes to the collection. The great phase of growth in the library's holdings began in the late 1450s with the arrival of Thomas Westhaw. His election as Confessor General may have initiated a process of gradual change in the composition of the community, for within two decades it went from being a convent which was essentially non-graduate with a sprinkling of university men, to a community in which graduates began to predominate among the choir brothers. The university men who entered Syon between 1459 and 1500 brought at least 400 volumes with them, including large donations by Thomas Westhaw (55 volumes, c.1459), John Lawsby (41 volumes, c.1476), Richard Terenden (36 volumes, 1488) and John Steyke (77 volumes, 1489).[105] During this period more than three-quarters of the new brothers gave books to the library, creating the 'intellectual treasure house' with which we are now familiar. This sudden influx of books was no doubt the reason that Thomas Betson was assigned the task of rearranging and cataloguing the library after his admission as a deacon-brother in 1481.[106] The years between 1500 and 1526 saw the addition of at least a further 300 volumes from donations by the professed brothers, the most intense period of growth in the library's history. The largest donations in this period came from Thomas Kirkhall (42 volumes), Richard Reynolds (95 volumes), and John Fewterer (76 volumes, c.1517).[107] By the mid-1520s, a century of book donations by the brothers of Syon had placed at least 960 volumes in their library, approximately 80 per cent of the books for which the names of donors are known.[108]

By the second decade of the sixteenth century the brothers' library at Syon was eminently equipped to assist the priest-brothers in their role as preachers and spiritual guides of the sisters. The great collection of manuscripts and books provided sufficient reference material for crafting the most erudite of sermons.[109] The enormous variety of classical and medieval authors quoted

---

104 Gillespie, *Syon Abbey Catalogue*, pp. 569–70, 578–9, 579.
105 *Ibid.*, pp. 590–1, 582, 588–9, 587–8.
106 *Ibid.*, pp. xlvi–li; Betson's catalogue of the books (Corpus Christi College Cambridge MS 141) has been described as 'one of the most thorough and complete catalogues surviving from the medieval period' (p. viii). For the ordinances approved for the new library see R. J. Whitwell, 'An Ordinance for Syon Library, 1482', *EHR*, 25 (1910), pp. 121–3.
107 Gillespie, *Syon Abbey Catalogue*, pp. 582, 585–6, 576–7.
108 Gillespie (*ibid.*, p. xliv) states that 1,200 of the more than 1,400 books listed in Betson's catalogue were assigned a donor's name.
109 Vincent Gillespie, 'The Book and the Brotherhood: Reflections on the Lost Library of

by Richard Whitford in *A dayly exercyse and experyence of dethe* (1537) gives a clear indication of the diversity of the library's contents and the use to which it was put by one of the most talented scholars in the last generation of brothers.[110] It has been noted above that the priest-brothers at Syon were constrained by their Rule to give the spiritual direction of the sisters first priority; study came second. Their days crowded with liturgical and sacramental duties, the brothers simply had very little free time to write and publish for a wider audience. Hence they concentrated on translating texts for the sisters right up until the dissolution, a good example being Thomas Precious's translation of David of Augsburg's *De exterioris et interioris hominis compositione* (c.1530s).[111] It would also seem that if any of the brothers scaled the heights of spiritual perfection they left very little written evidence of their mystical attainments.[112] Most of their literary output continued to take the form of translations into English of Latin texts for the spiritual guidance of the sisters, although in the sixteenth century this audience was widened to include the pious laity.

James Hogg and Vincent Gillespie have produced detailed surveys of the literary and spiritual writings of the Syon brothers, and their conclusions indicate a paucity of original spiritual compositions and an almost complete absence of mystical experience.[113] It must nevertheless be recognised that the final forty years of Syon's pre-dissolution existence brought an outpouring of publications, commencing with Thomas Betson's *A profitable treatise* (1500), and including such popular books as *The Mirror of Our Lady* (1530), William Bond's *Pilgrimage of Perfection* (1526) and *A Devout Treatise* (1534), and John Fewterer's *The Mirror of Christ's Passion* (1534). It was Richard Whitford, however, who proved to be by far both the most accomplished and the most prolific of all the sixteenth-century Syon authors. Starting with an English version of the Rule of St Augustine in 1525,

Syon Abbey', in A. S. G. Edwards, Vincent Gillespie and Ralph Hanna (eds), *The English Medieval Book: Studies in Memory of Jeremy Griffiths* (London, 2000), p. 202.

[110] James Hogg, 'The Contribution of the Bridgittine Order to Late Medieval English Spirituality', in James Hogg (ed.), *Spiritualitat Heute und Gestern*, Analecta Cartusiana 35 (Salzburg, 1983), pp. 168, 170. For Richard Whitford, see also James Hogg, 'Richard Whytford', in James Hogg (ed.), *Studies in St Birgitta and the Brigittine Order*, Spiritualitat Heute und Gestern 19 (Salzburg, 1993), vol. 2, pp. 254–66.

[111] Gillespie, *Syon Abbey Catalogue*, p. 584; this manuscript is now Cambridge University Library MS. Dd.2.33.

[112] Hogg, 'The Contribution of the Bridgittine Order', p. 174.

[113] See Hogg, 'The Contribution of the Bridgittine Order' and 'Richard Whytford'; Gillespie, 'Dial M for Mystic'. On humanism and the Syon library, see Vincent Gillespie, 'The Book and the Brotherhood' (2000) and 'Syon and the New Learning', in James G. Clark (ed.), *The Religious Orders in Pre-Reformation England* (Woodbridge, 2002), pp. 73–96.

Whitford published at least fourteen books in the next seventeen years, including a 1531 translation of Thomas Kempis's *Imitatio Christi* (titled *The Folowyng of Cryste*) which continued to exert a profound influence over most later English translations of this work until the early twentieth century.[114] Likewise, his *Jesus Psalter* (1529) and *A Werke for housholders* (1530) were printed several times in his own lifetime, and *The Pype or tonne of the lyfe of perfection* (1532) enjoyed great popular success. Whitford's literary output concluded with no fewer than three books in 1541, his greater concentration on literary activities after 1534–5 perhaps being explained by the curtailment of his other priestly activities by Thomas Cromwell's monastic visitors.

The Brothers of Syon and the Dissolution

If Richard Whitford was the most important spiritual writer in the years immediately before the suppression of Syon, it is probably no surprise to discover that he was also one of the most outspoken opponents of the religious changes which engulfed the monastery in the mid-1530s. Syon had been in high favour with Henry VIII until his marriage crisis in the late 1520s. The young king no doubt wanted to be seen supporting Henry V's foundation at Isleworth so both he and other members of the royal family were occasional visitors and donors to Syon. Queen Katherine and Princess Mary continued to visit the abbey during the divorce proceedings and the Syon community supported the queen's cause in the early 1530s.[115] As Cromwell's campaign of intimidation began to succeed in turning vocal opponents of the divorce into timid supporters, at least one lodger living within the outer court at Syon was won over to the king's side.[116] These ominous signs must have unsettled some of the brothers, especially the noted theologian Richard Reynolds who was in close contact with Bishop John Fisher concerning aspects of the proposed divorce.[117] The real problems began for Syon in 1533 when Elizabeth Barton, the 'Holy Maid of Kent', was imprisoned for prophesying that the king would die within a month of marrying Anne Boleyn.[118] The Confessor General, John Fewterer, and Thomas More had already made Barton's acquaintance at Syon and both men were impressed with her.[119]

---

114 Hogg, 'The Contribution of the Bridgittine Order', pp. 171–4.
115 *LP*, IV, 6795; John Lewis Vives accompanied the queen to Syon in 1530.
116 *LP*, IV, 3233, 3234, 3235.
117 *LP*, VIII, 1125.
118 *LP*, VI, 1468 (1).
119 More later changed his mind when he heard her confession at Paul's Cross; see *LP*, VII, 287.

Richard Reynolds may even have been implicated in the affair because his friend from Cambridge days, Henry Gold, was one of the men charged with spreading the prophesy who was tried with Barton and ultimately executed with her on 21 April 1534.[120]

By the beginning of 1534, however, the Syon community was facing a more immediate problem. The session of parliament which began on 15 January 1534 enacted a range of legislation which extended Henry VIII's control over the English church, but by far the most important of these legislative instruments was the First Succession Act which secured the royal succession through the offspring of the king and his new queen, Anne Boleyn. This Act required all subjects of the king to swear an oath confirming their acceptance of the new line of succession; failure to do so was to be regarded as treason.[121] It is not known what happened during the visit of the royal commissioners to Syon, but both the brothers and sisters must eventually have been induced to subscribe to the oath of succession, no doubt influenced by events at the London Charterhouse in early May 1534. Unfortunately, there were undercurrents of opposition to the community's acquiescence. On 23 August Richard Whitford, described by Thomas Bedyll as 'one of the most wilful' of the brothers, failed to mention the king's title during his sermon, but worse was to come the next day (St Bartholomew's Day). When Robert Ricote (or Rygote) preached on that day he 'did as he was commanded' and mentioned the king's title, but he also added that the person who had commanded him to do so should 'discharge his conscience'. Immediately nine of the brothers walked out of the abbey church in defiance: the priests John Copynger, Richard Lache, Anthony Little, Richard Parker, John Howell and Fr Bishop, and the lay brothers Richard Browne, William Turlington and Br Andrew. Whitford and Lache were identified as the ring-leaders of a substantial faction among the brothers who had joined together in opposing the Confessor General and rejecting the injunctions of the bishop. Such a revolt against superiors would have been considered to be an exceptionally grave fault under the Bridgettine statutes. While many later commentators have seen this snub to authority as the brave action of men of conscience, within the enclosed community at Syon it could only have been interpreted as the grossest act of disobedience and must therefore have scandalised the other more compliant members of the community. In Bedyll's opinion the only line of action open to Cromwell was to forbid the priest-brothers to do any further preaching unless chosen individuals could be

---

[120] *LP*, III, 2062.
[121] Knowles, *The Tudor Age*, pp. 173–7.

trusted to adhere to the party line. He further recommended that Whitford and Lache should be punished.[122]

The state papers are silent as to what happened next at Syon, but David Knowles is no doubt correct in suggesting that Cromwell moved slowly and cautiously against the troublesome brothers in the convent.[123] That Robert Ricote was given permission to leave Syon at this time is likely for he wrote to the king declaring that he had prayed for Henry as supreme head of the church and for his troubles had been branded by his confreres as a 'wretch and heretic'.[124] By mid-1534 it was clear to the king and Cromwell that they needed to take further action to secure the obedience of the church in general and the religious orders in particular. A revised Treason Act and a new Act of Supremacy were passed in November 1534 and from the end of that year until the middle of 1535 an oath of supremacy was administered to communities of regular clergy up and down the country in an attempt to enforce compliance.[125] Syon's turn came in the middle of April. Once again it is not known what happened when the commissioners arrived at the monastery, but Richard Reynolds clearly refused to sign the oath and by 20 April was incarcerated in the Tower of London where he was interrogated with the Carthusian priors and several other men from Syon and Isleworth. Reynolds was accused of declaring the previous year that the princess dowager (Katherine of Aragon) was still the true queen of England and that he could not accept the king as supreme head of the church.[126] He had received confidential papers on the king's divorce from Bishop John Fisher, and it later emerged that he had encouraged Sir George Throckmorton during confession to resist the divorce in parliament.[127] John Leek and Thomas Scudamore, secular priests at Syon, and John Hale and Robert Feron of Isleworth were also implicated in the anti-supremacy agitation in and around the abbey. Reynolds held fast to his beliefs throughout his interrogations and on 26 April openly declared to the king's commissioners present in the Tower that 'the King our sovereign lord is not supreme head in earth of the Church of England', the words which were to secure his fate as one of the five proto-martyrs of the English Reformation.[128]

The trial of Richard Reynolds and the three Carthusian priors has been

---

122 *Ibid.*
123 *Ibid.*, p. 216.
124 *LP*, VII, 1092.
125 Geoffrey Elton, *Policy and Police: The Enforcement of the Reformation in the Age of Thomas Cromwell* (Cambridge, 1972), pp. 227–8.
126 *LP*, VIII, 565 (2).
127 *LP*, VIII, 1125; *LP*, XII (ii), 952.
128 *LP*, VIII, 609 (vi).

related many times.[129] The special commission appointed to hear the charges of high treason met at Westminster on 28 and 29 April 1535. Reynolds was regarded as one of the greatest theologians in the land and showed no fear of his accusers in answering their questions. He stated that he had hoped to remain silent like Christ at his trial, but being forced to speak he was sure that all good men in the kingdom and the whole of Christendom were with him in denying the king's supremacy. He was found guilty of treason and condemned to death by hanging, drawing and quartering.[130] All five prisoners were taken to Tyburn on 4 May 1535 and executed. Their execution took the usual barbarous form as for all traitors, but on this occasion the witnesses were shocked by the fact that the four monks among the condemned were led to the gibbet in their religious habits. This was a significant break with the traditional practice of degrading religious before execution, and served as a potent warning to all who were watching that no one would escape punishment for opposing the king no matter what his rank or position. The three Carthusians were executed first, but throughout the bloody process Richard Reynolds, true to his vocation, 'preached a godly and noble sermon' 'with a constancy and courage more than heroic' in order to encourage his Carthusian brothers to the last.[131] His manful death greatly affected the crowds who were gathered to witness the executions and his constancy secured his reputation as the 'Angel of Syon'. For David Knowles, Richard Reynolds represented all that was best in the religious orders on the eve of the dissolution, for he died '… like the Carthusians, with heroic fortitude. In equanimity, in strength of character, and in constancy he takes rank with More and Fisher among the noblest of the age.'[132]

The trial and execution of Richard Reynolds must have had as profound an impact on Syon as the martyrdom of the Carthusian priors had on the London Charterhouse. Unfortunately, Syon did not have a Maurice Chauncy to

---

[129] See especially the full set of contemporary papers relating to the trial and execution of the Carthusians and Reynolds collected for their canonisation process: Melchior de Pobladura (ed.), *Cause of the Canonization of Blessed Martyrs ... put to death in England in Defence of the Catholic Faith (1535–1582)* (Rome, 1968), pp. 1–62. The most detailed account of the trial and the defence mounted by Reynolds is to be found in the Vatican MS (*LP*, VIII, 661), while shorter but moving accounts are to be found in Knowles, *The Tudor Age*, pp. 216–18, and F. R. Johnston, *Saint Richard Reynolds* (South Brent, 1961). A secular priest, John Hale, was executed with them.

[130] *LP*, VIII, 661.

[131] Maurice Chauncy, *The Passion and Martyrdom of the Holy English Carthusian Fathers: The Short Narration*, ed. G. W. S. Curtis (London, 1935), pp. 96–7.

[132] Knowles, *The Tudor Age*, p. 218.

record the events of the summer of 1535 and the modern historian is forced to rely upon the rather partisan testimony of the royal commissioners who were sent by Cromwell to ensure the compliance of the Bridgettine community. It seems that at this stage the community had still not subscribed to the oath of supremacy, and Cromwell himself went to Syon with Bishop Stokesley some time after the trial, no doubt hoping to take advantage of the recent executions as a means of striking fear into the hearts of the Syon community. The visit does not appear to have been a complete success, for Cromwell's agents were still trying to secure Syon's submission to the supremacy five months later. Thomas Bedyll was left behind to keep a watchful eye on the convent, but at the end of July 1535 he reported to Cromwell that although the sisters were 'conformable in everything' and the Confessor General and David Curson were working to bring the brothers into line with the royal supremacy, two brothers were causing trouble.[133] It is not clear exactly who these two brothers were, but clearly the sense of shock created by the events of the summer had begun to wear off. Trouble broke out again at the end of the year when Richard Layton was called in to bring the situation back under control. On 12 December Fr Bishop preached the usual Sunday sermon and 'declared the King's title' to an abbey church full of people, but Thomas Brownal, one of the lay brothers, publicly denounced him as a 'false knave' and was taken into custody by Layton. It later emerged that there was a serious scandal unwinding within the male community of which Brownal's outburst was just the beginning. It was alleged that the priest-brother Bishop had recently attempted to escape from the enclosure with two lay brothers as accomplices. He was also accused of having tried to procure access into the brothers' enclosure for a woman of doubtful morals, and hatching a plan to remove one of the iron bars from the grille in the locutory so that he could gain more intimate access to a sister to whom he was confessor.[134] All of these accusations, if true, represented grave lapses in observance of the Rule. Layton reported to Cromwell that Bishop was not the only one among the brethren who had grown weary of his habit, and a few days later a lay brother called Matthew was 'reformed in the hope of liberty'.[135] More disturbing discoveries were made in the week following Brownal's outburst in the abbey church.

Richard Lache and John Copynger were very quickly discovered to be particularly recalcitrant in the matter of the king's title and on 13 December

---

133 *LP*, VIII, 1125.
134 *LP*, IX, 954.
135 *LP*, IX, 986.

were dispatched to Bishop Stokesley at Fulham Palace for further persuasion after Layton's efforts failed. The king's physician and the queen's almoner arrived at the abbey to 'convert' Richard Whitford and Anthony Little on the 14th, and another four divines were sent by the king on the 15th to complete the task.[136] Whitford held out, however, and Thomas Bedyll in exasperation was forced to take him into the garden and use 'fair words and foul' in an attempt to break his obstinacy. Bedyll threatened Whitford with the disgrace of being charged with using 'bawdy words' to women in the confessional, and even suggested that such an accusation against the Bridgettine monk might be used as a pretext for abolishing the practice of auricular confession throughout England. Whitford and Little were henceforth banned from hearing the sisters' confessions, and Bedyll even suggested that the confessionals should be walled up and the practice of frequent confession for the sisters discontinued. A lay brother, William Turlington, was identified as being 'very sturdy against the King's title', but it is not known what action was taken against him. The sisters were keen to see Fr Bishop and Richard Parker discharged from the monastery, and after four days of upheaval in the brothers' community Bishop Stokesley arrived at Syon on 16 December for another visitation. This time he was determined to secure the submission of both the brothers and sisters. He achieved this object among the sisters by warning them as their bishop-visitor that they were imperilling their souls by remaining obstinate against the king. With the support of the Confessor General he enjoined them to consent to the royal supremacy, which they silently agreed to do.[137] No doubt this approach was also used in the brothers' chapter, although Stokesley was still 'continually labouring' with Copynger and Lache at Fulham in the middle of January 1536. Copynger seemed to care little for his own life and both Stokesley and Cromwell were aware that Copynger was 'in much favour with the brethren, and especially with the sisters' – a man of abundant 'modesty and passion'. His return to Syon would help stabilise the community, but only if he could be assured that the Bridgettine brothers and sisters would be allowed 'to keep their rule and their ceremonies as they have done hitherto'. Stokesley suggested to Cromwell that the only way of achieving this end was to remove Bishop and the other offending brother from the monastery so that Copynger could return in good conscience and at the same time lead Lache back into conformity.[138]

This was evidently the course of action which Cromwell took, and some

136 *Ibid.*
137 *Ibid.*
138 *LP*, VIII, 77 (wrongly dated as 1535 in *Letters and Papers*).

time in early February 1536 the two brothers probably returned to Syon.[139] A little later (but before early May 1536) Copynger and Lache, now reconciled to the royal supremacy, demonstrated their loyalty by writing to the London Carthusians to assist in Cromwell's ongoing campaign of securing their submission to the supremacy.[140] The two Bridgettines admitted their fault in having had too many scruples of conscience in the past and urged the Carthusian brethren to accept the more learned and wiser counsel of their religious superiors who had conformed themselves to the supremacy for the good of religion and the order of the realm. They emphasised that they had been won over by a combination of 'charity' and 'good and Catholic learning', and not by threats or fear. They were particularly concerned that the Carthusians should relinquish any wilfulness and submit to 'obey the prior that God hath set to be obeyed'. This no doubt indicates the means by which the brothers of Syon were brought into submission by Stokesley and their Confessor General – a simple and direct appeal to their vow of obedience to religious superiors acting according to the Rule and constitutions. That this process had weighed heavily on John Fewterer, the Confessor General, is evident from his postscript to this letter in which he admits to ill health. He would die only a few months later on 26 September 1536, and John Copynger would succeed him as Confessor General in an election presided over by Cromwell himself.[141]

This initial attempt by the Bridgettines to weaken the resolve of the Carthusians was, of course, unsuccessful and the monks of the London Charterhouse were dispersed for 'correction' in two waves during May 1536 and May 1537. Some of the Carthusians, including Bartholomew Burgoyn and William Broke, were dispatched to Syon for 'reformation' in mid-1536, and Maurice Chauncy and John Foxe were later sent there in September 1537 before being fully rehabilitated and returning to the London Charterhouse. On both occasions John Copynger was successful in bringing the Carthusians around to accepting the royal supremacy, reporting to Cromwell on 27 September 1537 that Chauncy and Foxe had ceased to be obstinate and were now 'conformable' to the king's will.[142] While Copynger no doubt believed that he had saved two impressionable young Carthusians from the certain

---

139 *LP*, X, 213; 31 January 1536: Stokesley to Cromwell asking that Copynger and Lache be put into someone else's custody so that he can return to London.
140 *LP*, VIII, 78 (also wrongly dated as 1535).
141 *LP*, XI, 501 confirms that Fewterer died in September 1536, dispelling any doubt arising from confusing entries in the *Syon Martiloge* which suggest that he left the monastery in 1536 but later took up residence at Termonde and died there in 1546. For Cromwell's presence at the election of Copynger see *LP*, XI, 501.
142 *LP*, VII, 1090 (incorrectly dated to 1534), and XI, 487

death that their confreres had earlier suffered, Maurice Chauncy was never reconciled to the fact that he had been seduced by Copynger's reasoning and had therefore failed in upholding the high standards of constancy which John Houghton and his other confreres had shown in winning their martyrs' crowns.[143]

It would appear that the brothers' community at Syon returned to its normal routine and was left in relative peace after the events of late 1535, although the king took the sensible precaution of forbidding any of the brothers to preach in the abbey church in order to prevent further problems from arising.[144] That Fr Bishop was released from his vows is certain, as was Robert Ricote either in 1536 or earlier.[145] It is likely that the lay brother known only as 'Matthew' was also given a dispensation, but the other priest who was unpopular with the sisters, Richard Parker, died at Syon on 4 April 1536. The outspoken Thomas Brownal was cast into Newgate prison and died there of gaol fever on 21 October 1537, recognised immediately by his confreres as a martyr for the faith.[146] The compliant Confessor General John Fewterer died in September 1536, and a lay brother, John Allen, died in January 1537. In the space of two short years, therefore, Syon lost one-third of its male convent, a much higher attrition rate than at any other time in its history and undoubtedly causing serious problems in providing for the spiritual needs of the still full community of sisters. Cromwell therefore gave the Confessor General permission to accept new brothers, but this act ultimately proved to be the undoing of the monastery and was used as a pretext in 1539 for its suppression.[147] That there were men who wanted to enter the community even after all the difficulties of the previous eighteen months says much for the high regard in which Syon continued to be held. On 5 February 1537, Bishop Stokesley admitted William Knotton as a priest-brother and Thomas Godfrey as a lay brother according to the traditional rites of the order; John Green was admitted as a priest-brother on 27 August; and Anthony Sutton and John Howell on 4 March 1538.[148] William Knotton almost immediately turned out to be a mistake, for on 9 June 1537 (barely four months after his profession) he climbed over the enclosure wall in an attempt to petition Cromwell personally

---

143 For Chauncy's guilty conscience, see Peter Cunich, 'Maurice Chauncy and the Charterhouses of London and Sheen Anglorum', *Analecta Cartusiana* 86:1 (Salzburg, 2007), pp. 53–7.
144 *LP*, XII (ii), 33.
145 Neither of their names is recorded in the *Syon Martiloge*.
146 FLE/12, p. 99.
147 *LP*, XIII (i), 1096.
148 *LP*, XIII (i), 1095.

for release from his vows.[149] This request was granted and a 'capacity' was awarded by the archbishop's prerogative court on 20 June, the only formal dispensation to leave the religious life granted to a priest of Syon.[150]

Whatever it was that induced William Knotton to leave Syon after such a short time, his apostasy must have had a heavy impact on the convent for it was the only successful attempt ever recorded in the long history of the monastery. Worse was to come. In May 1538, a charge of *praemunire* was brought against Bishop Stokesley, but listing as accessories the abbess, Agnes Jordan, one of the sisters, Margaret Dely, the Confessor General, John Copynger, and a senior brother, David Curson, for their parts in the profession of the five new brothers admitted to the convent since early 1537. The profession ceremony required the bishop to ask the brothers to observe the provisions of Martin V's bull (*Mare Anglicanum*) and this act represented a breach of the statute of Praemunire. Stokesley was able to obtain a pardon from the king, but for Syon there was to be no escape. Cromwell had already begun the process of wholesale suppression of the monasteries by early 1538, but he seems to have waited for an opportunity to play his hand at Syon. That opportunity came soon after John Copynger's death on 2 October 1539 when Cromwell finally launched his commissioners against Syon, and the abbey was suppressed under the year-old charge of *praemunire* in late November 1539.[151] Generous pensions were awarded to fifty-six sisters and seventeen brothers.[152] The number of priests had been reduced from thirteen to eight by the recent deaths of John Copynger (2 October 1539) and John Bramston (28 June 1539), and the impossibility of professing any new brothers after the charge of *praemunire* in mid-1538. Likewise, it was not possible to replace the lay brother Richard Mote who died on 26 July 1538, and it also seems likely that the newly professed lay brother, Thomas Godfrey, was forced to leave in 1538, because his name does not appear on the pension list.[153]

---

149 *LP*, XII (ii), 67.
150 D. S. Chambers (ed.), *Faculty Office Registers 1534–1549* (Oxford, 1966), p. 139.
151 See *LP*, XIV (ii), 424, 425 and 427, for Cromwell's intention to dissolve Syon on the charge of *praemunire*. Copynger's death is given as 2 October in the *Syon Martiloge*. The pensions were awarded on 29 November 1539, so the suppression must have taken place either on that day or a few days earlier; see *LP*, XIV (ii), 581 (1).
152 *LP*, XIV (ii), 581; the priest-brothers were David Curson, Richard Whitford, John Green, Anthony Sutton, John Stewkyn, Richard Lache, Anthony Little and John Howell; the deacon-brothers were Thomas Pollard, John Millet, Thomas Precious and John Selby; and the lay brothers were James Wooley or Wells, John Bartlett, John Massey, William Turlington and Richard Browne.
153 It should be noted, however, that Godfrey returned to the community after the dissolution, perhaps lodging with the abbess's community at Denham from 1540.

The community of brothers at Syon had proven remarkably resilient despite the efforts of Cromwell and his agents to sow discord and dissent, and they were able to avoid the terrible fate of the Carthusian houses where similar upheavals to the religious life had occurred from 1534. John Copynger appears to have discharged his duties as Confessor General responsibly in the three years during which he led the brothers' community, although with numbers so low and the priests being forbidden to preach it is open to question just how 'normal' the religious life at Syon really was during these years. The tantalising evidence of an almost total breakdown in regular discipline among the brothers from about 1534 until the return of Copynger and Lache in early 1536 must have made the reimposition of full regular observance difficult. The insurrection had also spilled over into the sisters' convent for a time as the priest-brothers used their control of the confessional in an attempt to strengthen the sisters' resolve against royal demands, but in the end it was among the brothers that the greatest defiance against the royal supremacy and the most serious lapses in regular discipline were uncovered. That so many of the brothers could have rebelled against the authority of their ailing Confessor General in such an observant and well-disciplined community provides us with perhaps the best example from the 1530s of just how divisive the succession and supremacy policies were for religious communities around the country.

The Brothers and the Survival of Syon

David Curson probably led the brothers as president in the weeks between Copynger's death and the suppression. He received the largest pension of all the brothers: £15 per annum. The three senior brothers – Richard Whitford, John Green and Anthony Sutton – received pensions of £8 per annum; the other priests and deacons were granted £6.13s.4d. per annum; and the lay brothers each received £2.13s.4d. per annum.[154] Whereas formal suppression by the crown marked the end of all other monastic communities in England, in the case of Syon the brothers and sisters hatched a plan in the days either immediately before or after the arrival of the royal commissioners which would enable them to maintain conventual life on a reduced scale. This was probably made possible by the comparatively large pensions which the Syon religious received, which meant that small groups of brothers and sisters would be able to maintain themselves quite comfortably as household-based religious communities in the secular world. The presence of priests to minister

---

[154] *LP*, XIV (ii), 581.

to the sisters in these smaller 'household' communities allowed the sisters to continue their daily office, Lady Mass and confessions as if the dissolution had not happened; and lay brothers were assigned where possible to each household to cater to the temporal needs of the sisters. Thus it was that in the early months of 1540 the brothers of Syon began to play a new role in sustaining the scattered remnants of England's only Bridgettine monastery. The first few years after the dissolution seem to have involved some experimentation with different groupings of male and female religious in several localities, but by the mid-1540s the survival of a number of small Bridgettine households provided the means by which the Syon community could be reconstituted in 1553 at Termonde (Flanders) as a functioning *conventus* until its eventual return to England in 1557.

Canon Fletcher was able to identify at least six discrete households of Syon sisters in the 1540s but was not able to trace the fortunes of these groupings with any accuracy.[155] Recent research using the Augmentations pension accounts has provided more detailed information about these six groups and one additional household. It is now possible, therefore, to say with greater certainty how the reconstituted Termonde community of 1553 evolved out of the various household groupings in England.[156] The abbess's household at 'Southlands' in Denham (1540–6) consisted of Agnes Jordan and six sisters, a secular priest from Syon and two lay brothers (Richard Browne and Thomas Godfrey). The prioress's household (1540–6) consisted of Margaret Windsor, three other sisters and the deacon-brother Thomas Precious. Richard Whitford acted as spiritual advisor for three of the sisters for a short time (1540–1) before going his separate way with the lay brother John Massey, perhaps in the household of Lord Mountjoy. He probably later joined the abbess's household until his death on 16 September 1542. The fourth household initially formed around the sister-sacristan, Bridget Fitzherbert, and consisted of five sisters, the priest-brother John Stewkyn, and the lay brother John Massey, but this group appears to have all but collapsed within a year of formation. John Massey soon transferred to the Dely household but later cared for Richard Whitford from mid-1541, while John Stewkyn stayed until 1542 but then disappears from view until the

---

155 Fletcher, *Syon Abbey*, pp. 137–9; see also FLE/12, pp. 110–14.
156 Canon Fletcher used the *Calendar of Letters and Papers* in his research on the post-dissolution Syon households during the late 1930s and early 1940s because the original documents were not available at that time due to wartime restrictions. The pension books (E315/249–62), treasurers' (E323) and receivers' accounts (LR6/62/1–2) give a more complete picture of the pattern of pension payments than the calendars and have been used to reconstruct the Syon households (1539–53) for this study.

refoundation of Syon in 1557. The fifth household consisted of the two Dely sisters, Margaret and Audrey, and three others. They managed without brothers to minister to them until 1542, when Anthony Sutton and John Millet were briefly members of the household. This household appears to have joined with the grouping led by John Green in 1545–6. The Green household, formed in 1544, initially consisted of just one sister (Rose Paget) and one other brother (Anthony Sutton), but it expanded after 1546 as other households began to collapse. The only household that did not include brothers was the one that formed around the several sisters from the Yate and Fetttyplace families at Buckland (Berkshire) and which survived intact until 1557. The transitional Syon households were, however, generally far from static in their membership, and the flexibility of these arrangements no doubt helped to ensure the survival of at least two sizeable groups of religious despite the various threats to their existence.

One of the biggest threats to the survival of these small households was the rapid demise of several brothers. Richard Whitford died in 1542, Thomas Precious on 12 March 1543, Anthony Sutton on 15 July 1544, and Richard Browne on 17 April 1545. Two of the more senior brothers, David Curson and Richard Lache, do not appear to have played a role in the spiritual direction of any of the households and certainly did not take over from their departed brothers when needs arose, so the spiritual direction of the sisters must have suffered as the 1540s wore on. Another problem was the passing of the older sisters who led each household. The consequent drop in pension income to support the several groups must have brought real hardship to the households in a time of rapid inflation. The elderly prioress died on 25 December 1545 and the abbess a few weeks later on 31 January 1546, necessitating the fusion of their households into a single group which was probably served by the lay brothers John Massey and Thomas Godfrey, but no priests. It was mainly the members of this combined household who eventually went under the leadership of Katherine Palmer to Termonde in stages between 1551 and 1553.[157] This new group consisted of at least six sisters and four brothers: Anthony Little and the three lay brothers Thomas Godfrey, John Massey and William Turlington. John Massey had proven particularly versatile in the years of survival between 1539 and 1553. He appears to have moved around frequently between the various households before finally going with Katherine Palmer to Flanders in 1551 as part of the advance party to secure a new home for Syon; he was, perhaps, a reliable and resourceful trouble-shooter who went wherever he was most needed. The regular life as

---

[157] 'Katherine Palmer', in *ODNB*.

practised by the small group of English Bridgettines established at the convent of Maria Troon at Termonde by 1553 must have been quite limited, but they nevertheless preserved a vital link of continuity with the pre-dissolution convent. Even though there were only six choir sisters and one priest-brother, they were able to maintain a semblance of their former liturgy until the middle of 1556 by which time two of the lay brothers and one of the sisters had died.[158] Cardinal Pole attempted to bring this remnant of the Syon community back to England with him in 1554, but it was only with the deaths in early 1556 that the decision was finally taken to return home.

Once this fragile Bridgettine community of five sisters and two brothers arrived back in England, Cardinal Pole and Queen Mary, who had already re-established the Carthusians under Maurice Chauncy at Sheen, encouraged Katherine Palmer and her companions to return to their former monastery at Syon.[159] A large number of sisters living in retirement in the home counties made their way back to Syon and joined the five sisters from Termonde, forming a new *conventus* numbering twenty-one sisters. John Green, who had stayed in England, was named as Confessor General in the refoundation charter of 1 March 1557 but was not enclosed with the community on 1 August 1557.[160] Anthony Little and John Stewkyn were the only priests available to minister to the sisters and they were assisted by the single surviving lay brother, Thomas Godfrey.[161] The full round of liturgical ceremonies could not have been possible among either the brothers or the sisters with only two choir brothers enclosed at Syon, and there is no indication as to whether any new brothers joined the community before the final exile from England early in 1559. At the second suppression of the convent, Anthony Little stayed in England, perhaps to care for the sisters who were too old or frail to make the trip into exile in Flanders, while John Stewkyn and Thomas Godfrey accompanied Katherine Palmer and the other exiles. Both Stewkyn and Godfrey died before the year was out, leaving the sisters in a foreign country

---

158 The sister was Margery Covert who died on 18 November 1555; the lay brothers were William Turlington (died 17 March 1556) and John Massey (died 6 April 1556).

159 The returning religious were the superior, Katherine Palmer, Dorothy Slight, Margaret Monington, Anne Daunsey, Mary Nevell and Anthony Little. It is possible that Thomas Godfrey was also with them.

160 John Green was still alive and receiving his pension of £10 per annum in 1568 so ill health or death must be ruled out as reasons why he failed to rejoin the community in 1557; see LR6/64/5, m.33v.

161 London Guildhall Library, MS.9531/12; Register of Bishop Edmund Bonner, fol. 147r. Eighteen of the twenty-one sisters named in the refoundation charter elected Katherine Palmer as abbess. Jane Rush and Elizabeth Faux were probably too ill to be enclosed and they both died soon after the event. The original refoundation charter is at Syon Abbey, South Brent.

without spiritual direction or masculine assistance in dealing with the outside world.[162]

How the sisters managed to secure new spiritual directors after 1559 is a question that cannot be answered with any certainty. It seems likely that at least six new brothers were professed in the years between 1559 and 1564, but the circumstances of their being admitted to Syon remain clouded in mystery.[163] These newly professed brothers were probably exiled Marian priests but very little is known about their origins or training. Clement Burdet was an MA of Oxford and had been rector of Englefield in Berkshire (1542–60) before being deprived of his living early in the reign of Elizabeth I.[164] The other new brothers probably had similar careers. Anthony Little, the last surviving brother from the Syon of 1539, finally made the crossing from England and rejoined the community at Mishagen in 1568 or 1569, but with his death on 27 January 1571 the last link with the old community of brothers at Syon was broken.[165] In the years that followed until the last brother of Syon died in 1695, a further thirty-three brothers were professed, twenty-seven choir brothers and six lay brothers.[166] It apparently became very difficult to recruit lay brothers after Syon went into exile and it seems likely that the community was without any lay brothers at all between 1559 and 1585 when Thomas Gower/Gore was professed. Even though the *Lisbon Additions* of 1607 continued to list the rota of duties for the eight lay brothers who would normally be present in an ideal Bridgettine monastery, it is unlikely that any more than two lay brothers were present in the community at any time during the whole of the seventeenth century.[167] The *Lisbon Additions* gave greater emphasis to the inferior status of the lay brothers in the community than the earlier Syon *Additions for the Lay Brothers*, so the seventeenth-century

---

[162] Stewkyn probably died on 23 August 1559, and Godfrey died on 2 January 1560; see BL Add. MS 22,285 fols. 51v and 21v.

[163] They were William Jolly who died 14 March 1567, Clement Burdet who died 20 December 1570, Stephen Marks who died 10 May 1570, Henry Herbert, Thomas Willan and John Johnson; see FLE/12, pp. 156–7.

[164] Emden, *BRUO 1501–1540*, p. 84.

[165] His last pension payment was in 1567–8 and he was listed as one of the six brothers at Mishagen in 1569; see FLE/12, p. 157. At the time of his death only Katherine Palmer, Dorothy Godrington, Audrey Dely, Margaret Monington and Eleanor Page remained from the Syon community of 1539.

[166] Twenty-five of these were identified by Fletcher from Syon's own records, and another two are given in Aidan Bellenger (ed.), *English and Welsh Priests 1558–1800: A Working List* (Downside, 1984), pp. 32, 112. The additional brothers are John Austin Abbot and William Sutton.

[167] Ellis, *Syon Abbey*, p. 135. The manuscript of the *Lisbon Additions* at Syon has not yet been published.

community in Portugal probably exhibited far less equality among the brethren than had been the case in England during the fifteenth century. The Syon brothers' community during the seventeenth century was therefore smaller than it had ever been in the pre-Reformation period and relations between choir monks and lay brothers probably became similar to those in other monastic orders. The last two lay brothers, Laurence Mason and Peter Hall, died within two months of each other in 1692, leaving a male community of just three priests who themselves would all be dead by 1695.

The Decline and Disappearance of the Brothers of Syon

Throughout the late sixteenth and seventeenth centuries the small male community of no more than five priests at any given time cared for the spiritual needs of a female convent numbering between twenty and thirty sisters.[168] All the choir brothers professed after 1559 appear to have been priest-brothers even though the *Lisbon Additions* continued to legislate for the traditional four deacons.[169] The new brothers were initially exiled Marian clergy, but increasingly from the 1580s they were priests who had been trained in the English seminaries on the continent. For example, the twelfth Confessor General (1584–1628), Joseph Seth Foster, was educated and taught at the English colleges in Douai and Rheims, and several of the brothers professed in the 1580s followed Foster from the English college in Rheims.[170] Very few of the new brothers had missionary experience in England because most of them entered Syon immediately after ordination, but David Kemp, John Marsh and John Vivian are known to have spent some time on the mission in England. David Kemp was active in London and Yorkshire, having been imprisoned at York (1585) and in the Marshalsea in London (1588) before being professed at Rouen in 1588; John Vivian was also imprisoned for a time in the Marshalsea (1585) before being banished from England.[171] After Syon settled in Portugal in 1594, brothers were drawn from many of the continental English seminaries, and after 1628 several of those professed were men who had trained at the new English College in Lisbon. These brothers included Francis Therall/ Thorold *alias* Benson, sixteenth Confessor General

---

168 There were three brothers at Mishagen in 1572–3, five brothers and twenty-four sisters in 1587 at Rouen, and five brothers and twenty-two sisters when Syon arrived at Lisbon in May 1594; see FLE/12, pp. 200, 167, 192.
169 Ellis, *Syon Abbey*, pp. 141–2.
170 Nicholas Barras (1585), John Marsh (1586), John Vivian (1586) and David Kemp (1588); see FLE/12, pp. 185–90.
171 FLE/12, pp. 189–90, 187–8.

(1662–86), George Griffin, seventeenth and last Confessor General (1686–95), and William Sutton.[172]

The roles played by the brothers during Syon's exile in the Low Countries, France and Portugal were both varied and important for the survival of the monastery. Their essential duties continued to be the celebration of the mass, the spiritual direction of the sisters, and provision of confession for both sisters and seculars.[173] When Seth Foster was professed in 1584, Syon had been without a Confessor General for more than a year after the death of Thomas Willan (eleventh Confessor General, 1575–83) on 22 February 1583. Foster was moved by the 'spiritual desolation' of the sisters who at that time could rely only on the elderly John Johnson for their spiritual direction and were desperate for another English confessor.[174] The revised Rule and *Lisbon Additions* of 1607 reinforced these roles and also that of preaching, duties which had always been central to the vocation of a Bridgettine brother.[175] The divine office of the brothers remained essentially the same after 1607 but that of the sisters changed dramatically.[176] The revised constitutions also took into account the decrees of the Council of Trent and the lessons learned from two hundred years of living the Bridgettine life within the cloisters at Syon, so there were some inevitable changes. From 1607 the brothers were given greater prominence in the affairs of the monastery and the Confessor General was expected to play a much wider role in administrative matters than ever before.[177] No longer limited to his primary role as 'conservator' of the spiritual life of the monastery, the Confessor General was now to be consulted by the abbess on a variety of issues including the appointment of sisters to obedientiary offices, and he began to act as procurator for the community in its business dealings with the outside world. Moreover he acquired authority to send brothers outside the enclosure and to admit lay people to the fraternity of the chapter. He also played an enhanced role in the ceremony of professing sisters, even acting as the bishop's deputy if necessary.[178] While some of these changes can be attributed to the application of Tridentine decrees, others must have been introduced in recognition of the central role played by Foster as Confessor General in keeping the Syon community together during the long

---

[172] FLE/12, pp. 209–10; see also Michael Sharratt (ed.), *Lisbon College Register 1628–1813* (CRS 72, 1991), pp. 197–8, 69–70, 194–5.
[173] Ellis, *Syon Abbey*, p. 141.
[174] FLE/12, pp. 178–9; see also Fletcher, *Syon Abbey*, pp. 72–4.
[175] Ellis, *Syon Abbey*, pp. 140–2; chapter 61 of the *Lisbon Additions* is devoted entirely to preaching and confession.
[176] Ellis, *Syon Abbey*, pp. 138, 129–30.
[177] *Ibid.*, pp. 124, 126.
[178] *Ibid.*, pp. 126–8, 132.

years of uncertainty. Strict enclosure of both male and female convents remained in force, however, and the Confessor General was only allowed to enter the sisters' cloister to administer the sacraments in cases of sickness.[179]

Newer roles were also undertaken by the brothers in response to the changed circumstances of Syon's tenuous day-to-day survival between 1559 and 1594. During this period Syon was forced to move first in 1564 from its initial haven at the Bridgettine monastery of Maria Troon at Termonde to an abandoned monastery called Bethany near Zierikzee in Zeeland, and then in 1568 to Mishagen near Antwerp.[180] Their life was no more settled at Mishagen (1568–72) or later at Mechelen (1572–80) where both monasteries were sacked by Calvinist rioters, and from 1575 only two elderly brothers survived to minister to the needs of the growing community of sisters.[181] From 1584, however, we know more about the activities of the brothers and the way in which they helped secure Syon's survival. The twelfth Confessor General, Seth Foster, 'a masterful Yorkshire man, young, able and energetic', immediately set himself the task of consolidating Syon's resources after his profession and election as Confessor General on 15 August 1584.[182] He was able to secure a new house for the community in early 1587 and a pension from the Rouen parliament to support the convent after four years of semi-starvation. Perhaps more important, however, he found new men to swell the ranks on the depleted brothers' side of the monastery. During his time as Confessor General (1584–1628) he professed at least nine new brothers, five of whom joined before the end of 1588. These men ensured a greater level of continuity in providing spiritual services for the sisters than had been possible since leaving Termonde in 1564. As well as the traditional role of spiritual 'conservator', Foster expanded his activities on behalf of the sisters and throughout his long Confessor Generalship acted as 'procurator' for the community, but his involvement in local politics and his loyalty to King Philip II of Spain also had its disadvantages. Foster had sedulously supported the Catholic League from the late 1580s, so when Henry IV finally triumphed and won the submission of Rouen early in 1594, Foster found himself *persona non grata* and Syon was faced with the difficult choice of staying and weathering the storm or moving once more. The community, having only recently elected a new

---

179 *Ibid.*, p. 142.
180 The most detailed account of Syon's wanderings in exile between 1559 and 1594 is to be found in Fletcher, *Syon Abbey*, pp. 43–111.
181 No new brothers were professed after c.1564; see FLE/12, p. 185. The two surviving brothers in 1575 were Thomas Willen, eleventh Confessor General (died 22 February 1583) and John Johnson (died 4 March 1593).
182 For Seth Foster, see Fletcher, *Syon Abbey*, pp. 72–122; and FLE/12, pp. 177–81.

abbess, chose to flee at a meeting presided over by Foster on 2 April. Under his leadership and after several adventures the whole community finally reached Lisbon safely on 20 May 1594. Once Syon had settled at Lisbon Fr Foster continued to be extremely active in providing for their temporal needs and as late as 1610 he was acting on behalf of the sisters in recovering their rents in the Spanish city of Valladolid.[183] The enhanced role of the Confessor General of Syon as manifested in the *Lisbon Additions* of 1607 therefore stemmed largely from the peculiar circumstances in which the community found itself during the 1580s and 1590s.

Several other choir brothers assisted in the temporal dealings of Syon during the long years of instability. John Marsh and John Vivian, both professed c.1585–6, were sent by Seth Foster in 1587 to collect Syon's unpaid Spanish pension from King Philip II, a mission which turned into a dangerous adventure and included incarceration at the Marshalsea before their return to Rouen in late 1588. It was during this trip that they met David Kemp who came with them to Rouen and soon entered the monastery as a brother.[184] The vicissitudes of exile, and especially the virtual disappearance of lay brothers from the community for long periods, therefore meant that the choir brothers were called upon to perform duties which had no precedent within the order's Rule or statutes. The *Lisbon Additions* even enjoined the non-existent deacons to assist the lay brothers in their chores when numbers were low.[185] The monastery's arrival at Lisbon in 1594 certainly brought more settled conditions and an opportunity to return to the older rhythms of Bridgettine observance, and the number of sisters in the community rose during the early seventeenth century. For the brothers, however, it was a different story. Although they no doubt continued to provide the sisters with ample opportunities for frequent confession, they were too few in number to perform the full choral office and other liturgical ceremonies according to Bridgettine custom. It is also doubtful that they continued to discharge their public preaching duties as stipulated by the Rule and the *Additions*. English-speaking congregations in the abbey church in Lisbon must have been quite small given the size of the English colony in the city, and although the brothers perhaps picked up some Portuguese during their time in Lisbon, it is unclear whether they were ever able to preach effectively in that language as required by the Rule. The biggest problem, however, was numbers.

---

[183] Michael E. Williams, 'Paintings of Early British Kings and Queens at Syon Abbey, Lisbon', *Birgittiana*, 1 (Naples, 1996), p. 132.

[184] Fletcher, *Syon Abbey*, pp. 79–81; FLE/12, pp. 186–90.

[185] Ellis, *Syon Abbey*, p. 142.

Despite the opening of a new English College at Lisbon in 1628 and an early promise of further vocations from this seminary, the flow of male aspirants from England to the Bridgettine order completely failed in the second half of the seventeenth century. The last profession of a Syon brother appears to have taken place in 1663, but this priest did not persevere.[186] Permission was sought in 1634 and 1652 for Syon brothers to travel to England in search of fresh male recruits, and in 1676 an attempt was made to secure a new Confessor General from Altomunster Abbey, but all these plans failed to augment the male community.[187] The six brothers (four priests and two lay brothers) who constituted the community in 1685 therefore faced the prospect of growing older with little hope of recruiting new men to replace them. When the penultimate Confessor General (Francis Thorold) died in early 1686, the remaining six brothers were all well into their sixties and cannot have constituted a particularly vigorous convent.[188] By 1692 the two remaining priest-bothers were both in their seventies. It became an urgent matter to find new younger confessors for the sisters and desperate appeals were made first to the English College in Lisbon and then to Altomunster Abbey in 1693. These petitions were all in vain, however, and with the death of the seventeenth Confessor General, George Griffin, on 24 June 1695 the brothers' community at Syon ceased to exist after nearly three hundred years of serving the spiritual needs of the sisters.

The decline in male vocations at Syon no doubt came as a result of several factors. The Iberian peninsula was perhaps a little too far off the beaten track for young Englishmen seeking to test their vocations to the priestly life. Even though English seminaries were established at Valladolid (1589), Seville (1592), Madrid (1611) and Lisbon (1628), none of these ever housed more than twenty students at a time and the Lisbon college was one of the smallest.[189] Most Englishmen wishing to undertake training for the priesthood during the seventeenth century were attracted instead to the Low Countries, France or Rome where the larger and more famous seminaries were to be found. The more prominent male orders such as the Jesuits, Benedictines and Franciscans were the most successful in attracting vocations, and it seems that

---

[186] This priest was John Mark, a former student at a Jesuit college.

[187] Fletcher, *Syon Abbey*, pp. 129–30

[188] At the time of his election in 1686 the last Confessor General, George Griffin, was approximately sixty-five; John Mark was also sixty-five (if he was still in the community at that time); James/Jerome Blount was sixty-four (died 17 August 1694); it is not known how old Robert Carlton (died 1693) was, nor the two lay brothers, Laurence Mason (died 26 July 1692) and Peter Hall (died 1 October 1692).

[189] Bellenger, *English and Welsh Priests*, pp. 6–7; Sharratt, *Lisbon College*, p. vii.

the Bridgettine order was neither particularly well-known, nor was it very attractive for recusant Englishmen aspiring to the religious life during the seventeenth century.[190] Indeed, it could be argued that the contemplative orders were generally less popular in recusant circles, for the Carthusians of Sheen Anglorum at Nieuport in Flanders also had difficulties maintaining numbers and eventually died out after the suppression of the house in 1783.[191] This should not come as too much of a surprise. For Englishmen, the attractions of the contemplative life had always been rather limited, and at the end of the Middle Ages there were only ten monasteries in England which were in any sense fully contemplative in their spirituality – Syon and the nine charterhouses. With the steep decline in the number of English Catholics during the seventeenth century the pool of possible recruits for the contemplative life also declined, but the emphasis on the active mission to Catholics in England must also have been a strong factor in rendering the contemplative life even less attractive to young men who burned with a desire to serve their fellow Catholics. That Syon continued to attract a constant stream of female vocations throughout the seventeenth and eighteenth centuries in stark contrast to the situation for men simply reinforces one of the essential differences which has been noticed between male and female contemplative life among English recusants. For women the 'passive' contemplative life was considered to be normal and appropriate, but for men it was the active life of the missionary priest which was most valued. It is this development within the culture of English Catholicism which best explains the decline and eventual disappearance of the Bridgettine brothers of Syon.[192]

The death of the last Confessor General created a new crisis for the sisters, a crisis that was far more serious than the shortage of spiritual direction that they had experienced in 1583–4. This time, although they were able to attract three secular priests and a Dominican friar to serve their needs in the period 1695–1717, none of these men wished to be professed as a Bridgettine brother.[193] The abbess therefore petitioned the president general of the English Benedictine Congregation for a chaplain and procurator, and from

---

[190] Bellenger, *English and Welsh Priests*, p. 248. The three largest orders account for 84 per cent of ordinations of regular clergy during the seventeenth century, and 48 per cent of all ordinations. Bellenger was able to trace only fifteen English Bridgettine professions for the entire seventeenth century, a negligible portion of the 3,056 ordinations in this period.

[191] Bellenger, *English and Welsh Priests*; there were only forty-four English Carthusians professed in the seventeenth century.

[192] Some female religious desired to be more actively involved in the mission, however; see Claire Walker, *Gender and Politics in Early Modern Europe: English Convents in France and the Low Countries* (Basingstoke, 2003), pp. 47–9, 118–24.

[193] FLE/12, p. 211.

1717 until 1768 the English Benedictines took over the spiritual direction of the Syon community. This represented something of a return to the early spiritual roots of the Bridgettines, for Benedictine spirituality had always been closely associated with St Bridget's order. The English Benedictines had already gained a certain amount of experience as chaplains to their own convents of English nuns from the early seventeenth century when the controversial Augustine Baker laid the foundations of modern English mystical spirituality.[194] Dom Augustine Sulyard was therefore appointed procurator and stayed at Syon until 1768. He and the four Benedictine monks who acted in succession as confessors at Syon between 1717 and 1768 do not appear to have had any prior experience as chaplains to nuns before being appointed to Lisbon, but they seem to have been genuinely appreciated by the sisters.[195] The spiritual direction of the Bridgettine nuns presented logistical difficulties for the English Benedictines, however, because the four monasteries of the congregation were all located in the north-western corner of Europe, far away from Lisbon. The English monks were therefore withdrawn after 1768 and priests from the English College in Lisbon took over their duties. These priests and the earlier Benedictine chaplains are all described as 'confessors' in the Syon obit book, as were those who came after them when Syon finally returned to England in 1861.[196]

The distinctive roles played by the Bridgettine brothers at Syon, beginning with the formal enclosure of the community in 1420 until the death of the last brother in 1695, demonstrate a strong element of continuity but also a surprising degree of flexibility which helped to save the community on more than one occasion. That Syon survived at all was an extraordinary achievement when compared with the persecution and collapse of the mother house at Vadstena and other Bridgettine houses elsewhere in Europe. The Vadstena community was largely spared from the first waves of Gustavus Vasa's rough reformation of the Swedish church, but several brothers are known to have been early apostates and by the 1540s only four priests remained at the abbey. Then in October 1543, less than four years after the suppression of Syon, Lutheran ministers were put in charge of the Vadstena abbey church and

---

194 Walker, *Gender and Politics*, pp. 143–7; David Lunn, *The English Benedictines 1540–1688: From Reformation to Revolution* (London, 1980), pp. 198–217.
195 FLE/12, pp. 211–12. For Augustine Sulyard, see Athanasius Allanson, *Biography of the English Benedictines* (Ampleforth, 1999), p. 197. The confessors were Bernard Quyneo (1717–25), Benedict Shafto (1725–42), Peter Wilcock (1742–53, 1761–8) and Francis Joseph Carteret (1754–61), for whom see Allanson, *English Benedictines*, pp. 158, 174, 206, 210–11.
196 See FLE/14, 'A Catalogue of the Dead both Brothers and Sisters in Ye Monastery of Syon'.

Catholic services including divine office, the mass and confessions were abolished. The four remaining priests were forbidden to act as spiritual directors for the sisters and eventually conformed to Lutheranism, but the abbess and her sisters struggled on as a community under harsh persecution until John III succeeded in 1568.[197] Although there was a partial revival at Vadstena between 1568 and 1615, the abbess and eleven nuns were finally forced to flee into exile at Maria Brunn Abbey near Danzig, and the community slowly died out just as Syon was re-establishing itself in Lisbon.

Vadstena was not therefore able to re-establish itself outside Sweden in the same way that Syon put down strong roots in Portugal. It is tempting to suggest that this was partly due to the absence of male religious in the Vadstena community to act on behalf of the sisters in temporal matters. At Syon the roles of the Confessor General and brethren were certainly enhanced during the years of exile from England, but this did not save the male wing of the community from extinction. Despite their increasing subordination to the Confessor General, it was the sisters' community that flourished in Lisbon during the seventeenth century and eventually brought Syon back to England in the nineteenth century. The different fates of Vadstena and Syon should not, however, mask the fact that in both cases the crisis of Reformation elicited a range of very different reactions from individual male religious. Some, such as Reynolds and Brownal, held fast to their beliefs and died for the old faith; others reluctantly embraced the new religion and made the most of the changed circumstances, escaping the strictures of the Bridgettine cloister and pursuing less demanding careers in the secular church. The majority, however, did what was required of them by their superiors and acted as obedient religious should. In the case of both Syon and Vadstena it was the sisters who demonstrated greater mettle, and it was they who were principally responsible for perpetuating the Bridgettine ideal beyond the Reformation. At Syon, however, the community's survival strategy was greatly aided by the mutual assistance and support which brothers and sisters living under one roof could provide for each other.

---

[197] FLE/23, pp. 133–8.

2

Syon Abbey: Women and Learning c.1415–1600

VIRGINIA R. BAINBRIDGE

Syon Abbey, founded by King Henry V in 1415, was the most important house for women religious established in England in the century before the Reformation. It was the only English house of Bridgettines, the Order of St Saviour, founded by St Bridget of Sweden (c.1303–73) as part of a contemporary movement for spiritual reform and renewal. Syon is renowned for its lavish endowment by Henry V, its principled opposition to Henry VIII's Reformation, and its significant role in forging recusant Catholic identity.[1]

Learned Women

Syon is perhaps most famous in the fifteenth and sixteenth centuries as a centre of Renaissance learning and an intellectual powerhouse of ecclesiastical reform. From the mid-nineteenth century, when research on Syon began in earnest, it was not the sisters, who constituted the main body of the community, but the smaller group of brothers which attracted academic attention. Syon's reputation was glamorised by the association of its brothers with the charmed circle of English humanists who welcomed Erasmus in the early sixteenth century.[2] Even *The Angel of Syon*, the only full-length biography of a member of the house, did not take one of the sisters as its subject, but the martyred brother St Richard Reynolds (d. 1535).[3] The significance of the

---

[1] G. J. Aungier, *The History and Antiquities of Syon Monastery, the parish of Isleworth and the Chapelry of Hounslow* (London, 1840), is still the standard history of Syon and this essay is part of a larger project which aims to summarise subsequent research in a new standard history; see also V. R. Bainbridge, 'The Bridgettines and Major Trends in Religious Devotion 1400–1600', *Birgittiana*, 19 (2005), 225–40.

[2] James K. McConica, *English Humanists and Reformation Politics under Henry VIII and Edward VI* (Oxford, 1965), esp. chs 3 and 4.

[3] Adam Hamilton, OSB, *The Angel of Syon: The Life and Martyrdom of Blessed Richard*

brothers' contribution to national history, especially during the early stages of the English Reformation, made their lives the obvious starting point for research on the house. Documentary sources on them are plentiful as many of them were educated at Oxford and Cambridge universities and a number were the authors of surviving manuscripts and books.[4]

The sisters remained the 'still small voice of silence' at the heart of the community.[5] Their lives of dedication to contemplative prayer were the reason for its existence, but the details of their lives were veiled by their enclosure and a comparative lack of documentation. Over the last hundred years, information has gradually been accumulated and the lives of the nuns have come into focus.[6] Research by manuscript scholars, notably Ann Hutchison, Christopher de Hamel, David Bell and Mary Erler, on books once owned by Syon's sisters has allowed a glimpse into their cloister.[7] Writing in the 1920s, Eileen Power presumed that most English medieval nuns were poorly educated and could not read Latin: they merely parroted the words of their service books without full understanding.[8] Her ideas remained influential until the late twentieth century.[9] However, the Bridgettine Rule allowed nuns to have an unlimited supply of books for study, despite their vow of poverty.[10] The *Syon Additions* to the Rule assumed that some of the nuns were unlettered, but equally that some were learned and that literacy in both English and Latin was required for important aspects of daily life, for service in the choir, for reading aloud in the refectory and for holding office.[11] The

Reynolds ... to which is added a sketch of the History of the Bridgettines of Syon, written by Fr Robert Parsons SJ c. 1595 (London, 1905).

[4] M. B. Tait, 'The Bridgettine Monastery of Syon (Middlesex) with Special Reference to its Monastic Uses' (Oxford University DPhil, 1975), esp. chs 6–8.

[5] I Kings, 19: 12.

[6] Exeter University library, MS 95, Canon John Rory Fletcher's mss. vols 10–12.

[7] Ann M. Hutchison, 'Devotional Reading in the Monastery and in the Late Medieval Household', in Michael G. Sargent (ed.), *De Cella in Seculum* (Cambridge, 1989), pp. 215–77; Ann M. Hutchison, 'What the Nuns Read', *Medieval Studies*, 57 (1995), 206–22; de Hamel, *Syon Abbey*; D. N. Bell, *What Nuns Read: Books and Libraries in Medieval English Nunneries* (Kalamazoo, MI, 1995); Mary C. Erler, *Women, Reading and Piety in Late Medieval England* (Cambridge, 2002).

[8] Eileen Power, *Medieval English Nunneries c. 1275–1535* (Cambridge, 1922), pp. 240–60, 277.

[9] Sally Thompson, *Women Religious: The Founding of English Nunneries after the Norman Conquest* (Oxford, 1991); Marilyn Oliva, *The Convent and the Community in Late Medieval England: Female Monasteries in the Diocese of Norwich 1350–1540* (Woodbridge, 1998), pp. 2–5. These two studies represent a new wave of scholarship on medieval nuns.

[10] Hutchison, 'What the Nuns Read', p. 208.

[11] Hogg (ed.), *Rewyll*, vol. 4, pp. 102, 147, 149, 152, 160–1.

Rule prescribed punishment for sisters who damaged any books and records show that these were carefully maintained.[12]

The Syon Martiloge and other sources name over 500 inmates and patrons of the house, around 300 sisters, 150 brothers, and the rest benefactors, in the period c.1415–1630. Biographical information on the sisters provides clues about their family background and their lives at Syon.[13] What is problematic about this data, in common with much data on medieval and early modern women, is that it is seldom directly about the nuns themselves, but more often about their kinsmen, who feature in the historical record. Nevertheless, some conclusions may be drawn. Preliminary findings show that many nuns came from London, Middlesex, where Syon was located, and the Home Counties, and their kinsmen were active in local and national government. Few sisters were of aristocratic origin. Most came from powerful families of royal courtiers, gentry, lawyers and merchants. These were the groups principally affected by rising literacy levels, for whom education was an important tool for social advancement. It is worth noting that the majority of Syon's patrons shared the same social profile. The evidence suggests that the sisters, as well as the brothers who served their sacramental needs, participated in a culture of learning, which began at home.[14]

Of the 300 nuns who belonged to the community between 1415 and 1630, forty (13 per cent) are currently known to have owned books in English, French or Latin, or to have received a humanist education.[15] The number who owned books was probably higher, as the *Syon Additions* to the Rule required the sisters to equip themselves with books before entering the monastery.[16] Elizabeth Skynnard (d. 1476), the daughter of wealthy London furriers, allowed 40 marks for the expenses of her profession in 1444, which included the cost of a Bridgettine service book and a processional.[17] She was one of

---

[12] *Ibid.*, vol. 2, pp. 42–3; M. C. Erler, 'Syon Abbey's Care for Books: Its Sacristans' Account Rolls 1506/7–1535/6', *Scriptorium*, 39 (1985), 293–307.

[13] BL, MS Add. 22285, The Martiloge of Syon Abbey; Exeter UL MS 95, vols 10–12; C. G. Gejrot and V. R. Bainbridge (eds), *The Syon Martiloge, British Library MS Add. 22285: A Critical Edition of Texts Relevant to its History*, Henry Bradshaw Soc. (forthcoming), will publish an appendix of short biographies of those named in the Martiloge, based on Canon Fletcher's work.

[14] Eileen Power, *Medieval Women* (Cambridge, 1975), pp. 68–80; Patricia Cullum and Peter Goldberg, 'How Margaret Blackburn Taught Her Daughters: Reading Devotional Instruction in a Book of Hours', in Jocelyn Wogan-Browne *et al.* (eds), *Medieval Women: Texts and Contexts in Late Medieval Britain* (Turnhout, 2000), pp. 228–34.

[15] Hogg (ed.), *Rewyll*, vol. 2, pp. 103–38, gives the postulant's responses at profession in both English and Latin.

[16] Hogg (ed.), *Rewyll*, vol. 4, p. 83.

[17] Guildhall Library, London, MS 9171/4, fols 153 v., 159 r.; Exeter UL, MS 95, vol. 12, p. 50.

three fifteenth-century sisters so far recorded as book owners. The second was Anne Charles or Karlsdottir, who came from Sweden in 1415, Syon's earliest known female scribe. She copied the manuscript of two works by Richard Rolle which she gave to the brothers' library.[18] The third was Anne de la Pole (d. 1501), the aristocratic seventh prioress about whom much has been written.[19] Book ownership became more common among the nuns in the course of the sixteenth century, as it did in gentry and merchant households outside the community. Dorothy Slight, the widow of a St Albans merchant, could both read and write. She signed the will she made when she entered Syon in 1535 and her name is in two fifteenth-century manuscripts, a *processional* and a copy of *Disce Mori*.[20] Ulla Sander Olsen's research on Bridgettine houses in the Low Countries shows that from their foundation the nuns were both authors and scribes of their own books. At the convent of Maria Troon in Flanders, where Syon sisters sheltered in exile after 1539 and again in 1558, Maria Van Oss, first Abbess (1466–1507), chronicled the history of the house, and Sr Joanna de Keyser was a diligent copyist of manuscripts for fifty-eight years before she died in 1526.[21]

Recent research on literacy in early modern society has developed a subtle understanding of what it meant to read and write. The two skills were not necessarily taught together, as they are today. A person who could read could not automatically write, and a person who could write a signature could not necessarily write more than that. When it came to reading, some people could follow a text when it was read out loud, or find their way through a book with the help of the rubrics and the pictures: hence the popularity of illustrated books of hours.[22] Others could understand more complex works for themselves. It is possible to identify three levels of literacy which Syon sisters are likely to have attained from the three main types of books they owned: first, liturgical books for use in choir and for private devotion; second, devotional

---

[18] Claes Gejrot, 'Anna Karlsdotters bönbok. En tvåspråkig handskrift från 1400–talet', in *Medeltida skrift- och språkkultur*, ed. I. Lindell (Stockholm, 1994). W. F. Pollard, 'Bodleian MS Holkham Misc. 41: A 15th-Century Bridgettine Manuscript and Prayer Cycle', *Birgittiana*, 3 (1996), 43–53; this MS seems to have been written by Sr Joanna of Syon.

[19] C. A. J. Armstrong, 'The Piety of Cicely, Duchess of York: A Study in Late Medieval Culture', in idem, *England, France and Burgundy in the 15th Century* (London, 1983), pp. 135–56, esp. p. 340.

[20] TNA, Prob. 11 25/30/226; Bell, *What Nuns Read*, pp. 196–7, 199.

[21] Hauptarchiv der Stadt Köln, MS Geistliche Abteilung, 178; U. Sander-Olsen, 'Handschriften en Boeken uit het Birgittinessen-Klooster Maria Troon te Dendermonde', *Ons Geestelijk Erf*, 64 (1990), 89–106.

[22] M. T. Clanchy, 'Images of Ladies with Prayer Books: What Do They Signify?', in R. N. Swanson (ed.), *The Church and the Book*, Studies in Church History 38 (Woodbridge, 2004), pp. 106–22, esp. pp. 121–2.

treatises written in English or French, divided into sections for use as the basis for daily meditation;[23] and third, books to read for pleasure in English or French and theological works in Latin, which all demanded a greater degree of understanding.

Liturgical books, chiefly psalters and books of hours, were the ones most widely owned by Syon nuns. These were especially suited to private devotion, because they contained personal selections of offices, including the Hours of the Holy Spirit, canticles, litanies and prayers. Even with limited literacy skills, women could use the books as prompts to remind them of prayer cycles they had memorised. In the sixteenth century lay sister Elizabeth Crouchley (professed 1521) owned a book of this type.[24] They were often handed down from mothers and other female relatives – for example Sr Clemence Tresham (d. 1567) owned a psalter which once belonged to her aunt Rose Tresham – and women used them to acquire at least a rudimentary education in the home.[25]

At Syon, education continued in the cloister, where the main purpose of the college of priests was to train the sisters for their contemplative vocation. Around half the sisters known to have owned books had copies of devotional treatises written or translated into English. *The Myroure of Oure Ladye*, written especially for the nuns by one of the priests, outlined the method of study at this more advanced level of literacy.[26] *The Orchard of Syon*, an English version of the *Dialogues* of St Catherine of Siena, divided into sections for daily meditation, was printed for the sisters in 1519 at the expense of their steward Sir Richard Sutton, co-founder of Brasenose College, Oxford.[27] It is likely that Sr Magdalena Baptista Boeria (professed by 1518, d. 1539), a native Italian speaker, helped to prepare the edition. Her father, John Baptista Boerio of Genoa, was a physician to Henry VII and Henry VIII and her two brothers were educated by Erasmus.[28] Sutton expressed his continued support for education at Syon in his will of 1524, which provided an income from property in neighbouring Brentford to 'teach nuns at Syon'.[29]

---

23 Ann M. Hutchison, 'Syon Abbey: Dissolution, No Decline', *Birgittiana*, 2 (1996), 245–59, esp. p. 255 n.
24 Bell, *What Nuns Read*, pp. 180–1.
25 Erler, *Women, Reading and Piety*, p. 146.
26 Hutchison, 'What the Nuns Read', pp. 208–13; eadem, 'Devotional Reading in the Monastery', pp. 221–4.
27 *ODNB*; Aungier, *Syon*, p. 81, addenda, pp. 531–3; Tim Thornton, *Cheshire and the Tudor State* (Woodbridge, 2000), pp. 35–6.
28 Erler, *Women, Reading and Piety*, p. 141; *LP*, I. no. 1477; II. i. nos. 338, 387, 542, 634, 635, 770, p. 1463.
29 W. Ferguson Irvine (ed.), *A Collection of Lancashire and Cheshire Wills* 1301–1752 (1896), pp. 41–6.

Several sisters owned the popular devotional works *The Chastising of God's Children* (1493) and *The Tree and Twelve Fruits of the Holy Ghost* (1534).[30] Syon's founders were inspired by the fourteenth-century English mystics, and at least four sisters owned Walter Hilton's *Scale or Ladder of Perfection* (printed 1494), a manual of contemplative prayer.[31] This too was divided into twenty-eight sections for daily use.[32] Cicely, Duchess of York, left her granddaughter, the prioress Anne de la Pole, Walter Hilton's *Mixed Life*, and English translations of Bonaventura's *Life of Christ*, made by Nicholas Love, and St Bridget's *Revelations*.[33] Sr Johanna Sewell (d. 1532) was given a number of Richard Rolle's works by James Grenehalgh, a Carthusian of Sheen, including *The Fire of Love* and a *Commentary on the Song of Songs*.[34] The literacy skills of the nuns who owned these books probably ranged from the capacity to meditate on a particular passage of devotional reading, to a more complex understanding of the subject matter. In her recent book, Mary Erler has presented a coherent picture of communities of readers, made up of both lay and religious, passing manuscripts and printed books between them in life and at death. Syon numbered Elizabeth de Vere (c.1410–75), Countess of Oxford, among its special benefactors.[35] She was the patron of Osbern Bokenham, for whom he wrote the *Legends of Holy Women*. She died in retirement at Stratford nunnery and left a French devotional manuscript to Barking abbey.[36] In pious circles there was little difference in the reading habits of lay and monastic women. Inscriptions show that the Syon sisters shared their books, passing knowledge between friends or from one generation to another.

In 1977 Joan Kelly asked the question 'did women have a Renaissance?'[37] Subsequent research has revealed that Renaissance culture did not extend far

---

[30] Bell, *What Nuns Read*, pp. 171–210.

[31] *Ibid.*

[32] Hutchison, 'Syon Abbey: Dissolution, No Decline', p. 255 n.

[33] D. Knowles, *The Religious Orders in England*, vol. 2 (Cambridge, 1955), p. 133; Armstrong, 'Piety of Cicely, Duchess of York', p. 340; Bell, *What Nuns Read*, pp. 199, 209–10.

[34] Bell, *What Nuns Read*, pp. 172–3, 178–9, 187–8, 198; Erler, *Women, Reading and Piety*, pp. 44, 121–3; Michael Sargent, 'Walter Hilton's *Scale of Perfection*: The London Manuscript Group Reconsidered', *Medium Aevum*, 52 (1983), 189–216; Michael Sargent, 'James Grenehalgh: The Biographical Register', *Analecta Cartusiana Kartausermystik und-Mystiker*, 4 (1984), 20–54.

[35] BL, MS Add. 22285, fol. 70 v.

[36] *Complete Peerage*, x. 236–9; Michael Hicks, 'The Last Days of Elizabeth, Countess of Oxford', *EHR*, 103 (1988), 76–95; Erler, *Women, Reading and Piety*, pp. 22, 44–5; A. I. Doyle, 'Books Connected with the Vere Family and Barking Abbey', *Transactions of Essex Archaeological Society*, NS, 25 (1958), 222–43.

[37] Joan Kelly, 'Did Women Have a Renaissance?', in *Women, History and Theory: The Essays of Joan Kelly* (Chicago, 1984), pp. 19–50.

beyond the narrow world of princely courts, even for men, and many of the women who participated in the New Learning were nuns.[38] According to Barbara Harris, few royal or aristocratic women between 1450 and 1540 became nuns because dynastic pressures obliged them to marry and bear children.[39] Instead, they deputised suitable candidates from their retinues to live a monastic life in order to share its spiritual fruits.[40] In 1429 Margaret, Duchess of Clarence, sponsored the profession of Margaret Wynter at Sopwell Benedictine convent, who may have transferred to Syon, where Simon Wynter, possibly her brother, was a priest.[41] Margaret of Clarence's granddaughter, Margaret Beaufort, sponsored a number of vocations to Syon from family estates in Cheshire and Flintshire.[42] In 1488 she had a suite of rooms built overlooking the interior of the abbey church.[43] There she and other women of the royal household could meet the nuns and it is clear from her sponsorship of publications for Syon that they shared a culture of religious learning.[44] Evidence from Syon overturns Eileen Power's assumption that English nuns were poorly educated. The Bridgettine nuns drawn from the circles of the Royal court did indeed have a Renaissance.[45]

Two of the sisters who came from families of courtiers owned books which reflected fashionable literary tastes. Anne Covell [Colvylle] (d. 1531), a relative of the diplomat Sir John Colvylle (c.1337–94), owned a book which included works by the poets Chaucer and Lydgate.[46] This later passed down to

[38] Lisa Jardine, ' "O Decus Italiae Virgo" or the Myth of the Learned Lady in the Renaissance', *Historical Journal*, 28 (1985), 799–819; Anthony Grafton and Lisa Jardine, *From Humanism to the Humanities: Education and the Liberal Arts in 15th and 16th century Europe* (London, 1986), pp. 29–57; M. L. King, *Women of the Renaissance* (Chicago, 1991), part ii; D. Sobel, *Gallileo's Daughter* (London 1999).

[39] Barbara J. Harris, 'A New Look at the Reformation: Aristocratic Women and Nunneries 1450–1540', *Journal of British Studies*, 32 (1993), 89–113.

[40] Geoffrey Baskerville, *English Monks and the Suppression of the Monasteries* (London, 1937), pp. 209–10.

[41] Exeter UL, MS 95, vol. 12, p. 18; for Simon Wynter see below.

[42] V. R. Bainbridge, 'Who Were the English Bridgettines: The Brothers and Sisters of Syon Abbey 1415–1600', in Mia Åkestam, Claes Gejrot and Sara Risberg (eds), *St. Birgitta, Syon and Vadstena: Proceedings of the International Conference Held in Stockholm October 2007* (forthcoming).

[43] TNA, SC6 ADDENDA/3485/3.

[44] Susan Powell, 'Syon Abbey and the Mother of King Henry VII: The Relationship of Lady Margaret Beaufort and the English Bridgettines', *Birgittiana*, 19 (2005), 211–24.

[45] Paul Lee, *Nunneries, Learning and Spirituality in Late Medieval English Society: The Dominican Priory of Dartford* (York, 2001); Oliva, *The Convent and the Community*. Both show that most convents were inhabited by nuns from lesser gentry or yeoman families, who did not share the cultural life of court circles.

[46] BL, MS Add. 22285, fol. 61 v.; Bell, *What Nuns Read*, p. 195; Erler, *Women, Reading and Piety*, p. 147; *History of Parliament: The House of Commons*, 1386–1421, ii. 635–7.

Sr Clemence Tresham. Sr Anne had another book which contained works by Walter Hilton and a treatise on the *Discernment of Spirits*.[47] Prioress Margaret Windsor's brother was Andrew, lord Windsor, Syon's steward, a renaissance scholar and favoured courtier of Henry VIII.[48] Margaret owned a French translation of Boccaccio's *De La Ruine des nobles Hommes et Dames* (Lyon, 1483), *The Tree and twelve Fruits of the Holy Ghost*, a psalter,[49] and a prayer book left to her by her aunt, Anne Sulyard or Bourgchier (neé Andrew).[50] This evidence suggests that some of the sisters were capable of reading both for edification and for pleasure.

Abbesses and prioresses were more likely to have owned theological works in English and Latin, which demanded the highest level of literacy. Copies of William Bonde's *Pilgrimage of Perfection* (1526)[51] and Richard Whitford's *Pipe or Tun of the Life of Perfection* (1532),[52] which were suitable for those who taught others about spiritual development in the framework of the monastic life, belonged to senior members of the community, Joan Spicer (d. 1534) and Eleanor Fettyplace (d. 1565) respectively. Elizabeth Gybbs (d. 1518), fifth Abbess, owned a manuscript copy of *Musica Ecclesia* by Thomas Kempis, founder of the *devotio moderna*.[53] This contained the first three books of his classic *The Imitation of Christ*, copied for her by William Darker, a Carthusian scribe of Sheen. Clemence Tresham, who led a group of nuns observing the Rule in her family home after the dissolution, possessed Thomas Kempis's *Complete Works* in Latin printed in 1523,[54] and Katherine Palmer (d. 1576), eighth Abbess, owned the *Complete Works* of Johannes Tauler, the fourteenth-century Rhineland mystic, printed in Cologne in 1548.[55] Those who were educated in Latin and humanist studies became abbesses and prioresses, like the thirteenth and fourteenth abbesses Barbara and Ann Wiseman, educated by their father Thomas Wiseman.[56]

Senior nuns owned a higher proportion of the books, and tended to own

---

[47] Bell, *What Nuns Read*, p. 190; Erler, *Women, Reading and Piety*, p. 147.
[48] Tait, 'Bridgettine Monastery of Syon', p. 341; *Complete Peerage*, xii. 792–4; *Harleian Soc.* xlii. Surrey, 186–7.
[49] Bell, *What Nuns Read*, pp. 183, 192, 193–4; Erler, *Women, Reading and Piety*, pp. 149, 182.
[50] C. Richmond, 'The Sulyard Papers: The Rewards of a Small Family Archive', in D. Williams (ed.), *England in the Fifteenth Century* (Woodbridge, 1987), pp. 199–228.
[51] Erler, *Women, Reading and Piety*, p. 142.
[52] Bell, *What Nuns Read*, pp. 194, 196.
[53] Hutchison, 'Devotional Reading in the Monastery', pp. 215–16; Bell, *What Nuns Read*, p. 186.
[54] Bell, *What Nuns Read*, p. 185; Erler, *Women, Reading and Piety*, pp. 148–9.
[55] Bell, *What Nuns Read*, p. 183; Erler, *Women, Reading and Piety*, p. 148.
[56] Hamilton, *Angel of Syon*, pp. 27–8.

more than one each.[57] Greater learning enabled them to oversee the education of junior sisters. However a more practical literacy was vital to their effectiveness in office. The Abbess managed an enormous property portfolio and retained a team of top lawyers, accountants and administrators to advise her. Such management skills could only have been acquired by women, or indeed by men, who received a practical education in powerful mercantile or noble households.[58]

A significant proportion of nuns were recruited from the intellectual elite. Their kinsmen included fashionable authors, cultural commentators and influential academics. Katherine Wey (d. 1509) was the niece of William Wey (d. 1476), the author of a pilgrimage guide to the Holy Land, a fellow of Eton College and later of Edington Priory, Wiltshire.[59] Katherine seems to have copied out her own service book,[60] and she gave a volume of William Wey's sermons to the Syon brothers' library.[61] Agnes Wriothesley (d. 1529) came from a family of heralds and was the aunt of Windsor herald, Charles Wriothesley, the chronicler.[62] Agnes Smythe (professed by 1518) was the great-niece of Bishop William Smyth of Lincoln, co-founder of Brasenose College with Syon's benefactor Sir Richard Sutton.[63] The Fettyplace sisters, Eleanor (d. 1565) and Dorothy (d. 1586), and their extended family have become well known through Mary Erler's research.[64] Their half-brother was the leading humanist, Sir Thomas Elyot, author of *The Boke named the Governour*. The intellectual and clerical elite from which such women came was shattered in the 1530s and their lives illustrate its effects. After Syon's dissolution, the Fettyplace sisters spent their later years in retirement in family homes living according to the Rule. Sr Joanna Dene (d. 1557) went to live in the household of Sir George Gifford, MP, where she had a position teaching Latin to his daughters and a niece.[65] Ursula Hoorde (d. 1598), whose powerful

57 Erler, *Women, Reading and Piety*, pp. 147–9.
58 Sylvia Lettice Thrupp, *The Merchant Class of Medieval London* (Ann Arbor, MI, 1948), pp. 169–74.
59 *ODNB*; W. Wey, *The Itineraries of William Wey 1458–62*, Roxburghe Club (London, 1857).
60 Bell, *What Nuns Read*, p. 208.
61 Gillespie, *Syon Abbey Catalogue*, p. 591.
62 Charles Wriothesley, *A Chronicle of England 1485–1559*, ed. W. D. Hamilton, Camden Society, 2nd ser. (London, 1875), p. ix.
63 R. Churton, *Lives of Bishop William Smyth of Lincoln and Sir Richard Sutton Kt.* (1800); M. C. Erler, 'Syon's Special Benefactresses and Friends', *Birgittiana*, 2 (1996), 217–20.
64 'Elyot, Richard, Thomas', in *ODNB*; McConica, *English Humanists*, p. 58; Erler, *Women, Reading and Piety*, pp. 85–99.
65 *Historical MSS Commission*, 12th Report, pt iv. *MSS of the Duke of Rutland*, vol. 1, pp. 307–14; *History of Parliament*, 1509–1558, pp. 212–13.

family produced several generations of lawyers, academics, monks and nuns, chose a radical route: she and her cousin William Hoorde participated in clandestine Catholic activities and she eventually joined Syon in exile abroad and became its thirteenth prioress.[66]

The nuns of Syon Abbey acquired education in a number of ways, informally by learning to read in the home, perhaps sharing education in accountancy or Latin and Greek with their brothers, growing up to administer a large household, moving on into the cloister, learning to meditate on prayers or short passages of devotional text, and gradually coming to understand more complex mystical and theological works.

A College of Priests

Syon was part of a network of educational establishments and its college of priests was an important link between the community of sisters and centres of learning beyond the enclosure. The chantry college was a fashionable institution in the later Middle Ages. Colleges were flexible in the activities they undertook, which included daily worship, the commemoration of founders and benefactors, education of the young and the advancement of learning.[67] Founders and benefactors paid to maintain a group of priests as part of their spiritual retinue, in return for prayers and learned counsel. St Bridget attached a college of priests to each of her monasteries, to minister to her sisters' spiritual and educational needs and to evangelise to the laity.[68]

From the start, Syon's brothers included men with expertise in women's education. St Jerome was a role model for the Bridgettine brothers.[69] He was a hermit famous for biblical scholarship, which the Bridgettine Rule encouraged the brothers to undertake. He was also the head and principal teacher of a

---

[66] Exeter UL, MS 95, vol. 12, pp. 58–60; *Calendar of State Papers Domestic 1547–80*, p. 688; Alan Davidson, 'Roman Catholicism in Oxfordshire c. 1580–1640' (unpublished PhD dissertation, University of Bristol, 1970), pp. 178, 256–9; *Harl. Soc.* xlii. Surrey, 222–3; Ann M. Hutchison, 'Beyond the Margins: The Recusant Bridgettines', in *Studies in St Birgitta and the Brigittine Order*, 2 vols, Analecta Cartusiana 35:19 (Salzburg, 1993), pp. 267–84, esp. pp. 281–2; David Knowles, *The Religious Orders in England*, vol. 3 (Cambridge, 1959), p. 238.

[67] Marian Campbell, 'Medieval Founders' Relics: Royal and Episcopal Patronage in Oxford and Cambridge Colleges', in Peter Coss and Maurice Keen (eds), *Heraldry, Pageantry and Social Display in Medieval England* (Woodbridge, 2002), pp. 125–42, esp. p. 125.

[68] Virginia R. Bainbridge, 'Women and the Transmission of Religious Culture: Benefactresses of Three Bridgettine Convents c. 1400–1600', *Birgittiana*, 3 (1997), 55–76, esp. pp. 56–7.

[69] G. R. Keyser, 'St Jerome and the Bridgettines: Visions of the Afterlife', in Daniel Williams (ed.), *England in the Fifteenth Century* (Woodbridge, 1987), pp. 143–52; Hutchison, 'What the Nuns Read', p. 212.

mixed monastic community which, like Syon, was comprised largely of devout widows and virgins. Fr Thomas Fishbourne (d. 1428), the first Confessor General, was a married layman before he followed a late vocation to the priesthood.[70] He became a recluse attached to St Alban's Abbey, where he was a spiritual director to noble ladies, including Eleanor Hull and Elizabeth Beauchamp, before entering Syon. Simon Wynter (d. 1448), one of the original brothers, wrote a *Life* of St Jerome for his patron Margaret, Duchess of Clarence.[71] This reflected Syon's mission to educate pious women, both those within and those associated with the house.

Syon Abbey was founded in the same wave of ecclesiastical and educational reform as a number of Oxford and Cambridge colleges. These included the foundations of several bishops of Winchester, the richest diocese in England. Bishop William of Wykeham (d. 1404) founded New College, Oxford, in 1379, and his college at Winchester in 1382. New College was an innovative institution with a strong theological emphasis, set up specifically to educate priests for ministry, rather than for a life of scholarship or administration.[72] Seventy scholars lived an austere semi-regular life, in what was an enormous complex of buildings for its time, with some architectural parallels to Syon. Throughout the fifteenth and sixteenth centuries, a significant proportion of Syon's brothers was educated at Winchester and New College. Presumably these men were drawn to Syon, with its mission to educate its sisters and lay associates, by the same motives which had drawn them to New College.

Pembroke Hall, Cambridge, also had a long association with Syon. Fr Thomas Westhaw (d. 1488), third Confessor General and doctor of theology, was the first in a line of fellows from Pembroke. Pembroke shared its founder, Marie de St Pol, with nearby Denney Abbey and the fellows traditionally provided spiritual direction for the nuns there.[73] Westhaw became Syon's Confessor General in 1460, the year after he was professed, suggesting he may have been recruited to fill this position. He helped to establish Pembroke College library with a gift of nineteen books, and his gift of fifty-three books to Syon brothers' library was one of the five largest

---

[70] Knowles, *Religious Orders in England*, vol. 2, p. 180; F. R. Johnston, 'Joan North, 1st Abbess of Syon 1420–33', *London and Middlesex Archaeological Society*, 85 (1995), 2–13; also in *Birgittiana*, 1 (1996), 47–65, esp. p. 57.

[71] *Cal. Papal Reg. 1427–47*, 174–5; Keyser, 'St Jerome and the Bridgettines', pp. 143–52; Johnston, 'Joan North', p. 57.

[72] J. Buxton and P. Williams (eds), *New College Oxford 1379–1979* (Oxford, 1979), pp. 3–43.

[73] *VCH Cambridgeshire*, ii. 295–302; *ibid.*, iii. 346–55; Erler, *Women, Reading and Piety*, pp. 109–10.

donations.[74] Syon's benefactor, Hugh Damlett (d. 1476), a fellow and subsequently master of Pembroke (1447–50), had links with several convents of nuns and his friends included the devout laywoman Margaret Purdans, a Norwich widow with a considerable library.[75] Syon's fifth and seventh confessors general, Stephen Saunder (d. 1513)[76] and John Fewterer (d. 1536),[77] were former Pembroke fellows, as was the priest William Bonde (d. 1530),[78] author of two treatises on the spiritual life. Bonde wrote *A Treatise for them that ben Tymorouse and Fearfull in Conscience* (1527, 1534), for the Denney nuns. The frontispiece of his more complex work for spiritual directors, *The Pilgrimage of Perfection* (1526, 1531), depicts a monk writing at a desk, in the traditional pose of St Jerome.[79] The Denney nuns were eager to read the works of Erasmus, who wrote his edition of St Jerome at Cambridge in 1511–16.[80]

Most of the works written by the Syon brothers were part of an educational agenda.[81] Thomas Betson (d. 1516), a deacon and Syon's best known librarian, was already circulating manuscripts around women's religious communities,[82] when the brothers began to utilise the new medium of printing. Works printed primarily for the sisters included the *Mirror of Our Lady*, written in the mid-fifteenth century and printed in 1530, which explained the Bridgettine liturgy to the nuns and potential recruits, and William Bonde's *Treatise for them that ben Tymorouse and Fearfull in Conscience*, which outlined common problems in the early stages of the mystical path. These joined a growing genre of books written for nuns in English. Richard Whitford (d. ?1543)[83] entered Syon in 1511 from the

---

[74] Knowles, *Religious Orders in England*, vol. 2, p. 347; Emden, *BRUC*, pp. 630–1; Tait, 'Bridgettine Monastery of Syon', pp. 225–6; J. Hughes, *Pastors and Visionaries: Religion and Secular Life in Late Medieval Yorkshire* (Woodbridge, 1988), p. 248; *VCH Cambridgeshire*, iii. 348; Gillespie, *Syon Abbey Catalogue*, pp. 590–1.

[75] Gillespie, *Syon Abbey Catalogue*, p. 574; Erler, *Women, Reading and Piety*, pp. 78–9, 177 n. 34.

[76] Emden, *BRUC*, p. 507; Gillespie, *Syon Abbey Catalogue*, p. 587.

[77] *ODNB*; Emden, *BRUC*, pp. 226–7; Erler, *Women, Reading and Piety*, pp. 109–10; Gillespie, *Syon Abbey Catalogue*, pp. 576–7; Knowles, *Religious Orders in England*, vol. 2, p. 347; Tait, 'Bridgettine Monastery of Syon', pp. 76, 215, 280–4.

[78] *ODNB*; Emden, *BRUC*, p. 72; Gillespie, *Syon Abbey Catalogue*, p. 569; Tait, 'Bridgettine Monastery of Syon', pp. 213–14.

[79] Erler, *Women, Reading and Piety*, p. 46, fig. 4, and see above fig. 1.2 (p. 30).

[80] *Ibid.*, pp. 107–8.

[81] J. T. Rhodes 'Syon Abbey and its Religious Publications in the 16th Century', *JEH*, 44 (1993), 11–25.

[82] Erler, *Women, Reading and Piety*, pp. 42–3.

[83] TNA, Prob. 11/17/5, fo. 39; *ODNB*, see also 'Blount, Fox'; Erler, *Women, Reading and Piety*, pp. 94, 98; Gillespie, *Syon Abbey Catalogue*, pp. 591–2; Tait, 'Bridgettine Monastery of

household of Richard Fox (d. 1528), bishop of Winchester. Fox, who founded Corpus Christi College, Oxford in 1517, had been master of Pembroke College, Cambridge from 1507 to 1518, and Whitford was probably involved in preparing the English translation of the *Benedictine Rule* for the nuns in his diocese.[84] Whitford belonged to a line of men who were drawn to a vocation at Syon because of an interest in teaching women religious: he joined a community which now had a century of experience in women's education.

Michael Tait has shown that Syon's priests were highly educated and from the mid-fifteenth century many were graduates.[85] In the sixteenth century eighteen out of thirty-two pre-dissolution Syon priests were graduates, nine of whom followed late vocations after holding fellowships at Oxford and Cambridge colleges.[86] Their educational level was comparable to that of clergy in London and the Thames valley, where the number of university-educated priests had risen to 75 per cent by 1500.[87] Syon Abbey was located in the county of Middlesex, in Isleworth hundred, where Winchester College had the right to present clergy to all three of the parish churches. A significant number of the vicars had taken the same route to Isleworth as their colleagues at Syon, through education at Winchester and New College.

A comparison may be made with Syon's clerical benefactors. They came from the same educational background as the brothers, many were educated at Winchester and New College and they included Oxford and Cambridge fellows both present and past. It seems to have been an established pattern among Oxford fellows to spend a few years in university administration and then to move on. Among Syon's clerical benefactors were Master John Temse (d. c.1482),[88] principal of St Edmund's Hall, Oxford, 1438–58, who went on to become Rector of Ross-on-Wye, and John Newcourt (d. 1485),[89] who was educated at Winchester and New College. He left a fellowship at New College to become a canon of St Paul's Cathedral, London. The medieval scholastic tradition had established a path from the university back to a life of service in

---

Syon', pp. 194, 215, 276–7, 289–94; James Hogg, 'Richard Whytford: A Forgotten Spiritual Guide', *Studies in Spirituality*, 15 (2005), 129–42.

[84] *ODNB*; Joan Greatrex, 'On Ministering to 'certayne devoute and religiouse women', in W. J. Sheils and Diana Wood (eds), *Women in the Church*, Studies in Church History 27 (Oxford, 1990), pp. 223–35; Barry Collett (ed.), *Female Monastic Life in Early Tudor England: With an Edition of Richard Fox's Translation of the Benedictine Rule for Women, 1517* (Aldershot, 2002).

[85] Tait, 'Bridgettine Monastery of Syon', chs 6–7.

[86] *Ibid.*, pp. 276–7.

[87] J. Mattingly, 'Cookham Brae and Isleworth Hundreds 1422–1558' (unpublished PhD thesis, University of London, 1994), pp. 172–207.

[88] Emden, *BRUO to 1500*, iii. 1858–9.

[89] *Ibid.*, ii. 1354.

the world or to a life of contemplation. St Thomas Aquinas set aside his writings and spent the last year of his life in contemplation. He apparently said, 'all that I have written seems to me like so much straw compared with what I have seen and with what has been revealed to me'.[90] Jean Gerson, the internationally renowned scholar and chancellor of the University of Paris, spent the last ten years of his life in retirement at Lyons, devoting himself entirely to spiritual life and parish duties. Jonathan Hughes has identified a group of fifteenth-century London clergymen who forsook the world in their later years to join the contemplative communities of Bridgettines and Carthusians.[91] These included Syon's third Confessor General, Thomas Westhaw (d. 1488), and priests John Lawsby (d. 1490), and John Pinchbeck, who joined Syon around 1459 but was granted a dispensation to join a mendicant order in 1463.[92]

The Syon brothers were both learned and worldly. Many combined the practical skills they had learnt as college fellows or parish clergy with contemplative practice. Although they had withdrawn to Syon, they maintained connections with networks of priests, whose careers had followed similar patterns. Through the brothers, Syon's sisters had access to the latest intellectual and theological trends.

Patrons of Learning

From its foundation Syon shared many benefactors with Oxford and Cambridge universities and in the course of the fifteenth and sixteenth centuries built up a dense network of associations through personal relationships.

Thomas Gascoigne (d. 1458), the chancellor of Oxford University, was an early devotee of St Bridget.[93] His interest in her writings helped to establish her cult in England and he composed a vernacular life of the saint. He was a friend of some of Syon's earliest brothers and left his books to their library. Fr Robert Bell (d. 1460), the second Confessor General, probably gave him two bones from a finger of St Bridget which he brought back from Vadstena, and which Gascoigne left to New College.[94] The bones were listed amongst the

---

[90] F. C. Copleston, *Aquinas* (Harmondsworth, 1955), p. 10.
[91] Hughes, *Pastors and Visionaries*, p. 248.
[92] *Calendar of Papal Registers relating to Great Britain and Ireland*, 1455–64, pp. 638–9.
[93] *ODNB*; H. Cnattingus, *Studies in the Order of St. Bridget of Sweden: I: The Crisis in the 1420s* (Stockholm, 1963), p. 132; Johnston, 'Joan North', pp. 55, 57, 58; W. Pronger, 'Thomas Gascoigne', *EHR*, 53 (1938), 606–26.
[94] BL, MS Add. 22285, fo. 1 r.; Johnston, 'Joan North', p. 58.

college's most valuable possessions, but were probably lost at the Reformation.[95]

The Syon Martiloge contains a list of around 100 special benefactors and
friends, which included major patrons of Oxford University like Archbishop
Henry Chichele (d. 1443), who founded several educational establishments.[96]
The Martiloge records that in 1420 he presided over the solemn enclosure and
first professions of the community, and in 1431 he con-celebrated mass with
the bishops of Rochester and Bath on the translation of the community to their
new site and held a banquet for the spiritual and temporal lords, to mark the
occasion.[97] In 1438 Chichele founded All Souls College, Oxford, to com-
memorate the souls of those who had died in the Hundred Years' War.[98]
Members of the Danvers family were among Syon's special benefactors and
they provided further connections between Chichele, Oxford and Syon.
Although their social background was comparatively humble, it was typical
of the majority of Syon's benefactors and inmates. The Danvers family were
wealthy gentry with lands in Oxfordshire and elsewhere, drawing additional
income from the practice of law, the London property market and trade.[99]
They were probably drawn into the orbit of Syon and the Oxford colleges as
clients of Chichele and other powerful men, with whom they shared cultural
interests. John Danvers (d. c.1449) and his second wife, the heiress Joan
Bruley, were benefactors of All Souls, where the arms of Danvers impaling
Bruley were carved on the east door of the cloister leading to the college
walks.[100] Joan also gave money for the new gate tower at University
College.[101] Danvers's son by his first marriage, the lawyer Robert Danvers
(d. 1467), served first Thomas Langley, bishop of Durham, another of Syon's
special benefactors, and later Chichele.[102] Robert Danvers oversaw
Chichele's foundation of All Souls, he was an executor of Chichele's will, and
he was also attorney for New College, Oxford.[103] Thomas Danvers (d. 1502),
eldest son of John Danvers and his wife Joan, fulfilled a similar administrative
position, assisting William Wayneflete, bishop of Winchester, with his

95 New College, Oxford, MS 9654, fo. 3 r.
96 BL, MS Add. 22285, fos. 70 r–71 v.
97 *Ibid.*, fos. 14 r.–v.
98 *ODNB*; E. F. Jacob, *The Register of Henry Chichele, Archbishop of Canterbury 1414–43*,
i–iv (Canterbury and York Society, 1937–47).
99 F. Macnamara, *Memorials of the Danvers Family* (London, 1895).
100 *Ibid.*, pp. 100–1, 104–5.
101 William Carr, *University College* (London, 1902), p. 65.
102 Macnamara, *Memorials of the Danvers Family*, pp. 102–14.
103 *History of Parliament*, 1386–1421, ii. 747–8.

foundation of Magdalen College, Oxford, established in 1458.[104] Thomas Danvers was not only a lawyer and a man of practical abilities, but his letters display Renaissance learning.[105] His brother William Danvers was associated with Magdalen's foundation, and William's wife Anne gave a 'Lollard Bible', an English translation of the New Testament, to Syon.[106]

Syon's special benefactors included patrons of Cambridge University. John Somerset (d. 1454), personal physician to Henry VI, assisted the king with the foundation of Kings College in 1441.[107] Richard Buckland (d. 1436), a London fishmonger and treasurer of Calais, was among the dozen or so richest Londoners of his generation, involved in shipping and army transport to Harfleur and Agincourt. A major supplier to the royal household, he was a client of John, Duke of Bedford and executor of his will. Buckland and his wife Joan (d. 1462) were connected with a number of religious and educational establishments and were some of the most generous benefactors of Syon Abbey.[108] Joan used a legacy from Richard to endow God's House, Cambridge, and John Brokle (d. 1444), another of Syon's special benefactors, a former Lord Mayor of London and a draper who supplied the royal household, was a trustee.[109] God's House was set up to educate grammar school masters in order to fill a shortage. It was later absorbed into Christ's College, one of Lady Margaret Beaufort's two Cambridge foundations.[110]

Syon's benefactors were equally concerned with theological education, at a time when increasing emphasis was laid on an educated clergy. Lady Margaret Beaufort is well known for her endowment of a public lecture in Divinity at Oxford in 1497 and a fellowship in the same subject in 1502.[111] Less well known, but extremely wealthy, is Sir John Crosby (d. 1476), a London grocer. Like many of Syon's special benefactors he was drawn from England's mercantile elite and endowed a fellowship in Canon Law at Lincoln College, Oxford in 1476.[112]

---

[104] Virginia Davis, *William Wayneflete, Bishop and Educationalist* (Woodbridge, 1993); Macnamara, *Memorials of the Danvers Family*, pp. 155–64.

[105] Macnamara, *Memorials of the Danvers Family*, pp. 156–7, 163–4, 169–70.

[106] *Ibid.*, pp. 173–85.

[107] *ODNB*; Anne Sutton and Livia Visser-Fuchs, 'The Cult of Angels in Late Fifteenth-Century England', in Lesley Smith and Jane H. M. Taylor (eds), *Women and the Book: Assessing the Visual Evidence* (London, 1996), pp. 230–65.

[108] Jenny Stratford, 'Joan Buckland', in Caroline M. Barron and Anne F. Sutton (eds), *Medieval London Widows 1300–1500* (London, 1994), pp. 113–28.

[109] *Ibid.*, p. 122; *History of Parliament*, 1386–1421, ii. 365–7.

[110] *VCH Cambridgeshire*, iii. 429–36; M. K. Jones and M. G. Underwood, *The King's Mother: Lady Margaret Beaufort* (Cambridge, 1992), ch. 7.

[111] *VCH Oxfordshire*, iii, 17.

[112] *ODNB*; *VCH Oxfordshire*, iii. 165.

Syon had important links with Oxford colleges throughout the sixteenth century, both before and after the house was dissolved in 1539. Sir Richard Sutton, steward and benefactor, co-founded Brasenose College with Bishop William Smyth of Lincoln. Sir William Cordall (d. 1581),[113] privy councillor to Mary and Master of the Rolls to Elizabeth, and William Roper (d. 1577/8),[114] St Thomas More's son-in-law, were both appointed visitors to St John's College by its Catholic founder, Sir Thomas White, and both were commemorated in Syon's Martiloge.[115]

New College, Oxford, a centre of humanist reform before the Reformation, swiftly became a centre of resistance to Protestant reform under the leadership of Fr Thomas Harding (d. 1572), professor of Hebrew.[116] It retained enduring links with Syon through the group of prominent fellows who left for exile in the Low Countries at the start of Elizabeth's reign. Harding, a generous benefactor of Syon in exile, settled in the university town of Louvain and helped to set up the English College of Douai.[117] Among the group were two leading Roman Catholic polemicists whose sisters were nuns at Syon, Thomas Stapleton,[118] who became professor of Divinity at the university of Louvain, brother of Sr Anne Stapleton,[119] and Nicholas Sanders or Sander,[120] brother of Margaret, eleventh prioress, and Sr Elizabeth.[121] William Rastall, a nephew of St Thomas More and a publisher at Louvain, was commemorated in the Syon Martiloge along with his scholarly wife Winifred, who was renowned for her knowledge of Greek.[122] John Fowler, another New College fellow, also settled at Louvain where he became the main publisher of English recusant

[113] *ODNB*; Davidson, 'Roman Catholicism in Oxfordshire', p. 637.

[114] Davidson, 'Roman Catholicism in Oxfordshire', p. 637; Thomas Stapleton, *The Life of Sir Thomas More*, trans. P. E. Hallett, ed. E. E. Reynolds (New York, 1928; London, 1966, 1984), pp. 65, 75, 145, 193 & n.

[115] BL, MS Add. 22285, fos. 54 r., 56 r.

[116] Emden, *BRUO 1501–1540*, pp. 265–6; Buxton and Williams, *New College Oxford*, pp. 44–51.

[117] BL MS Add. 22285, fo. 71 v.

[118] Stapleton, *Life of Sir Thomas More*, pp. xii–xiv; Hutchison, 'Beyond the Margins', pp. 267–84.

[119] *Harl. Soc.* xvi. Yorks., 293–7; Stapleton, *Life of Sir Thomas More*, p. vii; Hutchison, 'Beyond the Margins', pp. 267–75; Erler, *Women, Reading and Piety*, pp. 18, 39–42.

[120] *ODNB*.

[121] John Hungerford Pollen (ed.), Unpublished Documents Relating to the English Martyrs, vol. 1, 1584–1603, CRS 5 (1908), pp. 140–2; Joseph Gillow, *A Literary and Biographical History, or Bibliographical Dictionary of the English Catholics from the Breach with Rome, in 1534, to the Present Time*, 5 vols (London and New York, 1885–1902), v. 475; Hutchison, 'Beyond the Margins', pp. 268–72.

[122] Emden, *BRUO 1501–1540*, p. 475; Fuller, *Worthies*, pp. 362–3; Gillow, *Biographical Dictionary*, v. 390–2; Stapleton, *Life of St Thomas More*, pp. xvii n., 35–6 n.

literature.[123] He may have been a relative of Sr Dorothea Fowler, a Syon nun in the early seventeenth century.[124]

Of the recusant nuns who joined Syon in exile in the Low Countries and later in Lisbon, Portugal, many had brothers who were Jesuits or secular priests, educated in continental seminaries. These included the tenth Abbess Elizabeth Hart (d. 1609) and her sister Margery (d. 1628), who were probably sisters of the Jesuit Fr John Hart (d. 1594), and aunts of Rev. William Hargreaves, president of the English College at Lisbon (1634–7).[125] Sr Clare Dowman (d. 1627) was a niece of both Syon's twelfth Confessor General, Fr Seth Foster (d. 1628), and the prominent Jesuit Fr Richard Holtby, and her brother Seth Foster was also a Jesuit.[126]

The life of Lady Joanna Dormer (d. 1571), a benefactor of Syon, illustrates Syon's connections with both Catholic and Protestant intellectuals in England and abroad in the later sixteenth century.[127] She was the sister of Mary Newdigate (d. 1535) of Syon and St Sebastian Newdigate (d. 1535), the Carthusian martyr.[128] She supported leading Catholic intellectuals under Edward VI, who were promoted to important positions in the Church and the universities under Queen Mary.[129] Her family were courtiers to Mary, and her granddaughter Jane Dormer married the Spanish ambassador, the Duke of Feria, who used his position to arrange safe passage for the Syon community when they went into exile in the Low Countries in 1559.[130] On her journey to Spain, Jane, Duchess of Feria was received with honour at the cities and courts of the Low Countries and was welcomed to the French court, where she became acquainted with Mary, Queen of Scots.[131] Jane, Duchess of Feria was a cousin of Lady Frances Sidney, who co-founded Sidney Sussex College,

---

123 *ODNB*; A. C. Southern, *English Recusant Prose* (Oxford, 1950), pp. 342–4.

124 Hamilton, *Angel of Syon*, plate opp. p. 97; Dorothy Fowler may have been related to William Fowler, or alternatively descended from families with long associations with Syon, the Fowlers of Rycote, Oxfordshire, who were intermarried with the Windsors of Middlesex.

125 'Hart, John', in *ODNB*; Davidson, 'Roman Catholicism in Oxfordshire', pp. 117–18, 264–5, 293–5, 384; Henry Foley (ed.), *Records of the English Province of the Society of Jesus*, 7 vols in 8 (London, 1875–83), iii. 18, 24; John Morris (ed.), *The Troubles of our Catholic Forefathers, Related by Themselves*, 3 vols (London, 1872–7), ii. 28–34; *VCH Oxfordshire*, xii. 133, 152.

126 'Forster, Richard', in *ODNB*; Foley (ed.), *Records of the Society of Jesus*, iii. 3–17, 188–9; Hamilton, *Angel of Syon*, plate opp. p. 97.

127 Henry Clifford, *The Life of Jane Dormer, Duchess of Feria*, trans. E. E. Estcourt, ed. J. Stevenson, SJ (London, 1887), ch. 1; L. E. Whatmore, *The Carthusians under Henry VIII*, Analecta Cartusiana 109/1 (Salzburg, 1983), pp. 125, 131–2; *Harl. Soc.* xii. Warws. 39.

128 'Newdigate, Sebastian', in *ODNB*.

129 Clifford, *Life of Jane Dormer*, pp. 17–18, 43.

130 *Ibid.*, pp. 48, 101–8.

131 *Ibid.*, pp. 108–28.

Cambridge with her husband.[132] Probably on account of this family connection, Sir Philip Sidney, the poet and soldier, protected the Syon community from Calvinist troops at Mechelen in the 1570s.[133] Lady Joanna Dormer lived in exile until her death aged eighty at Louvain, where she continued to support Catholic intellectuals and was given a university funeral in 1571.[134] She was one of a succession of highly learned gentlewomen associated with Syon who participated in the culture of Europe's royal courts and universities.

When Syon is studied in the broader context of its benefactors and friends, it is apparent how strong the links were with intellectual communities beyond the enclosure. Many of the relationships forged in the fifteenth and early sixteenth centuries endured throughout the crisis of the Reformation and continued into exile. It was not only the brothers who were part of networks of learning; the sisters too were connected with them through family and social ties.

Libraries and Evangelism

The Bridgettines followed both monastic tradition and the emphasis of their foundress on the acquisition of knowledge. Starting with the mother house of Vadstena, they swiftly built up richly stocked libraries. From its foundation Syon attracted book collectors as brothers and patrons. An Italian visitor to the English court in around 1500 wrote that few except the clergy were interested in study.[135] It is therefore significant that Syon's benefactors, both clerical and lay, included major bibliophiles and scholars of their day.

The contents of Syon brothers' library are well known through the Catalogue written by the deacon Thomas Betson (d. 1516).[136] In just over a century it had become one of the largest libraries in England with around 1,450 volumes, an astonishing size, as David Knowles points out, for use by fewer than twenty men.[137] Five Syon brothers contributed 400 volumes between them and six others twenty to thirty each.[138] John Bracebridge, one of the earliest brothers, a scholar educated at Oxford whose interests ranged from theology to medicine and science, gave 111 volumes which formed the core

132 *Ibid.*, pp. 40–2, 63.
133 'Sidney, Philip', in *ODNB*; F. R. Johnston, *Syon Abbey: A Short History of the English Bridgettines* (London, 1964), p. 13.
134 Clifford, *Life of Jane Dormer*, pp. 50–4.
135 V. H. Galbraith, *The Literacy of the Medieval English Kings* (Raleigh Lecture, 1935), pp. 78–111.
136 Bateson, *Catalogue of the Library of Syon*; Gillespie, *Syon Abbey Catalogue*.
137 Knowles, *Religious Orders in England*, vol. 2, p. 350.
138 *Ibid.*, pp. 347–8.

of the collection.[139] The wealth of his family, a dynasty of York merchants, presumably afforded him what was an enormous quantity of books for this time. Four more Cambridge scholars brought substantial libraries with them when they became brothers, confessors general Thomas Westhaw and John Fewterer from Pembroke Hall, John Steyke (d. 1513), and the martyr Richard Reynolds.[140] William Asplyon (d. 1485), a fellow of University College, Oxford, brought eighteen books with him when he entered Syon, and he and Walter Skirlaw, bishop of Durham, who was involved with Syon's foundation, established the library at University College with their gifts of books.[141]

Friends, both clerical and lay, assisted in building up the library. The Martiloge records that special prayers were to be said for library donors, and the brothers' library catalogue functioned as a secondary necrology, naming the donors of each volume so they could be remembered in prayer. Syon was a house full of books: besides those in the libraries of the brothers and sisters, there were service books for use in the church, books to read out loud in the refectory and books kept in the cells for private devotion.

Syon's patrons included members of the royal family who collected books and had scholarly interests: Henry V, his two brothers, Humphrey, Duke of Gloucester, and John, Duke of Bedford, and his aunt, Margaret, Duchess of Clarence, and later Edward IV, Henry VII and their immediate families.[142] Humphrey, Duke of Gloucester,[143] and Thomas Kemp, bishop of London, who finished Duke Humphrey's work on the Oxford Divinity School building, were both commemorated in the Syon Martiloge.[144] Other patrons of both the Divinity School project and Syon Abbey were Edward IV, Archbishop Henry Chichele, and Thomas Chaundler, successively warden of Winchester and New College, chancellor of Oxford University and pioneer of humanism in England.[145] The list of special benefactors included notable bibliophiles, James Butler (d. 1452),[146] fourth earl of Ormond, a career

---

139 Exeter UL, MS 95, vol. 12, p. 16; *ODNB*; Gillespie, *Syon Abbey Catalogue*, p. 570; *History of Parliament*, 1439–1509, ii. 99; Hughes, *Pastors and Visionaries*, pp. 70, 110; Knowles, *Religious Orders in England*, vol. 2, p. 347; Tait, 'Bridgettine Monastery of Syon', pp. 242, 246–8.
140 Knowles, *Religious Orders in England*, vol. 2, pp. 347–8.
141 *VCH Oxfordshire*, iii. 70.
142 Janet Backhouse, 'Founders of the Royal Library: Edward IV and Henry VII as Collectors of Illuminated Manuscripts', in Daniel Williams (ed.), *England in the Fifteenth Century* (Woodbridge, 1987), pp. 23–41.
143 BL MS Add. 22285, fo. 5 v.; *ODNB*.
144 BL MS Add. 22285, fo. 70 r.; I. Philip, *The Bodleian Library in the Seventeenth and Eighteenth Centuries* (Oxford, 1983), p. 5.
145 BL, MS Add. 22285, fos. 70 r–71 v.; I am grateful to William Clennell of the Bodleian Library for sharing his unpublished research with me.
146 *ODNB*; *Complete Peerage*, x. 123–6.

soldier, a patron of the College of Heralds and a scholar of history and antiquities, and John Somerset, physician to Henry VI and a scholar of science and humanism. Joan, widow of Richard Buckland, whose mercantile wealth was equal to that of Syon's aristocratic patrons, was also a generous library donor.[147]

Thomas Bodley's new university library, founded in 1602, was originally viewed as a Protestant enterprise until research revealed a more subtle picture.[148] The Catholic Thomas Allen of Gloucester Hall encouraged Catholic scholars to give books to the Bodleian and some had strong connections with Syon.[149] The most substantial donors in Bodley's own lifetime included Charles Danvers,[150] descended from Syon's fifteenth-century patrons, Henry Wriothesley, third earl of Southampton, Shakespeare's patron, whose ancestors included Sr Agnes Wriothesley (d. 1529),[151] Sir Thomas Tresham, great-nephew of Sr Clemence Tresham, and Anthony, second Viscount Montague, whose daughters Bridget and Lucy were nuns at Syon in the 1620s.[152] Wriothesley's widow gave a manuscript copy of the Bridgettine *Rule* in English to the library of St John's College, Cambridge,[153] and Tresham was a major benefactor of the library of St John's College, Oxford.[154] The love of books and learning apparently transcended the sectarian divide between Protestant and Catholic members of a diverse literary elite, in which Syon Abbey still had a place after its dissolution and exile.

Conclusion

In this essay there has only been space to touch on a small proportion of the evidence linking Syon with Oxford and Cambridge and with other seats of learning. This evidence shows that the Syon nuns were from powerful families where literacy and learning were prized. With their patrons, they shared a

---

[147] De Hamel, *Syon Abbey*, pp. 81–2.

[148] N. R. Ker, 'Oxford College Libraries in the Sixteenth Century', *Bodleian Library Record*, 6 (1957–61), 459–515, esp. p. 505; A. Davidson, 'Catholics and Bodley', *Bodleian Library Record*, 8 (1967–72), 252–7; Philip, *Bodleian Library*.

[149] Philip, *Bodleian Library*, pp. 10, 16–18, 41–2.

[150] Davidson, 'Catholics and Bodley', p. 254; Philip, *Bodleian Library*, p. 19.

[151] Exeter UL, MS 95, vol. 12. p. 87; *Complete Peerage*, xii. 118–31; *ODNB*; James Hogg (ed.), *Rewyll of Seynt Saviour*, i, Analecta Cartusiana 183 (Salzburg, 2003), p. xvi; Aungier, *Syon*, pp. 81–2; Philip, *Bodleian Library*, pp. 8–9; Wriothesley, *Chronicle of England*, p. ix.

[152] Davidson, 'Catholics and Bodley', p. 252; Michael Questier, *Catholicism and Community in Early Modern England* (Cambridge, 2006), pp. 332–3.

[153] Hogg (ed.), *Rewyl of Seynt Saviour*, p. xvi.

[154] Kerr, 'Oxford College Libraries', pp. 511–15.

belief in education as a tool for social and spiritual reform. Their acquisition of learning was less formal than for men because they were educated in the private sphere of the family, household or monastic enclosure. There they had access to the counsel of some of the leading intellectuals of their day, which gave them the opportunity to become women of learning.

3

Syon and the English Market for
Continental Printed Books: The Incunable Phase[1]

VINCENT GILLESPIE

A book is a fragile creature, it suffers the wear of time, it fears rodents,
the elements, clumsy hands. If for a hundred and a hundred years
everybody had been able freely to handle codices, the majority of
them would no longer exist. So the librarian protects them not only
against mankind, but also against nature, and devotes his life to this
war against the forces of oblivion, the enemy of truth.

Abbot Abo, in Umberto Eco, *The Name of the Rose*

In a letter to Archbishop Matthew Parker written in July 1560, John Bale
spoke of the years leading up to 1540, which he called the 'tyme of the lamentable spoyle of the lybraryes of Englande', when he saw the collections of
suppressed religious houses broken up for resale or for use as binding fragments, scrap paper, 'in stacyoners and boke bynders store howses, some in
grosers, sopesellars, taylers, and other occupyers shoppes, some in shyppes
ready to be carryed over the sea into Flaunders to be solde'.[2] If such books
were indeed exported to Flanders in the years after the suppression, then in
many cases they would have been retracing the route by which they had
entered England in the first place, especially if they were printed books. The
established trade route of the Rhine, Flanders and Antwerp happened to link
together the major centres of the new technology – Basel, Mainz, Strasbourg,

[1] This essay is reprinted from *Religion and Literature*, 37.2 (2005), 27–49. I am grateful to the
editors, and especially to Paul Patterson and Kathleen Canavan, for their kind permission to
include it here. I have made some expansions in the argument and added some further examples
since its first publication. But this is still not a full study of Syon's printed book holdings, and
only focuses on books published up to 1500.
[2] Quoted by Honor McCusker, 'Books and Manuscripts Formerly in the Possession of John
Bale', *The Library*, 4th ser., 16 (1936), 144–65, at pp. 145–6.

Cologne, and the Low Countries – whose trade with England was dominated by the members of the Merchant Adventurers company: men like William Wilcocks, Roger Thorney and, of course, William Caxton, who also played a significant role in the new 'Latin trade' in imported continental printed books.[3] From very soon after the invention of commercial printing, England had been a good market for the new commodity.[4] This market included not only liturgical books (printed abroad in substantial numbers for the English market) and devotional books, but also Latin works of theology, philosophy, canon law, grammar and classical learning, aimed at and bought by the students or, more probably, the teachers at the great universities of Oxford and Cambridge and also by scholars and teachers in the great schools and monastic centres of learning with which fifteenth-century England was so richly endowed. Early continental printers seem to have sought trade agreements with stationers in such centres, or well connected to them. In Oxford, evidence survives from 1483 of books being supplied to Thomas Hunt by

---

3   See the brilliant overview of this commercial milieu in Anne F. Sutton, 'Caxton Was a Mercer: His Social Milieu and Friends', in Nicholas Rogers (ed.), *England in the Fifteenth Century*, Harlaxton Medieval Studies, 4 (1994), pp. 118–48.

4   The standard discussions of the English trade in continental printed books are: H. R. Plomer, 'The Importation of Books into England in the Fifteenth and Sixteenth Centuries', *The Library*, 4th ser., 4 (1924), 146–50; Nelly J. M. Kerling, 'Caxton and the Trade in Printed Books', *The Book Collector*, 4 (1955), 190–9; Howard M. Nixon, 'Caxton, His Contemporaries and Successors in the Book Trade from Westminster Documents', *The Library*, 5th ser., 31 (1976), 305–26; Graham Pollard, 'The English Market for Printed Books', *Printing History*, 4 (1978), 7–48; Elizabeth Armstrong, 'English Purchases of Printed Books from the Continent 1465–1526', *EHR*, 94 (1979), 268–90; Nicholas Barker, 'The Importation of Books into England 1460–1526', in Herbert G. Göpfert *et al.* (eds), *Beiträge zur Geschichte des Buchwesens im konfessionellen Zeitalter*, Wolfenbüttler Schriften zur Geschichte des Buchwesens, 11 (1985), pp. 251–66; Lotte Hellinga, 'Importation of Books Printed on the Continent into England before c. 1520', in Sandra Hindman (ed.), *Printing the Written Word: The Social History of Books circa 1450–1520* (Ithaca, NY and London, 1991), pp. 205–24; A. S. G. Edwards and Carol M. Meale, 'The Marketing of Printed Books in Late Medieval England', *The Library*, 6th ser., 15 (1993), 95–124; Anne F. Sutton and Livia Visser-Fuchs, 'Choosing a Book in Late Fifteenth-Century England and Burgundy', in Caroline Barron and Nigel Saul (eds), *England and the Low Countries in the Late Middle Ages* (Stroud, 1995), pp. 61–98. An invaluable biographical conspectus is provided by C. Paul Christianson, *A Directory of London Stationers and Book Artisans 1300–1500* (New York, 1990). See also the important essays in J. B. Trapp and Lotte Hellinga (eds), *The Cambridge History of the Book in Britain*, vol. 3: *1440–1557* (Cambridge, 1999), especially Margaret Lane Ford, 'Importation of Printed Books into England and Scotland', pp. 179–201; C. Paul Christianson, 'The Rise of London's Book Trade', pp. 128–47; Paul Needham, 'The Customs Rolls as Documents for the Printed-Book Trade in England', pp. 148–63; Elisabeth Leedham-Green, 'University Libraries and Book Sellers', pp. 316–53; Kristen Jensen, 'Text Books in the Universities: The Evidence from the Books', pp. 354–79. The following discussion is greatly indebted to these pioneering studies.

Peter Actors and John of Westfalia, apparently on a sale or return basis, and a similar list may describe books provided by the Parisian printer Pierre Levet in 1480.[5] Lotte Hellinga has noted that 'the first books printed at Mainz were aimed at a clearly defined market, a clientele largely confined to monastic houses', and there is no reason to doubt that continental printers were seeking to tap into a similar market when they began importing into England.[6]

No English monastic centre was richer (or indeed better endowed) than 'the Monastery of St. Saviour and St. Bridget of Syon' of the Order of St Augustine, founded by Henry V in 1415 as part of his tripartite plan to create a network of new religious houses around the royal palace of Sheen.[7] The first (and in the event only) Bridgettine house in England, Syon brought a new kind of monasticism to post-schism and post-Wyclif England. A double house consisting of sixty nuns, thirteen priests, four deacons and eight lay brethren, the monastery also had a double function. The strictly enclosed nuns gave themselves totally to contemplation interspersed with liturgical prayer and praise, using their own distinctive (and divinely revealed) office, based on the *Sermo angelicus*.[8] The brethren, meanwhile, said the office of London diocese (recently changed to the Sarum rite at the time of the foundation) and,

---

[5] Paul Needham, 'Continental Printed Books Sold in Oxford, c. 1480–3', in Martin Davies (ed.), *Incunabula: Studies in Fifteenth-Century Printed Books Presented to Lotte Hellinga* (London, 1999), pp. 243–70.

[6] Hellinga, 'Importation', p. 205. See also John L. Flood, ' "Volentes Sibi Comparari Infrascriptos Libros Impressos ...": Printed Books as a Commercial Commodity in the Fifteenth Century', in Kristian Jensen (ed.), *Incunabula and Their Readers: Printing, Selling and Using Books in the Fifteenth Century* (London, 2003), pp. 139–51 (text), 255–62 (notes).

[7] The standard account of the foundation of Syon is still G. J. Aungier, *The History and Antiquities of Syon Monastery, the Parish of Isleworth and the Chapelry of Hounslow* (London, 1840). More recently M. B. Tait, 'The Brigittine Monastery of Syon (Middlesex) with Special Reference to its Monastic Uses' (unpublished doctoral thesis, University of Oxford, 1975), studied much unprinted manuscript material and explored the spiritual and cultural life of the house. See also N. Beckett, 'St. Bridget, Henry V and Syon Abbey', in J. Hogg (ed.), *Studies in St. Birgitta and the Brigittine Order*, Analecta Cartusiana 35:19 (1993), 2. 125–50, for a more recent perspective on the politics of the foundation. On the fabric, see R. W. Dunning, 'The Building of Syon Abbey', *Transactions of the Ancient Monuments Society*, NS, 25 (1981), 16–26.

[8] See the masterly discussions by Roger Ellis, *Viderunt eam filie syon: The Spirituality of the English House of a Medieval Contemplative Order from its Beginnings to the Present Day*, Analecta Cartusiana 68 (1984); 'Further Thoughts on the Spirituality of Syon Abbey', in William F. Pollard and Robert Boenig (eds), *Mysticism and Spirituality in Medieval England* (Cambridge, 1997), pp. 219–43; 'The Visionary and the Canon Lawyers: Papal and Other Revisions to the *Regula Salvatoris* of St Bridget of Sweden', in Rosalynn Voaden (ed.), *Prophets Abroad: The Reception of Continental Holy Women in Late-Medieval England* (Cambridge, 1996), pp. 71–90.

in addition to attending to the spiritual needs of the nuns, were charged by the *Regula salvatoris* with more outward-facing public duties:

> Thes thrittene preestis owe to entende oonly to dyuyne office and studie & prayer. And implie them w*ith* none o*þ*er*e* nedes or offices. Whiche also are bounde to expoune iche sonday the gospel of the same day in the same messe to all herers in ther modir tounge.[9]

They were also 'opunly to preche' on solemn festivals. In addition to dominical and festal sermons, major opportunities for preaching to the laity at Syon arose on those special days associated with the various indulgences granted to those who attended the house, and in particular with the popular and generous *Ad vincula* indulgence.[10] The pilgrim crowds offered a large potential audience. Apart from occasional (and specially sanctioned) spiritual guidance to high-born women (such as Margaret, Duchess of Clarence) and probably to postulants to the sisters, preaching and confession were the main activities that would have brought the Syon brethren into public view.[11] Though little evidence of preaching by Syon brethren now survives, these public sermons were probably popular and influential events.[12] The brethren's

---

9   For facsimiles and transcriptions of English copies of the *Regula Salvatoris* and the *Syon Additions*, see James Hogg (ed.), *The Rewyll of Seynt Sauioure and Other Middle English Brigittine Legislative Texts*, vols 2–4, Salzburger Studien zur Anglistik und Amerikanistik (Salzburg, 1978–80). All citations in this essay are from this edition. See now also James Hogg (ed.), *The Rewyll of Seynt Sauioure and A Ladder of Foure Ronges By the Which Men Mowe Clyme to Heven*, Analecta Cartusiana 183 (2003), which reproduces and transcribes Middle English versions of the *Regula Salvatoris* from Cambridge University Library MS Ff. 6. 33 and London, Guildhall MS 25524, and Latin versions from London, British Library MS Harley 612 and Syon Abbey South Brent MS 7. The standard edition of the versions of the Latin is Eklund (ed.), *Regula Salvatoris*. Fragments of the Rule and Additions were more recently identified among the manuscripts still in possession of the sisters: N. R. Ker and A. J. Piper, *Medieval Manuscripts in British Libraries*, 4 (Oxford, 1992), pp. 348–9. This quotation is from Cambridge University Library MS Ff. 6. 33, fol. 57r; Hogg (ed.), *Rewyll*, p. 38; Eklund (ed.), *Regula Salvatoris*, cap. 15, section 174, p. 121. For the passage in the Latin Σ text, see cap. 13, section 171 (Eklund (ed.), *Regula Salvatoris*, pp. 161–2).
10   The preaching office of the Syon brethren has been carefully and thoughtfully studied by Susan Powell, 'Preaching at Syon Abbey', *Leeds Studies in English*, NS, 31 (2000), 229–67; see also her 'Syon, Caxton and the *Festial*', *Birgittiana*, 2 (1996), 187–207, which discusses Syon's possible involvement with printed sermons.
11   On Symon Wynter's relations with Margaret, Duchess of Clarence, see G. R. Keiser, 'Patronage and Piety in Fifteenth-Century England: Margaret, Duchess of Clarence, Symon Wynter and Beinecke MS 317', *Yale University Library Gazette*, 60 (1985), 32–46.
12   For some evidence of the political concern generated by the public preaching of the Syon brethren in the 1530s, see Vincent Gillespie, ' "Hid Diuinite": The Spirituality of the English Syon Brethren', in E. A. Jones (ed.), *The Medieval Mystical Tradition in England*, 7 (Cambridge, 2004), pp. 189–206.

library collection contained hundreds of sermon collections, including several attributed to Syon brethren themselves, though only one of these has been identified as surviving. The provision in the vernacular *Additions* for the brethren allowing a preacher three days' remission from choir duties 'to recorde hys sermon' suggests that this duty was both accorded a high priority and taken seriously by the brethren.[13]

In pursuance of these pastoral duties, they were to be allowed access to books, 'as many as be necessary to doo dyvyne office and moo in no wyse', and also to liturgical and academic books, 'Thoo bookes they shalt haue as many as they wyll in whiche ys to lern*en* or to studye'.[14] The *Regula Salvatoris*, *Additions* for the brethren and other Syon-related documents suggest that, certainly by the middle of the fifteenth century and probably before, Syon was seeking to exercise a high-minded and idealistic model of priesthood that stressed the importance of the lived example of priests reinforcing their teaching; which valued and encouraged scholarship alongside prayer and contemplation; and which was fully aware of the dangers of heresy but had learned some of the lessons of the *Wyclifisti* and their critiques of priesthood and monastic life. Some of this idealism was no doubt a reflection of the spirit of the age of the Councils of Constance and Basel.[15] This *zeitgeist* would have penetrated the house through new professions, through the books they brought with them, as well as through the house's wider personal contacts with the clergy, the hierarchy, and the aristocracy and, of course, through the many books the house continued to acquire by donation, bequest and targeted purchase.

Syon documents imply the emergence of a book culture early in the life of the house. The vernacular *Additions* to the Rule for the sisters and for the brethren, dating from the first half of the fifteenth century (though surviving

---

[13] The Syon *Additions for the Brethren* (Guildhall manuscript) record in a short chapter headed 'Of the offices of the prechours' that 'Eche of the prechours schal besyde the sermon day haue thre hole days at lest oute of the quyer to recorde hys sermon'; Hogg (ed.), *Laybrothers' Additions*, p. 122.

[14] Cambridge University Library MS Ff. 6. 33. fols. 62v–63r; Hogg (ed.), *Rewyll*, pp. 49–50. For the Latin text (Π version), see cap. 21, sections 227–8: 'Libri quoque, quotquot necessarii fuerint ad divinum officium peragendum, habendi sunt, plures autem nullo modo. Illos autem libros habeant, quotquot voluerint, in quibus addiscendum est vel studendum' (Eklund (ed.), *Regula Salvatoris*, p. 127). The Π version, cap. 18, sections 227–8, is substantially the same (*ibid.*, pp. 204–5).

[15] This *zeitgeist* is explored in Vincent Gillespie, 'The Mole in the Vineyard: Wyclif at Syon in the Fifteenth Century', in Helen Barr and Ann M. Hutchison (eds), *Text and Controversy from Wyclif to Bale: Essays in Honour of Anne Hudson*, Medieval Church Studies 4 (Turnhout, 2005), pp. 131–62. I intend to study it in detail in a forthcoming monograph, *Reverend History: Syon Abbey and the Religious Culture of England 1415–1539*.

only in much later copies), both include specific prescriptions against the mistreatment of books and require silence in what is explicitly called 'the lybrary'.[16] Thomas Betson (d. 1516), librarian or *custos librarie* of the brethren's collection, makes a point in his own surviving writings of stressing the need to treat books with care.[17] His *Ryght profytable treatyse*, printed by Wynkyn de Worde in 1500, and aimed at an audience 'that ben come & shall come to relygyon', closes with the exhoration '¶ Lerne to kepe your bokes clene &c'. A surviving letter in his informal hand, intended to serve as the preface to a collection of 'goostly writyngis' sent to a group of 'Welbiloved Susturs', exhorts them to 'oftymes rede hem & kepe hem clene and hole. And when tyme shall requyre repayre hem.'[18] Several surviving manuscripts from Syon show that Betson practised what he preached in his willingness to undertake quite major repairs to damaged books, rewriting whole quires or adding patches where necessary. As custodian of a large collection, Betson was aware that manuscripts were fragile, precious and vulnerable objects. Perhaps his message got through: a note in Rose Tresham's manuscript Psalter exhorts: 'Lerne to kepe your books fayre & ockapy them well & use to clasp them whan you have done.'[19] Even so, there is evidence that under Betson's

---

[16] A surviving 1482 ordinance for the making of books refers to 'the kepers of the libraris of the bretherne and [Sys]terne Sydes there', printed by R. J. Whitwell, 'An Ordinance for Syon Library, 1482', *EHR*, 25 (1910), 121–3; Hogg (ed.), *Sisters' Additions*, p. 72 (the Additions for the Sisters). The relevant entries are usefully collected by Mary C. Erler, 'Syon Abbey's Care for Books: Its Sacristan's Account Rolls 1506/7–1535/6', *Scriptorium*, 39 (1985), 293–307.

[17] On Thomas Betson, see A. I. Doyle, 'Thomas Betson of Syon Abbey', *The Library*, 5th ser., 11 (1956), 115–18. Betson probably entered Syon in or around 1481 and may have been involved with the library up to his death in 1516. For a summary of recent knowledge of the library, see Gillespie, *Syon Abbey Catalogue*, pp. xxix–lxv. The standard (and masterly) discussion of the Syon libraries is now de Hamel, *Syon Abbey*. There is a cursory account of the library in D. N. Bell, 'Monastic Libraries 1400–1557', in Trapp and Hellinga (eds), *The Cambridge History of the Book in Britain*, pp. 229–54, esp. pp. 245–7. Betson's initial recension of the list was complete by about 1504, after which new accessions were added into blank spaces or by the erasure of entries relating to volumes now lost, damaged or removed from the collection. In some cases it has been possible to reconstruct these erased entries by using Betson's Index (which was not systematically updated) and by recovery under ultraviolet light. In the new edition, surviving entries are numbered SS1, and reconstructed entries SS2. References here will be to the alphabetical class-mark in the *registrum* and to the numbering of the new edition.

[18] *A ryght profytable treatyse* (STC 1978); facsimile repr. with intro. by F. Jenkinson (Cambridge, 1905); Durham University Library MS Cosin V. iii. 16, fols. 118r–v, ed. A. I. Doyle, 'A Letter Written by Thomas Betson, Brother of Syon Abbey', in *The Medieval Book and a Modern Collector: Essays in Honour of Toshiyuki Takamiya* (Cambridge and Tokyo, 2004), pp. 255–67, p. 257. See also Ellis, 'Further Thoughts', pp. 219–43.

[19] Oxford, Bodleian Library MS Auct. D. 4.3., fol. 6v; cited by Mary C. Erler, *Women, Reading and Piety in Late Medieval England* (Cambridge, 2003), p. 146. Rose Tresham is not

guidance, the library of the Syon brethren systematically shed manuscript copies and replaced them with printed works.[20]

Printed books were not automatically considered to be more robust or long-lasting than manuscripts. Johannes Trithemius, writing in the 1490s, commented that while handwriting on parchment would be able to endure for a thousand years, printing was an unknown quantity because it used paper; 'if in a paper volume it lasts for two hundred years, that is a long time'.[21] But longevity was not the only consideration. Many of Syon's older manuscript books were academic and pastoral miscellanies compiled by the brethren themselves. For someone in Betson's position, the advent of printing may have offered real advantages and curatorial opportunities to replace damaged or imperfect copies of important texts, to supplement incomplete holdings, to acquire superior versions of well-used materials, or perhaps even to make available versions of texts that were easier to locate or perhaps simply more legible than those buried in the largely miscellaneous manuscript holdings. Enea Silvio Piccolomini, describing for Cardinal Juan de Carvajal the forty-two-line printed Bible he had seen in Frankfurt in 1455, commented that 'the script is extremely neat and legible, not at all difficult to follow. Your grace would be able to read it without effort and indeed without glasses.'[22] Ease of navigation and legibility must have been among the physical attractions of the new printed books, and the gradual emergence of 'collected works' or cumulative editions of patristic authors would also have been a welcome development for institutional libraries with a desire to foster sound scholarship and orthodox teaching.

Along with other religious orders, the Bridgettines were quick to see the potential of the new medium. In 1492, Bartholomaeus Ghotan printed at Lübeck the *editio princeps* of Birgitta of Sweden's *Reuelaciones* (*GW* 43910), an edition of 800 paper copies and sixteen on parchment (the latter perhaps destined for each of the order's houses) and apparently seen through the press by brothers from the Bridgettine mother house at Vadstena. A copy of this edition is probably reported in the Syon *registrum* at M.115 (SS1.848).

---

listed in the *Martiloge* as a nun of Syon, but there is a Clemence Tresham, so the book may have a Syon provenance.

[20] On the overhaul of the collection see de Hamel, *Syon Abbey*, pp. lv–lvi, and, in more detail, Vincent Gillespie, 'The Book and the Brotherhood: Reflections on the Lost Library of Syon Abbey', in A. S. G. Edwards, Vincent Gillespie and Ralph Hanna (eds), *The English Medieval Book: Essays in Memory of Jeremy Griffiths*, British Library Studies in the History of the Book (London, 2000), pp. 185–208.

[21] *De laude scriptorum*, cap. 7; cited in David McKitterick, *Print, Manuscript and the Search for Order 1450–1830* (Cambridge, 2003), p. 20.

[22] Cited in McKitterick, *Print, Manuscript and the Search for Order*, p. 31.

Mary Erler has commented that Syon 'appears to be the only English religious institution whose espousal of the new technology of printing is extensive enough to be described as adapting a continental model'.[23] The appeal of print was partly practical and partly pragmatic. The so-called 'wretch of Syon', Richard Whitford, commented in one of his many works published in the second quarter of the sixteenth century that, 'bycause that writynge unto me is very tedyous: I thought better to put it in print'.[24] From 1500 onwards, Syon increasingly embraced printing for its own publications. But its eager acquisition of printed books started well before this date, and printers and stationers were quick to make provision for the demand.[25]

The evidence of the surviving *registrum* of the brethren's library suggests that even in its manuscript phase the collection was already large, deep and rich. But it seems to have come into its own only in the years after 1471, when it rapidly became a treasure house of learning through the acquisition and accession of large numbers of printed books. It was the death in 1471 of Thomas Graunt, canon and precentor of St Paul's Cathedral, and a staunchly orthodox figure whose twenty-six donations recorded in the *registrum* constitute a substantial collection of multi-work miscellany manuscripts (and only manuscripts), that prompted the addition of a special provision for benefactors to the library, recorded in the *Martiloge* (which also served as the obit and record book of the brethren). The service of the dead with nine readings and a requiem mass were to be said for those who provided books for 'librarie sororum vel librarie fratrum' or who provided books for common use.[26] Graunt had been a fellow of Oriel College, Oxford from 1425 until 1435

---

23 Mary C. Erler, 'Pasted-in Embellishments in English Manuscripts and Printed Books', The Library, 6th ser., 14 (1992), 185–206, at p. 204.
24 *A dayly exercise* (STC 25414), sig. D. 6v; cited in J. T. Rhodes, 'Syon Abbey and its Religious Publications in the Sixteenth Century', *JEH*, 44 (1993), 11–25, p. 15.
25 Woodcuts using distinctive Birgittine iconography are found in books produced both for Syon and by Syon: Martha W. Driver, 'Pictures in Print: Late Fifteenth- and Early Sixteenth-Century English Religious Books for Lay Readers', in Michael G. Sargent (ed.), *De Cella in Seculum: Religious and Secular Life and Devotion in Late Medieval England* (Woodbridge, 1989), pp. 229–44; 'Nuns as Patrons, Artists, Readers: Bridgettine Woodcuts in Printed Books Produced for the English Market', in Carol Garrett Fisher and Kathleen L. Scott (eds), *Art into Life: Collected Papers from the Kresge Art Museum Medieval Symposia* (East Lansing, 1995), pp. 236–67.
26 The brethren's *Martiloge* survives as London, British Library, MS Additional 22285. The decision is dated 7 September 1471, and grants prayers 'inspeciali pro anima magistri Thome Graunte et pro animabus Iohannis et Helene parentum eius. In generali vero pro animabus eorum omnium qui librarie sororum vel librarie fratrum aliquem vel aliquos libros ad communem usum eorundem pro Dei honore ampliando contulerunt' (fol. 17v (*De exequiis pro benefactoribus librariarum.Capitulum 7*)). A new edition, by Claes Gejrot and Virginia Bainbridge, of those parts of the *Martiloge* manuscript relating to the history of the house is

(where he would probably have known the ultra-conservative and orthodox Thomas Gascoigne, another donor to Syon, who had rooms in the college) and might have known of the reputation at least of Reginald Pecock who was a fellow of Oriel from 1414 until 1424.[27] In 1452, Graunt was authorised to obtain 'books, letters, schedules or writings' belonging to one Andrew Teye and to examine them for 'heresy, error or treason', and as a functionary of St Paul's was probably involved in the process against Pecock, so he may have been attracted to Syon by its reputation for sound teaching and ascetic orthodoxy. Syon had strong links with the forces of orthodoxy at the universities and in London, the most powerful of such connections being the number of rectors from the city churches who gave books to the house or who themselves eventually felt called to join the community at Syon, and the steady stream of recruits from Pembroke Hall, Cambridge and Lincoln College, Oxford, both of which had established reputations as centres of austere orthodoxy and anti-heretical teaching.[28]

Whatever the reason for Thomas Graunt's gift to Syon, the period after the 1471 *Martiloge* decision emerges as a decisive one in the history of the library of the brethren. The evidence suggests that before 1471 the library at Syon was not the well-organised resource that it was later to become and that the real heyday of the collection coincides quite precisely with the advent of printing and, perhaps incidentally, with the growth of the New Learning in England.[29] This renaissance in the library may have been the work of a recent recruit to the house. Thomas Westhaw, third Confessor General, is described in the *Martiloge* as 'doctor theologie'. Embodying the twin streams of orthodoxy that often flowed into Syon, he had been a fellow of Pembroke Hall,

---

underway. I am indebted to Dr Gejrot for making available to me their preliminary transcriptions.

[27] Biographical data about known donors to the library of the brethren are gathered in de Hamel, *Syon Abbey*, pp. 567–94. Pecock, himself a London rector and first master of Whittington College before becoming embroiled in controversy, had an oblique connection with Syon through the Guild of All Angels founded on the Syon demesne. The documents relating to the foundation of the fraternity (and mentioning Pecock and other founders) are edited by Aungier (ed.), *History and Antiquities of Syon Monastery*, pp. 459–64 (letters patent, translated pp. 215–20). See also Anne F. Sutton and Livia Visser-Fuchs, 'The Cult of Angels in Late Fifteenth-Century England: An Hours of the Guardian Angel presented to Queen Elizabeth Woodville', in Leslie Smith and Jane Taylor (eds), *Women and the Book: Assessing the Visual Evidence* (London, 1996), pp. 230–65, which places the circumstances of the foundation of the fraternity into a wider devotional and social context.

[28] See further on this Gillespie, 'The Mole in the Vineyard'.

[29] Vincent Gillespie, 'Syon and the New Learning', in James G. Clark (ed.), *The Religious Orders in Pre-Reformation England*, Studies in the History of Medieval Religion 18 (Woodbridge, 2002), pp. 75–95.

Cambridge in 1436. He was subsequently rector of All Hallows, London and had moved to Syon by 1468 at the latest, becoming Confessor General from 1472 until his death in 1488. This period marks such a change and development in the library collection, including building works in 1479 on the fabric of the library and the arrival in 1481 of Thomas Betson (perhaps quickly appointed librarian), and in 1482 of the layman Thomas Baillie or Raille with a specific brief to care for the books, that it is tempting to suggest that it was Westhaw's reaction to the state of the brethren's library holdings that may have prompted the apparent reform of the collection in the wake of the 1471 *Martiloge* resolution.

Graunt's donations on his death in 1471 were all manuscripts. Westhaw's books (and he contributed over fifty) contained many prints, including several collections of early printed *sammelbände*. The change had happened in less than a generation. The impact of the new technology on the producers of manuscript books was significant. Philip Wrenne, a stationer of London, complaining against his imprisonment for debt sometime around 1487, lamented that, despite his years of work in 'lymnyng', 'the occupation ys almost destroyed by prynters of bokes'.[30] But the change from a manuscript culture to a print culture was neither immediate nor complete. Manuscripts continued to arrive at Syon after the invention of printing and there are some entries in the library *registrum* that seem to imply mixed printed and manuscript contents. N.65 (SS1.919), for example, is a printed collection of treatises by Jean Gerson, all printed in Nuremberg by Johann Sensenschmidt and Andreas Frisner between 1473 and 1476. The Nuremberg collection is supplemented by the *Flores Sancti Augustini* by François de Meyronnes, which may also have been printed. But the final item reported by Betson (a commentary on pseudo-Denys the Areopagite also attributed to Meyronnes) is still unprinted and must therefore have been a manuscript addition to the printed texts.[31] Similarly D.49 (SS1.227) appears to be a collection of printed canon law works supplemented by manuscript notes and texts relating to scholastic acts and academic exercises. The donor, Stephen Saunder, who had studied at Cambridge and Louvain, probably assembled this mixed-medium miscellany during his academic career.[32]

---

[30] Early Chancery Proceedings, Bundle 74, no. 50, cited in C. Paul Christianson, 'An Early Tudor Stationer and the "prynters of bokes" ', *The Library*, 6th ser., 9 (1987), 257–62.
[31] Cambridge University Library MS Ff. 1.19 was originally a similar mixture of the two media. Before being broken up, it contained manuscript devotional writings by John Whetham from London Charterhouse and a number of printed devotional works.
[32] Further to the description in the *registrum* edition (pp. 78–9), supplementary identifications of texts in this volume (including materials ascribed to John Wycliffe) are made in Gillespie,

Overall, however, the 'printed' quality of the post-1471 Syon collection is indeed striking, and the Syon brethren quickly embraced the potential of the printing press. Books printed in the 1460s and early 1470s are easily identified in the surviving *registrum* of the brethren's library.[33] Betson's good curatorial habit of including the *secundo folio* for each press mark (a practice continued in the post-Betson recension of the *registrum*) is invaluable in this regard as it usually allows discrimination between the various early printed editions of a particular work to pinpoint the precise printing that found its way into the library at Syon. Some of the earliest printed books will have entered Syon in the personal libraries of brethren professed after this period. The pattern of recruitment, especially in the later years of the fifteenth century and into the sixteenth century, shows a high percentage of graduate entrants, and some very high-powered academic recruits, including several former heads of house at Oxford and Cambridge. Many of these men brought all or part of their books with them on profession (some made selected donations to their *alma mater* on resignation). But the order also allowed brethren to receive books after their profession, and there is ample evidence to suggest that this happened (this can sometimes be calibrated by comparing known profession dates against publication dates of books given by particular brethren).[34] Syon brethren also kept in contact with friends and colleagues outside the house, and there seems to have been a steady stream of donations entering the house, sometimes for the use of 'the preachers' (as they were called) in general and sometimes for the exclusive use of an individual brother for the term of his life.[35] A donor inscription in a surviving Syon book records that Thomas Jan

---

'The Mole in the Vineyard', pp. 151–2.

[33] In addition to the Cologne *Sammelbände* discussed elsewhere in this chapter, see, for example, the identified early prints at A.45 (SS1.45): Cicero, Venice 1470 or Rome 1469; B.55 (SS1.132a–c): Bessarion, Rome 1469; K.13 (SS1.623): Valerius Maximus, Strassburg, not after 1470; N.66 (SS1.920): Bernardino of Siena, Cologne c.1470; O.11 (SS1.953): Ambrose, Cologne c.1470.

[34] For examples, see Gillespie, 'The Book and the Brotherhood', pp. 190–2.

[35] See, for example, O.16: SS1.958, a manuscript copy of William Peraldus, *Summa de uitiis et uirtutibus*, written in 1453 by the London scribe Peter Cederwalt, and given to Syon by Edward Lupton 'ad perpetuum usum predicatoribus in eodem'. The book is now in Lincoln Cathedral Library, MS 60. Edward Lupton (d. 1482) was a fellow of Magdalen College, Oxford but had vacated his fellowship by 1476. He was Collector of University Rents in 1472–3. From 1476 to 1479 he was rector of All Hallows, Honey Lane (London). In 1479 he became rector of St Michael Royal, and Master of Whittington College (London), remaining so until his death. He is typical of the secular clergy with an academic background who are found giving books to Syon. Whittington College had been founded precisely to improve the in-service training of the London clergy. For other examples of such donations, see Gillespie, 'The Book and the Brotherhood', pp. 192–4.

or Jane (d. 1500), a canon of St Paul's and archdeacon of Essex, gave a copy of Iacobus Philippus Bergamensis, *Supplementum Chronicarum* (Brescia, 1485 (Goff J209)) to Syon on condition that Richard Terenden (a former colleague) had the use of it in his life.[36]

Books may also have been given to the house by their printers and importers. A house of Syon's size and prestige might have offered a good opportunity for merchants wanting to break into the English 'Latin trade' and to impress an influential and potentially significant customer. Syon, while strictly guarding the enclosure of the nuns, was otherwise highly permeable to visitors and temporary residents. Many came for the public preaching of the brethren and for confession; others (like Margery Kempe) came for feast days and their associated indulgences. The abbey also had a large community of lay officers and servants. The large estate made provision for temporary residents who were not bound by the rules of enclosure but wanted to share something of the spiritual life of the place, and for those who were passing their year of external novitiate in the demesne of the house. Visitors were sometimes allowed to use the brethren's library, and it had a reputation for the richness of its holdings. The famous report of the Venetian Gasparo Spinelli concerning his visit to Syon in July 1527 to meet Richard Pace, dean of St Paul's, describes Pace as 'leading a blessed life in that beautiful place', surrounded by such a quantity of books the like of which Spinelli had never seen before.[37] Merchants, printers and importers may have donated books to Syon not just out of piety but also perhaps as a high-class shop window for their wares. As with the more formally advertised patronage of certain printed books by public figures such as Lady Margaret Beaufort, word-of-mouth knowledge of Syon's approval for and use of a particular book would surely have done no harm to its chances in the marketplace.

So what we have in the Syon collection is both the accumulated detritus of the brethren's previous lives (often as academics or as secular clergy) and books deliberately acquired by them or for the house more generally after their arrival there, alongside books given to them or left as bequests. This makes precise discriminations about the nature of the active collection

---

36 This book was probably once K.48 in the *registrum* (see note on SS2.123), occurring in a sequence of donations attributed to Terenden, but has subsequently been erased. It survives, and is now Xanten, Stiftsbibliothek 3970 B [Inc.] 241.

37 F. Stefani, G. Berchet and N. Barrozzi (eds), *I diarii di Marino Sanuto*, 58 vols (Venice, 1879–1903), 45 (1896), p. 631; Tait, 'Brigittine Monastery', p. 340; R. Rex, 'The Earliest Use of Hebrew in Books Printed in England: Dating Some Works of Richard Pace and Robert Wakefield', *Transactions of the Cambridge Bibliographical Society*, 9 (1990), 517–25. J. Wegg, *Richard Pace: Tudor Diplomat* (London, 1932).

especially hard.[38] As anyone who has worked in an institutional library well knows, only certain strata of the collection are active at any one time, with other layers of holdings barely disturbed or quietly superseded but not deaccessioned out of *pietas* or inertia.[39]

A collection dominated by Latin printed books from the period 1470 to 1525 was *de facto* a Christian humanist collection.[40] Was, for example, a real and informed choice of intellectual school actually possible for a potential buyer in England within the range of available printed editions; or was he at the mercy of what his stationer had or could obtain for him? It is surely probable that, especially in the years before 1500, printed editions were acquired as and when they became available, and the ownership of a particular edition may not be reliable evidence of a positive intellectual allegiance, though in the case of academic books it may reflect a particular intellectual caste and training. Given the background and training of many of the post-printing brethren, one needs to be cautious about attributing to the collection a deliberate intellectual character that may partly be the result of accidents of chronology and printing history: brethren may have bought the editions they did because that was what was available at the time they were studying or teaching. Even so, the kinds of books they bought, and the dates of the editions they acquired, are of considerable interest for historians of the later medieval book.

The first printed book known to be purchased by an Englishman was a copy of the 1459 Mainz edition of Durandus printed by Fust and Schoeffer, bought in Hamburg in 1465 by James Goldwell, fellow of All Souls College, Oxford and an early humanist (the book is still in the college library). The next documented purchase was made by John Russell, bishop of Lincoln and chancellor of England under Edward IV, who bought two copies of Fust and Schoeffer's 1466 edition of Cicero's *De officiis* in Bruges in April 1467. Between July 1466 and March 1468, Gerhard von Wesel, the agent of the London Hanse in Cologne, sent two printed bibles to London for 'my lord Worchester'. This

---

[38] The matter is further complicated by the survival of eight identifiable Syon books that appear never to have been included in the *registrum*, and two surviving books that were given by brethren of Syon to people outside of the house. For an account of these (including four incunables) see de Hamel, *Syon Abbey*, pp. lxxi–lxxiii. The movement of books into and out of the house may have been quite free.

[39] For a 'cynical' view of the growth of the Syon collection, see R. Lovatt, 'The *Imitation of Christ* in Late Medieval England', *Transactions of the Royal Historical Society*, 5th ser., 18 (1968), 97–121: 'the Syon library, impressive though it seems, had a more fortuitous character, and was basically little more than the sum of the libraries of its benefactors' (p. 112).

[40] This argument is developed in more detail in Gillespie, 'Syon Abbey and the New Learning'.

was John Tiptoft, Earl of Worcester, a sublime classical scholar as well as a consummate political thug, who is almost certainly the same 'Comes Wygorniensis' who gave a copy of Eusebius's *De preparacione Euangelii* to Syon (H.15: SS1.512), though that was probably a manuscript. So by the mid-1460s Englishmen were both buying printed books while abroad and ordering them for delivery from overseas.[41]

Printed books were probably being imported into England as early as July 1466.[42] But it seems to have been only in the late 1470s that the customs rolls began to record substantial imports of printed books into England, with Nelly Kerling misreporting the first extant reference in December 1477 (a date now corrected by modern scholarship to 10 January 1478) when the alien merchant Henry Frankenbergh and the Louvain printer John of Westfalia imported £6 worth of books (though the records for the preceding four years are missing).[43] It is, in fact, also from 1477 that the first record of a purchase of a printed book in England comes, when the newly-arrived papal collector Giovanni Gigli bought a copy of Diodorus Siculus, printed in that same year by Andreas de Paltasichis in Venice.[44]

The surviving evidence suggests that this market for imported books was dominated by foreign merchants. Frankenbergh, for example, in addition to importing other people's editions, commissioned the printing by William de Machlinia (another alien working in London, also known as William Ravenswalde) of the first English edition (STC 26012, of about 1484) of the pastoral manual *Speculum christiani*, a work compiled in England for parish priests about 1400, and including many Middle English verses, here printed 'ad instanciam necnon expensas Henrici Vrankenbergh mercatoris'. This looks like a good example of a collaborative and speculative printing venture by alien merchants targeted at the special needs of the English market.[45]

Other significant alien importers of books included another 'docheman', John of Westfalia (otherwise known as John of Acon), who appears alongside Frankenbergh in customs rolls from early in 1478 through to 1491. It may be an indication of the scale of John's activities as a printer in Louvain and as an

41 For these purchases, see Barker, 'Importation', pp. 253–5; Armstrong, 'English Purchases'.

42 Unsurprisingly by a German, Gerhard von Wesel of (equally unsurprisingly) Cologne, who was alderman of the German community in London; Ford, 'Importation', p. 197, on the authority of Graham Pollard and Albert Ehrman, *The Distribution of Books by Catalogue from the Invention of Printing to A.D. 1800*, Roxburghe Club (1965).

43 Kerling, 'Caxton', p. 192; Christianson, 'Rise', p. 137; Needham, 'Customs Rolls', p. 151.

44 Armstrong, 'English Purchases', pp. 272–3.

45 Needham, 'Customs Rolls'; Christianson, 'Rise', pp. 136–8; Sutton, 'Caxton Was a Mercer', pp. 134–8. The information on printers and merchants outlined in the following paragraphs is assembled from the studies listed in note 4.

importer in London that at least eight of his prints can be found recorded in the Syon *registrum*, in editions dating from 1474 (given by the sixteenth-century brother Richard Whitford) through to 1484/5.[46] Another initiative by alien merchants (in this case the innovative Cologne adventurers who sought to establish satellite presses across Europe to print and import Cologne materials) was the relatively short-lived Oxford press of Theodoricus Rood. His work is represented at Syon by a copy of the first printed edition (?1483) of William Lyndwood's *Prouinciale* (T.15: SS1.1355), a codification of English canon law as it developed in the decade after the founding of Syon in 1415, and one of the favourite canon law books at Syon, witnessed in no fewer than seven printed and three manuscript copies. This was a book that was first produced in the heady atmosphere of pastoral zeal surrounding the great reforming councils of Constance and Basel in the first half of the fifteenth century. Its emphases continued to sit comfortably with Syon's mission to be a centre of orthodox excellence, and the presence of multiple printed copies alongside manuscript versions is all the more noteworthy given that the canon law section of the Syon collection was comprehensively re-ordered early in the sixteenth century (probably in the first decade), with many older law books being discarded or de-accessioned.[47]

Early in his printing career (1481–2) William de Machlinia had been in partnership with John Lettou before striking out on his own until 1486. But Lettou had set up in business as early as 1480, supported by the wealthy merchant William Wilcocks.[48] One of the books printed by Lettou at Wilcocks's commission is recorded in the Syon *registrum* as F.19 (SS1.400):[49]

400 Bonde F.19.   2° fo. *caritatem*

g.63.// Valentius super psalmos vsque ad *dixi custodiam*, cum tabula.

Thomas Waleys, *Expositio super duos nocturnos Psalterii*, a commentary on Ps. 1–38: pr. London 1481 (*STC* 19627) as 'Doctor

---

[46] Westfalia books are apparently described in the following Syon *registrum* entries (donor's name in brackets): C.44: SS1.176 (Whitford); D.49: SS1.227a (Saunder); N.45: SS1.899 (Steyke); ?R.31: SS1.1223b–h (Butler); A.47: SS1.47 (Steyke); K.65: SS1.675 (Terenden); P.57: SS1.1097 (Trowel); S.44: SS1.1311 (Terenden).

[47] On this revision process, see Gillespie, 'The Book and the Brotherhood', p. 199, and the entries under section T of the edited *registrum*.

[48] On Lettou and Wilcocks, see now Sutton, 'Caxton Was a Mercer', pp. 134–6.

[49] Entries from the *registrum* are reproduced from my edition, and follow the layout of the manuscript, with the cataloguing conventions of the *Corpus of British Medieval Library Catalogues* superimposed.

Valentius'; Kaeppeli 3890; Stegmüller *Bibl*.8245; Sharpe, *Latin Writers*, 686. There is a table to this work at 146d.

This *secundo folio* agrees with the edition printed in London by John Lettou for William Wilcocks in 1481 (*STC* 19627).

As with the 1474 Westfalia, given by a sixteenth-century brother, this book was given to Syon by William Bonde (d. 1530), a fellow of Queens' College, Cambridge between 1503 and 1507 and of Pembroke Hall thereafter, serving as university preacher in 1509–10. Bonde, one of the most prolific authors in Syon (admittedly not a hard contest to win), and a member of a theologically conservative college with strong links to Syon, presumably acquired this book second-hand, though it was a rare edition of a rare text so it might have been old stock. But Bonde's provenance and status suggest that Wilcocks was aiming at (and apparently hitting) a specific academic market in commissioning volumes of this kind from Lettou (whose usual stock in trade was law books). Wilcocks, whose wife Johanna was described as 'Theutonicus' in the alien's return, was quite an entrepreneur. As a member of the Draper's Company and its warden in 1486 and 1493, and (like Caxton) also a leading member of the Merchant Adventurers, Wilcocks may have stood surety for Lettou as was necessary for aliens wishing to be admitted to the freedom of the city, and may even have invited him to come to London in the first place. As a Merchant Adventurer, Wilcocks, like Caxton and Roger Thorney, who also speculated in the book trade, would have been able to import paper on his own account and thus cut out the middle man in printing and publishing. He may also have been a book lover, if he can be identified with the donor of B.55 (SS1.132) to Syon, which seems probable as there is no reported member of either house at Syon with this surname:

132 Wilcokkes   B.55.   2° fo. *tionibus et*

b.28.// **a** Bessarionis cardinalis in calumpniatorem platonis libri 4ᵒʳ. **b** Item eiusdem examinacio legum platonis translacionis et errorum eius declaracio. **c** Item eiusdem de natura et arte aduersus Georgium Trapezuntium. **d** Item liber quadripartiti Ptholomei. **e** Centiloquium eiusdem. **f** Centiloquium hermetis. **g** Eiusdem de stellis beibeniis. **h** Centiloquium bethem et **i** de horis planetarum, **j** de significacione triplicitatum ortus. **k** Centum quinquaginta proposiciones Almansoris. **l** Zael de interrogacionibus **m** de eleccionibus, **n** de temporum significacionibus in iudiciis. **o** Messahallach de recepcionibus planetarum, **p** de interrogacionibus. **q** Epistola eiusdem cum 12ᶜⁱᵐ capitulis. **r** Et de reuolucionibus annorum mundi.

a–c Bessarion, *Aduersus calumniatorem Platonis*, *Correctio* *librorum Platonis de legibus Georgio Trapezuntio interprete* and *De natura et arte aduersus Georgium Trapezuntium*: pr. together Rome 1469 (*GW* 4183). **d–r** The remainder of this volume is as 124.

This *secundo folio* agrees with the edition of items **a–c** printed in Rome 1469 (*GW* 4183). The remainder of this volume is the omnibus edition of Ptolemy printed in Venice 1493 (Goff P1089).

This composite volume would have been close to the cutting edge of modern printing of natural philosophy, and the great Ptolemy collection in particular was one of the triumphs of early humanist printing. So this would have been a prestigious and intellectually significant gift. It is not recorded whether the brethren had the heart to tell the donor that they already had a copy (B.47: SS1.124).

Caxton does not feature in the Syon *registrum* either as printer or as donor. But when Caxton returned to London in 1476, he brought with him experience of the book trade in Cologne and in Bruges, and it is likely that he imported books into England as well as printing them himself. Johann Veldener, who had supplied Caxton's types was, by this date, printing on his own account in Louvain, and Nicholas Barker has suggested that Veldener books in Caxton bindings 'suggest that this link provided an early source of import'.[50] The possible presence of a Johann Veldener edition of Werner Rolewinck's *Fasciculus Temporum* printed in Louvain probably about 1475 at K.22 (SS1.632) of the *registrum* offers a tantalising hint of that connection and trade. (It must be admitted, however, that the *secundo folio* of that edition is shared by five others of similar date from presses in Cologne and Venice.) Similarly it has been suggested that Gerard Leeu of Antwerp printed some Caxtons immediately after his death in 1492, perhaps to cover a hiatus in supply while the succession was effected. His work was certainly achieving some kind of exposure in England as his 1488 edition of the *Morticellarium aureum* of Michael Francisci was in the Syon collection at Q.61 (SS1.1174), with the lack of a named donor suggesting that it may have been purchased on behalf of the community or given anonymously (perhaps even by its importer). The French printers who flooded into the London trade after Caxton's death are represented at Syon by Richard Pynson's 1499 edition of Lyndwood's *Prouinciale* (T.16: SS1.1356).

Caxton's successor Wynkyn de Worde appears in the *registrum* both as a printer and as a donor.[51] De Worde was himself a major importer of printed

---

[50] Barker, 'Importation', p. 255.
[51] He gave A.74: SS1.75, his own 1500 edition of the *Hortus vocabulorum* (STC 13829); and M.30: SS1.763, his own 1516 edition of the *Noua legenda Anglie* (STC 4601).

books, with twenty-nine shipments in his name recorded in customs rolls between 1503 and 1531. Given the strong links that existed between de Worde, Syon and Lady Margaret Beaufort, he may well have been a supplier of imported books as well as his own printing to Syon, but perhaps not until after 1500, when Wynkyn printed Thomas Betson's *Ryght profytable treatyse,* the first printed work to emanate from identifiable Syon authorship. The book seems to have initiated a substantial and ongoing commercial relationship between Wynkyn and Syon.[52]

Although the Syon *registrum* preserves these partial traces of the developing English trade in printing and importing books, the bulk of its printed books, drawn from major cities and presses across the length and breadth of Europe, are largely mute about the entrepreneurial endeavours that brought them to the banks of the Thames at Isleworth. The richness of Syon's holdings is all the more striking when we notice that other religious houses in England sometimes found it difficult to compete in the market for imported printed books. In 1532, John Houghton, prior of London Charterhouse, wrote to the vicar of the Cologne Carthusians asking him to acquire and send ten copies of all the printed texts of Denys the Carthusian and twenty copies of two other para-mystical texts because the demand for them among 'the pious and learned' in England was so great that the English Carthusians had trouble buying them when they arrived and often had to 'go hungry'.[53] (Syon had had printed copies of works by Denys for several decades by this date.[54])

The impact that printing had on the reading of the Syon brethren and on the developing resources of the library can be explored by looking at brief case studies of the books donated by four brethren who were professed in the decades after 1450. These snapshots show how the physical makeup of a brother's collection changed across the decades from 1460 to 1500 as the number of manuscripts declined and the number of printed books increased. They also show how the presses and publishers represented in their collections changed over the years, and how the kinds of books they were acquiring

52 G. R. Keiser, 'The Mystics and the Early Printers: The Economics of Devotionalism', in Marion Glasscoe (ed.), *The Medieval Mystical Tradition in England,* 4 (Cambridge, 1987), pp. 9–25; Susan Powell, 'Lady Margaret Beaufort and her Books', *The Library,* 6th ser., 20 (1998), 197–240; see also Powell, 'Syon, Caxton and the *Festial*'. Lucy Lewis, ' "For No Text Is an Island, Divided From the Main": Incunable Sammelbände', in Barry McKay, John Hinks and Maureen Bell (eds), *Light on the Book Trade: Essays in Honour of Peter Isaac* (London, 2004), pp. 13–26, discusses an incunable *sammelband* of de Worde editions with strong Syon affiliations.
53 E. M. Thompson, *The Carthusian Order in England* (London, 1930), pp. 329–30. The other works he requested were called *De contemptu mundi* and *Scala religiosorum.*
54 E.g. in M.50 (SS1.783 c, d); M.109 (SS1.842); R.31 (SS1.1223h).

changed, from manuscript miscellanies in the earlier period to multi-volume printed editions of major works at the end of the incunable period.[55]

The first example is the same Thomas Westhaw who may be responsible for the rearrangement of the library at Syon in the 1470s. After his distinguished career in Cambridge, Westhaw had in 1448 succeeded the great preacher (allegedly of 3,038 sermons) William Lichfield as rector of All Hallows the Great in the city of London before joining Syon, perhaps as early as 1459, and certainly by 1468, where he became third Confessor General in 1472. Westhaw's life (he died in 1488) and career thus straddle the invention of printing. Of his fifty-two identified gifts to the brethren's library, forty must have been manuscript books, while only ten were certainly printed books. Of these ten, the latest dateable item was printed in 1477 (that is, the year of the first reported purchase of a printed book in England, and just before records of the import trade start to occur).[56] Westhaw's printed books precisely trace the Rhenish trade route which was the main artery bringing early printing into England: presses in Basel, Cologne, Nuremberg, Esslingen, Utrecht and the Netherlands are all represented in his collection. No books from France or Italy are represented, and the overwhelming majority of his books come from Cologne, most of which are grouped into (and were probably bound and sold in England as) *Sammelbände*.[57] N.60 (SS1.914) is a typical theological miscellany, probably the output of a number of Cologne presses in the early 1470s. Augustine rubs shoulders with Jean Gerson. A papal bull on the Jubilee year sidles up alongside a marian sermon. Pseudo-Aquinas nestles against pseudo-Cicero. There is nothing particularly coherent about this book apart from the date and point of origin of most of its contents. N.61 (SS1.915), however, consistently addresses very contemporary anxieties about heresy and the spread of Islam, with its recent papal utterances calling for a new crusade against the Turks in the wake of the fall of Constantinople in 1453, penned by that same Piccolomini who had enthused over the forty-two-line Bible and who was now Pius II. N.62 (SS1.916) has a bundle of Cologne editions (items a–g) of confessional and sacramental works, all from the press of Ulrich Zel, with the late and slightly eccentric addition of another unrelated Cologne print, of Plutarch on a liberal education. N.65 (SS1.919) appears to be a *sammelband* of Nuremberg editions of the works of Jean Gerson (popular at Syon for his intelligent and

---

[55] All the identified books given by particular donors (including some not listed in the *registrum*) are listed in the index of donors in Gillespie (ed.), *Syon Abbey*, pp. 567–94.

[56] N.62: SS1.916b, Bonaventure, *de triplici uia* (*Gesamtkatalog der Wiegendrucke*, 7 vols (Leipzig, 1925–38); 8 (Stuttgart, 1978–), no. 4706).

[57] This topic would richly repay further examination.

highly academic orthodoxy), with the addition of two works by Francois de Meyronnes. Westhaw's books are a valuable witness to the penetration of early commercial printing into the English market.

Stephen Saunder was Syon's fifth Confessor General, and came from a similar academic background to Westhaw. Stephen incepted as a Master of Arts in 1468, and was a fellow of Pembroke Hall, Cambridge c.1470–3, serving as treasurer in 1471 and 1472. He received grace to proceed to the Bachelor of Theology degree in 1471–2. In 1475 he matriculated at the University of Louvain to study theology. From 1473 to 1478, he is recorded as rector of Welwyn (Hertfordshire). Like Westhaw, he also gave books to Pembroke. He was elected Confessor General shortly after the death of his predecessor in 1497, serving until his own death in 1513. Only four of his nineteen gifts to Syon seem likely to have been manuscripts, and only two of these are securely so.[58] The remaining fifteen or seventeen books were probably all printed. Although seven of these are from as yet unidentified presses, the remaining identified books show a much wider spread of presses. Two books each come from Cologne, Venice, Paris and Strassburg, with single books from Lyon, Rome, Esslingen, Louvain and Nuremberg. The Louvain book (D.49: SS1.227) is of particular interest, as we know that Saunder studied theology there in 1475. It would be tempting to suggest that he might have bought his copy of Iohannes de Ligniano's *De pluralitate beneficiorum ecclesiasticorum* while studying in the town, but as this edition was printed by Johannes de Westfalia, who had a thriving London-based import trade, that temptation must be resisted, though it is striking that the edition was printed in the very year he began his studies at Louvain.[59]

The third example comes from a near contemporary of Saunder. John Steyke is yet another member of the distinguished Cambridge cohort of Syon brethren in the late fifteenth century. Having studied at Cambridge, John Steyke was rector of St Lawrence's (Norwich) from 1480 to 1484, and rector of Brundell (Norfolk) from 1483 to 1489. He may, therefore, have joined Syon in 1489. His death is recorded in the Syon *Martiloge* on 31 March 1513, just six days before Saunder died. Of his seventy-five gifts, thirty-three appear to have been manuscripts while forty-four were probably printed books, though only half of these have had their edition identified to date. The identified editions in his collection comprise five books from Venice, four from

---

[58] SS2.104 and 105, erased from the *registrum*, were almost certainly manuscripts. A.42: SS1.42 and D.64: SS1.242 may perhaps be printed books, though as yet unidentified.

[59] Another edition (Paris, 1474–5) has the same *secundo folio* as the Louvain edition, but the date of purchase would probably have been the same in either case.

Cologne (including an interesting *sammelband* volume of Augustine texts (N.44: SS1.898)), three from Deventer, two from Nuremberg, and single witnesses from presses in Louvain, Brussels, Leiden, Augsburg, Basel and Rostock. N.44 offers an interesting collection of early single editions of Augustinian texts useful in catechisation and preaching, supplemented by Jacobus de Voragine's bibliographical treatise on the Augustine canon. These are probably all from the press of Bartholomaeus de Unkel and all appeared for the first time in 1482. Steyke seems to have had a modest but genuine interest in printed books of science and astronomy: among his donations are copies of Euclid's *Elementa* and a run of eight books (B.44–51) including Pliny, Ptolemy in the 1493 omnibus edition, the ten tracts on astronomy by Guido Bonnetti in the Augsburg 1491 edition, the Venice 1497 edition of the *Mathesis* and a print of Boethius's *De institutione arithmetica* (probably from Augsburg). Although he lived until 1513, the latest dated edition that has been identified among his gifts was printed in 1497, though some of the unidentified editions may come from post-incunable printing.

The fourth example is N.41 (SS1.895). The book was probably given by Dominus Richardus Grene, reported by the *Martiloge* to be a priest of Syon who died in April 1487, but was perhaps the property of the lay brother John Grene who lived until April 1508. This time the volume reflects more classicising interests, though still in the context of a deeply miscellaneous collection of prints, bound together (perhaps literally) only by their common origin from Cologne presses in and around 1470. Perhaps this was Grene's 'classical library', to which he later added his manuscript copy of William Flete's remedies against tribulation. This addition must have been made after he joined Syon, as the title reported in the *registrum* reflects that of a surviving copy (Oxford, St John's College MS 77) known to have been used and owned by John Dygon, recluse of the neighbouring Carthusian house of Sheen, and probably reflects a distinctive Sheen/Syon textual tradition.

What these examples show is that theological *Sammelbände* may have arrived in England in some quantity, probably aimed at the academic and monastic market. The existence of probably manuscript additions in these books further illustrates that the change from a manuscript culture to a print culture was neither immediate nor complete. But the attraction of printed *Sammelbände* to readers and to librarians is clear. They offered instant miscellaneity and easy accessibility in a uniform and legible format. This appealed to academics and to preachers. Syon, of course, was full of both.

The final example is provided by Richard Terenden, a rare example of a late fifteenth-century Syon brother with an Oxford background. A scholar of Winchester in 1467 and of New College, Oxford in 1471, before becoming

Bachelor of Civil Law, Terenden was a fellow of New College in 1473 but had vacated his fellowship by 1483. He was rector of St Leonard's (Hastings) from 1477 to 1482 and of several Essex parishes between 1482 and 1488. From 1487 to 1488 he was a canon of St Paul's Cathedral (London) and prebendary of Ealdstreet. He may have joined Syon in 1488. Terenden gave twenty-seven volumes to the library. His collection has two striking differences from those of his contemporaries Saunder and Steyke. First, and perhaps most significant, not one of the twenty-seven gifts attributed to him appears to have been a manuscript, although ten of the books are in editions yet to be identified. Terenden seems, therefore, to demonstrate a shift from manuscript to print culture more dramatic than that of his Cambridge colleagues. Whether Oxford was more advanced in the transition to printed books is hard to say. But in addition to the evidence provided by the Oxford press of Theodoricus Rood, we do have much better documented evidence of stationers selling continental printed books in Oxford. Rood's partner Thomas Hunt, as we have seen, was supplied books for sale in 1480 by the Parisian printer Pierre Levet and in 1483 by Johannes de Westfalia and his business partner and fellow importer into London, Peter Actors, who in 1485 received a patent from Henry VII as Royal Stationer. Though there would probably have been similar stationers in Cambridge, they are less visible in the early documentary record than their Oxford counterparts, and the known names of Cambridge stationers come from the 1530s and 1540s.

The exclusively printed nature of Terenden's collection may be no more than an accident of donation or survival (perhaps he had given his manuscripts elsewhere), but the nature of those printed books reflects a more deliberate change of emphasis. Whereas Westhaw's Cologne *Sammelbände* from the 1470s replicated the contents and appearance of late medieval miscellany manuscripts, Terenden's books include several multi-volume editions of collected works or major summae, such as his three-volume edition of Antonius Florentinus's *Summa moralis* (D.71–3: SS1.249–51); or his three-volume Nuremberg edition of the same author's *Chronicon siue Summa historialis* (K.49–51: SS1.659–61); or his four-volume printed Bible from Venice (E.60–3: SS1.366–9), accompanied in a fourth volume by a recent and sophisticated finding aid (E.64: SS1.370). Terenden's identified books represent a spread of presses: five editions from Nuremberg, three from Venice, three from Cologne, three from Louvain (all published by Johannes de Westfalia), two from Strassburg and one each from Alost and Rostock.

As the appendix shows, when considered overall, the identified incunable holdings at Syon map closely on to the recent statistical work on English imports by Margaret Lane Ford for the *Cambridge History of the Book*.[60] Her finding that Cologne books dwindled in numbers towards the end of the century is borne out at Syon, where thirty-six Cologne books from the 1470s are identified, and not a single Cologne book from the 1490s. Her finding that Paris books remained steady through the 1470s and 1480s and increased modestly in the 1490s is also supported by the Syon materials, which show figures of nine, five and sixteen copies. Ford found that import and ownership of Venice books rocketed in the 1490s, and at Syon a similar increase is observed in Venice editions produced in the 1490s (from five to nine to twenty-eight across the three decades). There are still huge gaps in our knowledge and understanding of the market for continental printed books in England, but the Syon collection is an underused resource that witnesses to hundreds of identified (and dozens still to be identified) printed books (including over 270 identified incunables) which can be placed and dated with considerable accuracy because of Thomas Betson's diligence in recording their *secundo folios* and in replicating their title pages in his descriptions of the books. Of course care is necessary in interpreting such data. Books printed in the 1470s in some cases only entered the collection at Syon on the profession of brethren joining in the first decades of the sixteenth century and so belong to the cultural milieu of their previous lives as much as to that of Syon. But used with care the Syon collection may add considerably to our understanding of the 'Latin trade', not just during the incunable period which is the subject of this essay but also in the heady and exciting years when humanism and printing revolutionised the structures and resources of learning, those unexpectedly few years before 'the tyme of the lamentable spoyle of the lybraryes of Englande' laid waste the great collection of the Syon brethren.

Appendix: Identified Incunables in the Syon *Registrum*

c.1467–1469
Total: 3

Cologne	2
Rome	1

1470–1479
Total: 82

Cologne	36
Paris	9

---

[60] Ford, 'Importation', pp. 179–201, especially table 8.1 (p. 185). See similar tables in Barker, 'Importation', pp. 263–6; Hellinga, 'Importation', pp. 211 (fig. 7.2), 222–4.

Louvain	5
Nuremberg	5
Strassburg	5
Venice	5
Basel	4
Netherlands	3
Esslingen	2
Utrecht	2
Brussels	1
Deventer	1
Lübeck	1
Mainz	1
Padua	1
Zwolle	1

1480–1489
Total: 84

Cologne	16
Strassburg	10
Nuremberg	9
Venice	9
Basel	6
Brussels	5
Louvain	5
Paris	5
Speyer	3
Deventer	2
Netherlands	2
Ulm	2
Alost	1
Antwerp	1
Gouda	1
Heidelberg	1
Leiden	1
London	1
Mainz	1
Oxford	1
Rostock	1
Treviso	1

1490–1500
Total: 112

Venice	28
Paris	16
Basel	15
Strassburg	14
Hagenau	10
Nuremberg	9
Lyon	5
Brescia	2
Augsburg	1
Bologna	1
Cremona	1
Florence	1
Freiburg	1
London	1
Lübeck	1
Mainz	1
Modena	1
Rome	1
Toulouse	1
Pavia	1
Westminster	1

4

'Moche profitable unto religious persones,
gathered by a brother of Syon':
Syon Abbey and English Books

C. ANNETTE GRISÉ

Syon Abbey's involvement in the early printed book market has generated scholarly interest from a few angles. The classic, essential treatments of the topic, Doyle's discussion of the larger role of religious orders in the printed book trade and J. T. Rhodes's survey of Syon's involvement in the publication of pre-Reformation books, are an excellent starting point for this topic, providing lists and descriptions of texts and authors. Critics such as George R. Keiser and myself have examined the publication of Middle English mystical and visionary books, including those printed from Syon manuscripts. Vincent Gillespie's recent work on the printed books in the brothers' library includes discussions of Syon brothers whose books are printed before the Reformation. In addition, Martha Driver has studied the woodcuts used in Syon books, arguing that Syon sisters and brothers played an important role in the production of devotional texts from their abbey.[1] The wealth of materials available

---

[1] A. I. Doyle, 'Book Production by the Monastic Orders in England (*c.* 1375–1530): Assessing the Evidence', in L. L. Brownrigg (ed.), *Medieval Book Production: Assessing the Evidence* (Los Altos Hills, CA, 1990), pp. 1–19; J. T. Rhodes, 'Syon Abbey and its Religious Publications in the Sixteenth Century', *JEH*, 44 (1993), 11–25; George R. Keiser, 'The Mystics and the Early English Printers', in Marion Glasscoe (ed.), *The Medieval Mystical Tradition in England*, vol. 4 (Cambridge, 1987), pp. 9–26; C. Annette Grisé, 'Holy Women in Print: Continental Female Mystics and the English Mystical Tradition', in E. A. Jones (ed.), *The Medieval Mystical Tradition in England*, vol. 7 (Cambridge, 2004), pp. 83–96; Vincent Gillespie (ed.), *Syon Abbey*, with *The Libraries of the Carthusians*, ed. A. I. Doyle, Corpus of British Medieval Library Catalogues 9 (London, 2001); Vincent Gillespie, 'The Book and the Brotherhood: Reflections on the Lost Library of Syon Abbey', in A. S. G. Edwards, Vincent Gillespie and Ralph Hanna (eds), *The English Medieval Book: Essays in Memory of Jeremy Griffiths* (London, 2000), pp. 185–208, and 'Syon and the English Market for Continental Printed Books: The Incunable Phase', *Religion and Literature*, 37 (2005), 1–23 (reprinted as Chapter 3,

from Syon allows for further work to be done on Syon's contribution to the pre-Reformation English book market. This essay goes some way toward making this tradition better known to students and scholars, offering some suggestions about its importance in late medieval piety and the pre-Reformation print tradition.

The essay begins with a short chronological survey of the texts and authors of printed devotional works associated with Syon.[2] After briefly summarising the major characteristics of Syon printed books I will analyse the framing materials for the texts and how they defined their readers and authors, leading into a consideration of why the Syon texts consciously self-identify themselves. Although there are other monastic authors, texts and reading communities specified in the devotional print tradition in late medieval England, Syon's role was far greater than that of any other religious house.[3] Factors that may contribute to this impact were the abbey's location close to London and its printers, the wealth and connections of Syon's patrons and clientele, the learning of the brothers and sisters and their access to religious manuscripts and books, and the pastoral duties of the brothers – both to the sisters and to the laity. The devotional texts supported and expanded the brothers' spiritual responsibilities to their sisters by providing multiple copies of significant texts for the nuns to read, while at the same time the texts allowed the brothers to seek a broader base for their message as they actively courted a wider audience in their texts. The brothers enhanced their roles as fathers, teachers and preachers in the new medium of print; however, the new medium meant the brothers potentially could reach readers who had no monastic training and were not reading the texts within the controlled environment of the monastery. They often did not change their texts drastically for the print versions, but this awareness informed their choices of texts and the contextualising they did in the framing materials.

Syon's contributions to vernacular printed books began early in the incunable period, but it was not until just before the 1520s that the abbey

---

above); Martha W. Driver, 'Nuns as Patrons, Artists, Readers: Bridgettine Woodcuts in Printed Books Produced for the English Market', in Carol Garrett Fisher and Kathleen L. Scott (eds), *Art into Life: Collected Papers from the Kresge Art Museum Medieval Symposia* (East Lansing, MI, 1995), pp. 244–57, and *The Image in Print: Book Illustration in Late Medieval England and its Sources* (London, 2004).

[2] See Rhodes's essay 'Syon Abbey' for a more complete treatment of this aspect of the tradition.

[3] See, for example, Henry Bradshaw's lives of Werburgh and Radegund, both printed in 1521 by Pynson (STC 3506 and 3507), and Bishop Richard Fox's translation of the Benedictine rule for the nuns of his diocese, printed also by Pynson in 1517 (STC 1859).

played a substantial role in this new medium. In the incunable period printers chose classic, popular texts for printing, ones that were tried and true in manuscript form and were likely to have a solid audience in print form. John Flood's study of early German printers concludes that '[t]hey tended to be conservative rather than innovative "agents of change", catering for existing markets rather than creating new ones',[4] and scholars such as Lotte Hellinga have established that the English printers followed the same pattern.[5] In the early sixteenth century there were more printers publishing more books (but England's was still a relatively small market by continental standards) and although publishers did not take substantial risks they were ready to try other formulae for success, such as Syon texts that had some popularity in manuscript and had the potential to appeal to a solid group of religious readers and/or a wide devout audience. By the 1520s Syon's reputation as a supplier of texts for the printed book market was cemented. The 1530s see the Syon authors become their most prolific (with Richard Whitford at the forefront), publishing advice for living a good Christian life, justifying the monastic life, and drawing connections between lay piety and the monastic life. However, just when the Syon tradition gained its momentum it was cut short by the suppression of the monasteries.

The incunable period offers relatively few publications that can be linked directly to Syon. The first known Syon author wrote in Latin: Clement Maidstone's *Directorium sacerdotum* (1487–1508), the first Latin guide for priests to the office and calendar printed in England, is viewed as a significant development in the tradition of the Directorium or Pye (*Pica*), providing access for priests in printed form to the rules for determining which offices and feast days were to be performed when.[6] It is only at the turn of the sixteenth century that we find vernacular printed books expressly associated with Syon. The first Middle English devotional text associated with Syon is Simon Wynter's *Life of Jerome* (1499), originally written for Margaret, Duchess of Clarence (who late in life became a vowess living near Syon ministered to by Wynter, a Syon brother), and printed to be made available to

---

4   John L. Flood, ' "Volentes sibi comparare infrascriptos libros impressos ...": Printed Books as a Commercial Commodity in the Fifteenth Century', in Kristan Jensen (ed.), *Incunabula and Their Readers: Printing, Selling and Using Books in the Fifteenth Century* (London, 2003), pp. 139–51, at p. 146.
5   See, for example, Lotte Hellinga, *Caxton in Focus: The Beginning of Printing in England* (London, 1982).
6   Christopher Wordsworth (ed.), *The Directorium Sacerdotum of Clement Maydeston*, Henry Bradshaw Society (London, 1902), and *The Tracts of Clement Maydeston*, Henry Bradshaw Society (London, 1894).

other like-minded readers.[7] In the introduction to her abridged edition of the *Life*, Claire Waters notes that 'Symon's willingness to compose this *Life* for Margaret no doubt stemmed from his personal interest in her welfare, but it was also part of a larger trend of monastic compositions for laypeople'[8] which offered advice on how to live a good, pious life. Jerome's legend is offered as an exemplar, a typical function for hagiography, a useful text for the pious laity – and one that furthermore supported Bridget's cult in England through Wynter's use of Bridgettine materials in the text.[9]

Following from Wynter's instructional hagiography we see in the 1500 publication of Thomas Betson's *Ryght Profitable Treatyse* the beginning of the Syon tradition of printing vernacular advice for female religious about living a devout life.[10] A. I. Doyle explains that Betson's *Treatyse* 'was the prelude to a succession of books printed primarily, yet not solely, for the benefit of the [Syon] sisters and chiefly at the initiative of the brothers, until the time of the Dissolution'.[11] The majority of books associated with Syon Abbey provide instructions on living a good Christian life, many originally written for religious but adapted (or simply made available) to a larger pious lay audience by virtue of their being printed and sold to those who can afford to buy them. Within this rubric there is a wide range of texts published, from hagiography to monastic rules, to guides for living a good Christian life.

The publication of the *Orcharde of Syon* in 1519 by Wynkyn de Worde was a turning point for the Syon printed tradition in English. It is the first book to showcase its association with Syon and its nuns: its preface explains that

---

[7] Westminister, Wynkyn de Worde, 1499? (STC 14508). For biographical information on Margaret, see George R. Keiser, 'Patronage and Piety in Fifteenth-Century England: Margaret, Duchess of Clarence, Symon Wynter and Beinecke MS 317', *Yale University Gazette*, 60 (1985), 32–53.

[8] Claire Waters (intro. and trans.), 'Symon Wynter: The Life of St. Jerome', in Anne Clark Bartlett and Thomas H. Bestul (eds), *Cultures of Piety: Medieval English Devotional Literature in Translation* (Ithaca, NY and London, 1999), pp. 141–63 and 232–49, at p. 142.

[9] Keiser explores the Bridgettine aspects of this text in 'St Jerome and the Brigittines: Visions of the Afterlife in Fifteenth-Century England', in Daniel Williams (ed.), *England in the Fifteenth Century: Proceedings of the 1986 Harlaxton Symposium* (Woodbridge, 1987), pp. 143–52. Some further examples of the use of hagiography written by male religious and published for a wider audience are Henry Bradshaw's work: *The Holy Lyfe and History of Saynt Werburgh*, printed by Richard Pynson in 1521 (STC 3506) and *The Lyfe of saynt Radegund*, also published by Pynson in 1521 (STC 3507). See Christina Carlson, 'Of Ministers and Mistresses: Henry Bradshaw's Abbesses and the Hagiography of the Household' (unpublished PhD dissertation, Fordham University, 2005).

[10] For brief treatments of Betson and his text see H.S. Bennett, 'Notes on Two Incunables: The Abbey of the Holy Ghost and A Ryght Profytable Treatyse', *The Library*, 5th ser., 10 (1955), 120–1; A. I. Doyle, 'Thomas Betson of Syon Abbey', *The Library*, 5th ser., 11 (1956), 115–18.

[11] Doyle, 'Book Production', p. 15.

when the steward of Syon found a manuscript of the revelations of Catherine of Siena (a fellow visionary to Bridget of Sweden) that had been written for the Syon sisters he had it published at his own expense. The nuns are addressed in the second prologue and epilogue by the anonymous Syon translator, and the woodcuts include a scene of Catherine with a group of nuns – they are not Bridgettines, but the depiction of a female religious community reminds the reader of the Syon manuscript context (Figures 4.1 and 1.3).

The works of Richard Whitford, the self-titled 'wretch of Syon', began to be printed in the 1520s. His first publications are Middle English translations of Latin monastic books used at Syon: the *Rule of Saynt Augustyne* (1525, 1527) and *The Martiloge in Englysshe* (1526).[12] Since St Bridget of Sweden received her revelation to create a new monastic order at a time when the Pope was not allowing new orders, Bridget established the Bridgettines under the umbrella of the Augustinian order. The Augustinian rule was therefore read at Syon, along with additions specifically for the Bridgettines (included in the print edition), and was held in common with other Augustinian houses. The martyrology was an important ritual for the monastery as it commemorated founders, patrons and other important figures. These initial Whitford texts are significant for they show a typical use of printed texts for monasteries: producing books in sufficient number for the use of all (or many) members of a religious house.

Another Syon author active in the 1520s was William Bonde, whose *Pylgrymage of Perfeccyon* (a lengthy, elaborate treatise on living the religious life) was published by Richard Pynson in 1526 and again in 1531 by Wynkyn de Worde, the second time with the passion meditation *Rosary of Our Savyour Jesu* appended (Figure 4.2).[13] Bonde was also the author of the *Directory of Conscience*, first published in 1527 by Lawrence Andrews, then twice in 1534 by Richard Fawkes as *A Deuoute Epystle or Treaty for Them That Ben Tymorouse and Fearefull in Conscience*. This text advises the reader on how to turn fear of God into a positive force. The *Pylgrymage of Perfeccyon* does not explicitly identify its author, but Richard Whitford mentions in his *Dayly Experyence of Dethe* that the author of the *Pylgrymage* is his colleague William Bonde.[14]

The 1520s therefore saw a productive start to the Syon tradition of English printed books. Publication of Syon works increased dramatically in the 1530s,

---

12 Wynkyn de Worde prints the *Rule* in 1525 and 1527 (STC 922.3, 922.4; formerly STC 13925 and 25417). De Worde prints the *Martyloge* in 1526 (STC 17532).
13 STC 3277, STC 3278. The latter includes the *Rosary*, which is not listed separately in the STC or on Early English Books Online.
14 Fol. D.5.b. Found in his 1537 collection of works printed by Robert Redman (STC 25413).

Figure 4.1: *Here begynneth the orcharde of Syon in the whiche is conteyned the reuelacyons of seynt [sic] Katheryne of Sene, with ghostly fruytes [and] precyous plantes for the helthe of mannes soule* (London, [1519]), title page, sig. A1r.
© The British Library Board. All rights reserved. British Library shelfmark C.11.b.6.

Figure 4.2: William Bonde, *Here begynneth a deuout treatyse in Englysshe,
called the Pylgrimage of perfection very p[ro]fitable for all christen people to
rede: and in especiall, to all relygious p[er]sons moche necessary* (London,
1526), sig. A1v. © The British Library Board. All rights reserved. British Library
shelfmark G.11740.

beginning with the printing in 1530 of the *Myrroure of Oure Ladye* by Richard Fawkes (STC 17542) (Figure 4.3). This Middle English translation of and commentary on the Bridgettine Lady Office was an important marker of Bridgettine ritual distinction, and the framing materials – woodcuts, prologues and epilogues – make specific reference to Syon, its founder and its inhabitants. This text was the only major printed book in English that comes from Bridget's corpus. It was also during this decade that Whitford turned to producing advice on living a good Christian life (for religious and/or lay readers). He was at his most prolific, having at least one book printed each year (including reprints) from 1530 to 1537 – in each of 1530, 1531, 1533 and 1537 three or four texts with his name attached were printed or reprinted.[15] It was in this decade that Whitford's major devotional works were published. *The Pype or Tonne of the Lyfe of Perfection* is a lengthy treatise on how to be a religious which includes some direct attacks on the Protestant reformers (STC 25421). *The Golden Epistle*, Whitford's translation of a letter attributed to Bernard of Clairvaux containing some advice on living a religious life and addressed to a brother, became popular with both religious and lay readers during the late Middle Ages (STC 1912–14). Two books that were reprinted several times during the 1530s are *A Werke for Housholders*, containing advice for the urban laity on living a devout life (STC 25421.8–25425.5), and *The Folowynge of Cryste*, a trendy *devotio moderna* text on the *imitatio Christi* tradition, translated earlier in the century by Lady Margaret Beaufort

---

[15] In 1530 are published Whitford's *Golden Epistle* (Wynkyn de Worde, STC 1912), *Short Monycyon or Counsayle of the Cure & Gouernaunce of a Housholde* (Robert Wyer [dating uncertain]), *An Alphabete or Crosrowe Called an A.B.C.* (Richard Fawkes), and *A Werke for Housholders* (Robert Redman [dating uncertain] STC 25421.8, de Worde STC 25422). 1531 sees the *Golden Epistle* again (Wynkyn de Worde STC 1913, Robert Wyre STC 1914), *A Werke for Housholders* (Peter Treueris [dating uncertain] STC 25422.3, Robert Redman STC 25412), four editions of *The Folowynge of Cryste* (Robert Wyer (and Peter Treueris?) STC 23961), Robert Redman (2 editions, STC 23964 and 23964.3), Thomas Godfray STC 23963; the dating is uncertain for all 1531 editions), and *A Werke of Preparacion vnto Communion or Howselyng* (Robert Redman STC 25422.5). In 1533 we see Whitford's most popular works printed again: *A Werke for Housholders* (Wynkyn de Worde STC 25423, Redman STC 25423.5) and *The Folowynge of Cryste* (Selections, Robert Wyer [dating uncertain]). 1537 is Whitford's last good year of publishing: *A Werke for Housholders* (Robert Redman STC 25413, John Wayland STC 25413.5), *A Werke of Preparacion vnto Communion or Howselyng* (Robert Redman STC 25425, John Wayland STC 25425.5) and *A Dayly Exercise and Experience of Dethe* (John Wayland STC 25414). For an excellent online bibliography of Richard Whitford's works, see Stephan Borgehammar and Ulla Sander Olsen, 'Texts and Translations by Richard Whytford, Taken from (R)STC', in *On-Line Bibliography of St Birgitta and the Birgittine Order*, http.//www.sanctabirgitta.com/media/424.pdf (accessed 13 March 2006). This bibliography does, however, include two texts attributed to Whitford but not written by him: *The Fruit of Redemption* and *The Pomander of Prayer*.

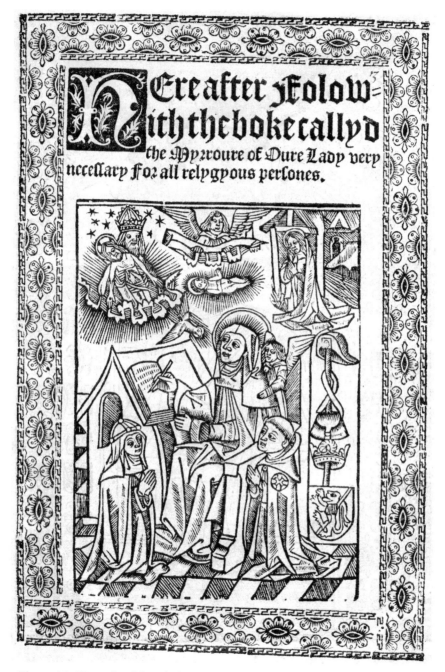

Figure 4.3: *Here after folowith the boke callyd the myrroure of Oure Lady very necessary for all relygyous persones* (London, 1530), sig. A1r. © The British Library Board. All rights reserved. British Library shelfmark C.11.b.8.

(STC 23961–8.5). Whitford was the most prolific contributor to the Syon printed English book tradition and it is in his books that we see the active promotion of a Syon author and identification with Syon as part of marketing the texts. It was a formula that worked: as Driver notes, Whytford's works were 'bestsellers'.[16]

John Fewterer published *The Myrroure or Glasse of Christes Passion* with Robert Redman in 1534 (STC 14553). Like Whitford's *Pype* and Bonde's *Pilgrymage*, this book uses an allegorical conceit to structure the text. It is a passion meditation dedicated to Lord John Hussey, but originally written for nuns.[17] This was the last new text to come from Syon, although Whitford's works continued to be reprinted until the second half of the 1530s. 1537 – one year after the first act of Parliament dissolving the smaller monasteries had come into effect and one year before Parliament would order all monasteries closed – was the last year Syon texts made a substantial contribution to the printed devotional tradition. Whitford's *A Werke for Housholders*, *A Werke of Preparacion vnto Communion or Howselyng* (both printed by Robert Redman and John Wayland), and *A Dayly Exercise and Experience of Dethe* (published by John Wayland) all made their way into print again that year: these were works geared toward the newer kinds of readers and contemporary practices found in this time of transition.[18] They all addressed a general audience and were published together with some other minor works as a collection of Whitford's works, the typical way his devotional treatises were published in the late period. Thus Whitford and Syon still claimed their relevance as the authorities stepped up their attacks against the monasteries.

The Syon texts often went against the typical anonymity of devotional manuscripts and books by including specific references to the authors and original readers and patrons. Many of the books from Syon were the usual kind of devotional materials favoured in the late Middle Ages, although they seem to do a better, more consistent job. Because they were a visible representation of the printed devotional tradition some anonymous texts have been attributed to Syon authors or presumed to be written for the Syon nuns. For

---

[16] Driver, 'Pictures in Print', p. 233.

[17] Vincent Gillespie discusses this text in 'Strange Images of Death: The Passion in Later Medieval English Devotional and Mystical Writing', in *Zeit, Tod und Ewigkeit in der Renaissance Literatur*, Band 3, Analecta Cartusiana 117 (Salzburg, 1987), pp. 111–59, at pp. 124–6 and notes.

[18] *A Werke for Housholders* (Robert Redman STC 25413, John Wayland STC 25413.5), *A Werke of Preparacion vnto Communion or Howselyng* (Robert Redman STC 25425, John Wayland STC 25425.5) and *A Dayly Exercise and Experience of Dethe* (John Wayland STC 25414).

example, *The Dyetary of Ghostly Helthe* appeared in 1520, a year after the *Orcharde* was printed, exploiting the trend of addressing a female religious audience in the prefatory materials and using woodcuts of holy women associated with Syon, Catherine of Siena and Bridget of Sweden. This was a savvy strategy considering the popularity the *Dyetary* gained, as it was reprinted three times that decade.[19] The text provides meditations and offers useful information for how to live a good life of religious perfection. The author and original readers were anonymous, however, so scholars have not been able to positively identify this text with Syon.

Whitford's popularity and productivity have led scholars and readers to attribute other printed books to him. Two important examples are *The Fruyte of Redempcyon* and *The Pomander of Prayer*. *The Fruyte of Redempcyon* states that it is written by Simon [Appulby], the Anchorite of London, but it has been attributed to Whitford likely because of its similarity to other Syon books: it is a conventional set of meditations on Christ's life and death printed four times (1514, 1517, 1530, 1531; STC 22557–60). *The Pomander of Prayer* has also been attributed to Whitford, but Horsfield has refuted this, noting that the text itself says that it was written by a Sheen Carthusian, with a preface written by a Syon brother as a kind of endorsement.[20] The text itself deals comprehensively with the topic of prayer, addressing a more general audience of devout people rather than a strictly monastic audience, and was popular enough to be printed four times as well (1528, 1530, 1531, 1532).[21] Given Whitford's insistence on including his name with his printed books, it seems unlikely that these texts were written by him.

There are two other texts associated with Syon readers which I will mention here. Sir Thomas Elyot dedicated *A Swete and Deuoute Sermon of Holy Saynt Ciprian of Mortalitie of Man* to his half-sister Susan Kyngeston, a vowess at Syon. In the prefatory epistle he asks Susan to communicate it to their other two sisters, both of whom were nuns at Syon.[22] Scholars have also written about John Ryckes's *The Ymage of Loue*,[23] sixty copies of which were

---

[19] Wynkyn de Worde, 1520, STC (2nd edn) 6833; Henry Pepwell, 1521, STC (2nd edn) 6834; Henry Pepwell, 1523, STC 6835; Wynkyn de Worde, 1527, STC (2nd edn) 6836.

[20] Rev. Robert A. Horsfield, '*The Pomander of Prayer*: Aspects of Late Medieval English Carthusian Spirituality and its Lay Audience', in Michael G. Sargent (ed.), *De Cella in Seculum: Religious and Secular Life and Devotion in Late Medieval England* (Cambridge, 1989), pp. 205–13, at p. 207.

[21] The last three editions are found in STC 25421.3–25421.6. The 1528 edition is discussed by Horsfield, '*Pomander*', p. 207 and n.11.

[22] 1534, 1539 (STC 6157, 6158), London, Thomas Berthelet. See Mary C. Erler, *Women, Reading, and Piety in Late Medieval England* (Cambridge, 2002), pp. 87–9.

[23] 1525, 1532 (STC 21471.5, 21472).

bought by the nuns of Syon. This text has received scholarly notice because it was suspected of being heretical and recalled by the authorities. *The Ymage of Loue* presents a very compelling allegory about the various kinds of love, leading to the true image of love which is God. The book ends with an address to 'you good ladyes' asking them to pray for the author and have mercy on him.[24]

Wynkyn de Worde was the printer who had the greatest involvement with Syon authors and texts right from the beginning, and it was his ubiquitous woodcut of Bridget that was borrowed and copied by many printers for many texts.[25] By the 1530s other printers played key roles in introducing important Syon works: Robert Redman (who took over Pynson's shop and materials after the printer's death) was the first to print the *Werke for Housholders*, *Pype or Tonne of the Lyfe of Perfection* and Fewterer's *The Myrrour or Glasse of Christes Passion*; while the *Myrroure of Oure Ladye* was published by Richard Fawkes.[26] Richard Pynson's participation was minor, publishing Bonde's *Pylgrymage of Perfeccyon* in 1526, as was Robert Wyer's, being involved in the *Golden Epistle* and *Folowynge of Cryste*. Other printers played roles as well, for example, by issuing reprints or publishing a text or two. For example, Laurence Andrews printed the *Directory of Conscience* in 1527, although his output was rather small.[27] As Syon texts became more popular and were being reprinted more often, more printers became involved in publishing Syon works. By the 1530s Syon books were becoming known as a good venture, especially if a first edition had done well. The Syon sisters were a ready audience and lay readers were also interested in Syon productions.

The printed texts associated with Syon share many characteristics. Many of them have a didactic, practical focus appropriate for their original monastic context. The texts reveal the medieval penchant for *divisio* and *collectio* – useful for the purposes of instruction and also contributing to the tendency for these texts to be lengthy. These texts often are all-inclusive volumes – one-stop devotional books that would keep orthodox readers busy for a long time. In these all-inclusive texts we also find a concern to cover the basic elements of Church doctrine, found for example in the *Ryght Profytable Treatyse*, *Werke for Housholders* and Whitford's collected works: providing

---

[24] For a recent treatment of this topic, see Rebecca Krug, *Reading Families: Women's Literate Practice in Late Medieval England* (Ithaca, NY and London, 2002), pp. 202–6.
[25] See discussion below. This woodcut is no. 457 in Edward Hodnett, *English Woodcuts 1480–1535* (Oxford, 1973 edn; first published 1935).
[26] Hodnett, *English Woodcuts*, p. 54.
[27] Hodnett only credits two works to him: *English Woodcuts*, pp. 68–9.

pastoral teaching for lay or religious readers written in the vernacular. There are also some shorter texts which provided advice and reading on specific elements of devotion and instruction. For example, the incipit for the 1534 general edition of the *Directory of Conscience* explains that it is 'A deuote treatyse for them that ben tymorouse and fearefull in conscience whiche treatyse yf yt be well red ouer and folowyd wyl brynge þe reders out of al scrupulosite of conscience & seruyle feare/ & brynge them to the holy feare and Love of almighty God' (STC 3275). These treatises targeted specific topics and practices of interest, such as redirecting affect to God or supplying meditations and prayers on Christ. For example, Fewterer explains in the prologue to his *Myrroure*,

> I thought this boke shulde be moche profytable to the readers and edefyeng to all that wolde diligently hear it, And to say the treuth: I know nothynge more comfortable to man, For amonges all the exercyses that helpe the spirite to obteyne the loue of God, and specially to hym þat wolde begyn & use a spiritual lyfe: no thynge is thought more frutful, than the continual meditacion of the passion of our lorde god Jesus Christ, for exercyses of all other spirituall meditacions may be reduced and brought unto this. (Fol. +i.a)

This text sees the part standing in for the whole, while others, like the *Directory*, offer advice on specific topics of interest.

The Syon printed tradition also made an effort to produce high quality, well-written, conservative texts. They demonstrated a wealth of knowledge and experience, revealed for example in the liberal use of quotations and references from biblical and patristic sources (and others), often cited in the margin: Rhodes's explanation for why '[t]he margins of Bonde's *Pilgrymage*, Fewterer's *Myrrour* and Whitford's books are peppered with references to the source texts to an unprecedented degree for vernacular works' is that it provided an 'assertion of orthodoxy' during a time of 'increasing doctrinal uncertainty and controversy'.[28] Bonde writes in his prologue to the *Pilgrymage* his rationale for producing a summa as follows:

> The cause that moved me to wryte this treatyse was this. After my entraunce to religion, considering to what I had bounde myselfe and howe (as Saynt Thomas sayth), Every religiouse persone shulde intende the perfeccion of his soule, which is the very peas of the spirit. I thought it necessary to drawe a treatyse for myself, that shulde conteyne in somme the sentences of illumined doctours, concerning

---

[28] J. T. Rhodes, 'Syon Abbey and its Religious Publications in the Sixteenth Century', *JEH*, 44 (1993), 11–25, at p. 17.

perfection, as Saynt Austen, Saynt Gregory, Saynt Bernard, Saynt Thomas, Saynt Bonaventure, Saynt Anselm, and Antonine, which doctours I folowe most commonly in this pore treatyse/ Joynynge also therto the gostly exercise and experience of holy fathers, as I thought them to make most for my purpose, thynkynge that if I had them compyled in one treatyse I shuld have a singular jewel to bere in my bosom, wherin dayly & hourely I might loke, as a mirour or lokyng glasse for my edificacion/ and perceive myne owne imperfeccions, howe farre I am euery day from the lyfe and perfeccion of holy fathers. (fols A.i.b–A.ii.a)

Bonde's monastic training was put to good use in the first place in creating a beneficial text for his own use, but then he made it available to friends by writing in Middle English and passing on this orthodox, authoritative, yet accessible treatment of the religious life. In this passage we also see the use of entertaining allegories such as the mirror – or orchard, wine vessel or barrel, or pilgrimage – to describe aspects of religious living and devotional practices and to organise their materials. Not only did this increase the accessibility of the difficult materials, but also these texts could write about piety from different perspectives, repackaging similar instructions in a variety of frames.

One must bear in mind, however, that many of the characteristics of Syon texts were found more widely in the printed devotional tradition and may not be attributed solely to books from Syon. This can make it difficult to determine the provenance of some of the devotional books written originally for a female religious audience but not identified as Syon in the printed texts themselves, especially if they were also known to have been available at Syon in manuscript form. For example, the *Lyf of Kateryne of Seenys* and the *Treatyse of the Tree and XII. Frutes* both address an unidentified community of religious women.[29] There is some circumstantial evidence supporting a Syon source for these texts. Catherine of Siena was well known at Syon and the *Lyf* is a lengthy volume concerned with detailing her life and showing Catherine as exemplary – an example of hagiography as instruction for a community of women religious.[30] *The Tree and XII. Frutes* instructs on the religious life through the use of allegories and this pair of treatises was read at Syon: two copies of the printed book are known to have been owned by Syon sisters.[31]

---

29 London: Wynkyn de Worde, 1492? and 1500 (STC 24766 and 24766.3); London: R. Copland and M. Fawkes, 1535 (STC 13608).
30 This text was edited in the nineteenth century: C. Horstmann (ed.), 'The Lyf of Saint Katherin of Senis', *Archiv für das Studium der Neueren Sprachen und Litteraturen*, 76 (1886), 33–112, 265–314, 353–91.
31 David N. Bell, *What Nuns Read: Books and Libraries in Medieval English Nunneries*

Nevertheless, we do not have solid proof that Syon was involved in the print production of these texts. Still it seems worthwhile to acknowledge that there are some standard characteristics associated with Syon books, even though the texts cover a wide variety of devotional subgenres – from hagiography to devotions to instructions on the religious life or living devoutly – and these characteristics are not exclusive to Syon.

This essay focuses on those books that make specific reference to or association with Syon or are included in the Syon printed tradition by later authors or texts. Vernacular Syon texts took care to distinguish themselves through some reference to their original audience or to their author, using framing materials – prologues, prefatory letters, woodcuts, incipits, explicits and title pages – to make direct associations with Syon. In these books there was a move to create a Syon oeuvre of vernacular devotional literature, where the Syon monk as author and the Syon nun as reader were represented as exemplary models for the audience, providing an example of a positive relationship of spiritual equality between figures of authority and seekers of understanding. For these works the abbey is a paradigm of spiritual contemplation and learning; therefore, reading its books brings the audience closer to these ideals.

We shall now consider the framing materials before we move into a discussion of the representations of readers and authors. The Syon books generally used their illustrations in the traditional way: to frame a text or mark book or treatise divisions. The illustrations usually related to the content or had a general devotional theme. Yet they performed other functions as well. The woodcuts, prefaces and the texts proper often used holy women such as Bridget of Sweden and Catherine of Siena as their subject (or made reference to them), drawing links visually and textually between the contemplative role of the Syon nuns as readers and the spiritual authority and literary activities of their predecessors and models.

Martha Driver's research on the woodcuts in books associated with Syon has been an important contribution to our understanding of the framing materials of these texts.[32] I have argued earlier in this essay that it was only with the

---

(Kalamazoo, MI, 1995): Syon A) 3. is a printed *Tree and XII. Frutes* owned by Dorothy Godrington, a nun of Syon, and no. 14 is a copy of the same book owned by Margaret Windsor. This text has been edited: J. J. Vaissier (ed.), *A Devout Treatyse Called the Tree & xii Frutes of the Holy Goost* (Groningen, 1960).

[32] Her book *The Image in Print* includes a chapter titled 'Representations of Saintly Women in Late Medieval Woodcuts', pp. 115–50, which provides important discussions of illustrations of Bridget of Sweden and Catherine of Siena. See her earlier work as well: Martha W. Driver, 'Nuns as Patrons, Artists, Readers', and 'Pictures in Print: Late Fifteenth- and Early Sixteenth-Century English Religious Books for Lay Readers', in Sargent (ed.), *De Cella in Seculum*, pp. 229–44.

Orcharde (1519) that Syon became a marketing entity for print tradition. Before that time there was no concerted effort to market Syon-associated texts as such, but after this time references to Syon became more prominent in incipits and prefaces. Interestingly, these findings have a parallel in the use of Bridgettine woodcuts. After 1520 most of the Syon texts included one or more woodcuts depicting Bridget of Sweden, the most common one being an illustration of Bridget having a revelation while she is writing at a desk flanked by a kneeling Bridgettine nun and monk (Figure 4.2).[33] Although Bridget of Sweden was the usual representative for Syon texts, Catherine of Siena starred in the woodcuts of the *Orcharde* since this book is a translation of Catherine's revelations. It produced several woodcuts using Catherine of Siena as its subject, including one of Catherine with twelve Mantellate nuns, the only example of a female community illustrated in Syon printed books (Hodnett no. 863).[34] The title page woodcut, where Catherine receives a revelation from God as she sits in front of an open book on a prie-dieu (Hodnett no. 862; Figure 4.1) was used in two other texts: *The Doctrines out of the Lyfe of Saynt Katheryn*, the Middle English extracts from the Legenda Minor, published by Pepwell in 1521 with several other devotional treatises (including the extracts from the Book of Margery Kempe); and *The Dyetary of Ghostly Helthe*, published in 1520 and 1527 and addressed to a community of religious women. The editions of the *Dyetary* include one woodcut each of Bridget of Sweden and Catherine of Siena.[35] I have already mentioned that the topical similarity and female religious audience suggest this text is affiliated

---

[33] Hodnett, *English Woodcuts*, no. 457. He provides a full description of the woodcut: 'St Bridget of Sweden. (L) A nun kneeling. (C) St Bridget, facing left, wearing a double nimbus, and writing in a book on a desk. At her left shoulder a small angel. (RC) A monk kneeling. (R) A pilgrim's staff and shield, crown, wallet, and hat. Shaded tile floor. (Above) (L) In a cloud and radiance God the Father wearing a crown with a dotted bamd, and holding the body of Christ, who wears a double, cruciform nimbus. Eight stars, five of which have six points. (LC) The Dove descending. (C) The Infant Jesus in a radiance. An angel with a scroll. (R) The Madonna kneeling in a manger.' Pepwell and Treveris produced copies: Hodnett, *English Woodcuts*, no. 2277, no. 2379.

[34] The series of woodcuts is numbered 862–9 in Hodnett, *English Woodcuts*. See Driver, 'Nuns as Patrons, Artists, Readers', *The Image in Print*, and 'Pictures in Print', for discussions of this and related woodcuts.

[35] The first woodcut is of Bridget of Sweden flanked by a Bridgettine nun and monk (Hodnett, *English Woodcuts*, no. 457, and Driver, 'Pictures in Print', plate 23, copied by Pepwell for his editions, Hodnett, *English Woodcuts*, no. 2277), which is used in many Syon books, and the second is of Catherine of Siena: in the first edition she is receiving inspiration from the Trinity (Hodnett, *English Woodcuts*, no. 454 – this one is not used elsewhere) – she has a book in front of her, as do the three figures of the Trinity – while in later editions the woodcut from the *Orcharde* of Catherine receiving the stigmata with the Dove descending from God the Father is used (Hodnett, *English Woodcuts*, no. 862; Pepwell's copy is no. 2275).

with Syon. Based on woodcut subjects we also find that this text could be a Syon work – or at the very least it was working to appear to be by capitalising on recent interest in Catherine and the abbey.

The *Myrroure of Oure Ladye*'s programme of Bridget of Sweden woodcuts is similar to the *Orcharde*'s use of illustrations of Catherine of Siena. Like the *Orcharde*'s woodcuts, the *Myrroure*'s illustrations serve as separators for the sections of the book and show Bridget writing and receiving revelations. Bridget often has a figure of inspiration or revelation above her as she writes or reads the open book. She is often shown as a reader or writer, caught in the act of receiving revelations and writing them down – a simplified depiction of the process which usually involved one or more amanuenses and spiritual confessors to write down and authorise the revelations. Catherine of Siena also has an open book in front of her on the title page woodcut and in many of the other woodcuts in the *Orcharde*. In fact, the common feature of the illustrations in this text is Catherine's place at the front (left or right) with an open book in front of her, gazing up at the scene from her book depicted in the woodcut, with God (often surrounded by angels) directing the vision from above. In these woodcuts holy women are reading, having revelations, meditating and contemplating. They function as exemplars as well as intermediaries for the readers, demonstrating the powerful effects of piety, reading and devotions for the audience.

The *Pylgrymage of Perfeccyon* also contains woodcuts of Bridget, including the most popular Syon one. The 1526 printing of the *Pylgrymage* shows Bridget writing with angels surrounded by pilgrim iconography, the trinity and Madonna and Child (Hodnett 1349; Figure 4.3). It is a simpler arrangement than the ubiquitous Bridget illustration. This woodcut is also found in the 1506 *Life of Seynt Birgette*, published with Capgrave's *New Kalendar of England*, and the *Lyfe of Saynt Werburgh* published in 1521 and written by Henry Bradshaw. Since Bradshaw's works were not written for the Syon nuns we see here that one holy woman could easily substitute for another in the woodcuts. The *Pylgrymage* would have been a costly book to produce: it is well over 400 folios, with about a dozen woodcuts in the first edition. This suggests some kind of assured market for the book, for example that there was a backer or a guaranteed group of buyers – perhaps similar to the printing context for the *Orcharde*, *Myrroure of Oure Ladye* and the *Rule of Saynt Augustyne*. Moreover, when this long volume was reprinted it included three lavish fold-out woodcuts and a passion meditation at the end. *The Rosary of Our Savyour Jesu* (STC 3278) is a simpler meditation and may have made the book more accessible, as some of the discussion of good Christian living may have been difficult for some readers to understand. It is an add-on, practical application of what has come before, especially given the strong emphasis on the importance of Christ's passion in the text. The wood-cuts work in a similar way, illustrating the more difficult theological concepts presented in the book rather than being just something to entertain the reader. In the second edition the book became more comprehensive, offering not only instruction but also application, theory and practice, intellectual arguments and devotional exercises.[36]

The *Orcharde* and the *Myrroure of Oure Ladye* not only illustrate the holy woman subject of their text in their woodcuts, they also introduce the Syon nuns as the identified original audience of the text by addressing the nuns of Syon in prologues and epilogues. The *Orcharde* begins the second prologue with a gracious, flattering address to the sisters and Lady Abbess, portraying the writer of the manuscript as a lowly scribe unfit to include his name in the text:

> Relygyous moder and deuoute sustren/ called & chosen besyly to labour at the house of Syon/ in the blessed vyneyerde of our holy sauyoure/ his parfyte rule whiche hymselfe endyted/ to kepe continu-ally vnto oure lyues ende/ under the gouernaunce of oure blessed lady/ her seruyce onely to rede & to synge/ as her specyall seruauntes and doughtren. ¶ And she youre moste souerayne lady & chefe Abbes of her holy couent/ I synfull unworthy to bere any name to the worshyp of that holy saueoure/ and at the reuerence of his glorious moder/ to youre ghostly recreacyon/ with helpe of youre prayes [*sic*] (compelled by charyte) for ghostly affeccyon/ purpose to wryte to you after my simple felynge/ the reyelacyons of oure lorde to his chosen mayde Katheryne of Sene. (fol. iii.a–b)

This lovely portrayal of the sisters and Abbess presents them as close to the writer, a relationship built on respect and the pursuit of shared goals. It is an idealised portrait of this community, one that supported Syon's efforts to improve the reputation of monasticism and monastic houses. The orchard allegory is introduced shortly after this passage and tied to the nuns' reading practices, as the reader is encouraged to browse through the text as though wandering in an orchard. In this way the organisation of the text and the reading of the text are aligned. The addresses in the *Myrroure* are similar but not as extensive as those in the *Orcharde*. For example, the preface addresses the community as the 'moste dere and deuoute systres/ ye that ar the spouses

---

[36] J. T. Rhodes, 'Prayers of the Passion: From Jordanus of Quedlinburg to John Fewterer of Syon', *Durham University Journal*, 85 (1993), 27–38, p. 30, mentions a reference to Bonaventure as a source for this text.

of oure lorde Jesu chryste/ and the specyall chosen maydens & doughtres of his moste reuerence mother' (fol. A.iii.b). This text brings in the allegory of the mirror, tying it to the nuns' reading practices as well: the more devoutly and perfectly the nuns perform their office, the clearer and more perfectly they will see the Virgin Mary in the 'mirror' of their devotions. The nuns functioned as exemplars of female monasticism, just as Bridget of Sweden and Catherine of Siena acted as exemplars of holy women. The woodcuts and the prefaces establish a connection between the readers and the holy women: just as Bridget and Catherine hold books on their laps or on a desk, so the reader holds this book on her or his lap or on a desk. Moreover, the nuns act as intermediaries for this connection, helping to illustrate the proper attitudes for reading and devotional practices for the audience. I have argued else-where that in these texts the Syon sisters are represented as meek and obedient in a double-layering of their reading and living practices: just as they are exhorted to be meek and obedient to their superiors, so they are to obey humbly the instruction offered in their book.[37] The dynamics between the author and audience developed in these texts are multiple, however, since we also see the writers display respect and caring for their readers within the bounds of spiritual friendship – what Anne Clark Bartlett calls a 'discourse of familiarity'.[38] Part of the authors' use of the humility topos was to position themselves as inferior to their charges, humbly submitting themselves to the readers' authority while they read the text offered to them. This was some-times accomplished by referencing the Abbess as the figure of authority for the nuns and putative patron figure for the text. She held power and prestige within the community of nuns and thus transferred this to the text. Neverthe-less, the position reverses itself in the text proper, where the writer becomes the authority discoursing on the subject of the text. For the Syon oeuvre this is accomplished in part by using the author's name in the text, incorporating numerous references to authoritative sources, and adopting the tone of the paternalistic spiritual father in the body of the text. Although these gestures of authority may appear to contradict the prefatory positioning of reader and writer, masking authority under the guise of equality, it may be more correct to view the reader–writer dynamics as multiple – the texts offer the readers

---

[37] C. Annette Grisé, ' "In the Blessid Vyneȝerd of oure Holy Saueour": Female Religious Readers and Textual Reception in the Myroure of Oure Ladye and the Orcherd of Syon', in Marion Glasscoe (ed.), *The Medieval Mystical Tradition in England*, 6 (Cambridge, 1999), pp. 193–211.
[38] Anne Clark Bartlett, *Male Authors, Female Readers: Representation and Subjectivity in Middle English Devotional Literature* (Ithaca, NY and London, 1995), p. 96. See the discussion of this topic in Krug, *Reading Families*, p. 198.

more than one way to view their role and to develop their reading practices. In the end, however, all positions function within the larger dynamic of the writer as authority and the reader as student.

Devout readers in late medieval England were accustomed to adapting devotional texts written for another audience to their own circumstances as they read. *The Directory of Conscience*, or *A Deuote Treatyse for them that ben Tymorouse and Tearefull in Conscience*, provides a fascinating example of this adaptability played out in the prefaces to the three editions. The 1527 edition published by Andrews begins with a prologue written by the printer himself, explaining that the book was originally 'louyngly, & tenderly endyted to one of the Systres of Syon' and is now being printed at the request of another religious man 'for the ghostly edifycacyon of all them that be or entende to be the spowses of our Redemour Jhesu cryste' (fol. A.i.b). This edition also includes the popular woodcut of Bridget of Sweden flanked by a Bridgettine nun and monk that is found in numerous Syon texts (Hodnett no. 457). In the 1534(?) editions the title is changed to 'A deuote treatyse for them that ben tymorouse and tearefull in conscience' and the book is divided into chapters.[39] There are some other very minor changes and the editions use different woodcuts and prefaces: one issue did not include a preface (STC 3275), addressing instead a general readership of 'them that ben tymorouse and fearefull in conscience' and ending with common woodcuts of Christ,[40] while the other issue included a copy of a prefatory letter addressed to a nun of Denney who was sent a copy of the text by the author Bonde. Erler has noted these differences and found connections between Bonde and the abbey of Denney, arguing that his fellow Syon inhabitant, John Fewterer, is likely to be the religious man who persuaded Bonde to send the text to the nun.[41] In this version we see an antithetical example of the author-reader model found in the *Myrroure of Oure Lady* and the *Orcharde of Syon*, for Bonde tries to distance himself from this religious woman instead of displaying an intimate spiritual relationship of friendship and equality. He states he was reluctant to send this text to her since there was not a personal relationship between the two of them. Yet the nun had been pestering the author, sending him unwanted gifts and asking her go-between (the spiritual friend required for this tradition) to present her request. The gift exchange is portrayed as foisted upon the author, interrupting his attempts at living a spiritual life away from worldly concerns and material possessions. His unwillingness to undertake the project is

---

[39] Hodnett, *English Woodcuts*, puts the other edition as 1535: p. 102.
[40] An image of Pity and Christ in the garden; the Bridget of Sweden woodcut is not included in this edition.
[41] See Erler, *Women, Reading, and Piety*, p. 109.

overcome by his own friendship with the nun's spiritual friend. Perhaps he was clear to distance himself from this woman because she was from another monastery, but this attitude is far removed from the affection usually shown in Syon prefaces between monk-authors and nun-readers. It was appropriate in one way, because a monk should demonstrate proper decorum – as should a nun, who is here presented as an unwelcome lover, showering him with gifts and unwanted attention and sending others to press her suit. She is not the embodiment of meekness we see in the portrayals of the Syon nuns in the *Orcharde* and *Myrroure*.

The *Directory* runs the gamut of audience possibilities, from nuns (both from Syon and another house) to religious brothers to a general audience. This was the ideal kind of circulation for such a printed book, finding ever wider circulation and reaching all kinds of devout readers, female and male, religious and lay. Another author whose works addressed a wide audience was Richard Whitford. Whitford is a useful example for understanding the importance of authorship in the early print period. He used the epithet 'poor wretch of Syon' to describe himself in virtually every text he had printed: Horsfield claims that Whitford 'made it a fetish to publish under his own name'.[42] Whitford declares it is not for reasons of vanity but so that his works can be identified and attributed to their source – that is, an orthodox, well-learned Syon brother. He also was careful in detailing the provenance of his texts. Whitford explains in his preface 'Unto the deuout reders' for the 1537 edition of *Dayly Exercyse and Experyence of Dethe* (STC 25414) how the text became published:

> In our lorde god, & moost swete sauyour Jesu salutacyon. This lytle tretie, or draght of deth, dyd I wryte more then .xx. yeres a go/ at the request of the reuerence Mother Dame Elisabeth Gybs/ whome Jesu perdon/ the Abbes of Syon. And by the oft calling upon/ and remembraunce of certeyne of hyr deuout systers. And nowe of late I haue ben compelled (by the charytable instance and request of dyuers deuout persones) to wryte it agayne & agayne. And bycause that wrytynge vnto me is very tedyouse: I thought better to put it in print/ whereunto I was rather moued/ that I perceyued by the printers: you haue thankfully taken suche other poore labours: as we before haue sende forth. (fols A.i.b–A.ii.a)

This passage illustrates the textual production and reception of this text in a way that we do not usually see in the manuscript devotional tradition. It has become more precise in some ways when compared to the typical address to

---

[42] Horsfield, 'Pomander', p. 206.

an anonymous religious sister, yet it has opened up to include pious lay people who have also asked for a copy of the text. He sees the print publication as advantageous – not only to his weary hands and eyes, but also to those 'dyuers deuout persones' who can benefit from the instruction offered in the text. Whitford describes the movement from an exclusive audience for the first manuscript to a more general one in the print edition as an inevitable expansion process of a popular text, where print could make the texts available more easily and effectively than manuscript production could. The original creation of the text was authorised by the Abbess and her sisters, while the publication was justified not only by its popularity in manuscript but also by Whitford's previous success with printed books. While many Syon books kept the original details of the manuscript source production intact in the new print context, Whitford often reworked the spiritual friendship model, demonstrating his awareness of the need to find a new relationship between the author and the print audience. He offered the spiritual authority of the author-monk who provided pastoral care for devout, literate religious and the lay audience (which was anonymous and multiple). This new model was still paternalistic, but the power dynamic becomes more explicitly hierarchical. Whitford thus expanded his authorial role in pastoral care from Syon inhabitants and patrons to the wider print audience. This anticipated the development of the post-Reformation author function in texts. In the late Middle Ages the author played a role in secular and religious poetry and mystical treatises, while devotional prose texts often remained anonymous. Whitford's conscious attribution of his works allowed for a public author to be published with his corpus, one that instructed the readers of his printed text in a direct way and constructed a relationship between the author and the new audience – addressing not only his original charges (that is, the Syon nuns) but also often the new print readership of the books.

Vernacular translations of rules (such as Whitford's Augustinian rule and Fox's Benedictine rule) addressed a specific audience of religious professed in an order. Other texts that served a monastic function, like the *Martiloge*, also played a similar role, being written so that illiterate religious persons could read it and know what they recited in Latin: instructing them about their rituals and regulations so they had knowledge and increased their devotion, showing it in outward signs of performing rituals and following the regulations of their order. Monasteries presented a ready audience for such pre-Reformation printed texts. Printing texts written for nuns was a way of expanding the *cura monialium* to make it more efficient, allowing the brothers to reach more female religious (as well as pious laity) and make more copies of necessary texts available. The bottom of the title page of the dual Latin–English version of the *Rule of Saynt Augustyne* sets out the advantages for all Augustinians owning an individual copy of the book. It emphasises the portability and affordability of the book: 'The translatour doth aduyse and counseyll all þe disciples of this rule to bere always one of these bokes vpon them syth they ben so portatyue and may be hadde for so small a pryce' (STC 922.3, pt 2, fol. A.i.a). The pre-Reformation audience for printed texts was similar to what was found previously in the manuscript period, except now it was potentially bigger and the readers were not necessarily known to the authors and printers (as Bonde's preface to the nun of Denney explains). Moreover, although the *cura monialium* was an essential part of the responsibilities of the Syon brothers – their basic *raison d'être*, essentially – they also had a responsibility to preach to laity in weekly vernacular sermons. The printed books helped to expand the monks' pastoral responsibilities for the *cura pastoralis* as well to an audience that was interested in Syon and piety, whose abilities and knowledge base were unfamiliar and varied more widely than that of the nuns. In this way, the devotional literary tradition originally written for the pastoral care of nuns was made available to the mixed print audience, touted as being much profitable for all devout persons.

Many other Syon texts also referred specifically to their audiences, drawing attention to their original readers and taking care actively to seek a larger market in these printed versions. For example, the incipit of the *Pylgrymage of Perfeccyon* states: 'Here begynneth a deuoute treatyse in Englysshe/ called the Pylgrimage of Perfection: very profitable for all christen people to rede: and in especiall/ to all relygious persons moche necessary' (fol. A.i.a). Fewterer's *Myrroure or Glasse of Christes Passion* is dedicated to Lord John Hussey but in the preface the author explains that it is profitable to all who will listen to it. This is generally the attitude taken in the texts, encouraging religious and lay readers to take what they can from the texts – and it was what readers had been doing for at least a century already. Horsfield explains in his discussion of the prayer manual printed by a Carthusian and endorsed by a Syon brother,

> [t]he *Pomander [of Prayer]* is an example of the late medieval practice of adapting monastic practices and traditions to meet the needs of the newly literate laity who were striving to achieve a piety outside the walls of the cloister. This 'outreach' by the English Carthusians had been developing throughout the fifteenth century. ... The effect of this activity was to break down their isolation and give some credibility to the monastic ideal at a time when the standing of many other orders in England was low. The fact that the *Pomander* ran into four editions

within a space of five years supports the claim that the Carthusians had an audience enthusiastic for their work.[43]

Books like this one came out of and found a place in the 'exclusive and tightly-knit spiritual aristocracy' made up of 'some of the Carthusians, some of the Bridgettines, and the circle, religious and literary, which grouped itself around Lady Margaret Beaufort, bishop John Fisher and later Sir Thomas More'.[44] Printers must have hoped to reach these and similar kinds of readers with their devotional books. Erler states: '[t]he female audience for early English printing had been developed in the fifteenth century – nuns and aristocrats with an admixture of gentry. It seems clear that the early printers' choice of texts to publish often relied on and acknowledged this audience'.[45] Driver has pointed out that often the first reader or owner of a printed devotional work was religious, but a secondary reader or owner of a printed devotional work could be secular, concluding that there was a 'vital and exciting transition made possible by printing: the movement from lay ignorance to lay literacy'.[46]

Although the Syon books often sought a wider audience, the Syon sisters provided the model for the print audience and acted as a form of original patron as well in the texts that addressed them. These addresses legitimated the text and attached the Syon name and reputation to the books as a context for the print audience.[47] The texts represent the relationship between the Syon sisters and brothers as based on spiritual equality and friendship, with the nuns as meek, obedient readers and the monks as kindly, paternal figures of authority and learning: the male religious authors are brothers as well as fathers to the women. Furthermore, in the prologues to these texts the Syon nuns are represented as readers, the original audience reading the text; they are connected not only to the visionary women in the woodcuts through their shared reading practices, but also to the readers of the printed book. The books suggest the print audience is on an equal footing with the original readers: if the readers are not nuns themselves they are still literate, pious and wealthy enough to afford to buy and read these books – or at least well connected

---

43 *Ibid.*, pp. 208–9.

44 Michael Sargent's article on the devotional literary activities of the English Carthusians references Roger Lovatt's term for this 'spiritual aristocracy': 'The Transmission by the English Carthusians of Some Late Medieval Spiritual Writings', *JEH*, 27 (1976), 225–40, at pp. 239–40.

45 Erler, *Women, Reading, and Piety*, p. 133.

46 Driver, 'Pictures in Print', pp. 230, 244.

47 Driver states in her discussion of the most popular Bridgettine woodcut that it 'functions as an imprimatur or seal of approval, a bookplate that assures the reader or purchaser of the authenticity of the text contents': *Image in Print*, p. 149.

enough to borrow them. Moreover, just as the books were no longer hidden in the monasteries when they were printed and made available to a wider audience, so the readers were not necessarily enclosed in cells (but could be reading in chambers or shared spaces in households) when they read the books. The physical freeing of devotional books, reading and readers from the monastery nevertheless resulted in an increased desire to exert control over the readers and their devotional reading. We see this enacted through the enhanced authority of the paternal author and an increased understanding of the importance of providing general instruction to the readers. By the 1530s Syon books had moved from focusing on a female monastic audience to consider more frequently a wider audience, as Whitford's textual progression illustrates. Although this progression had been occurring in the fifteenth-century manuscript tradition, it became more evident and common in the print tradition which allowed for the production and circulation of more copies. We nevertheless see that the original monastic audience retained its importance to the end of this tradition for displaying provenance, providing authority and illustrating exemplarity.

Where Syon made its most significant contribution to the print tradition was in providing instruction on living a good Christian life – especially in texts that could do double-duty and be read by religious and lay readers. The incipit to the *Ryght Profitable Treatyse* explains its scope and aims, offering virtually a definition of the vernacular devotional printed tradition dominated by Syon works:

> Here begynneth a ryght profitable treatyse compendiously drawen out of many & dyuers wrytynges of holy men to dyspose men to be uertuously occupyed in theyr myndes & prayers. And declared the Pater noster. Aue. & Credo. In our mother tonge with many other deuoute prayers in lyke wyse medefull to relygyous people as to the laye people with many other moost holsomest Instruccyons as here after it shall folowe. (fol. A.ii.a)

Syon texts regularly included instruction on basic Church teachings as well as gathering excerpts from a variety of orthodox sources to provide advice, 'moost holsomest Instruccyons', on right living. They often contained prayers and meditations, commenting on devotional practices as well as giving examples. The brothers had both the training and the resources to compile many sources and then translate and prepare them for a pious audience interested in living a devout life. They had access to meditations and prayers and could advise on their use for the devout. These texts provided the print audience with examples of and instruction on proper devout behaviour and ritual performance. They supplied the audience with reading resources and devotions to keep them busy and offered them materials that could substitute for or complement performing monastic hours. While Protestant works championed biblical learning and scriptural instruction, these late medieval Catholic texts prioritised instruction in living a good Christian life; offered meditations, prayers and other devotions; explained (even justified) the vocational options available to Catholics; and provided more space for lay piety and lay imitation of monastic practices.

Can we support Rhodes's claim that Syon provided a 'co-ordinated programme of publication' and 'a positive programme for Catholic reform'?[48] Syon offered a more programmatic attempt to publish devotional works than any other monastic house produced, and tied it directly to its monastic name. The Bridgettine monks expanded their role of providing for the spiritual wellbeing of the nuns in the early print era. Their mandate to preach to the laity in English also may have encouraged them to utilise the new print medium to spread their words. They printed a variety of vernacular devotional books that answered the needs of religious and the devout literate laity in the late fifteenth and early sixteenth centuries. It may not have been a consciously worked out curriculum or programme, but it did provide a comprehensive corpus of instruction and resources for their audience – reading materials, devotional exercises and devotional instruction. The print audience responded well to this corpus, establishing Syon books as a popular, conservative tradition that served the needs of devout readers until the Reformation established different standards for devotional literature in print.

---

[48] Rhodes, 'Syon Abbey', pp. 17, 24.

5

Continuity and Isolation:
The Bridgettines of Syon in the Sixteenth
and Seventeenth Centuries[*]

CLAIRE WALKER

> We know, feel and have experienced for more than seventy years the full hardships of this our exile; of which our many afflictions, sorrows, and tears are true witnesses and, with our injuries, sufferings and dangers on land and at seas, true testimony of how much we have had to suffer; finally the aching loss of our native land, families and mother tongue, as well as our extreme poverty in foreign lands and kingdoms, declare and make evident the burdens and great difficulties we have experienced and carried on our shoulders.
>
> 'The Petition to her Royal Highness the Princess of Wales whom God Preserve', in de Hamel, *Syon Abbey*, p. 25

The heartfelt words of Prioress Barbara Wiseman and the Bridgettine sisters in Lisbon to the Spanish Infanta might have been written by any of the exiled English nuns during the seventeenth century. As members of a religious minority which was not permitted officially to practise its faith, hundreds of women left their homeland to join expatriate religious communities abroad. The exodus began in the aftermath of Henry VIII's dissolution of the monasteries when groups of Bridgettines, Dominicans, Poor Clares and possibly nuns of other orders travelled abroad to continue their pious vocation in continental cloisters. Likewise, individuals determined to maintain their vows

* I would like to thank the Reverend Mother Anna Maria O.Ss.S. of Syon Abbey for permission to obtain copies of the Fletcher MSS from the Hill Museum and Monastic Library at St John's University. I am also grateful to Betty Travitsky for copies of Sister Elizabeth Sander's letters, and Peter Cunich for advice about the Fletcher MSS. Finally, I am indebted to Alex Walsham and Eddie Jones for their patience and assistance during the writing of this essay.

settled in foreign houses.[1] The numbers of English Catholics desiring a monastic life for themselves or their female kin were so high that by the late sixteenth century the first post-Reformation abbey was established for Benedictines in Brussels. An English Poor Clare convent was founded at St Omer in 1608, and in 1609 the English women resident in the Flemish cloister of Augustinian canonesses in Louvain departed to form their own community. By the end of the seventeenth century, there were twenty-two contemplative English convents which had survived the vicissitudes of exile and poverty described by the Bridgettine nuns eighty years earlier. Twenty-one were located within a relatively small part of north-western Europe, in the Low Countries and in France, while the Bridgettines resided to the south in Lisbon.

The history of the English Bridgettines is thus closely connected with that of the other expatriate cloisters, yet it is also distinct. Unlike the other post-Reformation religious houses which had tenuous links with the pre-dissolution monastic orders, the Bridgettine nuns could claim direct continuity with pre-Reformation Syon Abbey in Isleworth. The Bridgettine story of exile was also dramatically different from that of the other religious orders in timing and setting. A group of the sisters began their quest to retain their monastic identity in the Low Countries and France upon the dissolution of their house in 1539, but during the religious upheavals of the late sixteenth century they struggled to locate a permanent and safe home there, and this resulted in the 1594 decision to move to Portugal (then under Spanish rule) to be closer to their principal patron, Philip II. Their residence in Lisbon made them something of an isolated outpost in the history of post-Reformation English monasticism. Although supported by the English seminaries in Spain and, after 1638, Lisbon College, they lacked the female support networks provided by other English convents.[2] They were also short of the immediate support of the larger clusters of exiled English Catholics and their networks which operated in the Spanish Netherlands.

This essay seeks to examine the experience of the Syon nuns in comparison with those of the other exiled religious orders. The Bridgettines' much earlier experience of exile makes it difficult to offer a chronological comparison. Moreover, the loss of their archives in a convent fire in 1651 means that it is difficult to unravel their experiences in Lisbon in any considerable depth. The study will necessarily adopt a more thematic approach and consider their

---

1 Claire Walker, *Gender and Politics in Early Modern Europe: English Convents in France and the Low Countries* (Basingstoke, 2003), pp. 13–14.
2 There were Irish Dominican friars in Lisbon from 1600, and a cloister of Irish Dominican nuns from 1639.

experiences of foundation, exile, poverty, patronage, and sense of mission from their 1559 second departure for the continent, and the ways their pioneering experiences were shared with or differed from the houses which were founded forty or more years later.

Pioneers of Monastic Exile

The dramatic insecurity of the Bridgettine sisters' decades of exile in the sixteenth century hardly needs to be recounted. Initially in Antwerp and Termonde before their recall to England during the reign of Mary Tudor, their resumed exile when Elizabeth came to the throne led them back to Termonde (1559–1564), Zierikzee (1564–1568), Mishagen (1568–1571), Antwerp (1571–1572), Mechelen (1572–1580) and Rouen (1580–1594), before they finally set sail for Lisbon in 1594.[3] The nuns' peregrinations were largely the result of confessional conflict in the Reformation's aftermath, which was particularly intense in the Low Countries as the Dutch sought independence from Spanish rule. The sisters hurriedly departed Mishagen for Antwerp after continued harassment by local mobs incited, according to Fletcher, by Calvinist preachers. Religious strife in their new haven persuaded them to relocate to Mechelen, where they were at the mercy of both Protestant rioters and violent Spanish soldiers. In November 1676, following the Spanish sack of Antwerp, the Bridgettine convent was invaded by angry locals searching for arms the nuns were supposedly storing. The resultant destruction and pillage of the cloister proved too much for the elderly abbess, Katherine Palmer, who passed away the following month. Two years later a number of the younger members of the house were sent home to England to collect alms to support the besieged monastery, and in 1680 the remaining nuns fled Mechelen when it fell to the Protestants. They settled in Rouen and remained there for fourteen years before fear of religious uncertainty under Henry IV, and possible political difficulties resulting from the house's association with the Catholic League, led to their departure for Lisbon in 1594.[4] The Syon exiles sought refuge abroad in the Southern Netherlands and France during a period of intense insecurity caused by the Dutch Revolt and the French Wars of Religion. Their decision to settle in Spanish territory which was not beset by warfare and which was closer to Spain was therefore made in part for reasons of security.

---

[3] John Rory Fletcher, *The Story of the English Bridgettines of Syon Abbey* (South Brent, 1933), pp. 37–112.

[4] Fletcher, *English Bridgettines*, pp. 46–54, 96–7.

Yet the protection of their persons and their property was not the sole reason for their departure south. Extreme poverty was a significant factor behind their instability in the Low Countries and France. As exiles the nuns had very little income to sustain their livelihood and were dependent upon the charity of kin, English expatriates, and supportive locals to make ends meet. The sisters were reliant upon abodes located by others, and those available to foreigners with little means were often entirely unsuited to monastic life, necessitating costly renovations or another move to a better site. The Syon nuns spent the initial years of their second exile living alongside Flemish Bridgettines in their hosts' cloister. The arrival of nine additional English nuns made the two communities living under the same roof, each with their own abbess, unworkable and resulted in their departure for Zierikzee. There they were provided with an abandoned monastery which was located on marsh land and accordingly so damp and unhealthy that it had been forsaken by its previous residents. The 'unwholesome' air led to widespread sickness and the deaths of some sisters. In her plea to Rome for permission to move somewhere more wholesome, Abbess Palmer also noted that it was difficult to obtain the necessities of life in Zierikzee. They moved to Mishagen where with friends' help they purchased a convent previously inhabited by Augustinian canonesses.[5] Constant threats by Calvinist mobs made this abode unsafe, so in the autumn of 1571 the nuns abandoned it and fled to Antwerp and sought shelter with the Augustinian canonesses at the Falcon convent, where they had found refuge in 1539.[6] During the nuns' fourteen years in Rouen, they occupied three different premises.

On several occasions the community was unable to meet the cost of rent or they were in danger of starvation. Income from England was precarious at the best of times, so the sisters increasingly settled in places with an expatriate English Catholic population which would support them. Yet these refugees were not always well placed to assist them sufficiently. In July 1578, Pope Gregory III wrote to Don John of Austria, the recently appointed governor of the Low Countries, requesting that the nuns' Spanish pension which was in arrears be reinstated because they suffered tremendous poverty in Mechelen, and their plight had worsened since the lay English exiles had fled the town.[7] When they arrived in Rouen in July 1580, their penury was such that they were given permission by the local ecclesiastical authorities to beg.[8] The same

---

5 Hill Museum and Monastic Library, St John's University (hereafter HMML), England 682, Canon Fletcher MS 6, fols 4–14; Fletcher, *English Bridgettines*, pp. 43–5.
6 HMML England 682, Canon Fletcher MS 6, fols 34–48.
7 HMML England 682, Canon Fletcher MS 6, fol. 122; Fletcher, *English Bridgettines*, p. 51.
8 HMML England 683, Canon Fletcher MS 7, fol. 65; Fletcher, *English Bridgettines*, p. 70.

year the great benefactor of persecuted English Catholics, George Gilbert, visited the Bridgettines on his way to the English College in Rome. He found them in 'great necessity' and left them 600 scudi and persuaded a friend likewise to donate alms.[9] Yet, the infrequency of this kind of generosity meant that by 1587 the community's circumstances were so straitened that they appealed to English Catholics for assistance to ensure their survival, writing, 'if help does not come they must be utterly dissolved and dispersed'.[10] By 1590 the nuns could not afford the rent for their convent and moved to a confiscated Huguenot property provided rent-free by the Catholic League's military leader, the Duc de Mayenne. Renovations to the new residence finally gave them an abode which suited their needs. Yet a few years later, after the defeat of the League, they faced losing it to its former owner, another factor which prompted the transfer to Lisbon.[11]

In contrast, the majority of the post-Reformation English foundations remained in the towns and cities where they had been established. Economic necessity, warfare and disease caused some communities to relocate, like the Benedictine abbey founded at Boulogne in 1652 which moved to Pontoise in 1658 because the 'sea ayre' gave them all 'agues' and the town 'was subject to surprises of war and many other casualtyes', including the presence of Cromwell's soldiers in nearby Dunkirk.[12] The Third Order Regular Franciscans came closest to the Bridgettine experience. Founded at Brussels in 1621, the nuns moved to Nieuport in 1637 to escape the high cost of living and the supposed negative impact on recruitment of successive outbreaks of plague. In 1658 the community split, with sick nuns returning to England, some nuns going to Paris to establish a new convent, others relocating to Bruges, and the remainder staying at their war-ravaged cloister for another four years before joining the sisters who had gone to Bruges.[13] Among those houses which remained in their original location, some were forced to abandon their premises temporarily at times of war or natural disaster. Part of the Augustinian convent temporarily fled Louvain for Bruges during a siege in

[9] Henry Foley (ed.), *Records of the English Province of the Society of Jesus*, 7 vols in 8 (London, 1878), iii. 691.

[10] *Calendar of State Papers Domestic (Elizabeth), 1581–1590*, p. 435; HMML England 683, Canon Fletcher MS 7, fols 203–15; Fletcher, *English Bridgettines*, pp. 76–7.

[11] HMML England 683, Canon Fletcher MS 7, fol. 61; Fletcher, *English Bridgettines*, pp. 84–5, 97.

[12] 'Abbess Neville's Annals of Five Communities of English Benedictine Nuns in Flanders, 1598–1687', ed. Justina Rumsey, in *CRS Miscellanea V* (London, 1909), p. 48.

[13] Convent of Poor Clares, Arundel, Franciscan MS Annals, fols 25–6, 31, 35–43, Annals of the Religious of the 3rd Order of St Francis of the Province of England from the Year 1621 to (1893); Walker, *Gender and Politics*, pp. 18–19.

1635.[14] The Poor Clares of Gravelines had to contend with the destruction of their monastic buildings twice in the seventeenth century. In 1626, a fire destroyed everything but the choir, kitchen and infirmary, and the nuns were forced to seek refuge temporarily in a neighbouring house.[15] Then in 1654 the powder arsenal explosion which destroyed a large proportion of the town flattened much of the convent. Some of the sisters moved to St Omer while it was rebuilt.[16] Yet these disruptions aside, most convents were able to weather the turmoil caused by political unrest, economic difficulties and disease. Patronage was often the key to success in this respect.

Patronage and Identity

The fire and gunpowder explosion in Gravelines highlighted the importance of patronage in the survival of the Poor Clare community. After the 1626 debacle, when appeals were sent even to the Pope for assistance, the chronicle reported that, 'after a yeare or two by Gods speciall Providence, & the Alms of charitable persons their house was completely built again'.[17] In 1654, there was another appeal to Rome, and Louis XIV assisted with a grant for the reconstruction of the house.[18] Three years earlier, the Bridgettines had faced similar tragedy when their monastery was largely destroyed by fire. The community's brothers solicited alms on a journey through Portugal to Spain, and the generosity of both the Portuguese crown and Lisbon's populace gave rise to a new convent and church. In 1755 the abbey was again demolished, this time by an earthquake which reduced much of the city to rubble. In a letter to her mother detailing the horror of the tremor, the destruction it wrought, and the nuns' new lodgings in a hut in the garden where three months after the event they still wore the same clothes they had been wearing when the earthquake struck, Sister Catherine Witham added the postscript, 'I wish some that has it, and can afford it, could send us a brace of hundred pounds to repair the Convent.' The religious community appealed to their countrymen and women

---

[14] Adam Hamilton (ed.), *The Chronicle of the English Augustinian Canonesses Regular of the Lateran, at St Monica's in Louvain (now at St Augustine's Priory, Newton Abbot, Devon), 1548–1644* (hereafter *Chronicle of St Monica's*), 2 vols (London, 1906), ii. 139–47.

[15] St Clare's Abbey, Darlington, MS Gravelines Chronicles, fols 150–3.

[16] Darlington, MS Gravelines Chronicles, fol. 215; Buckfast Abbey, Pontoise MS, 'An Account of the Blowing-up and Destruction of the Town of Gravelines'.

[17] Darlington, MS Gravelines Chronicles, fol. 163; Archives of the Archdiocese of Wesminster (hereafter AAW), A, vol. XX, fol. 179, Petition to the Pope, on behalf of the Poor Clares of Gravelines, after the fire in their Convent AD 1626.

[18] Peter Guilday, *The English Catholic Refugees on the Continent, 1558–1795* (London, 1914), p. 300.

for aid, noting that they had to do so, 'it being out of the power of our friends and benefactors to relieve us, they all having undergone the same misfortune and disaster'.[19] This eighteenth-century plea to England is telling. It suggests that previously, as was the case with the fire of 1651, the community had relied very heavily upon the patronage of locals, both English exiles and Portuguese supporters. The collective appeal of the convent and that of Catherine Witham hints that prior to the 1755 débâcle, patronage from England itself had not been as important.

Indeed patronage is one area where the Bridgettines stood slightly apart from the other cloisters. From the beginning of their exile, they had always considered the Spanish as their principal patrons and allies. This is not surprising, given the assistance of the Spanish monarchy and its officials. In 1559 it was the Spanish ambassador who secured their safe passage out of England. In the 1560s, Margaret of Parma, the Spanish governor in the Netherlands, negotiated an annual pension for the community of 1,200 florins from the Spanish crown.[20] Spain again supported them upon their transfer to Lisbon, and in their time of need in 1651. Other cloisters were similarly patronised by Spain either directly or indirectly through the rulers of the Low Countries. In the Southern Netherlands, the Archdukes Albert and Isabella assisted English foundations, like the first post-Reformation house in Brussels established by the Benedictines in 1598.[21] The English in the Low Countries eventually found other patrons as Spanish influence waned in north-western Europe. Conversely the Bridgettines, who had allied themselves so closely with the Iberian peninsula, remained dependent upon their royal patrons in Spain and Lisbon. Their continuing links with the Spanish, as opposed to the other monasteries to the north, clearly demonstrate the significance of local patronage and the exiled cloisters' necessary ties to the places they lived.

Yet despite the expatriate nuns' obvious need to foster indigenous connections, they emphasised their distinctiveness as religious exiles. Indeed they retained their identity as English Bridgettine nuns who were in exile awaiting the opportune time to return to their homeland and their former monastery. This meant that from their first experiences of emigration when they cohabited with Flemish sisters of their order in Termonde, subsequently stayed with Augustinian canonesses in Antwerp, and then initially in Lisbon resided with

---

[19] Fletcher, *English Bridgettines*, pp. 124–7, 135–8.

[20] HMML England 682, Canon Fletcher MS 6, fol. 120; Fletcher, *English Bridgettines*, p. 44.

[21] Paul Arblaster, 'The Infanta and the English Benedictine Nuns: Mary Percy's Memories in 1634', *Recusant History*, 23 (1997), 522; Paul Arblaster, 'The Archdukes and the Northern Counter-Reformation', in Werner Thomas and Luc Duerloo (eds), *Albert and Isabella 1598–1621: Essays* (Turnhout, 1998), pp. 88–90.

the nuns of Esperança for five years, they aimed to set up their own English cloister.[22] Moreover, such an establishment would be occupied by English women. Like some of the later English convents, the Bridgettines did accept a few local women. The community list provided by Thomas Robinson in his 1622 scurrilous account of the house included two 'Dutchwomen' and three 'Portugeses'.[23] Dowries generally provided the English cloisters with their primary source of income, so it was not surprising that they should turn to 'foreign' locals if there were insufficient English recruits. Such women and their families might also provide much needed local patronage networks. However, from early in its exiled existence, Syon was supposed only to profess English women.[24] The presence of the Netherlander and Portuguese women points to the severe financial stress under which the community laboured which presumably led to the relaxation of this rule. What is more, one Portuguese recruit, Leonor de Mendanha, who was professed in 1602 as Sister Bridget, was described as 'wealthy'. In 1649, and again in 1651, she was elected abbess. The 1640s proved difficult for all the exiled religious communities, with the civil war severely restricting recruitment and income from England. Like the Third Order Regular Franciscans who accepted a local woman with the dowry of a farm, and the Canonesses of the Holy Sepulchre at Liège, where well-connected native entrants proceeded to hold significant offices during times of economic strain, the Bridgettine sisters clearly recognised the wisdom of selecting a superior who would be able to secure local patronage to assist during these straitened times.[25] Such insight proved invaluable in the face of the 1651 fire. Abbess Bridget de Mendanha secured the means from Lisbon's residents to rebuild the monastic premises which were finished in 1656.[26]

The reasons why the English convents wished to recruit solely from England were varied. Often this was the requirement of the local ecclesiastical and civic authorities, concerned that the English establishment in their town would draw recruits from local monasteries. Approval for the foundation of an English Augustinian cloister in Paris was given in 1633 on the express

---

22 Fletcher, *English Bridgettines*, pp. 113, 125.
23 [Thomas Robinson], *The Anatomy of the English Nunnery at Lisbon in Portugall* (London, 1622), p. 32.
24 Fletcher, *English Bridgettines*, pp. 118, 124, 154n.
25 R. Trappes-Lomax (ed.), *Franciscana: The English Nuns, 1619–1821 and the Friars Minor of the Same Province 1618–1761*, CRS (London, 1922), pp. 31, 141–2, 195–6; R. Trappes-Lomax (ed.), 'Records of the English Canonesses of the Holy Sepulchre at Liège, Now at New Hall, 1652–1793', *Miscellanea X*, CRS (London, 1915), pp. 3, 32–4, 49, 105, 173–7, 179, 181, 183.
26 Fletcher, *English Bridgettines*, pp. 124–6.

understanding that it would accept only English subjects. Even after this stipulation was modified in 1655, presumably to assist the house financially at a time of severe economic distress during the Interregnum, the sisters' preference for recruiting only those from their homeland meant that between 1634 and 1700 only one choir nun and two lay sisters were French.[27] There were also linguistic and cultural considerations which often made shared cloisters unworkable. Mary Ward's experience as an external lay sister in the St Omer Poor Clare community was soured in part by language difficulties. She had a Walloon confessor and they were unable to communicate effectively enough to assuage her growing doubts regarding her vocation in the house.[28] The English Augustinians in Louvain's Flemish cloister struggled to become accustomed to the local diet, and they found the laundering work they had to perform too onerous.[29] The nuns, however, had more ideological reasons for preferring those of their own nationality. Founded, or in the case of the Bridgettines exiled, with the express intention of returning to England once Catholicism was tolerated in their homeland, the cloisters wanted women who understood their experience as members of a minority faith in a Protestant country to become their monastic sisters. They were English cloisters and as such preserved their own national identity in a way that partially separated them spiritually from the local environs and populace. For practical reasons they could not isolate themselves totally. They needed provisions, services and patronage from the townspeople. But first and foremost they were English and did all they could to secure patrons and support from among the expatriate English and from their homeland.

This was arguably easier for the post-Reformation houses founded in the seventeenth century to achieve. Established after the institution of the early English seminaries and colleges, and with the assistance of exiles who had often been abroad for several years and were therefore well connected locally, the Benedictines, Augustinians, Franciscans and Carmelites had a range of clerical and lay supporters who fully understood the difficulties of English Catholicism and the vagaries of exile. Moreover, generally they were founded in towns with sizeable communities of English émigrés.[30] Conversely, the

---

[27] B. Whelan, *Historic English Convents of Today: The Story of the English Cloisters in France and Flanders in Penal Times* (London, 1936), pp. 89–90; Antony F. Allison, 'The English Augustinian Convent of Our Lady of Syon at Paris: Its Foundation and Struggle for Survival during the First Eighty Years, 1634–1713', *Recusant History*, 21 (1993), 480–1.

[28] Mary Catherine Elizabeth Chambers, *The Life of Mary Ward (1585–1645)*, ed. H. J. Coleridge, 2 vols (London, 1882), i. 128, 159.

[29] *Chronicle of St Monica's*, i. 34–5, 64.

[30] For a discussion of the English expatriate community in the Southern Netherlands, see my 'Priests, Nuns, Presses and Prayers: The Southern Netherlands and the Contours of English

Bridgettines were the pioneers for both the male and female religious exiles. They faced the difficulties encountered by the later houses but without the well-established networks to sponsor their cause. Paul Arblaster has pointed out that war and rebellion in the Southern Netherlands between 1570 and 1590 made it difficult for refugees to settle, and many, like the Bridgettines themselves, fled for France.[31] Thus, while the nuns might access valuable human resources in the form of other expatriates, such connections were never entirely secure. In 1568, Abbess Katherine Palmer was able to purchase a property at Mishagen with the assistance of the Catholic controversialist, Dr Nicholas Sander, brother to one of the nuns, who had been an exile in Rome and Louvain since 1559 or 1560.[32] In 1572, the community moved to Mechelen upon the advice of Sir Francis Englefield, the former Marian courtier who was paid by the Spanish crown to advise the Duke of Alva on English affairs. Englefield and a small number of English Catholics lived there and offered succour to the nuns until he was expelled from Spanish territory in the light of a joint 1574 English and Spanish protocol to deport the 'rebels' of each other's countries.[33] As this example demonstrates, the security of the lay expatriates was often as tenuous as that of the religious community they sought to assist, and the English patrons were at the mercy of the same kinds of military and political actions as the nuns.

The Bridgettines' early years in Rouen were characterised by poverty and hunger which resulted from the paucity of patrons willing or able to succour them with alms. Fletcher notes that although they had the goodwill of English Catholic émigrés in the town, their exiled coreligionists largely lacked the means with which to support themselves, let alone the impoverished nuns.[34] The local townspeople had seemingly been persuaded by English Protestant merchants in Rouen that the sisters were wealthy, so they did not offer much support. The degree of truth in this claim is unclear but, as Fletcher has suggested, the paucity of local charity to the English nuns was perhaps more an issue arising from their nationality than malevolent rumour.[35] Fletcher might be correct in asserting that traditional antipathy between the French and

Catholicism', in Benjamin Kaplan, Bob Moore, Henk van Nierop and Judith Pollman (eds), *Catholic Communities in Protestant States: Britain and the Netherlands, c. 1570–1720* (Manchester, 2009), pp. 139–55; see also Paul Arblaster's chapter in the same book.

[31] Paul Arblaster, 'The Southern Netherlands Connection: Networks of Support and Patronage' in Kaplan *et al.* (eds), *Catholic Communities in Protestant States*, p. 127.

[32] HMML England 682, Canon Fletcher MS 6, fol. 4; *ODNB*.

[33] HMML England 682, Canon Fletcher MS 6, fols 58, 70, 94; *ODNB*.

[34] HMML England 683, Canon Fletcher MS 7, fols 73–4, 205.

[35] HMML England 683, Canon Fletcher MS 7, fols 71–3.

the English underpinned local reluctance to support the nuns, but it most likely can be attributed to a preference for endowing French religious houses and supporting local charitable causes. The nuns' associations with Spain may well have worked against French support as well. Moreover, the English women were just some of many impecunious religious exiles and their plight did not necessarily move their neighbours to charity in the way that the plight of later cloisters with more powerful connections and patrons did. As the length of exile extended, and news of Protestant 'persecution' of England's Catholics spread, sympathy for the sisters' tragic circumstances increased. The later cloisters played on this compassion, making much of their own and their families' suffering in petitions and pleas for help. Religious refugees, especially convents of women, had to learn strategies for survival in foreign lands and, lacking any example of other cloisters' experiences, the Bridgettines were forced to be inventive. Their survival despite the odds was a testament to their success. An English visitor to Lisbon in the 1670s related in his journal that 'in the esteem of the Portuguese and strangers [the convent] is of very good report'.[36] An exemplary reputation, powerful patrons and the capacity to use these valuable resources to their best advantage were essential to long-term survival.

As women, the sisters were more needful of informed and well-connected sponsors than their priestly counterparts who could act on their own behalf in secular society. Although they were adrift in foreign countries before the Tridentine decrees regarding women religious were implemented, as Bridgettines they were subject to enclosure. They were fortunate in that there were men who shared their experiences – the brothers of Syon which had been a double monastery. Three priests had accompanied Katherine Palmer's group of sisters which travelled abroad in 1539, but by 1583, when Thomas Willan, the community's Confessor General, died, there was only one brother left alive. While women had joined the refugee convent, no priest or lay brother had been professed in twenty years.[37] In 1584 this changed when Seth Foster entered the community and became its new Confessor General. In addition to securing the arrival of three more priests and a lay brother, he took charge of the nuns' affairs in Rouen. They moved into larger accommodation, petitioned England's Catholics for alms, and sent two of the new fathers to Spain to seek resumption of the Spanish pension which had been in arrears for

---

[36] Fletcher, *English Bridgettines*, p. 128.
[37] Profession registers are not complete for this period so recruitment figures have to be gleaned from surviving documents. In 1587 twenty-four sisters and six brothers signed a petition. See Fletcher, *English Bridgettines*, pp. 38, 71–2, 76–7; George J. Aungier, *The History and Antiquities of Syon Monastery* (London, 1840), pp. 102–3.

nine years. By allying the house with the Catholic League Foster secured it the patronage it had formerly lacked from the city's elites who supported the League.[38] He was later instrumental in the move to Lisbon and secured not only the permission of the city's governors for the community to stay there, but also the arrears of the Spanish pension and a promise of 700 crowns a year for six years from Philip II.[39]

Seth Foster's pre-eminence in guiding the nuns was not without disadvantages. It was his close alignment with the League during the French Wars of Religion that necessitated the community's exodus from Rouen. Moreover, his influence was targeted specifically in Thomas Robinson's attack on the cloister. Although written in the tradition of salacious accounts of the goings on in convents, particularly in the aftermath of the Reformation, Thomas Robinson's account of his time spent with the Bridgettines in Lisbon depicted Foster as the figure of authority in the cloister who was able 'to play *rex*' over all the nuns.[40] The anti-Catholic propagandising of this account aside, it nevertheless points to the significant position occupied by the Confessor General and hints that he had usurped the authority normally held by the abbess in the double monastery. Robinson claimed that Foster influenced the triennial elections to make sure one of his 'creatures' would hold the post and thereby 'dispose of the House as he thinketh fit'.[41] The veracity of Robinson is questionable and it is highly unlikely that Foster would have held such sway without complaints from disaffected nuns reaching the church authorities. In any case, nuns were commonly wary about allowing the confessor too much power. While Richard White, confessor to the Augustinian canonesses in Louvain, advised Prioress Winefrid Thimelby that 'nothing can begett a greater traine of miseries and disorder in a Cloister, then the superiours ruling the gostly father', she did not always heed his counsel. By the time the Paris Augustinian convent was established in 1634, its confessor was 'not to medle with the administration of the temporalities of the Monasterie' unless asked to do so by the abbess.[42] Nuns often recognised the dangers of permitting male supervisors too much authority. In the seventeenth century, the founder of six French Ursuline convents, Antoinette Micolon, warned: 'if one yields to them

---

38 HMML England 683, Canon Fletcher MS 7, fol. 73.

39 Fletcher, *English Bridgettines*, pp. 72–7, 96–114.

40 [Robinson], *Anatomy*, p. 14. For an incisive discussion of anti-Catholic polemic targeting nuns which includes analysis of Robinson, see Frances E. Dolan, 'Why Are Nuns Funny?', *Huntingdon Library Quarterly*, 70 (2007), 525–8.

41 [Robinson], *Anatomy*, p. 28.

42 Priory of Our Lady of Good Counsel, Sayers Common, St Monica's MS Qu2, fol. 2, Instructions for a Religious Superior; [St Augustine], *Rule ... Together with the Constitutions of the English Canonesse Regular's of Our B. Ladyes of Sion in Paris* (Paris, 1636), p. 139.

in the least, they wish to govern everything and that everything be done according to their ideas and opinions'.[43] Clearly a woman as strong as Letitia Tredway who founded the Paris Augustinians concurred and was determined not to allow her cloister's confessor the same rights that White had opined for the Louvain convent and Robinson claimed for Seth Foster in Lisbon.[44]

Whatever disadvantages the Confessor General's influence in the Bridgettines' affairs might have wrought, the convent had a distinct advantage over many of the later religious houses simply by having priests on the premises who would perform the sacraments for them. Many of the post-Reformation cloisters struggled to find priests who could say mass for them, particularly in their early years of existence. The English Augustinians in Louvain were unable to pay for a confessor and were fortunate when the retired Fr Fenn offered to serve them gratis. They relied on his spiritual advice, musical prowess and ability to perform the sacraments for some time. A poor Irish priest studying in Louvain and the newly-founded Irish Franciscans who lacked somewhere suitable to celebrate the sacrament also said masses for them.[45] The importance of having priests closely associated with a convent was recognised by Letitia Tredway of the Paris Augustinians who assisted in the foundation of St Gregory's College for the secular clergy. It adjoined the nuns' cloister and in return for her patronage Tredway persuaded the priests to perform the sacrament for no fee.[46]

Yet even Tredway who was so determined not to permit the confessor undue authority accepted the advice of her cloister's first two confessors, Miles Pinkney and Edward Lutton. Lutton in particular was instrumental in securing the cloister's political and economic survival. As women and enclosed nuns, no matter how talented and energetic the abbess or prioress, the exiled convents needed the aid of a competent male assistant and he was usually the confessor. Constrained by their gender and their religious vows, the women could not conduct all the business necessary to establish their house and to maintain (and sometimes save) it thereafter. As with the later cloisters, the Bridgettine nuns required help at a difficult time and Seth Foster fulfilled an important role. His legacy was perhaps most evident in the sisters' move to Portugal.

---

[43] Linda Lierheimer (ed.), *The Life of Antoinette Micolon* (Milwaukee, 2004), p. 89.

[44] One might also note that the sources which promote Foster's prominence (Robinson's *Anatomy* and Fletcher's accounts) are not without bias or blindness to the possibility that the nuns might have made more of the decisions than are credited to them.

[45] *Chronicle of St Monica's*, i. 60, 71–2.

[46] A. F. Allison, 'The Origins of St Gregory's, Paris', *Recusant History*, 21 (1992), 19–20.

The Bridgettines were welcomed by the governors of Lisbon who bestowed a grant of five ducats a day to support them, and they obtained 800 ducats from the king. They secured accommodation with a local religious community until their own house was obtained five years later. Later in the year Seth Foster travelled to Madrid to inform Philip II of the nuns' situation, and the king promised further financial support. The ecclesiastical authorities were similarly supportive of the sisters' plight. However, the apparently smooth transition from France to Portugal stalled in March 1595 when the archbishop refused to profess a novice, Dorothy Shelley, who had travelled with them from Rouen. The main sticking point lay in the non-compliance of the Bridgettine rule and constitutions with the Tridentine decrees. This had not been a problem in France where the Church did not enforce Trent's laws until 1615. Despite constant negotiation and the support of powerful friends in France and Rome, the dispute was not resolved until June 1597 when Pope Clement VIII placed the community under papal protection, approved its rule and constitutions subject to their Tridentine revision, and changed the term of the abbess from perpetual to a three-year position. Subjection to papal rather than episcopal authority meant that it was possible for the convent to profess only English women and thus maintain its identity as a recusant cloister.

Yet the wrangle over Sister Dorothy's profession revealed many of the issues which were to trouble the later female religious foundations in the Low Countries and France. Fletcher notes that the ecclesiastical authorities in Lisbon were alarmed at the poverty and insecure income of the Bridgettines and feared that the nuns might become a financial burden upon the local Church.[47] This was a very real concern for religious and civic leaders when it came to the later English foundations. Lacking solid endowments and with uncertainty about ongoing income, founding nuns often met firm opposition from the very bodies they had hoped would support the fight against Protestantism in England. Thus, like the Bridgettines in 1595, the Benedictine sisters who arrived in Boulogne from Ghent in 1652 faced antipathy from the bishop who, knowing of the impoverished Ghent convent, suspected that Abbess Mary Knatchbull of Ghent had 'sent out those Religious as ye scum of their Cloyster to shift for them selves in his Dioces'.[48] Eventually he accepted the nuns after the indefatigable efforts of Mary Knatchbull secured income for the house from local merchants, a clerical council in Paris ruled that a strict interpretation of Tridentine law was not applicable in the case of

---

47 Fletcher, *English Bridgettines*, p. 117.
48 Buckfast MS, Mary Knatchbull, 'An Account of the Foundation of the Convent of Boulogne: First Filiation from Ghent' (1653), fol. 34.

the exiled English nuns, and the women themselves had impressed him with their piety and virtue.[49]

The special case accorded the Boulogne Benedictine nuns with respect to regulations governing the establishment and jurisdiction of English cloisters reflected several decades of compromise by Church officials since the Bridgettines had required similar dispensations in the late sixteenth century. In spite of very real concerns regarding the exiled religious women's capacity to support themselves, the determination of Church officials and Catholic rulers to oppose Protestant regimes mitigated against a strict insistence upon Tridentine law and overcame local opposition to allow the convents to settle there. In this sense the exiled religious houses were at the forefront of the confessional battle lines which breathed new life into England's troubled relationships with both Spain and France. The Spanish had supported the Syon community from the accession of Elizabeth. Although payments were not always made, Madrid also provided financial support and other forms of assistance when requested. The sisters' gratitude for this help was evident in the story of their exile prepared in the early 1620s during the proposed match between the Infanta Maria and Prince Charles, in which they attributed their survival thus far to Philip III, and to the deeds of his father.[50]

Indeed the community's ties with Spain were so strong that when the Portuguese rejected Spanish rule in 1640, and the Duke of Braganza became King John IV, the sisters considered leaving Lisbon for Spain to ensure the continuation of their Spanish pension. Significantly, the new Portuguese king was reluctant for them to leave his dominions and promised that Portugal would pay the income previously received from Spain.[51] The reasons for the king's determination to keep the Syon nuns in Lisbon are unclear. It is possible that they were highly regarded by the city's inhabitants and thus considered a spiritual asset. More likely, he did not want to concede anything to Spain. He reputedly declared he was a king like Philip and thus would pay the nuns what Philip had given them.[52] However, it is also possible that he considered supporting the English exiles for the kudos it conferred upon the Catholic rulers who nurtured persecuted foreign religious minorities seeking refuge in their realm. Like the kings of Spain and the Archdukes Isabella and Albert in the Low Countries, John considered patronage of embattled

---

49 Knatchbull, 'Account of the Foundation ... of Boulogne', fols 61–3.
50 'The Petition to her Royal Highness the Princess of Wales whom God Preserve', in de Hamel, *Syon Abbey*, pp. 28–30.
51 Fletcher, *English Bridgettines*, pp. 122–3.
52 Fletcher, *English Bridgettines*, p. 123.

Catholic minorities a vital badge of confessional solidarity with obvious political overtones.

The Politics of Exile

When the Bridgettines left England in 1559 with the Duke and Duchess of Feria the political boundaries for Catholics in their homeland had not been clearly defined. As professed nuns they did not see a promising future under Elizabeth I, and so they returned to the continent to wait for an appropriate time to return. In 1578 when a small group of sisters returned to England from their war-ravaged cloister in Mechelen to collect alms for their community, the situation was very different. Some were arrested upon arrival at Dover and Colchester and detained, and they were all forced to move regularly to avoid detection.[53] The intervening twenty years had politicised the maintenance of Catholic belief and practice, and the determination of the state to fine, imprison and execute Catholics for offences related to recusancy and the support of the outlawed fugitive missionary clergy continued to harden in the years to come. The foundation of the seminaries and colleges on the continent and the activities of the lay expatriate Catholic communities abroad were of considerable interest to government spies. Even the cloisters of women which were not founded with the explicit intention to proselytise in England were scrutinised, and their location and size reported.[54] By their very existence, these religious cloisters of women were thus deemed a threat. The convents' role in educating girls later came into the spotlight in legislation which prohibited parents from sending their children to Catholic establishments abroad for education.[55] The authorities were also keen to prevent women travelling abroad to join the religious communities, and suspects were detained at ports and even imprisoned. Thus, despite a reluctance to admit that these women might engage in political activity, measures against the convents and the women who belonged to them suggested otherwise.

Obviously the women's religious houses were founded with a politically-charged goal to return to their homeland once Catholicism was tolerated there again. Indeed the Syon nuns had demonstrated this when they went back

---

[53] BL, Add. MS 18,650, fol. 10v, 'The Life and Good End of Sister Marie'; 'The Coppy of S. Elizabethe Sanders letters unto your wor. of her being in England', English College, Valladolid, Spain, Ser. II, L.5, no. 12, fol. [1] (Betty Travitsky kindly sent me copies of both a photocopy of the letter from the archive and a typed transcription of it); HMML England 682, Canon Fletcher MS 6, fols 171–5.

[54] Guilday, *Catholic Refugees*, pp. 30–3.

[55] Walker, *Gender and Politics*, p. 120.

to England during Mary Tudor's reign. Therefore, although across the Channel, the cloisters were a reminder that English Catholic institutions had survived the Reformations and might re-establish themselves easily should the opportunity arise. Some cloisters were not prepared to wait that long. In the seventeenth century certain houses sent members to England and Ireland in the hope of setting up small convents to assist the mission. The Gravelines Poor Clares sent sisters to Dublin in 1625, and the Third Order Regular Franciscans dispatched three nuns to England in 1639 for the same purpose. In the case of Mary Ward and the sisters of her Institute, there were houses with schools at Hammersmith in 1669, and in Yorkshire in 1677. In the 1620s individual sisters of the first Institute had used the guise of education to secure converts for Rome.[56] As in so many other instances, the Bridgettines had pioneered women's missionary work. Although the nuns sent to England in 1578 went to garner alms for their stricken Mechelen cloister, their presence among English Catholics inevitably attracted devotional attention and the ire of the government.

Much recent scholarship on the Syon nuns focuses on these women, in particular Mary Champney and Elizabeth Sander, for whom we have biographical and autobiographical accounts.[57] The extremely pious Mary Champney had been a visionary since childhood and, although raised in England, she travelled to Flanders in her late teens. Her travels abroad which were not originally for the purpose of entering a religious house culminated in her profession at Mishagen in 1569. Champney's return to England was short-lived; she died from tuberculosis in 1580. However, we know about her from a hagiographical account of her life and death, written soon after her death to inspire English Catholics to remain steadfast in their faith, but perhaps also as a means of advertising the virtue and plight of Champney's troubled Bridgettine cloister. Conversely, we know about Elizabeth Sander's eventful time in England from two letters she wrote to Sir Francis Englefield, one of Syon's patrons, who sought information about the Catholic networks in England which assisted the fugitive clergy and those wishing to escape England for religious establishments abroad.[58] Sander was the sister of the

---

56 'Registers of the English Poor Clares at Gravelines, including those who Founded Filiations at Aire, Dunkirk and Rouen, 1608–1837', in *CRS Miscellanea 9*, CRS (London, 1914), pp. 34–5; R. Trappes-Lomax (ed.), *Franciscana: The English Franciscan Nuns, 1619–1821 and the Friars Minor of the Same Province 1618–1761*, CRS 24 (London, 1922), p. 23; M. Wright, *Mary Ward's Institute: The Struggle for Identity* (Sydney, 1997), pp. 47–8; Chambers, *Life of Mary Ward*, ii. 27.
57 See also Ann Hutchison's essay below (Chapter 8).
58 For a discussion of these letters, see Betty S. Travitsky, 'The Puzzling Letters of Sister Elizabeth Sa[u]nder[s]', in Zachary Lesser and Benedict S. Robinson (eds), *Textual Conversations*

controversialist, Nicholas Sander, and her piety was of a more active nature than Mary Champney's, which meant that she spent most of her eight and a half years in England in prison. Despite their very different experiences in their homeland, the stories of Champney and Sander reveal much about the status of the Syon Bridgettines in Elizabethan England, the kinds of missionary work women might perform, and the ways English Catholics practised their religion in the absence of public spaces, like churches, for worship.

Mary Champney died surrounded by several people, and, as Ann Hutchison has commented, her elaborate funeral arrangements further indicate the esteem in which she was held.[59] 'The Life and Good End of Sister Marie' makes abundantly clear the way Champney's death provided a focal point for recusant devotion. While the 'Life' does not imply a shortage of priests in the circles which sheltered the dying nun, the many visitors to her sickbed do suggest that without free access to the sacraments and rituals of their religion, Catholics were drawn to alternative sources of spiritual sustenance. These pilgrims 'thoughte themselves the better for it … to saye any prayers with her or for her, in her presence'. In return she charitably offered child-rearing advice to parents, exhorted sinners to reform, and castigated the latest female fashions as dangerous to the health of potential nuns who needed to be fit and strong for the obligations of the choir.[60] Hence the presence of a nun on English soil in 1580 was potentially as threatening to Protestantism and the state as the missionary priests. Although she did not convert anyone upon her deathbed, Champney was considered a spiritual authority and her actions and advice not only inspired her immediate audience but also the later readers of the account written by someone present at her deathbed. Moreover, the saintly dying nun's access to God was considered so efficacious that she was asked to pray for 'the speedie conversion of Englande' and even for Mary Queen of Scots, the latter displaying obvious political overtones.[61] The lesson of Champney's worthy demise makes it abundantly clear that such a religious woman did not have to proselytise actively; her piety drew people to her in such a way that her deathbed comprised both religious ritual and political subversion.

Elizabeth Sander took a more overt stance in her defence of her beliefs. She was arrested for distributing copies of Edmund Campion's 'Challenge', and

---

in the Renaissance: Ethics, Authors, Technologies (Aldershot, 2006), pp. 131–45.

[59] Ann Hutchison, 'Three (Recusant) Sisters', in Anne Clark Bartlett *et al.* (eds), *Vox Mystica: Essays on Medieval Mysticism in Honor of Professor Valerie M. Lagorio* (Woodbridge, 1995), p. 155.

[60] BL, Add. MS 18,650, fol. 11v.

[61] BL, Add. MS 18,650, fol. 8.

then spent several years in prison before escaping to return to her convent when it was safely situated in Rouen. Sander's stout refusal to implicate Catholics who had sheltered her during her time in England, and her spirited determination to escape prison and rejoin her cloister, reflects the heroism of the recusant age when women as well as men defied the authorities to practise their faith against all odds and protect the fugitive clergy from arrest. Nancy Bradley Warren has argued that Sander's dissemination of subversive material 'went a long way towards making this women [sic] of God into a woman of arms'.[62] Sander herself denied any such intent, arguing upon her arrest that she was a woman and a nun and therefore no threat to the state.[63] But her actions belied her words. Circulating Catholic controversialist literature was most certainly a challenge to the Church of England and the government. However, I do not concur with Warren's conjecture about the Bridgettines' wider involvement in subversion.[64] Sander and the other sisters went to England to collect alms for their beleaguered and destitute cloister in Mechelen, and not to assist the papal military expedition to Ireland, despite Nicholas Sander's involvement in it.

Moreover, Elizabeth Sander was above all committed to her cloister and sisters. She arguably challenged the state more in her determination to escape prison to join the Syon community in Rouen, than in distributing polemical tracts. She reiterated that her objective was to obey her abbess above all else, and considered that this obligation legitimated her escape, perhaps even to the detriment of those, like the prison governor's wife, who assisted her. She recalled arguing with Catholic priests, who said she was legally bound to remain in prison until released, that 'I (beying Religious) am bound to obey to my power, notwtstanding any other lawe what so ever, ffor my professyon is to lyve in a cloister, and not abroade, nor in prysone'.[65] Eventually her persistent endeavours to escape prevailed and she rejoined her community at Rouen. She thus defied the authorities who had arrested her to return to the monastic enclosure from whence she came. Indeed, despite her adventures, Elizabeth Sander remained pious throughout. In prison she used her suffering as a form of religious devotion, commenting that after a failed attempt to

---

62 Nancy Bradley Warren, *Women of God and Arms: Female Spirituality and Political Conflict, 1380–1600* (Philadelphia, 2005), p. 144.
63 'The History of Syon (continued) Englefield Correspondence – English College, Valladolid: Sister Elizabeth Saunders' "Second Letter" to Sir Frances Englefield', trans. Adam Hamilton, in *The Poor Souls' Friend and St Joseph's Monitor* (March/April 1966), 43–4. The original of this letter is lost and Adam Hamilton translated a Spanish copy at Valladolid.
64 Warren, *Women of God*, p. 147.
65 'The Coppy of S. Elizabethe Sanders letters', fol. [5].

secure her release through bribes, '[I] made up my mind to stay there all my life, and look upon my prison as my convent'.[66] Like the nuns who belonged to the later English religious foundations, who stressed prayer as a very powerful weapon against the Protestants, Sander in her determination to return to the continent clearly considered her activism just as potent from within the enclosure as outside it. She was intensely conscious of her religious profession as a nun and considered that above all to legitimate all her actions.

Mary Champney, Elizabeth Sander and the other Bridgettine nuns who lived in England in the late 1570s and 1580s may well have conducted covert missionary work of the kind performed some forty years later by Mary Ward's sisters, like Sister Dorothea who claimed to have gained many souls for Rome through her underground missionary work among gentlewomen, children, and the poor. Disguised as the companion to a gentlewoman, Sister Dorothea used the educational, medical and social skills expected of women to conduct her mission.[67] Upon her arrest, Sander's request to 'returne unto my brothers howse agyne' was denied by the authorities who feared 'I would infect my brother, syster, and others' with Catholicism.[68] Even if they did not engage in proselytising, the accounts of the Bridgettine sisters' heroic feats in death, prison and gentry houses fed the emerging Catholic narrative of struggle, both in England and in religious houses abroad, to maintain the faith against all odds. A report to the English College in Douai in 1579 noted that although some had questioned the young nuns' return to England, the women demonstrated such 'greate constancy in there fayth, singuler modesty in ther behaviour and wise and discreete awnswers the are thorow owte the Realme talked of and commended'.[69] A visitor at Mary Champney's deathbed commented that the Bridgettine sisters' exemplary virtue during their time in England 'had donne more good to their cowntrye ... than ever their tarryinge in Machlin had bene able'. He hoped the other sisters in England with Champney would work 'to the further comforte, and consolacion of many good howses' across the country.[70] Plaudits such as these, the circulating manuscript copies of Mary Champney's visions and inspiring final weeks, and stories of Elizabeth Sander, which spread among the recusants in England and expatriates abroad, defined religious women's responses to the

---

[66] 'Sister Elizabeth Saunders' "Second Letter" ', p. 47.
[67] Chambers, *Life of Mary Ward*, ii. 27–39.
[68] 'The Coppy of S. Elizabethe Sanders letters', fol. [1].
[69] T. F. Knox (ed.), *The First and Second Diaries of the English College, Douay* (London, 1878), p. 149.
[70] BL, Add. MS 18,650, fol. 15.

difficulties of maintaining the beliefs and practices of a minority religion. They showed their compatriots that the innovative use of ritual and space pioneered by Elizabethan Catholics might be translated by women into religious cloisters abroad which would provide alternative loci for devotion during the years of Protestant ascendancy in England, but that these religious women could readily return to their homeland when toleration was granted, to restore the female monastic tradition on English soil. Indeed they might even return before such a wholesale repatriation was possible, to offer spiritual sustenance to their kin and the wider Catholic community.

In spite of the Bridgettine sisters' insecurity on the continent, they nonetheless survived, and their endurance and their story gave hope to their countrymen and women, and to those who twenty years after Champney and Sander arrived in England began the foundation of post-Reformation religious houses for women. It is perhaps an irony that the pioneering Bridgettines abandoned the Southern Netherlands and France only four years before the landscape there became dotted with several other English establishments. However, the Syon sisters remained intensely conscious of their pioneering role in establishing the early parameters of monastic exile. In their address to the Infanta Maria in c.1623, they pleaded that they might be the first expatriate cloister to return to England under her patronage, writing, 'our case is unique, since not only were we the first exiles for our Holy Catholic Faith, but also the only ones, of all the orders and convents of English nuns, who have continued and persevered in this very hard exile from its first inception until now'.[71] Their hopes were dashed by the collapse of the marriage negotiations. Yet their fervent desire to return to their homeland remained. Captain James Jeneefer, who visited the cloister during a sojourn in Lisbon in the 1670s, commented, 'such is the fondness of these real devouts, that they hope to return to the original foundation; but I doubt their harps will rust upon the willows before they will be able to tune that song of Syon alright'.[72]

Distinctive to the end of their exile, unlike their compatriots in France and the Southern Netherlands who fled to England from the French revolutionaries, the Syon community (by then only nuns after the last Confessor General died in 1695) remained in Lisbon until fears of a renewed occupation of Lisbon by Napoleon's forces in 1808 led to the departure of all but four choir nuns and three lay sisters for England. This initial return was not successful and extreme poverty led to the break-up of the community; and all those who had returned to England had died by the 1830s. Syon continued, however, in

71 'The Petition', in de Hamel, *Syon Abbey*, p. 25.
72 Fletcher, *English Bridgettines*, pp. 128–9.

the small community which had remained in Lisbon. It grew with an intake of new recruits from England until the political situation in Portugal became so difficult that, after 267 years in Lisbon, they sold their house in 1861 and departed for England. Thus, in spite of the economic, political and spiritual anguish of exile, Syon Abbey survived to achieve the nuns' goal of returning to their native soil.

6

Books and Reading at Syon Abbey, Lisbon, in the Seventeenth Century

CAROLINE BOWDEN

St Bridget (c.1301–1373) placed study at the heart of her version of the monastic day when establishing her order and, as a result, from the time of its foundation by Henry V in 1415, books and learning were of central importance in the religious life at Syon Abbey.[1] C. Annette Grisé, one of a number of historians who have discussed the importance of books at Syon, has described the convent as an important site of literary production and reception and a significant reading community.[2] Syon nuns participated in the production of devotional and instructional manuscripts as readers, patrons and role models, although there is no surviving catalogue for the nuns to indicate what was in their library before their dissolution in 1539. Following the closure, the determination of a small group of Bridgettines to continue living as a community led them into a lengthy period spent largely in exile during which

---

[1] The research for this chapter was made possible by the hospitality and support of the abbesses and archivists of a number of convents: I wish to acknowledge in particular Mother Anna Maria at Syon Abbey who answered many questions and showed me sources which I would not have found otherwise. The community also granted permission for the publication of images from their books held at Exeter University Library.

[2]   C. Annette Grisé, 'Syon Abbey in Late-Medieval England: Gender and Reading, Bodies and Communities, Piety and Politics' (unpublished PhD thesis, University of Western Ontario, 1998); Grisé, 'Women's Devotional Reading in Late-Medieval England and the Gendered Reader', *Medium Aevum*, 71 (2002), 209–25; Mary Erler, 'Syon Abbey's Care for Books', *Scriptorium*, 39 (1985), 293–307; Erler, *Women, Reading and Piety in Late Medieval England* (Cambridge, 2002). J. T. Rhodes, 'Syon Abbey and its Religious Publications in the Sixteenth Century', *JEH*, 44 (1993), 11–25. James Hogg, 'Brigittine Manuscripts Preserved at Syon Abbey', in James Hogg (ed.), *Studies in St Birgitta and the Brigittine Order*, vol. 2 (Salzburg, 1993), pp. 228–42; Hogg (ed.), *A Book of Uses of Syon Abbey*, Analecta Cartusiana 35:13 (Salzburg, 1991); Ann Hutchison, 'What the Nuns Read: Literary Evidence from the English Bridgettine House, Syon Abbey', *Mediaeval Studies*, 57 (1995), 205–22; Rebecca Krug, *Reading Families: Women's Literate Practice in Late Medieval England* (Ithaca, NY 2002).

the maintenance of order and the performance of the liturgy were extraordinarily difficult. When they finally settled in Lisbon in 1594, the community entered a new period of stability which allowed them to rebuild their collection of books and revive the reading habits they had followed in England. This essay will focus on evidence of reading practices from the first hundred years in Lisbon and set the Bridgettines in the context of the new English foundations established in exile from 1598.

The Bridgettine community left accounts of the period following their dissolution which show that in spite of the considerable difficulties they experienced in Flanders they continued to perform divine office and follow the rule.[3] There are several references to the problems of keeping religious observance going during these years, with the shortage of books and other deprivations: one observer wrote, 'all their portable Bookes for theyr private use ar so rudely written, that it pytythe me to see them'.[4] Ann Hutchison has found evidence that Abbess Katherine Palmer was actively seeking to improve the situation by commission or purchase: for instance, she had Henry of Herph's *Directorium aureum contemplativorum* recopied at Mishagen in Flanders.[5] They had hoped that by moving to Rouen they would find a place where they could follow their religious practice in more secure surroundings. However, their hopes were misplaced.

The experience of two sieges and the handing over of Rouen to the Protestant Henry of Navarre and his troops led the Bridgettines to reconsider their situation, and a group of thirty left Rouen in haste on Good Friday 1594.[6] They later explained that one of the reasons they chose to go to Portugal rather than return to Flanders was so that they could carry with them 'nuestras alhajas, y los libros y ornamentos de la Iglesia' (our precious objects, our books and church ornaments), arguing that it was less dangerous to transport themselves and their belongings by sea rather than face the uncertainties of travelling overland through war zones.[7] Portugal in 1594 was ruled from

---

[3] Described in Exeter University Library, Syon Abbey MS (unnumbered) in Box 28. 'An Account of The Travels dangers and wonderful Deliverances of the English Nuns of the famous Monastery of Sion From their first leaving England to their Settlement at Lisbon in the Kingdom of Portugal'.

[4] Quoted in de Hamel, *Syon Abbey*, p. 128.

[5] Hutchison, 'What the Nuns Read', p. 221; and see J. T. Rhodes, 'Religious Instruction at Syon in the Early Sixteenth Century', in James Hogg (ed.), *Studies in St Birgitta and the Brigittine Order*, vol. 2 (Salzburg, 1993), pp. 151–69, p. 64, n. 28.

[6] Robert Parsons, *Relacion Que Embiaron Las Religiosas Del Monesterio De Sion De Inglaterra, Que Estavan En Roan De Francia*, trans. Sacerdote Ingles Del Colegio De Valladolid Carlos Dractan (Madrid, 1594), p. 35v. I am grateful to Father Peter Harris, archivist at the English College, Valladolid, for this reference.

[7] *Relacion*, p. 30v (author's translation).

Madrid by their long-standing benefactor Philip II, giving them reason to hope they might find support and stability, albeit continuing as exiles.

The group that arrived in Lisbon led by Father Seth Foster as Confessor General and Abbess Elizabeth Hart, according to their own account, created an impression on the locals:

> ... [that] 30 persons viz 22 women, & 8 men should suddenly appear in the haven of Lisbon, in a Catholick Country wherein the Inquisition flourished against all counterfeits, & be so bold as to appear in their Religious habits, saying they were Religious persons, and bringing with them the Reliques, Rules & Monuments, Service books, Choir books, Libraries, Bulls, Records & Church furnitur of Sion.[8]

Although it was in effect a re-foundation and, as the extract demonstrates, they brought much that was essential to furnish their new house, the convent they established in Lisbon faced many of the same problems as the new English convents in Flanders. The community had to obtain permits, find or build appropriate premises, locate funding and establish a reputation in order to attract sufficient English recruits to ensure its survival. The Bridgettines remained an English community in exile, this time in Portugal, a country which had no previous experience of hosting an English religious institution either male or female. Indeed by 1594 Syon was the last surviving monastic community from England. It had been a precarious existence and by this time they carried little in the way of possessions or money by comparison with their time in England. However there were also significant links with the past and strong elements of continuity: the nuns carried with them enough of their monastic practices, books and relics to protect and reinforce a collective memory of their past. It was a community with more than forty years' experience of religious life in exile. Moreover they carried into Portugal, a country with a long tradition of political and trading relations with England, the prestigious reputation of Syon Abbey as a royal foundation with a tradition of scholarship and study which had attracted recruits from elite families from the beginning and had continued to do so even during the hard times in Flanders and France.

Although the Bridgettines emphasised their history and continuity with the past, both the circumstances in which they were living and the books that were available to them in seventeenth-century Lisbon were very different from those in late medieval England: perhaps most strikingly, living in exile away

---

[8] Exeter University Library, Syon Abbey MS (unnumbered) in Box 28. 'An Account of the Travels', p. 176. See also Ann Hutchison's chapter below (Chapter 8).

from immediate sources of English patronage, and secondly the changes in book production and the availability of printed books on a much bigger scale. This study of the Syon book collection in the seventeenth century has drawn on the methodology of recent work of several historians of early modern reading, in particular Heidi Brayman Hackel who seeks to understand reading practices and the ways that lay readers engaged with their books; and Heather Wolfe who published an important paper on the reading practices of the English Benedictine convents at Cambrai and Paris in the mid-seventeenth century.[9] The relationship between early modern English nuns and their books is complex and takes place on many levels. The Bridgettines, like the other members of the English convents in exile, can be seen from evidence in manuscripts and from the books themselves as buyers, recipients of donations, librarians, readers, annotators, performers of texts, listeners, donors, translators, compilers and editors, authors, patrons, dedicatees, subjects, repairers and copyists of the books in their collection.

In some ways the libraries created by religious lay English women and nuns overlap: recent scholarship has shown that the collections made by educated lay women, both Protestant and Catholic, in the sixteenth and seventeenth centuries contained many devotional works as well as literary texts, recreational readings and advice books. There were few Catholic books in English available to buy in this period.[10] The fact that English law forbade the publication or import of Catholic books severely restricted the market. One result of this was that authors in their prefaces often emphasised the wide appeal of their work in order to maximise their potential readership. However, although they might read some of the same texts, the nuns were very different from lay women readers. The criteria for selecting titles for the convent were clearly different from those for a lay household: the nuns' reading was directed towards the purpose of monastic life and while English convents owned a few seventeenth-century secular volumes, their libraries were more focused in their selection than those for even the most devout lay women. We need to approach the monastic reader differently from the lay reader. Whereas

---

[9] Heidi Brayman Hackel, *Reading Material in Early Modern England: Print, Gender and Literacy* (Cambridge, 2005); Heather Wolfe, 'Reading Bells and Loose Papers: Reading and Writing Practices of the English Benedictine Nuns of Cambrai and Paris', in Victoria Burke and Jonathan Gibson (eds), *Early Modern Women's Manuscript Studies* (Aldershot, 2004), pp. 135–56.

[10] Thomas H. Clancy, 'A Content Analysis of English Catholic Books, 1615–1714', *Catholic Historical Review*, 86 (2000), 259. See also the discussion in Alexandra Walsham, ' "Domme Preachers"? Post-Reformation Catholicism and the Culture of Print', *Past and Present*, 168 (2000), 72–123.

Hackel stresses the importance of considering the individual reader, her identity and her response to her books, the monastic rule subsumes the individual
within the conventual whole. Hackel describes the reading of male professional scholars as 'goal-orientated reading' in contrast to the reading of
most women which was recreational.[11] I would argue that the term 'goal-
orientated' also describes the situation of women religious, whose reading
was directed and purposeful: the selection of texts, the time devoted to
reading and the places where it happened were governed by the vows made at
their profession to fulfil the requirements of the religious life as laid down in
the constitutions and rules. Nuns' reading was prescribed: books were
selected and ways of reading them set down by their superiors and spiritual
directors. Nuns were not allowed to own any books individually: the buildings
and all their contents were held in common. Nevertheless, it is still possible to
see marks of individual Bridgettine readers in seventeenth-century volumes:
nuns who donated books to the convent; and others who were allocated books
for a period of time and wrote their names on the title pages. There are also the
unnamed individuals who inscribed additional material for the liturgy, added
marginalia or made repairs to books suffering wear and tear.[12] In addition to
printed works, the nuns in Lisbon had access to manuscript copies of works
specially translated and copied for them by the Bridgettine brothers in the
seventeenth century, and also volumes including compilations which they
transcribed themselves.[13]

Heather Wolfe's study of reading in the English Benedictine convent in
Cambrai in the mid-seventeenth century analysed documents from their
confessor Father Augustine Baker and his advice to the nuns, directing them
to particular passages and discussing interpretations. Wolfe's study considers
how one group of nuns interacted with their texts and we are able from Father
Baker's directions to identify the volumes they had in their library, although
few of the books survive. No equivalent documents of spiritual direction have
yet been found for the seventeenth-century Bridgettines. Instead we need to
look for some of the indicators recommended by Hackel in the books themselves for evidence and to bring together supporting contextual evidence
regarding the practice of religious life and governance of the convent to
understand the importance of books to the Bridgettines at Lisbon and the ways
they were read.

[11] Hackel, *Reading Material*, see pp. 2–3.
[12] See the discussion on pp. 188–92 and 195–6 below.
[13] Several of these are collected at Syon Abbey, Devon in Box 28: they are described by James
Hogg in 'Brigittine Manuscripts Preserved at Syon Abbey', pp. 232–42.

Although the history of the book and libraries is a growing area of research, the study of collections owned by early modern English women is still at an early stage. In recent years more evidence has been uncovered which has allowed a few collections to be reconstructed, but each one has had to be approached differently because of the nature of the surviving evidence.[14] This is also true for conventual libraries. The survival of books (as for manuscripts) was dependent on many different factors, often outside the control of the nuns. Catastrophic events took a variety of forms: for the Bridgettines it was a serious fire in 1651 and the Lisbon earthquake in 1755 which destroyed much of the convent, followed by a decision at the beginning of the nineteenth century over the return to England which split the community and divided their remaining heritage. In spite of these events, 253 titles published between 1540 and 1700 survive from the Bridgettine library, although there is little surviving data relating to provenance or the dates when the books were added to the library and few contextual documents which would allow us to understand how the books were read.[15]

As in England, the brothers had a separate library in Lisbon. A reference in the annals suggests that the brothers' library may have been sold off after the death of the last Bridgettine brother (George Griffin) in 1695, by Abbess Ursula Sutton, in order to pay for alterations to the buildings. The author of the annals explains: 'The Abbess was then very zealous about the building of the berrandays [verandahs] and, it may be suposed thought that the lybery was of littell proffitt to the Cumunity.'[16] This comment raises questions about why the sisters did not incorporate the brothers' library into their own at that stage: why were the brothers' books of little value to the nuns? For instance, does this mean that many of the brothers' books were in Latin and therefore inaccessible to the sisters? If that was the case how do we explain the survival of the volumes in Latin in the nuns' library from the sixteenth century? It is worth considering how we might understand the concept of Latinity among English women religious here. The lack of formal schooling for English girls, whether Catholic or Protestant, at the beginning of the seventeenth century

---

[14] Among them, David McKitterick, 'Women and Their Books in Seventeenth-Century England: The Case of Elizabeth Puckering', *The Library*, 7th ser., 1 (2000), 359–80; Paul Morgan, 'Frances Wolfreston and "Hor Bouks": A Seventeenth-Century Book-Collector', *The Library*, 6th ser., 11 (1989), 197–219; Caroline Bowden, 'The Library of Mildred Cooke Cecil, Lady Burghley', *The Library*, 7th ser., 6 (2005), 3–29; Heidi Brayman Hackel, 'The Countess of Bridgewater's London Library', in Jennifer Andersen and Elizabeth Sauer (eds), *Books and their Readers in Early Modern England* (Philadelphia, 2002), pp. 138–59.

[15] Limitations of space make 1700 an arbitrary cut-off point.

[16] Exeter University Library, Syon Abbey MS (unnumbered and untitled), 'Annals' in Box 28, p. 86.

meant that any girl with a classical education would have received it at home. We have evidence that a number of girls had been taught Latin before they joined convents. Among them were four daughters of Sir Thomas Wiseman of Braddocks, Essex, who became nuns; two of them, Ann and Barbara, became abbesses in Lisbon.[17] Mary Gough, who became the first Abbess of the Poor Clares at Gravelines, was taught Latin by the chaplain when she lived with her grandmother. According to the annals, in 1594 she was sufficiently fluent to hold a conversation with the bishop of St Omer over dinner, 'of England, of what the Catholicks underwent & of her own happy call to Religion'.[18] For most entrants there is no evidence regarding the standard they reached before joining. However, once they entered, part of the training of the choir novices included the reading of liturgical texts in Latin, including correct pronunciation and fluency. The daily performance of the liturgy required familiarity with a wide range of Latin texts including biblical readings, motets and antiphons. Repetition built on a grounding of Latin teaching would over time produce a basic understanding of the meaning of the texts even if a nun could not undertake a full translation.[19] There is little evidence either from manuscripts or books that outside the liturgy there was much familiarity with Latin. Few of the documents relating to the administration of the convent written by nuns are in Latin, and books, both printed and manuscript, selected for study and reading either privately or communally were mostly in the vernacular.

Early Years at Lisbon

From the start the Bridgettines were anxious to obtain full legal status for the foundation in order to secure their future after so many years of uncertainty. However they faced strong objections locally from the archbishop of Lisbon which they only overcame by securing permission from Rome to be answerable directly to the papacy through the Nuncio. Despite this setback they became established, receiving an annual grant from Philip II of Spain which

---

[17] Adam Hamilton (ed.), *The Chronicle of the English Augustinian Canonesses regular of the Lateran, at St. Monica's in Louvain: 1548 to 1644* (Edinburgh, 1904–6), vol. 1, pp. 47–8.
[18] St Clare's Abbey, Darlington, MS 'Fragment Annals', fol. 6.
[19] The discussion in Jane Stevenson's chapter, 'Women Catholics and Latin Culture', in Ronald Corthell *et al.* (eds), *Catholic Culture in Early Modern England* (Notre Dame, IN, 2007), pp. 52–72, I believe, exaggerates the level of Latin expertise among English women religious in the seventeenth century. Although undoubtedly there were some English nuns who could translate from Latin and were able (like Mary Gough) to conduct conversations in Latin, for the majority the limit was understanding texts associated with the liturgy.

was continued by his son, and a substantial gift of property from Isabel de Azavedo where they built their convent. They were determined to set standards in their religious life and follow the rules even while they were building. They placed emphasis on the monastic office and on reading but, as we have seen, they had arrived in Lisbon with few of the books they needed. A priority was a new version of the rules which would provide a framework for daily life and the liturgy. In 1607 the convent agreed the rules together with the Bridgettine 'Additions': several contemporary translated versions of the rules and associated commentaries were made which allow us to understand how the Bridgettines practised their religion.[20] To some extent, the rules reiterated what had happened in England, but they also added changes required by the Council of Trent, such as enclosure for women and the acceptance of lay sisters. In addition the religious authorities required the use of the Roman rite by the nuns for divine office as practised in the diocese of Lisbon. The rules regarding books remained much as they had been in England: appointing a librarian to look after the books belonging to the common library, with the Chantress responsible for books associated with the liturgy.

A measure of the importance of books to the Bridgettines can be seen by their reception of two dedications before 1620. The first was the dedication in 1609 to the Abbess (Elizabeth Preston) by the Franciscan, William Fitch, known in religion as Benet of Canfield, of *The rule of perfection.* Fitch had two Wiseman cousins who were senior members of the convent. If it were the only dedication we might take it as a sign of family feeling, but there is a second. This was the dedication of Thomas Everard's 1618 translation of Pinelli's *Mirrour of religious perfection* to: 'Barbara Wiseman Abbess and to the rest of the religious sisters of that holy house and family'. Its purpose is explained in the preface:

> In this Religious mirrour, you may behould rare Vertues and accordingly draw in your selves the forme of highest Perfection ... Here you will find whatsoever may help to the spirituall advancement of your soules: and by reading attentively reape condigne fruites of your devout labours.[21]

---

[20] A later manuscript copy of this text in English is published in James Hogg (ed.), *A Book of Uses of Syon Abbey*, Analecta Cartusiana 35:13 (Salzburg, 1991): its early date can be verified from internal signature evidence to 1607 (p. 26). See also Hogg (ed.), *Brigittine Legislation for Syon Abbey Lisbon*, Analecta Cartusiana 35:14 (Salzburg, 1991); and Roger Ellis, *Syon Abbey: The Spirituality of the English Bridgettines*, Analecta Cartusiana 68 (Salzburg, 1984), pp. 124–5.
[21] Lucas Pinelli, *The Mirrour of Religious Perfection* (1618), p. 3v.

Four copies of the book remain in the Syon library and it can also be found in the Sepulchrine library from Liège.[22]

It is important in this context when placing such emphasis on Bridgettine observance and reputation to consider the veracity of the vitriolic attack made by Thomas Robinson in *The Anatomy of the English Nunnery* in 1622. According to Robinson, lascivious books were read by the brothers and sisters who spent time together behaving inappropriately, and the convent fell far short of fulfilling the aims of the founders.[23] If Robinson is to be believed, it would be impossible to consider Syon Abbey as a well managed community, leading an orderly life. However there are several reasons to doubt Robinson's version of events. Although it was not published at the time, a lengthy response was drawn up, probably by the Confessor General Father Seth Foster, citing evidence that Robinson was an opportunist, inconsistent in his religious beliefs and generally unreliable.[24] Secondly, some of Robinson's claims were far-fetched: any flagrant breaches of the rules would have been picked up in official visitations by the bishop or his representatives. If rules were ignored or broken, it is hard to see how the convent could have earned its good reputation. Thirdly, the timing of the publication coincides with a burst of extremist Protestant polemic generated partly by concerns regarding the relaxation of laws against Catholics in England during the negotiations with Spain for the marriage of Prince Charles. Robinson used a tone and language in the pamphlet which can be seen in similar attacks on Catholics such as Gee's 1624 *Foot out of the Snare*.[25] Coming from the strand of polemic portraying Catholic priests or regulars as sexually predatory because of celibacy, Robinson's pamphlet fed extremist Protestant notions regarding the way religious life was lived within the enclosure, particularly since Syon was a double house with monks as well as nuns.[26] In opposition to Robinson's claims, as we have suggested, the convent appears to have been well regarded by outsiders, regularly attracting new members.

This view of sound management is supported by an illustrated petition

---

[22] I am grateful to Sister Mary Magdalene for sharing her library catalogue of the books from Liège with me.

[23] Thomas Robinson, *The Anatomy of the English Nunnery at Lisbon in Portugal* (London, 1622), reprinted in 1623, 1630, 1637 and 1662.

[24] This response has now been published as: '*Answer to an attack on the nuns of Sion contained in a book entitled "The Anatomy of the English Nunnery at Lisbon"*, by Thomas Robinson ...', in James Hogg (ed.), Analecta Cartusiana 244 (Salzburg, 2006), pp. 85–121.

[25] I am grateful to Professor Michael Questier for his comments on similar inflammatory anti-Catholic pamphlets in the 1620s.

[26] This is discussed in Frances Dolan, *Whores of Babylon: Catholicism, Gender, and Seventeenth-Century Print Culture* (Ithaca, NY, 1999), pp. 85–94.

almost contemporary with the Robinson pamphlet. When the Bridgettines learned of the negotiations of a possible marriage for Charles, Prince of Wales in 1622–3, they prepared a petition signed by the Abbess to be sent to the future Princess of Wales in Madrid. It was to be given to Philip III when the nuns considered there was a real possibility they could return to England. It has a presentation binding, was copiously illustrated and written in an elegant italic hand using language that shows how well they understood the rhetoric of supplication and how to maximise their chances of success.

> ... grant us permission, Most Clement Princess, to hear us say ... that we know, feel and have experienced for more than seventy years the full hardships of this our exile; of which our many afflictions, sorrows, and tears are true witnesses ... set us free, to put an end to our exile and lead us back to happy and greatly desired rest in our former home, Syon ... our case is unique, since not only were we the first exiles for our Holy Catholic Faith, but also the only ones, of all the orders and convents of English nuns, who have continued and persevered in this very hard exile from its first inception until now.[27]

The tone was humble, emphasising their poverty as a result of exile but with an underlying sense of pride in the fact that they were the only religious to have survived as a community. The petition remained in Bridgettine hands because the negotiations in Madrid broke down, but it serves as a reminder of the willingness of the Lisbon convent to engage with the political world outside at the highest level to protect and further their interests. The preparation of such an elaborate offering to a royal princess suggests that the Bridgettine nuns were politically aware and had sufficient resources to commission this lavish but well-chosen gift. Although their hopes were misplaced and the marriage negotiations failed, they were not alone: other English Catholics made similar judgements. Even though Charles married a Catholic princess, she was French: there would be no homecoming for the Bridgettines.

Their contacts with other English institutions in the Iberian peninsula brought the nuns a collection of twelve portraits of kings and queens of England via connections with the English College in Seville. This was a significant donation, emphasising their royal past. Like the presentation manuscript it was carefully chosen and would not have been made to a badly managed institution.[28]

---

27 De Hamel, *Syon Abbey*, p. 25.
28 This collection has been the subject of some research and currently forms part of a larger research project by Dr Elizabeth Perry on the artistic patronage of the Bridgettines in exile. I am

Bridgettine success in maintaining standards in religious life and earning a reputation for good governance is reflected in the number of professions that took place of women from prominent English families. Even during the peripatetic years, candidates from well known families, such as Elizabeth Vaux, daughter of the third Lord Vaux, who professed at Rouen, had sought them out. Between 1600 and 1630 at least twenty-five women joined the convent.[29] Among them were Ann and Lucy (professed 1614), daughters of Sir Anthony Browne, second Viscount Montague. They also attracted a few members from respected Portuguese families, including Bridget de Mendanha who professed in 1602. These associations brought patronage and connections which allowed the convent to survive in the long term. In spite of the challenges of operating in exile the Bridgettines continued to attract English women as recruits during the seventeenth century, although fewer brothers joined than was allowed for in the rules: around twenty-seven male names before 1695.[30]

Reading Spaces and Reading Practices

In Lisbon, as in all the English convents founded in the seventeenth century, a diversity of reading practices took place daily: silently and out loud, using printed books and manuscripts, in communal spaces such as the refectory and chapter house and privately in cells. In the church, the liturgy was either spoken or chanted, with the listener involved as an active participant with the reader or singer. Roger Ellis argues that for the Bridgettines, public worship in the chapel and private study were part of a dialogue which brought together different facets of the religious life, with reading at the centre of it. While the sisters were reading or following the office, they were also to look within themselves and see God in their souls.[31] The performance of divine office was intended to edify and instruct: it required attentive listeners as well as singers and readers, 'so that the voice of the Divine praise, may, as it were, continually tend to the love of God and men'.[32] As I have suggested, familiarity brought a certain level of understanding of Latin texts.

---

indebted to Dr Perry for sharing her preliminary thoughts. See Michael Williams, 'Paintings of Early British Kings and Queens at Syon Abbey, Lisbon', *Birgittiana*, 1 (1996), 123–34.

[29] This is a provisional total based on current research: the final number is undoubtedly higher.

[30] Full details of membership for the seventeenth century are difficult to verify, although the names and dates of death of most members have survived in the manuscripts.

[31] Ellis, *Syon Abbey*, pp. 110–11.

[32] Detailed regulations for daily life in Lisbon in the seventeenth century appear in two main published sources: first, Hogg (ed.), *A Book of Uses of Syon Abbey* (Salzburg, 1991); and

The complexity of arrangements for the performance of the office with its seasonal variations required detailed instructions for the Chantress to manage the books in the chapel and train readers and singers. In order to follow and participate in the liturgy effectively, it was essential for the choir nuns to be able to read and sing Latin as well as learn by heart. The Chantress (a senior figure in the convent hierarchy) ensured that there were sufficient books and that the voices were balanced: she helped the Abbess intone the antiphons, appointed readers and kept a record of the members for the purpose of observing anniversaries. The books were to be carefully handled, and all readings and singing should be well rehearsed in order to be reverent. According to the rules, the Chantress should report to the Chapter Meeting any deficiencies in the performance of the liturgy, whether singing or reading. The singing was to be beautiful but there was to be nothing flamboyant about it: it was for the glory of God rather than to display individual talents. Although books and learning were central to Bridgettine religious life, it was recognised in the rule that some sisters (probably lay sisters) might be 'unlettered' and would need to recite parts of the office from memory and participate by listening rather than reading.[33]

Communal readings also took place in the refectory at noon and in the evening; texts were to be in the vernacular so that all should understand. Once grace had been said:

> the reader without delaie shall beginne to reade distinctlie and plainelie ... eaverie daie through the yeare there shall bee had the reading of the historie or lives of the saintes or of some other spirituall matter whatsoever ... There shall be read also the Rules of Saint Augustine and the Constitutions of Saint Brigitt and also this Book of Additions.[34]

In this way prescriptive reading reinforced conventual ideals through repetition in a communal space in order to secure acceptance of the core values of Bridgettine religious life and to reinforce the collective memory of the community. Chapter Meetings provided further occasions when a reader would read out the appointed part of the rules.

Among the books for these public readings at Lisbon were two works: the

---

second, Hogg (ed.), *Brigittine Legislation for Syon Abbey Lisbon* (Salzburg, 1991). The quotation is from the former, p. 48.

[33] Extensive instructions for the performance of divine office were given in the Lisbon Additions to the constitutions, in Hogg (ed.), *Brigittine Legislation for Syon Abbey Lisbon*, pp. 99–145; and the office of Chantress was defined in the same work on pp. 152–4.

[34] Hogg (ed.), *Brigittine Legislation for Syon Abbey Lisbon*, p. 165.

first, *The Holy Court, Fourth Tome*, published in 1638, was inscribed specifi-
cally, 'Sister Mary Smith Book given for the reading stand in the Refectory
Sion' (Figure 6.1). Originally written in French by the Jesuit Nicholas
Caussin it was translated by Sir Thomas Hawkins. It is a handsome volume
bound in vellum containing texts of lengths very suitable for public reading.
We can identify approximately the date of its arrival in the library from
supporting membership data: Mary Smith professed in 1643, later becoming
Abbess. The second was a two-volume manuscript work of more than 1,100
pages: 'English Saintes of Kinges & Bishopps in the primitive times of the
Catholique Church ...' (Figure 6.2). It was translated by two Bridgettine
monks and copied for use in Lisbon by Brother Henry Mease and completed
in 1662. Among the female exemplary lives, it included several queens whose
portraits were part of the series sent from Seville: among them St Margaret of
Scotland (d. 1093) and St Ediltrudis, otherwise known as Etheldreda (d.
679).[35]

Sisters who were confined to their beds in the infirmary and thus unable to
participate in the daily office or come to the refectory to hear readings, could
read to themselves. There was a special dispensation for those unable for any
reason to read: they could listen to a sister reading to them in a quiet voice.[36]
Outside the infirmary, private reading also took place in the cells where the
sisters were permitted to have a candle and read silently.[37]

Bridgettine rules refer to a library with a register of books to be cared for by
a librarian appointed by the Abbess, although no list has survived. It was
possible with the permission of the Abbess for a book to be taken out of the
library for private reading.[38] In 1656 Father Charles Dimock made a list of
thirteen works headed 'Bookes of my own handwriting lent to the sisters'.
They included 'The life of St Thomas of Canterburie' to Sister Catherine
Knightlie (professed 1612, died 1664) and to Sister Marie Carnabie
(professed 1634, died 1669) 'The Soliloquies of Thomas à Kempis with
mysteries of the Christian faith of Titleman' and 'A little Inglish Catechisme'

---

[35] N. Caussin, *The holy court fourth tome* (Rouen, 1638). Exeter University Library, Syon
Abbey unnumbered MS: English Saintes of Kinges & Bishopps in the primitive times of the
Catholique Church when our Countrie of England was governed by Heptarchie of seaven
Kinges translated out of Surius Carthusianus his eight tomes of the lifes of Saintes by revrd
Father Brother Bibianus alias John Bibian moncke of the holy order of St Birgitt our Holy
Mother. Revived by the helpe & industrie of P Frey Estevan of the conception Moncke of the
same order on the 41 year of his profession being 69 yeares of age, borne in 1593 the yeare
before this monasterie removed to Lisbon 1594.

[36] Hogg (ed.), *Book of Uses*, p. 87.

[37] *Ibid.*, p. 29.

[38] *Ibid.*, p. 88.

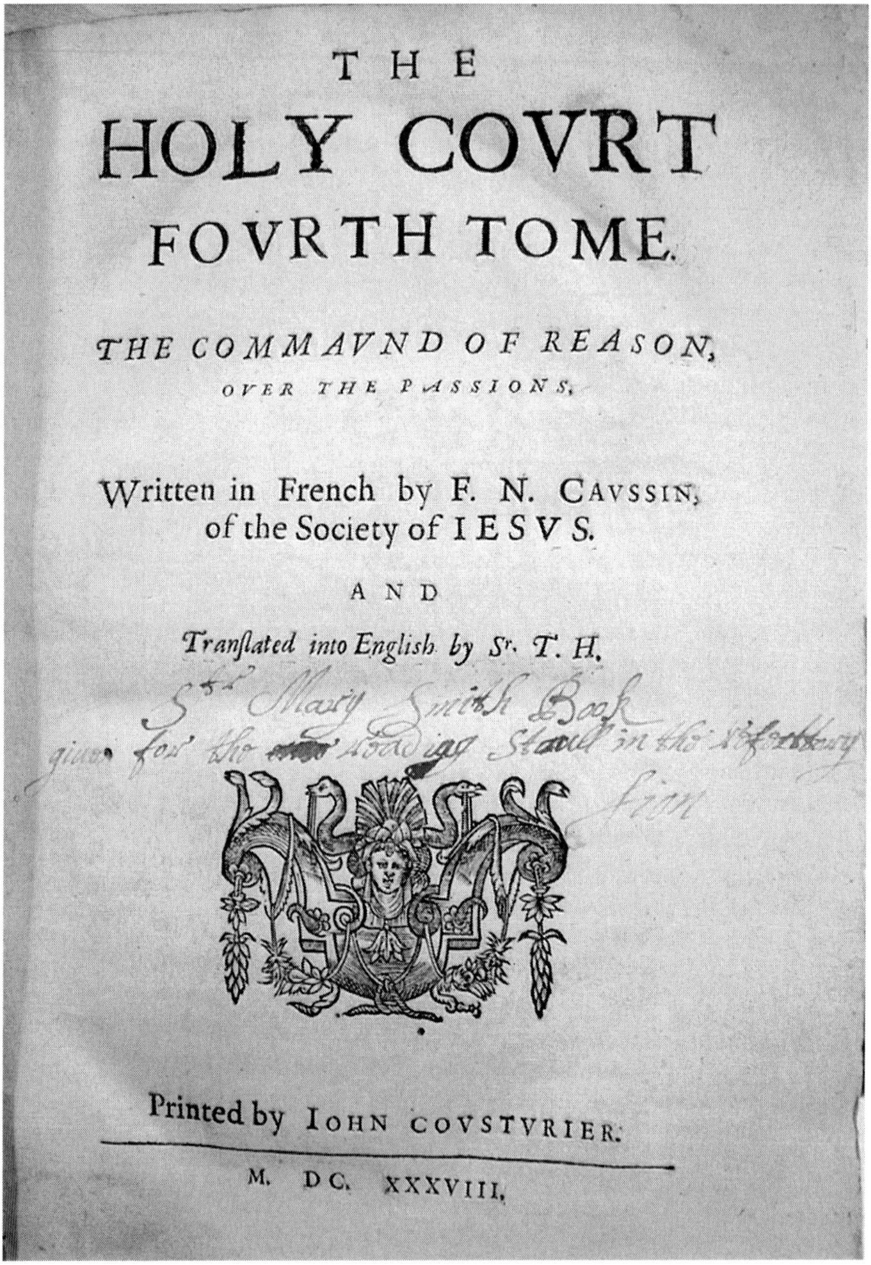

T H E
HOLY COVRT
FOVRTH TOME.

THE COMMAVND OF REASON,

OVER THE PASSIONS,

Written in French by F. N. CAVSSIN,
of the Society of I E S V S.

A N D

Tranſlated into English by Sr. T. H.

Printed by IOHN COVSTVRIER.

M. DC. XXXVIII.

Figure 6.1: N. Caussin, *The holy court fourth tome* (Rouen, 1638). Exeter University Library shelfmark Syon Abbey 1638/CAU/X. By permission of the Abbess of Syon Abbey, South Brent, Devon.

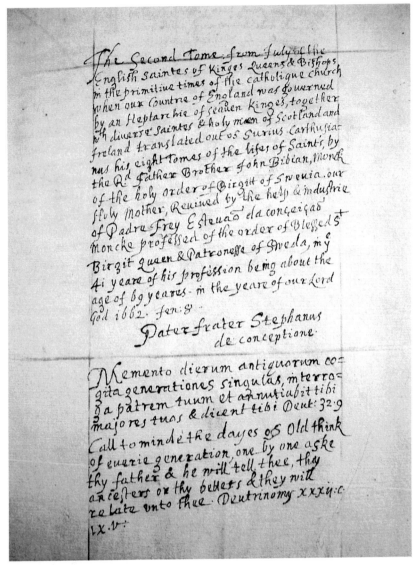

Figure 6.2: Exeter University Library, Syon Abbey unnumbered MS: 'English Saintes of Kinges & Bishopps in the primitive times of the Catholique Church when our Countrie of England was governed by Heptarchie of seaven Kinges translated out of Surius Carthusianus his eight tomes of the lifes of Saintes by revrd Father Brother Bibianus alias John Bibian moncke of the holy order of St Birgitt our Holy Mother. Revived by the helpe & industrie of P Frey Estevan of the conception Moncke of the same order on the 41 year of his profession being 69 yeares of age, borne in 1593 the yeare before this monasterie removed to Lisbon 1594', title page of vol. 2. By permission of the Abbess of Syon Abbey, South Brent, Devon.

to Sister Dorothie.[39] Although some of these manuscripts have not survived, the existence of the list demonstrates not only the activities of the Bridgettine brothers but also, more generally, the importance of manuscript works in conventual libraries in the seventeenth century.

The Context: The New English Convents and Their Books

By 1607 when the new rules for the convent at Lisbon were drawn up, the Bridgettines were no longer the only foundation open specifically for English women. The first new convent was founded by Lady Mary Percy in Brussels in 1598 as a Benedictine house, and before 1630 a further eight convents had been opened professing a total of around 345 members. The demand for places continued, and by 1680 twenty-one enclosed convents for English women had been opened in Flanders and France, and by the end of the century well over 2,550 women (virtually all English) had been professed.[40] In addition, Mary Ward's Institute attracted women who wished to join a congregation where the emphasis was on teaching and the active apostolate: in spite of its suppression in 1631 women continued to join the sisters, albeit living ostensibly as lay women, and the Institute opened a number of schools for girls in Europe.

A study of the constitutions governing these convents indicates the importance of books and reading to the practice of religious life in all the English foundations; and a number of the convents have left evidence of substantial libraries in spite of some catastrophic events associated mainly with the French Revolution. For instance, although very few books remain from the Benedictine convent at Cambrai, a catalogue in manuscript from the seventeenth and eighteenth centuries lists over 1,000 items.[41] The Canonesses of the Holy Sepulchre (Sepulchrines) from Liège brought to England a library which still contains 263 books published before 1699. The English Carmelites from Antwerp and Hoogstraete have a collection of 1,300 books from the seventeenth and eighteenth centuries.[42] Three hundred and forty-four books published in the seventeenth century survive in York from the collections of

---

[39] The list is recorded in the calendar of the manuscripts in Box 28 at Syon Abbey, Devon; see also Hogg (ed.), 'Brigittine Manuscripts ...', p. 238. 'The soliloquies of Thomas à Kempis ...' has survived: Box 28 No. 3. Dimock also translated the 1607 version of the 'Rules and Syon Additions' for the use of the nuns; see Hogg (ed.) *Book of Uses*, p. 194.

[40] These statistics are derived from the author's lists of the members of all the English enclosed convents; they do not include members of any of the houses of the Mary Ward Institute.

[41] Bibliothèque Municipale de Cambrai, France: Catalogue of the books of the English Benedictine nuns' library, MS 901, 519 fols.

[42] http://www.loc.gov/rr/main/religion/carmelit.html (accessed 10 September 2007).

the Mary Ward sisters in spite of their troubled history in the period – an indication of the importance of reading in their daily lives and their work in schools.[43] It is important to recognise that we have no hard evidence regarding the provenance of the books in the libraries and we cannot ascertain when they entered the collections. However the fact that so many have survived argues that practice followed prescription regarding books and reading in the English convents.

The printed works in the conventual book collections from the period can be divided into six broad categories: liturgical works mainly for use in the chapel; scripture and exegesis; devotional and instructional literature including meditations; exemplary lives and martyrologies; church history; and finally a miscellaneous section including (at least for the Bridgettines) medical texts, a herbal and secular history.

As one would expect, most of the authors of the books in conventual libraries in this period were male, but a few of the English nuns themselves contributed in different ways to printed books for others to read and study as well as manuscript compilations. For instance, the writings of Gertrude More, a Benedictine from Cambrai, were published incorporated into the writings of her confessor Augustine Baker. She explained attitudes towards reading at Cambrai in *The holy practises of a devine lover*, published in 1657:

> What Bookes, or Parts or Parcells of Bookes relish with our Spirits, breed discreet fervour and Devotion in us, those wee are to make use of and be conversant in; such as breed Feare, Scruples, Troubles, Confusion, and disquiet of Mind &c they are not for our purpose, neither do they concern us.

Twenty authors and books were listed in order to help, comfort and increase the devotions of contemplative spirits. Among those particularly recommended were St Catherine of Siena, St John of the Cross, the revelations of Saint Bridget and the writings of St Teresa.[44] Two copies of Gertrude More's 1658 text, *The spiritual exercises*, are found in the Bridgettine library along with lives of most of the role models listed by Baker. The Franciscan Conceptionist nuns in Paris specified in their constitutions that the Mistress of the Quire should be very skilful in reading Latin and in Gregorian chant: part

---

43 I am grateful to the late Sister Gregory Kirkus, CJ, at the Bar Convent, York, for this data.
44 Gertrude More, *The holy practices of a devine lover or The sainctly ideots devotions* (Paris, 1657), pp. 32, 34–7. For a discussion of the problems over authorship, see for example Ben Wekking, *Augustine Baker OSB: The Life and Death of Dame Gertrude More Edited from all the Known Manuscripts*, Analecta Cartusiana 119:19 (Salzburg, 2002), introduction, pp. xiv–xv.

of her work was to teach sisters how to read in the choir and practise with them.[45] As well as reading printed books, members of the English convents created manuscript copies both of whole texts and compilations for personal use: in so doing they were creating new editions of texts for private reading as well as adding to the stock of books in the convent.[46]

The existence of English convents in exile together with expatriate English Catholics created a new and expanding market in the seventeenth century for religious texts in the vernacular, in addition to the continuing demand in England: it was part of reaching the widest possible audience to increase sales. Devotional texts might appeal to laity as well as religious, men as well as women, and perhaps cross the religious divide and appeal to Protestants.[47] Women religious were thus able to take advantage of a larger number of texts available for purchase for those who did not know Latin. In some cases they provided translations themselves; for instance Mary Percy was responsible with Anthony Hoskins for *An abridgement of Christian perfection*, translated from a French version first published in 1612 and dedicated to 'Religious men and women of our nation'.[48]

The habit of writing names in the books has raised questions for some historians with regard to the ownership of property and the application of the monastic rule of poverty. It seems to have been widely recognised in the English convents that a book could remain in the hands of one sister for a long period of time with the permission of the Abbess and could be passed on to another sister at her death. It should perhaps be seen more as guardianship of a precious object rather than ownership. Sometimes the permission of the Abbess is formally stated; at other times it is implied. Two seventeenth-century Carmelite volumes demonstrate the variation: the first, Henry More's *Life and doctrine of our Savior Jesus Christ* of 1656, is inscribed 'Teresa Francisca de Jesu' and 'Maria Teresia de Jesu 1743 aetatis 65'; whereas Lanspergius's *Epistle or Exhortation of Jesus Christ* of 1610 is inscribed 'Sister Anastasia's Booke with leave' and Sis^r Winny with leave'.[49] The practice of writing names became more widespread in the eighteenth century.

---

[45] J. Gillow and R. Trappes-Lomax (eds), *The Diary of the Blue Nuns ... 1658–1810*, CRS 8 (London, 1910), pp. 295 and 302.

[46] Many of these survive in Archives Départementales du Nord, Lille, France, Séries H, Fonds Benedictins et Cisterciens.

[47] For discussion of Catholic publishing in this period see Walsham, ' "Domme Preachers" ', esp. pp. 81–8, 93–100 and 108–10.

[48] *Breve compendio intorno alla perfezione cristiana* (An Abridgement of Christian Perfection) ([St Omer] [English College Press], 1612 and 1625).

[49] Both these volumes are now at the Huntington Library, California, having been purchased from the Carmelite convent in Darlington.

Books at Lisbon

The collection of Bridgettine books at Exeter University Library comprises the library of printed rare books (253 volumes before 1700) as it existed at the convent at South Brent in 1990, together with twelve manuscript volumes mainly from the pre-dissolution period. They were handed over to the University for safe-keeping and to make them available for study.[50] No conventual catalogue for the books survives from the seventeenth century, leaving many questions unanswered regarding provenance and dates of acquisition. We do not know the size of the library at Lisbon which was damaged both by the fire of 1651 and the earthquake of 1755.[51] The proportion of books in Latin in the collection declined markedly over the seventeenth century. Fifty-four of the titles published before 1650 are in Latin; nearly half of these were printed before the arrival in Lisbon in 1594. Only fifteen titles in Latin were published between 1650 and 1700; of these ten are associated with the liturgy. There are some major gaps in the collection, such as the absence of bibles and paucity of liturgical works, particularly from the first half of the seventeenth century. No evidence has yet been found explaining what happened to them, although it is thought probable that they were brought back to England by the first group of returners in the nineteenth century and may have been dispersed at that stage.[52] Some copies of the printed office for Holy Week and a few psalters are still in the collection. However from surviving books we can gain significant insights into Bridgettine reading practices in the first century at Lisbon.

Some volumes bear no marks of ownership or readership and few other signs of use. Others have multiple signatures, annotations and signs of heavy wear and mending, indicating a book with considerable use over the centuries. It is worth considering reasons why nuns may have inscribed their names in particular books. It may be to demonstrate the importance of that text in the spiritual life of an individual, or to show they identified strongly with the views expressed by the author. One of the two Spanish copies of *Oficio de la semana santa* (1648), from the Plantin press in Antwerp, has been much used. A small pocket-sized book with red and black printing, it was inscribed 'Cicely Liddell', a choir nun who professed in 1729. The clasps are missing

---

50 The manuscripts have been described by James Hogg in 'Brigittine Manuscripts Preserved at Syon Abbey', pp. 228–42. See further the Appendix.

51 The presence of three seventeenth-century books from Lisbon in the Benedictine convent library from Brussels, located by the author (now at Douai Abbey), is an indication that books were dispersed at some stage either by gift or sale, but there is no indication of when it happened.

52 I am grateful to Abbess Anna Maria, Syon Abbey, for her comments.

and the spine is repaired with fabric. Another copy of this book (now with the books from the Benedictine convent in Brussels) can be identified as a Bridgettine book from the name in the flyleaf: Barbara More (professed at Lisbon 1696). This copy, in Latin, has been heavily annotated for singing and much mended.[53] This raises the interesting question of how many other books migrated between the convents at different times. It would be surprising if Sister Mary Teresa Clare Isabella Butt who inscribed her name and the date 'Feb 27 1791' was the first nun to use *The rule of the holy virgin S Clare* (1621). Inscriptions in the second edition of *The holy court* (1638) link the lay donor (Ursula Fermor) who gave the book to the nuns in 1664 with two Bridgettines: Sister Mary Harnage (professed 1662) who passed on the work to Sister Placida Huddleston (professed 1720). Other seventeenth-century Bridgettine names are found in manuscript texts: for instance Jane Carr (professed 1634) and Mary Carr who professed in 1653 both signed their names on the title page of the manuscript containing 'Life of the Spirit and How to obtaine the Gift of Prayer and Union with God', a translation made specially for the Bridgettines and completed around 1655.[54]

Several other volumes bear signs of having been mended early in their lives. For instance, the leather-bound manuscript miscellany dated 1655 containing among other things 'The Life of the Spirit' and 'How to obtaine the Gift of Prayer', translated by 'N N', has a section of leather inserted near the spine with large even, but rather inexpert, stitches, suggesting an untrained conventual hand. The binding of Gerard's *Herball* has been patched with brown fabric in a number of places. The binding of the 1624 Plantin *Psalter*, a work which would have received much use, has been mended on the spine and is missing its leather tying straps.

In conventual books, marginalia tends to take the form of additional material inserted either in the form of prayers or changes to liturgical practice rather than commentary on the adjacent text. Forty-two pages of additional material in manuscript are to be found at the end of Bonilla's *A short treatise of the quiet of the soul* ... of 1658; at the other extreme is the brief comment on the 1608 copy of *The History of Our Blessed Lady of Loretto*, which simply says 'Sion to be rade on saterdays'. Several of the translations and transcriptions made by brothers at Lisbon for the nuns in the seventeenth century contain lengthy introductory contextual material, for instance explaining the purpose of the manuscript.[55]

---

[53] The three works now at Douai Abbey are *Officium hebdomade sanctae* (1644), *Oficio de la semana sancta* (1648) and Serenus Cressy's *The church history of Brittany* (1668).

[54] Exeter University Library, Syon Abbey MS, Box 28, No. 7.

[55] From the 'Commentary on the exhibition of the Library of Syon Abbey in the Special

One striking contrast between the nuns' library from the pre-Reformation period and the seventeenth-century books at Lisbon is the relative absence of donations and presentation volumes. Although there were a number of large printed books at Lisbon, they were less expensively produced than the manuscript donations to Syon in England. The long volumes in manuscript at Lisbon were handsomely rather than elaborately bound, they have no illuminations and few illustrations. The books in Lisbon were books for a working library, varying in size from small pocket books to large folios, such as Cressy's *Church-history of Brittany* and Ribadeneira's *Lives of saints*, which needed to be placed on a stand for communal readings.[56]

The books at Lisbon came from the most significant continental presses publishing in English, including Antwerp, St Omer, Rouen, Douai and Paris. A few Catholic works in English were printed in England after Elizabeth's accession and in the first half of the seventeenth century, but the penalties for operating a Catholic press were severe and enforced. Some of these English editions found their way to Lisbon. Robert Southwell's *An epistle of comfort*, probably from 1587, was one such work. It bore a false imprint, Paris. The translation of Richeome's *Holy pictures of the mysticall figures of the most holy sacrifice and sacrament of the Eucharist* of 1619 is thought to have been printed at the Birchley Hall Press in Lancashire. Only one year later (1620), the second edition of the translation of Augustine's *Citie of God* was printed in London. An indication of the effects of the religious views of the later Stuarts on Catholic printing can be seen in the increase of identifiably Catholic texts printed in England after 1670, with a further steep rise during the reign of James II (1685–8). Both the *Dayly exercise of the devout Christian* and an English version of *De imitatione Christi* by Thomas Kempis were printed in London in 1673, followed in 1675 by *The holy life of Gregory Lopez, a Spanish hermit* and *The second part of the works of St Theresa*, all of which are in the collection.

The earliest ten volumes in the Bridgettine library date from the period before the suppression of the convent in 1539: nine of these are in Latin, including four copies of the complete works of St Jerome. Forty-two volumes

Collections Reading Room', Exeter University Library, 8–9 April 2002; O. Torsellino, *The history of our B. Lady of Loreto* ([St Omer] [English College Press], 1608); see, for example, Exeter University Library, Syon Abbey MS (unnumbered), 'English Saintes, Kinges & Bishopps', translated by John Bibian and transcribed by Henry Mease, and MS Box 28, No. 9, 'The life of the just in the practice of a lively faith'.
56 Serenus Cressy, *The Church-history of Brittany: from the beginning of Christianity to the Norman Conquest* ([Rouen], 1668); Pedro de Ribadeneira, *The lives of saints ...* (S Omers, Joachim Cartier, 1669).

(of which twelve are in English) were published before the death of Elizabeth I in 1603. John Roberts has observed that the majority of the devotional works in English in this period were intended for the laity, both those living in England and refugees on the continent. Many lay Catholics (unlike the Bridgettines) would not have had permanent regular access to priests for guidance, making the publication of works of spiritual guidance of great importance.[57] One of the books was a copy of *Dyvers holy instrucyons and teachyngs* (1541) by Richard Whitford, one of the brothers from Syon, printed in London. The Bridgettines owned two volumes by the Jesuit martyr Robert Southwell (1565–1591). One of them, *Marie Magdalen's funeral teares*, a volume of lyric poetry based around Mary Magdalene's grief on Christ's death, was a popular work among Catholics, with two editions from secret presses as well as twenty-four others. The collection includes two versions in translation of the Spanish Dominican preacher Luis de Granada's *Of prayer and meditation* (1584), published in Rouen.[58] Granada was an author whose works were in the libraries of several other English convents including the Benedictines at Dunkirk and the Augustinians in Paris.[59]

As we have seen, with the new rules drawn up at Lisbon the nuns were required to change the daily office they used to the Roman rite as used in the diocese of Lisbon rather than the Bridgettine office they had used formerly. This necessitated the purchase of new books. Among the few liturgical works held at Exeter is *Officium hebdomadae sanctae completum* (the office for Holy Week) of 1596. Another edition from 1578 bears two eighteenth-century signatures, an indication of how long books could be in use. Changes could sometimes be accommodated by manuscript additions in the margins or on blank pages. At the end of the seventeenth century the nuns appear to have commissioned the printing of liturgical works for their own use. In 1690 they bought from the Lisbon printer of religious texts, Joannis Galraō, forty-two copies of *Officia Propria sanctorum et aliarum festivitatum ... recitata a Monialibus Anglicanis Civitatis Ulyssiponensis*.[60] The nuns appear to have bought them with the long term in mind, only binding copies when they were needed, since twenty-one remain unbound. At about the same period they

---

[57] See, for example, John R. Roberts (ed.), *A Critical Anthology of English Recusant Devotional Prose 1558–1603*, Duquesne Studies Philological Series 7 (Pittsburgh, 1966), p. 26.

[58] Granada's influence is discussed in *ibid.*, pp. 4–5, 12–15, 42–3.

[59] Both these libraries are held at Downside Abbey. I am grateful to Father Boniface Hill for his assistance in identifying seventeenth-century volumes.

[60] [... recited by the English nuns of the city of Lisbon] Joannis Galram (fl. 1670–9?) published mainly religious works in Portuguese, Spanish and Latin. This work for the Bridgettines does not appear on the main list of ninety-six known works on http://opac.porbase.org/#focus search on 'Galrao' (accessed 13 September 2007).

bought at least nine copies of the Office of the Blessed Virgin Mary, of which three remain unbound.

The languages represented in the books printed before 1700 are mainly English with a substantial minority in Latin and other languages including Spanish (nineteen titles). Among them were Puente's (1665) life of the Spanish visionary, ... *la venerable virgen Dona Marina de Escobar* (1554–1633), who founded the Spanish Bridgettine convent in Valladolid, and several liturgical works based on the Latin missal, for instance *Oficio de la semana santa* published by the Plantin press in Antwerp in 1679.[61] The nuns also owned a few books in Portuguese.

A number of exemplary lives, both male and female, appear in the collection. Some of them were appropriate for reading communally at meal times, others more suitable for private reading and meditation. Among the lives of women are three copies of the 1609 edition of the life of St Catherine of Siena (1347–1380); the life and writings of St Bridget (c.1303–1373), foundress of the Bridgettines; St Teresa of Avila, foundress of the reformed Carmelites (1515–1582); St Winifred (d. 660), patroness of Wales, whose well drew pilgrims to Holywell, Flintshire; St Elizabeth (1207–1231), daughter of the King of Hungary, described as a chaste wife, a holy widow and a glorious saint; and the life of St Catherine of Bologna, foundress of the Poor Clares (1413–1463), which was published with the rule of St Clare in 1621. The lives of St Catherine of Siena and St Teresa of Avila feature among the books owned by most of the English convents in the seventeenth century.[62]

The library at Lisbon contained a number of works that confessors and spiritual directors had originally prepared for their own communities and which were subsequently published and appear in a number of conventual libraries. For instance, John Fenn who translated *The life of ... St Catherine of Siena* (1609) described himself as confessor to the Augustinian canonesses founded at Louvain in the year of publication. Three copies of Miles Pinkney's work, *Sweet thoughtes of Jesus and Marie or meditations for all the feastes*, prepared for the nuns in his care at the Augustinian convent in Paris,

---

61 Andres Pinto Ramirez, *Vida maravillosa de la venerable virgen Dona Marina de Escobar* (Madrid, 1673).
62 *The life of the blessed virgin, Sainct Catherine of Siena* ..., trans. John Fen (Douai, 1609); *Revelationes caelestis seraphicae matris S Birgittae* (Monachii [Munich], 1680) and *The most devout prayers of St Brigitte* ... (Antwerp, 1686); *The lyf of the Mother Teresa* ..., trans. W. M. (Antwerp, 1611); *Obras de la s. madre Teresa de Jesus* ... (Lisboa, 1654); *The second part of the works of St Teresa of Jesus* ([London?], 1675); *The admirable life of Saint Winefride, virgin, martyr, abbesse* ..., trans. J. F. ([St Omer], 1635); *The history of S Elizabeth ... distributed into iii bookes by H.A.* ([Rouen], 1632); *The rule of the holy virgin S Clare togeather with the admirable life of S Catharine of Bologna* ([St Omer], 1621).

appear in Lisbon: one with an inscription indicating its use more than a hundred years later in 1786. The presence of these books suggests that confessors had found ways of presenting material which was particularly relevant to nuns and that although the Lisbon convent may have been geographically isolated, it was nevertheless linked to the intellectual and spiritual life of other English women religious through common reading practices.

These English connections can be seen in the number of books of meditation in the mystical tradition found in the Benedictine conventual libraries at Cambrai (founded 1623) and Paris (1651) as well as in the Lisbon collection. Several of the authors included by Augustine Baker in his list of approved reading for the nuns at Cambrai, such as Tauler (c.1300–1361), Fitch (also known as Benet of Canfield; 1562–1611) and Teresa of Avila, also featured in the Bridgettine library.[63] Two copies of Gertrude More's *Spiritual Exercises* of 1658 were at Lisbon: she was Baker's disciple at Cambrai. There are also six copies of *Sancta Sophia or, Directions for the prayer of contemplation* (1657) which incorporate Gertrude More's writings with his own. The presence of multiple copies suggests that the books must have been used as part of formation by the confessor or novice mistress at Lisbon. The continuing Bridgettine interest in mysticism can be seen in the presence of a work with long-standing Syon connections, Hilton's *Scale (or ladder) of perfection* (1659 edn). It had been re-published in England after a gap of 120 years, edited by Serenus Cressy (1605–1674).

Among the books to guide the nuns' meditation was the 1669 *Journal of Meditations* which claimed to be 'a plain and easy method of meditating' by the Jesuit, Nathaniel Bacon, originally written in Latin and later translated into English by Edward Mico for the general reader. There are traces of earlier inscriptions on the title page but wear has made them illegible; only the name of 'Sister Rosa Hodgshon' who professed in 1749 is still clear. The book has been so well used that there is much mending to the first few pages and to the spine. In his Preface, Mico explains how the text should be used:

> ... at least take the pains to read every day one of these pages, and for the space of a quarter of an hour, either sitting or walking, onely to reflect or ruminate upon what you have read, applying what you may, to your self, and thinking what may serve for your own practise ...[64]

He gives three separate points to consider on a theme for each day throughout the year. Intended originally as a straightforward guide for devout laity

---

[63] See the discussion in Wolfe, 'Reading Bells and Loose Papers', pp. 137–8.
[64] Nathaniel Bacon, *A journal of meditations for every day of the year, written first in Latine by N B and newly translated into English by E M* [Edward Mico] (London, 1669), sig. A3v.

seeking to improve the quality of their religious life, this was a work that the nuns could also use.

The secular works in the seventeenth-century collection at Lisbon were few in number; among them medicinal texts to support the work of the sisters responsible for preparing medicines and caring for the sick, and several historical works. They had a copy of the first edition of John Gerard's *Great Herball* of 1597, which not only helped to identify the plants, but also indicated what ailments could be treated with them. They also acquired the fourth edition of Elizabeth Grey Countess of Kent's manual of practical advice relating to health care, *A choice manuall ...*, published in 1654. It was a popular work in England which went into nineteen editions. The nuns owned several historical works including Francis Bacon's *Historie of the reigne of King Henry the Seventh*, and seven volumes of Rushworth's *Historical Collections*, which covered the period 1618 to 1649. It is easy to see the practical value of William Camden's *Britain; or A chorographicall description of the most flourishing kingdomes, England, Scotland and Ireland ... beautified with mappes ...* (1637) to an institution in exile wishing to maintain practical knowledge of its sources of recruits, support and patronage.[65]

Conclusions

The Bridgettine book collection in Lisbon in the seventeenth century confirms the reputation earned by the Syon nuns in England as a reading community. Outside the liturgy for the daily office the nuns preferred on the whole to read in the vernacular, as did the other communities of English women religious. The nuns in Lisbon assembled a collection of printed books from small beginnings, assisted by the brothers of the community who made a number of manuscript translations and copies of the longest texts for them. In addition they made their own transcriptions of prayers, meditations and compilations for their personal use. The size and range of their collection is comparable with other English female religious communities of the period and the titles in the collection show that they bought many of the same books, thus demonstrating connections between the convents in exile in spite of the physical distance between Lisbon and the other houses. There are significant

---

65 John Gerard, *Great Herball* (London, 1597); Elizabeth Grey, *A choice manuall or, Rare and select secrets in physick and chyrugery* (London, 1654); Francis Bacon, *Historie of the reigne of King Henry the Seventh* (London, 1629); John Rushworth, *Historical Collections* (London, 1659–1722); William Camden, *Britain; or A chorographicall description of the most flourishing kingdomes, England, Scotland and Ireland ... beautified with mappes of the severall shires of England* (London, 1637).

lacunae (notably liturgical works and bibles, both essential to the religious life) in the collection now at Exeter University, which may be explained by the impact of either the major disasters experienced by the convent in Lisbon or loss resulting from the initial return to England in the nineteenth century. Other losses are more difficult to pinpoint. However there remains to this day a collection of great historical significance with sufficient marks of wear and tear and marginalia to show the centrality of books and reading in the daily lives of the English Bridgettines in the seventeenth century.

7

The Syon Martiloge

CLAES GEJROT

Introduction

Some kind of written record is a natural and almost required instrument in a community formed with serious intentions, where a small or large number of people have decided to co-operate. This is no less true if we go back to the Middle Ages. For a medieval monastery, a roll of all members and a list of benefactors that were to be remembered would seem a necessary tool. Syon Abbey, of course, was no exception. Among the preserved books from its fifteenth-century collections there is a volume that records the English Bridgettines and their friends. Scholars in search of firsthand information from Syon are grateful for this manuscript, and quotes are constantly found in books and articles. But few have discussed the source in itself. In the following pages I will try to describe how and when this book was arranged, explain its use in the monastery, and present some of the material it contains.

The *Syon Martiloge* is a parchment manuscript in small folio comprising 193 leaves.[1] The traditional name of the book is a short and easy English form

1   BL, MS Additional 22, 285. Until the first part of the nineteenth century the manuscript still belonged to the nuns of Syon. It was then (c.1829–37) sold to the Earl of Shrewsbury. In 1858 the British Museum bought it from his estate; see de Hamel, *Syon Abbey*, p. 121. The book has 'its original thick wooden binding covered with a contemporary soft white leather chemise wrapper with its metal clasp and catch intact' (de Hamel, *Syon Abbey*, p. 72). Brief descriptions of the manuscript are found in J. H. Blunt (ed.), *The Myroure of our Ladye*, EETS, extra ser. (London 1873), introduction, pp. xlv–xlvi, and in F. Procter and E. S. Dewick (eds), *The Martiloge*, Henry Bradshaw Society, vol. 3 (London 1893), introduction, pp. xxv ff. An edition of the historical parts of the manuscript with biographies of the people mentioned is being prepared by myself and Virginia Bainbridge. All quotations from the Martiloge are taken from a preliminary version of this edition, which will include a detailed description of the manuscript. I am grateful to Roger Andersson, Virginia Bainbridge, Vincent Gillespie and Peter Ståhl for valuable discussions and comments.

deriving from the Latin word *martyrologium*,[2] and, as is to be expected, a martyrology proper occupies a large portion, over 200 pages, of the volume. These stories taken from the lives of martyrs were intended for the use of the brothers at Syon.[3] Furthermore, a later hand has added to the martyrology texts short lections about various moralising and educational topics.[4] But the book also had other purposes. Substantial sections of the manuscript are filled with a variety of annotations relevant to the history of the English Bridgettine house and its inhabitants. In a central position among these, we find a long series of obits, forming an *obituarium*.[5]

Contents of the Manuscript

fol. 1	Certificate concerning a relic of St Bridget. Three seventeenth-century obits.
fol. 2r	List of abbesses and confessor generals of Syon (seventeenth-century hand).
fols 3r–4v	Remarks on some obsequies (with changes decided in 1440 and in 1471).
fol. 4v	Notes on the correct use of the words *kalendae, nonae* and *idus*.
fols 5r–10v	Calendar (with added material about Syon including obits that were later erased).
fols 11–12	Bookmark.
fols 13r–v	Notes on dates and the correct reading of the martyrology texts and the obits.
fols 14r–15r	Some important events in the early history of Syon, from 1415 to 1431.

---

[2] Naturally enough, a Latin form *martilogium* was also in use; cf. the quotation below taken from fol. 17v. On martyrologies (also in combination with obituaries, as in our case), see *Lexikon des Mittelalters*, 6 (München 2002), s.v. 'Martyrologium', cols 357–60.

[3] There was also a martyrology in English intended for the nuns at Syon (cf. e.g. *utrisque martilogiis* in the quotation below). This text was printed in 1526, and again in Procter and Dewick, *The Martiloge*. The martyrologium itself falls outside the scope of this essay which will instead concentrate on the obituary and other historical parts of the Martiloge manuscript.

[4] These marginal lections are analysed and discussed in V. Gillespie, ' "Hid diuinite": The Spirituality of the English Syon Brethren', in E. A. Jones (ed.), *The Medieval Mystical Tradition in England*, 7 (Cambridge, 2004), pp. 196 ff.

[5] On the various names for medieval rolls showing names of the dead (*obituarium, necrologium, liber vitae*) and their use in churches and monasteries, see *Lexikon des Mittelalters*, 6, s.v. 'Necrolog', cols 1078–9. In the present essay the English form 'obituary' will be used.

fols 15r–18r	Remarks on offices: a revised version of the text on fols 3r–4v.
fols 18v–20r	Latin and English forms for the vows of obedience that were to be taken by new members.
fol. 21r	Notes on graves in the cross-aisles (1485–8).
fols 21v–69v	Obituary.
fols 70r–71v	List of benefactors.
fols 72r–v	Notes on offices for certain benefactors (1490).
fols 77r–188r	*Martyrologium.*
fol. 188v	Prayers.
fols 189r–192r	List of Syon brothers and sisters buried in the monastery (1485–1557).

The main sets of historical texts, the oldest parts of the obituary included, as well as the calendar and the martyrology were written by fifteenth-century hands. Later entries were added gradually until the seventeenth century by a number of people, and this scribal activity clearly shows how the volume became a silent, but probably much consulted, companion to the Syon community from its first century and a half in England, and through the wanderings in Europe until the long stay in Lisbon.[6] What appears to be the very last entry in the book deals with 1647, and this obit must have been written that year or shortly thereafter.[7]

Practical Use of the Martiloge

The language used in the historical parts of the Martiloge is typical of a monastic, everyday Latin[8] without literary ambitions. The book had a specific and explicit daily use. After the reading of the *De profundis*, the martyrology text for this day was to be read aloud. The reader would then cite the names of the dead that were to be remembered on this day. It seems very likely that this procedure continued during the exile, perhaps in a modified form. The fact that annotations were still made in the middle of the seventeenth century is an

---

6 On the long exile of the inhabitants of Syon after the dissolution, see J. R. Fletcher, *The Story of the English Bridgettines of Syon Abbey* (Bristol, 1933), and the informative list in U. Sander Olsen, 'Birgittinorden och dess grenar', *Birgitta av Vadstena* (Stockholm, 2003), p. 381.
7 Fol. 65v, 30 November: *Soror Prissilla Dimmocke obijt anno 1647 Ulix<ipone>* ('in Lisbon').
8 Latin is used throughout the book with only a few exceptions: the English version of the obedience oaths and two items in the obituary (mentioned below).

unambiguous indication that the manuscript was utilised in some way, at least until that time. The intended use of the book is clearly displayed in two fifteenth-century passages, taken from different contexts in the Martiloge:

> *Martilogium legatur post De profundis cotidie exceptis duobus diebus ante pascha et die pentecostes.* (fol. 13v)

'The Martiloge should be read every day after *De profundis*, except on the two days before Easter [i.e. Good Friday and Easter Eve] and Whitsunday.'

> *Concessum est eciam, quod nomen dicti magistri Thome[9] inseretur et inscribetur utrisque martilogijs, scilicet tam sororum quam fratrum. Et eo die, quo obijt, omni anno recitabitur post leccionem martilogij, sicut nomina sororum et fratrum professorum mortuorum recitari solent.* (fols 17v–18r)

'It was also agreed that Master Thomas's name be introduced and written in both Martiloges, in the sisters' book as well as in the brothers'. And his name is to be pronounced every year, on the day of his death, after the reading of the Martiloge, as is the case with the names of deceased professed sisters and brothers.'

The persons in charge of this reading must have appreciated the practicality of having both these assignments – the martyrology sections and the obits – in the same book. And there was a further useful detail: the martyrology texts for daily reading have been supplied with the Latin word *obitus*, which is found in the margin whenever there is a name in the obituary to be remembered and recited after the lection. It seems that a recital of the names of the dead was often part of the duty of the preaching priest brothers, and in this case too, the Martiloge, or a similar record, would have been consulted.[10]

The book was equipped with other practical tools. Grammatical advice on the reading of various dates was probably a welcome contribution. For those unfamiliar with the use of the Latin words *kalendae, idus* and *nonae* this manual also explains the inflections and the etymology of these words.[11] There is also a very useful bookmark. When the reading of the martyrologium

---

[9] On Master Thomas (Graunt) see further below.

[10] Cf. the continuation of the passage just quoted (fol. 18r): *Similiter fiet in sermonibus fratrum, qui nomina omnium professorum mortuorum et specialium benefactorum, dum eorum annua dies aduenerit, recitare et pro eis orare consuescunt* ('The same procedure is to be used in the sermons of the brethren, who usually recite the names of deceased professed [brothers and sisters] and special benefactors on their anniversaries, and pray for them').

[11] Fols 4v and 13r–v.

was finished the reader could easily look up the corresponding place in the obituary. On the bookmark itself he found further help, if needed, in the form of carefully inscribed nominative forms of some frequent words to be used together with the verb *obiit* (plural *obierunt*):

obijt	*obierunt*
fundator	*abbatisse*
soror	*sorores*
focaria[12]	*focarie*
benefactor	*benefactores*
benefactrix	*benefactrices*
huius monasterij	

sacerdos	*sacerdotes*
diaconus	*diaconi*
frater	*fratres*
focarius	*focarij*
huius congregacionis	

The correct reciting of the name to be remembered – preceded by the words *eodem die* – was then made very easy. Further rules for the reading of the obits are found under the rubric *Modus legendi martilogium*.[13] A short excerpt from this text will suffice here (with the letter N denoting the name of any deceased person/s):

> *Tunc pronuncietur obitus, si habeatur, sic: Eodem die obijt N quondam soror/frater istius congregacionis, vel sic: Eodem die obierunt N quondam frater/fratres et soror/sorores istius congregacionis, vel sic: Eodem die obijt/obierunt N quondam benefactor/benefactores vel benefactrix/benefactrices huius monasterii.*

'Then the obit will be recited, if there is one, in the following way: "On this day, the late sister/brother N of this congregation died", or like this: "On this day, the late brother/brothers and sister/sisters N of this congregation died", or like this: "On this day, the late benefactor/benefactors or benefactress/benefactresses of this monastery died." '

---

12 A focary (Lat. *focarius* or *focaria*) was a brother or sister serving in the kitchen (cf. U. Westerbergh and E. Odelman (eds), *Glossarium mediae latinitatis Sueciae / Glossarium till medeltidslatinet i Sverige* (Stockholm, 1968–), s.v. *focarius*. Cf. also below, p. 217, the introduction of Margaret Berington.
13 Fols 13r–v.

It is interesting to note the slight difference in terminology. On the one hand, the words on the bookmark show that a nun should be cited as 'of this monastery', while the expression 'of this congregation' was to be used for members on the male side of Syon, in a way marking a closer relation with the reader. The instructions quoted next, on the other hand, do not make this distinction, but combine *soror* with *istius congregacionis*.

The Origin of the Martiloge

The martyrology and the initial calendar (which lacks original Bridgettine elements[14]) seem to be produced outside Syon.[15] But what is the origin and background of the historical writings in the Martiloge? We have no knowledge of any decision taken by Syon to set up the obituary and make the annotations concerning the history and practices of their monastery.

In some ways the Syon manuscript reminds us of the memorial book of the Vadstena brothers, the *Diarium Vadstenense*.[16] But the differences are many. Filled with annotations about the Bridgettines in Sweden, this book was not – as its Syon counterpart – mainly arranged as obits structured after a calendar. Instead, as the word *diarium*[17] indicates, it is throughout a chronological presentation of abbey events from the early days onwards, year by year, often day by day. The book was written and preserved in the male convent in Vadstena until 1545, at the time when the last brothers left the monastery.[18] It was used for a large number of informative entries of varying length and content, and, as has already been indicated, not only obits. In the Diarium, we find among other things an almost complete manifestation of all the introductions of new members into the abbey. Descriptions of ordinary monastic life alternate with reports of memorable occasions in the history of the monastery and glimpses of events in the outside world. For a limited period (the

---

[14] St Bridget's canonisation is added by a later hand in the margin of the feast for 7 October, *(festum) sanctorum Marci et Marcelli*.

[15] Cf. de Hamel, *Syon Abbey,* pp. 48 ff., on the external production and purchase of manuscripts.

[16] Claes Gejrot (ed.), *Diarium Vadstenense. The Memorial Book of Vadstena Abbey*, Acta Universitatis Stockholmiensis. Studia Latina Stockholmiensia XXXIII (Stockholm, 1988; with an introduction in English); and Claes Gejrot (ed.), *Vadstenadiariet. Latinsk text med översättning och kommentarer,* Kungl. Samfundet för utgivande av handskrifter rörande Skandinaviens historia. Handlingar del 19 (Stockholm, 1996; with a commentary and a translation into Swedish).

[17] This name was first used in the eighteenth century. The medieval Latin name for the book was *Liber memorialis* (Gejrot, *Diarium Vadstenense*, p. 74).

[18] Gejrot, *Diarium Vadstenense*, p. 13.

mid-fifteenth century) the latter kind of external material takes up a considerable part of the text. All in all, it is clear that the Diarium cannot have been the model for the Syon scribes working with the Martiloge annotations and obituary.

But there is another possible link to Vadstena. In a preserved document, probably emanating from the opening ceremonies in 1384, we learn about the establishment of a Bridgettine official *Liber vitae* that was to contain the names of deceased members of the monastery and also the names of the abbey benefactors and founders.[19] The document itself forms the beginning of the book. Here is a central passage:

> *Et ne obliuionis exemplar successoribus nostris relinquamus super qualitate primorum huius monasterii fundatorum, benefactorum et precipuorum promotorum, nomina eorundem cum nominibus sororum et fratrum defunctorum infra in hunc librum conscribi iussimus.*

> 'And, in order to make our successors remember who were the first founders, benefactors and principal promoters of this monastery, we have decided to write in this book the names of these persons together with the names of deceased brothers and sisters.'

Referring both to biblical passages[20] and to Bridget's Revelations,[21] the quoted Vadstena document ends by giving the names of the royal founders, King Magnus Eriksson and Queen Blanka.[22] This *Liber vitae*, or obituary, so

---

19 Cod. A 20, fols 189r–189 ½ r, National Archives, Stockholm. The text was first discussed in T. Höjer, *Studier i Vadstena klosters och Birgittinordens historia intill midten af 1400-talet* (Uppsala, 1905), p. 93 with footnote.

20 E.g. Ad. Phil. 4,3: ... *quorum nomina sunt in libro vitae.*

21 The document quotes Bridget's Revelations, book 6, chapter 70, 12, a passage where Christ tells Bridget that he will reward benefactors of the church: ... *Ideo ego animabus illorum, quorum bona illa fuerunt, ex mensa gracie mee et passionis prouidebo et miserebor* ('Therefore, out of my grace and passion I will provide for the souls of those who owned the property (that was donated), and I will have mercy on them'). The text is printed in B. Bergh (ed.), *Sancta Birgitta: Revelaciones, Book VI* (Stockholm, 1991), p. 231.

22 ... *fundatores enim huius loci erant rex Magnus filius Erici ducis quondam Swecie et regina Blancha eius coniungx* (sic), *qui sceptra regalia regnorum Swecie et Norwegie tenuerunt circa annos Domini MCCCL. Hii duo post beatissimam matrem nostram beatam Birgittam feruenciores erant erga huius monasterij fundacionem et dotacionem* ('... the founders of this monastery were King Magnus, son of the late Duke Erik of Sweden, and Queen Blanka, his wife. They ruled the kingdoms of Sweden and Norway around 1350. After our holy mother Saint Bridget, these two persons were most deeply committed in working for the foundation and dotation of this monastery'). It may be noted that the royal founders are otherwise seldom referred to in preserved Vadstena material. On Bridget's – and Vadstena's – aversion towards King Magnus, see O. Ferm, *Olaus Petri och Heliga Birgitta. Synpunkter på ett nytt sätt att*

formally introduced, is regrettably not preserved; we know today only the prefatory document. It would be very tempting to see the obituary and other historical parts of the Syon Martiloge as the result of a similar decision made in the English monastery. The scope is the same: the names and days of dead members, founders and benefactors.[23]

The links between Syon and Vadstena were initially very strong, beginning at the time of the marriage between Henry IV's daughter, Philippa, and Eric of Pomerania, king of the three Nordic countries. Until the 1420s, when the English Bridgettines in several ways separated themselves from Vadstena and the other monasteries of the order,[24] there had been a number of visits to England by representatives from the Swedish monastery.[25] These connections culminated, as it were, in 1415 when seven women from Vadstena emigrated permanently to England where they were among the first nuns to be connected to the new Bridgettine foundation.[26] In the mid-1420s, a small delegation from Syon visited Vadstena to discuss certain matters relating to the Rule and to the daily monastic routines.[27] This would have meant a good opportunity to see and study the practice of records and rolls in Vadstena. Perhaps they also looked at the Vadstena obituary mentioned above.

It seems likely that there were other Syon sources from which the Martiloge scribes could have taken material. In the Martiloge transcriptions of the Syon brethren's vows of obedience, which will be further discussed

---

skriva historia i 1500-talets Sverige, Runica et mediævalia: Scripta minora 15 (Stockholm, 2007), pp. 14–15 (with further references).

[23] It is perhaps interesting to compare the Syon Martiloge with other preserved English examples in the genre, e.g. the one of Durham and the one of New Minster/Hyde Abbey near Winchester. Although both these books concern institutions with a much older history than the relatively young Syon Abbey, they display traits that are at least partly similar to the Martiloge. The two mentioned manuscripts have in recent years been the object of new editions and investigations: David Rollason *et al.* (eds), *The Durham Liber Vitae and its Context* (Woodbridge, 2004); Simon Keynes, *The Liber Vitae of the New Minster and Hyde Abbey, Winchester* (facsimile edition), Early English Manuscripts in Facsimile 26 (Copenhagen, 1996).

[24] See H. Cnattingius, *Studies in the Order of St. Bridget of Sweden. I. The Crisis in the 1420's* (Uppsala, 1963).

[25] On the early contacts between Syon and Vadstena, see M. Hedlund, 'Vadstena kloster: ett fönster mot England', in Hedlund, 'Katillus Thorberni, a Syon pioneer and his books', in *Birgittiana*, 1 (1996), 67–87; and E. Andersson, 'Birgittines in Contact. Early Correspondence between England and Vadstena', *Eranos*, 102 (2004), 1–29.

[26] On the female emigrants, who were accompanied by two priests, see Claes Gejrot, 'Anna Karlsdotters bönbok', in *Medeltida skrift- och språkkultur*, ed. Inger Lindell, Runica et mediævalia: Opuscula 2 (Stockholm, 1994), pp. 38–43. The Swedish sisters all died in Syon, and their names are found in the obituary.

[27] The resulting answers from the Vadstena brothers have been preserved (Uppsala University Library, Cod. C 74 and C 363). An edition of these *Responsiones* is being prepared by Elin Andersson, Stockholm.

below, we meet a phrase showing the existence of another official Syon register: *signum meum manuale in communi registro domus nostre capitularis impressi* ('I have put my own signature in the common register of our chapter house'). In this case we have apparently to do with a register kept in the brothers' part of the monastery. Another relevant instance of the word *registrum* is found in an additional remark made to an obit on 18 February, but it is not clear if it is the same register that is referred to. The book mentioned in this case may have served as a direct source for the scribe: the words *vide plura in registro nostro* ('see further details in our register') point in this direction. The comment concerns a death that occurred during the convent's stay in Mechelen (1572–80), and it is possible that the source it refers to was produced after the escape from England.[28] Anyway, the book or books alluded to in these passages have not survived to our day.

We will now turn to the question of *when* the texts in the book were written down. It will not be possible to give a detailed answer. A complete analysis of the various scribes writing in different parts of the book would then be necessary, and this essay is not the place for such an extensive investigation. It will be sufficient here to look at some of the more important scribal hands that were active before the year 1500. Among the several fifteenth-century scripts that meet the reader, it is, in my opinion, possible to single out one scribe of particular interest.[29] As we will see, this anonymous scribe was at work in the 1470s and 1480s, when he made several major contributions to the Martiloge manuscript. First of all, he – or perhaps someone deciding for him – seems to be behind the setting up and arranging of the 'new' routine for the monastery obits, which replaced an older system.

These older obits had been inserted into the calendar at the beginning of the book, but they were later erased from these pages.[30] The deletion process must

---

28 Fol. 27v: Joanna Danister Maura soror obijt Mechlini; et ibi sepulta est apud fratres Augustinenses. De ea, vide plura in registro nostro.

29 Some distinctive letters of this script: *a, A, S, J, T*. In my opinion, it may be characterised as a subtype of Anglicana; cf. A. Derolez, *The Palaeography of Gothic Manuscript Books* (Cambridge, 2003), p. 140. The only scribal hand of the Martiloge so far identified with some degree of certainty seems to be that of the Syon librarian Thomas Betson, who c.1500 wrote an entry on fol. 72r. On this identification see Vincent Gillespie (ed.), *Syon Abbey: The Libraries of the Carthusians*, ed. A. I. Doyle, Corpus of British Medieval Library Catalogues 9 (London, 2001), p. xliii, n. 36. Gillespie (*Syon Abbey*, p. xlvii, n 48) also suggests that two sixteenth-century hands found in the Martiloge are identical with other scribes discerned in the Library Register (Cambridge, Corpus Christi College MS 141).

30 The calendar (decorated with an ornated initial for Kal/endae/ at the top of every page) is set up with one page for one month. There was only very limited space for the obits. It has been possible to read these erased obits with the help of ultraviolet light.

have taken some time – there were over seventy items to take away. It is likely that the work was done not long after 1474, which is the last death year found among the deleted entries.[31] In connection with this deletion, it may be assumed, the obits were transferred to the new obituary.[32] In fact, most of the Syon obits, if not all, concerning persons deceased before this time (the 1470s) seem to have been written by the same scribal hand – the scribe already mentioned. Of course, before writing down their names, he had to prepare a *mise-en-page*, a pattern for the altered way of recording obits, by providing rubrics for every page. It would be natural to assume that the setting up of the new obituary took place some time, perhaps a couple of years, before the erasure process.[33] We will return to this question below.

At this point it is important to add that there are Syon obits also in a calendar in another manuscript, today kept in Magdalene College, Cambridge.[34] No year numbers were used in these obits. It may be deduced, however, from a comparison with the Martiloge obituary that nothing was entered in the Cambridge calendar after 1451, or shortly afterwards.[35] As we have just seen, the calendar at the beginning of the Martiloge manuscript was also used as an obituary until the mid-1470s. Consequently, it appears that the Syon community had (at least) two separate lists for the recording of the deceased before the Martiloge obituary was set up. It is possible that these earlier obituaries were written separately and used at the same time. But another, and perhaps more plausible, explanation would be that the Cambridge obits were the first to be recorded, covering as they do the Syon deaths to 1451. Then, these items were taken into the Martiloge calendar, which has material until 1474.[36] Finally, all obits were moved into the Martiloge obituary.

An interesting internal reference point can be seen on fol. 21r of the Martiloge manuscript. Right before the main obituary, there is a short list revealing some burial places in the church transepts at Syon. The list was

---

[31] The phrase *Obitus Willelmi Blythe diaconi 1474* was erased from the calendar (fol. 6v), and the information is instead found in the new set of obits: *Dominus Willelmus Blythe diaconus 1474* (fol. 35r). The relevant date is 19 April.

[32] And, in a few cases, to the benefactors' list discussed below.

[33] On the structural pattern of the 'new' obits, see below.

[34] MS F.4.23, fols 7r–12v. As is the case with the Martiloge calendar, one page in the Cambridge calendar covers one month.

[35] The Martiloge entry for 17 September carries the year 1451 and seems to be the last obit that exists in both sources.

[36] The Cambridge calendar and the Martiloge calendar obits use similar formulae, e.g. 13 February: *Obitus Alicie Denham sororis professe* (Cambridge calendar), *Obitus Alicie Denham sororis* (Martiloge calendar).

written not earlier than 1485, probably by the obit scribe mentioned above. The year is explicitly stated in the rubric: *De iacentibus in ambitibus fratrum et sororum ab anno Domini 1485*. The first item in this list concerns the burial of William Asplyon: *In ambitibus fratrum loco primo, qui est prope fenestram primam, iacet magister Willelmus Asplyon, vt patet in presenti martilogio in festo sancti Ricardi, iii die Aprilis* ('In the first grave in the brothers' transepts, close to the first window, lies master William Asplyon, as is seen in this Martiloge, under the feast of St Richard, on 3 April'). The reference to the Martiloge obits is quite correct, and it gives us a definitive *terminus ante quem* for the start of the obituary recording.[37] The burial list mentions only four more graves. It then ends with the comment that further information on these burials is to be found in the following Martiloge (i.e. the obituary) with the respective death days.[38] The last of the deaths mentioned in the list occurred in 1488.[39] There is an interesting fact to take into account here. The consecration of the abbey church took place the same year, on 20 August.[40] Perhaps the idea of a list of burial places in the church was realised during the final preparation of the church for the consecration ceremonies.

The facts presented above lead us to the following hypothesis: between the first part of the 1470s and the mid-1480s our scribe had set up the framework for the Martiloge obituary, and he had filled in all the obits concerning a period of about half a century – starting with the years after the first professions, the early 1420s.

Furthermore, at the same time as this section was written down, or shortly afterwards, it seems that the obit scribe wrote the list of benefactors that follows directly after the obituary. His work resulted in a series of names of donors and friends of the monastery until the middle of the 1480s; at this point other scribes appear to take over. On one of the pages we come across a rewarding point of internal reference: *De duce Eboraco, quere superius folio 6 post kalendarium in principio libri* ('On the Duke of York, see above, fol. 6, after the calendar, at the beginning of the book').[41] This passage is a distinct indication that the main sets of texts in the first part of the manuscript – with the exception of a few later additions – already existed when our scribe did his work.

---

37 On 3 April: *2° Dominus Willelmus Asplyon sacerdos, 1485. Et iste est primus, qui sepelitur in ambitibus ecclesie ex parte fratrum loco primo* (fol. 33r).
38 *Idem intelligendum est de ceteris ibidem iacentibus aut in ambitibus sororum. De quibus patet apercius in martilogio sequenti cum diebus, quibus dormierunt* (fol. 21r).
39 *Loco 4° infra dictam fenestram prope parietem Robertus Brydde*; corresponding to fol. 38v, on 16 May: *Robertus Brydde ffrater laicus, 1488*.
40 The Martiloge, annotation on fol. 96; Fletcher, *Story*, p. 28.
41 Fol. 70v.

Let us now turn to these initial historical texts, found on both sides of the calendar.[42] It appears palaeographically evident that these parts are not the work of the obit scribe.[43] Fortunately, we are helped in our search for dating evidence by several year numbers that are included at different places in the texts themselves. The first block of text, apparently written on one and the same occasion, narrates the background of some changes in liturgy routines concerning specific offices for the founders, benefactors and friends of the monastery as well as general offices for the Syon members and their parents. The Syon community is reported to have reached agreements in these matters in 1431 and 1440. There is no break in the text flow here, and the text was perhaps written down not long after the joint decision was made in 1440. Then, after a change of scribes, we read about agreements reached in 1471. After the calendar, and again after a scribal change, another set of texts follows which seems to be the work of a single scribe. This section is where we meet the passages on the history of Syon that will be further discussed below. But in this scribal part, some of the previous information (on liturgy) is also repeated but revised and with additions. Here, 1484 is the latest year mentioned. Thus, it seems that these three sections were written, or, as would appear more likely, were copied from other sources into the Martiloge manuscript on three separate occasions: after 1440, 1471 and 1484.[44]

It would not be surprising if much of the recording in the Martiloge – the obituary as well as the list of benefactors – was in fact a direct result of the settlements of 1440 and 1471. Of these two, 1471 is especially important. This year, the community decided on a last addition to the special offices for friends and benefactors. The reason was Thomas Graunt, a canon of St Paul's in London who died in 1471. He bequeathed to Syon a significant collection of books, a donation which in its turn led to the decision that especially Graunt himself, but also all book donors in general, should be remembered with offices.[45] Here we find the permission, also quoted above, to inscribe master Thomas's name in both Martiloges: *Concessum est eciam, quod nomen dicti magistri Thome inseretur et inscribetur utrisque martilogijs.* Now, the wording here implies that some kind of recording had started in the Martiloge. Perhaps it would not be too far-fetched to take the interpretation of

---

[42] Fols 3r–18r.

[43] Although he may have been partly involved (making some additions).

[44] It is possible, but not very likely, that the texts in question were copied (by different scribes) into the Martiloge at the same time. One then has to answer the question why anyone would bother to copy also the old liturgy decisions that had been replaced by new ones.

[45] On Thomas Graunt and the book collections of Syon at this time, see Gillespie, *Syon Abbey*, pp. xliv–xlvi.

this even further. The explicit mentioning of writing things down in the Martiloge makes the reader see this recording process as something relevant and important at the time. It could, in fact, indicate that the recording *started* at about this particular time. This would fit in well with the discussion above about the setting up of the Martiloge before the erasure of the older calendar obits.

Our results as to the time of the writing down of the various historical parts of the manuscript, including the obituary and list of benefactors, may now be summarised. It seems that most of this work was made in the period between 1471 and 1485. The exception to this is a shorter text (two and a half pages) that was probably written down after 1440 but before 1471. After the mid-1480s, when the Martiloge had been arranged and set up for further annotations, and the earlier obituaries had been abandoned, we must assume that the continued recording took place not long after the described events.

The Martiloge Obituary

The largest section of the manuscript – apart from the martyrology itself – is the obituary with information about deceased members of Syon Abbey.[46] The obits recorded here are not restricted to the brothers and sisters living within the monastic *clausura*; they also include quite a few persons from the outside world – benefactors and friends of the monastery.

The pages of the obituary are structured in a calendarial and homogeneous way. On every page there is room for at least four days. New months always start with a new page. On the first line we find a letter and a figure. The letters are repeating, in strict order, a series from the letter *a* to the letter *g*;[47] the figures give the date of the month (always written with Arabic numbers). The name of the relevant month is written at the top of every page of the manuscript. A liturgical dating is also used, saints' days and ecclesiastical feasts having been inserted after the letter and date on the first line. On the following lines, the scribes filled in the names of persons who died on that day. The pages are spacious, and for most days there is place enough for further names (Figure 7.1).

There are a few standard types of annotations. The first and most common

---

46 Fols 21v–69v.
47 On this chronological system ('Tagesbuchstaben'), see H. Grotefend, *Taschenbusch der Zeitrechnung des deutschen Mittelalters und der Neuzeit* (1st edn 1898; 13th edn Hannover, 1991), pp. 4 and 135. The same lettering is found in the older calendars, in the first part of the manuscript and in the Cambridge calendar (see above), and it is quite possible that it was copied from there into the obituary.

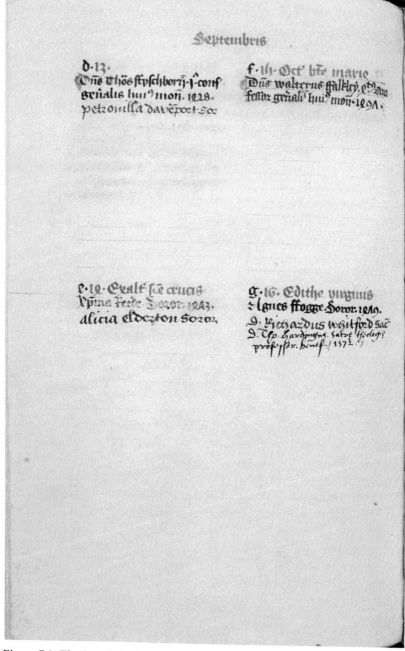

Figure 7.1: The Syon Martiloge: British Library, MS Additional 22, 285, fol. 55v: (Septembris). © The British Library Board. All rights reserved.

group consists of short and formulaic entries, giving only names, titles and – in many cases – years of death of the abbey members. The date, of course, is seen from the rubric of the relevant day.

Characteristically, these items often omit a main verb like *obiit*, as is seen in this short, but typical example from 5 March: *Dominus Thomas Bould sacerdos, 1476*. The abbesses, confessor generals and prioresses of the abbey are mentioned (with a few exceptions) until the beginning of the seventeenth century. The usual expression includes a sequence number: *Domina Elizabethe Muston 4:a abbatissa, 1497*. Only once, we read about the election of an abbess of the abbey. On 25 February, 1606, in Lisbon, Elizabeth Preston was chosen in the presence of ecclesiastical authorities: *Electa est in abbatissam soror Elisabitha Præston Vlyssipone per breve Pauli pape quinti ...* ('Sister Elizabeth Preston was elected as abbess in Lisbon through a *breve* issued by Pope Paul V ...'). The reason for the unusual entry in the Martiloge is most probably the papal decision alluded to in the text, which changed the extent of the office of abbess into a three-year term.[48] After this, there are no more obits for abbesses.[49] More surprising is, perhaps, the introduction of a kitchen maid, found on 13 May: *Margareta Beryngtone admissa in focariam* ('Margaret Berington was admitted as a focary'). There is no year added to this note, but the scribal hand seems to belong to the second half of the sixteenth century.

A second group of entries would be those of the parents of abbesses and confessors, e.g. 6 March: *Johannes Trowel et Matilda uxor eius, parentes magistri Iohannis Trowel 6:i confessoris generalis* ('John Trowel and his wife Matilda, parents of the sixth Confessor General, Master John Trowel'); 25 July: *Magister Edwardus Palmer et Alicia vxor eius, parentes domine Katherine Palmer 8:e abbatisse huius monasterij* ('Master Edward Palmer and his wife Alice, parents of the eighth abbess of this monastery, Lady Katherine Palmer'). The recording in this category starts at the time of the fourth abbess and the third confessor, i.e. in the last decade of the fifteenth century, and continues for about a century.

A third group would be the benefactors and founders. As has been pointed out above, the name of the benefactor Thomas Graunt was to be included in both Martiloges by a joint decision in 1471, and we meet his name on 8 July: *Magister Thomas Graunte, benefactor, 1471*. After this, the recording of

---

48 Fletcher, *Story*, pp. 117–18.
49 The last obit for a Confessor General is that of Joseph Seth Foster in 1628 (24 May): *Pater Josephus Seth Foster confessor generalis nostri ordinis obdormiuit in Domino, Vlissipone 1628. Et fuit 12 confessor generalis monasterij de Sion.*

benefactors continued. The last obit with the word *benefactor* or *benefactrix* written out is from 1616.[50]

A married couple would have been remembered on the death day of the husband, as is the case with Sir Edward Walgrave and his wife Lady Frances Paulet, who survived her husband by thirty-eight years. Her obit is added, by another scribe, directly after Edward's: *Dominus Edwardus Walgraue miles benefactor, qui captiuus propter catholicam fidem obijt primo Sept. 1561. Benefactor. Domina Francisca Paulet vxor eius, benefactrix huius monasterij, quæ obijt anno Domini 1599* ('Sir Edward Walgrave, knight and benefactor, who was imprisoned for his Catholic faith and died on 1 September 1561. A benefactor. His wife, Lady Frances Paulet, a benefactress of this monastery, who died in the year of the Lord 1599'). The same man appears as a testamentary executor of another English Catholic in a more elaborate obit on 18 September (1556): *Edwardus Curtney comes de Deueshere, qui dedit huic monasterio annuatim imperpetuum xl libras sic, quod semel in anno celebrentur exequie pro anima eius; similiter in eisdem exequijs oretur pro animabus quatuor executorum eius post mortem eorum, quorum nomina sunt: Fransiscus Ynglefylde miles, Edwardus Walgrave miles, Wylelmus Cordall, Jacobus Basset* ('Edward Courtenay, Earl of Devonshire, who gave to this monastery a yearly and perpetual gift of £40, provided that an office for his soul was to be celebrated once every year; furthermore, in this office prayers are to be read for the souls of his four executors after their death. Their names are: Francis Englefield, knight, Edward Walgrave, knight, William Cordall and James Basset'). There is a clear tendency to write longer texts in the later, post-medieval entries.

The persons regarded as the founding fathers of the monastery, King Henry V and Sir Henry FitzHugh, are remembered on their death days – the king on 31 August: *Dominus Henricus rex Anglie quintus, fundator huius monasterij primus. Obijt anno Domini 1422* ('Lord Henry V, King of England, the first founder of this monastery. He died in the year of the Lord 1422'), and Sir Henry on 31 December: *Eodem die obijt dominus Henricus Ffitzhughe, qui primo hunc ordinem adduxit in Angliam. Obijt anno Domini 1426* ('On the same day, Sir Henry FitzHugh died, who first moved this order into England. He died in the year of the Lord 1426'). Apart from Henry V, only one other reigning royal individual was included in the Martiloge obituary.[51] On 17 November (1558) we find, not surprisingly, an entry on Queen Mary Tudor,

---

[50] 29 October: *Domina Isabella de Mendanha obijt anno Domini 1616, benefactrix.*

[51] However, it deserves to be mentioned that Edward IV, although not mentioned in the obituary, is remembered as a second founder of the monastery in an historical passage on fol. 15r.

who made a brief return possible for the Syon members, in 1558–9, and also on the cardinal, Reginald Pole. The period 1539–57, when the community was driven into their first exile, is typically referred to as the 'schism'. The text, in all probability written before the Syon convent was again forced to flee, is worth quoting:

> *Regina Maria, que restaurauit monasterium et religionem nostram post schisma et fuit noua fundatrix et restauratrix eorundem. Eodem die obijt Reginaldus Polus cardinalis et legatus a latere. Qui et reconsiliauit totum regnum nostrum Anglie ad vnitatem ecclesie catholice et constituit nouam incorporacionem de religiosis personis, que superstites fuerunt, prius ante dissolucionem pertinentibus ad istum nostrum monasterium. 1558°*

> 'Queen Mary, who restored our monastery and order after the "schism" and who was their new foundress and restorer. And on the same day died Reginald Pole, cardinal and papal legate. He brought the whole of our kingdom of England back to the unity of the Catholic church, and he created a new community consisting of those pious persons who had survived and who before the dissolution belonged to our monastery.'

Two pre-1500 comments on ecclesiastical leaders may exemplify a fourth group. On 26 March [1489], we find a diocesan bishop of Syon: *Thomas Kempe episcopus Londoniensis* ('Thomas Kemp, bishop of London'). On 12 April [1443], Syon has remembered the archbishop of Canterbury who performed their first professions (in 1420): *Henricus Chicheley archiepiscopus Cantuariensis, qui hic fecit primam professionem, 1443* ('Henry Chichele, archbishop of Canterbury, who officiated during the first profession here, 1443').

In some instances, in the later entries, at a time when the Syon community was constantly moving, we learn some of the burial places of deceased persons, as on 2 May: *1592 Jana Barley soror. Sepulta est Rothomagi in ecclesia sancti Loi, in medio, coram crucifixo* ('1592 Sister Jane Barley. She was buried in the church of Saint Eloi in Rouen, in the middle of the church, in front of the Crucifix'); and on 14 July: *1594 Francisca Shelly soror. Iacet apud Carmelitas excalseatas[52] Vlyssiponæ* ('1594 Sister Frances Shelly. She rests with the Discalced Carmelites in Lisbon'). Sometimes, an obit can give us more information than just the place of death: 31 July (1572) *Margareta Mannyngton soror obijt in monasterio Ffacons Antuerpiæ conuentu tunc*

---

[52] I.e. *excalceatas* ('discalced').

ibidem commorante propter seuitiam hæreticorum tunc vbique grassantium in Belgico ('Sister Margaret Monington died in the Falcon convent[53] in Antwerp while the convent was living at this place because of the cruel heretics that were ravaging everywhere in Belgium').

The Martiloge obits remember the names of two Syon martyrs. Richard Reynolds,[54] a priest brother of Syon, is found on 4 May: *Dominus Richardus Raynold sacerdos, qui mortem sustinuit apud Tyburne propter catholicam fidem, 1535. Martir* ('The priest, Sir Richard Reynolds, who was executed at Tyburn because of his Catholic faith, in 1535. A martyr'). On 21 October, the Syon community celebrated the memory of Thomas Brownal[55] who perished two years after Reynolds: *Thomas Bownell frater laicus, 1537, qui incarceratus propter catholicam fidem in Newgate ibidem ex squalore carceris obijt. Martyr* ('Lay brother Thomas Brownal, 1537, who was put in prison in Newgate for his Catholic faith and died there because of the filthy jail. A martyr').

Only a few obituary texts are written in English. On 8 September the names of a series of benefactors are found on a separate leaf that has been pasted to the manuscript:

> The obyt of M:r Jhone Roper and Jane his wyffe, father *and* mother to M:r Willi*a*m Roper; also of S*i*r Jhone Fyneoy knighte, his grandfath*er*; also of olde M:r Jhon*e* Roper his aunceter, founder of certeyn chantryes dissolved; also the obytt of M:rs Margaret Roper wyffe to M:r Willi*a*m Roper.

The hand seems to belong to the late sixteenth century. On 2 November we find another text in English; it bears the year 1611:

> Note well*e* that in this covent uppon all sowles daye is dewe to be sung one masse of Requiem yerely for the sowle of mownsier Chevaler do Mal [d'Aumale?], that gave his lif for the catholik league and gave his almes of one hundrid cronones of the sun*n*e for a foundation of one

---

[53] On the Falcon sisters in Antwerp, see Fletcher, *Story*, p. 38.

[54] On Richard Reynolds see Adam Hamilton, *The Angel of Syon. The Life and Martyrdom of Blessed Richard Reynolds, Bridgettine Monk of Syon, Martyred at Tyburn, May 4, 1535* (London, 1905); Vincent Gillespie, 'The Book and the Brotherhood: Reflections on the Lost Library of Syon Abbey', in A. S. G. Edwards, Vincent Gillespie and Ralph Hanna (eds), *The English Medieval Book: Studies in Memory of Jeremy Griffiths* (London, 2000), pp. 190–1; and Gillespie, 'Hid diuinite', p. 206.

[55] Thomas Brownal was jailed because of his open protest 'against a sermon supporting the king's title' (*A Royal Foundation. Syon Abbey, Past and Present. By the Bridgettine Nuns of Syon* (South Brent, Devon, 1959), p. 12. Cf. D. Baxter, *Syon Abbey* (Chudleigh, 1907), p. 11 n; and Fletcher, *Story*, p. 34).

masse of Requiem yerely forever to be sung for his sowle and all Christen sowles. ...[56]

A Selection of Texts Outside the Obituary

History of Syon Abbey

Some important events in the early history of Syon Abbey are presented in an annalistic way in the coherent section found after the calendar.[57] Not surprisingly, the first item fittingly concerns 1415, when King Henry V officially marked the start of the construction work at Syon.[58] He was accompanied by the bishop of London, Richard Clifford, who, according to the Bridgettine rule, as the diocesan bishop of Syon was to be the official visitor of the monastery.

> *Anno Domini m° cccc° xv°, in festo cathedre sancti Petri, littera dominicali f, positus fuit primus lapis in monasterio sancti Saluatoris et sanctarum Marie virginis et Birgitte ordinis sancti Augustini sancti Saluatoris nuncupati per Henricum quintum regem Anglie presente episcopo Londoniensi Ricardo Clyfford.*

> 'In the year of the Lord 1415, on the feast of the Chair of Saint Peter [*i.e. 22 February*], the dominical letter being F, the first stone was laid in the monastery dedicated to Saint Saviour, the saints Virgin Mary and Bridget, of the order of Saint Augustine that is called Saint Saviour, by Henry V, king of England, in the presence of Richard Clifford, bishop of London.'

Then follow entries on the ceremonies on 21 April 1420, when twenty-seven nuns were professed, and on the male side, five priests, two deacons and four lay brothers. The death of Henry V in 1422 is recorded, and the founder is remembered as a particular friend of the Bridgettines at Syon and as a pious Christian seeing religion behind his good fortune: *Hic habuit singularem deuocionem ad hunc ordinem, presertim ad hoc monasterium, reputans beneficio religionis, quicquid euenerat sibi prosperum* ('He had a particular devotion for this order, especially for this monastery, and he regarded every successful thing that had happened to him as a gift from religion').[59] A passage from his last will is quoted, in which the dying king asks Syon to pray for him and his family.

---

56 Presumably a reference to Charles de Guise, duc d'Aumale, though it must be his cousin, Charles duc de Mayenne (d. 1611) who is intended
57 Fols 14r–15r.
58 King Henry's foundation charter is printed in *A Royal Foundation*.
59 The same words are used about Edward IV further down.

Under 1426 we find a report on the start of the new monastery buildings. The foundation-stone ceremony was now performed by the dead king's brother John, Duke of Bedford. The first Confessor General, Thomas Fishbourn, died in the same year, as did Henry FitzHugh. A longer passage describes his early efforts for the order, for instance his arrangements for bringing in Vadstena brothers for the preparation of Syon.

In 1431, the community was solemnly transferred to the new buildings. The ceremony was led by Henry Chichele, the archbishop of Canterbury, *in omnia gloria et honore*. The passage goes on to show the celebrations that continued:

> *Ffinitaque missa vestimentum, in quo celebrauit, cum tunica et dalmatica et tribus capis sericis vnicoloris, scilicet albi, dedit monasterio. Deinde, sine aliqua mora adijt mansionem suam ex altera parte Tamisie vocatam Mortlake[60] ducens secum ad prandium plures dominos spirituales et temporales. Obijt autem xij° die Aprilis, anno Domini 1443.*

> 'And after mass, [the archbishop] gave to the monastery the clothes he wore during the ceremonies including a tunic and a dalmatic and three copes of silk in a single white colour. He then immediately went to his residence, called Mortlake, on the other side of the Thames, bringing with him to dine many distinguished men of the church and of the world. He died on 12 April, in the year of the Lord 1443.'

The ending clearly shows that these passages were written long after the recorded events. As already shown above, in the dating discussion, they were in fact probably written down in the 1480s. In addition to these texts, there are other shorter entries on Syon's history written on different occasions and scattered here and there through the manuscript.

Thomas Gascoigne's Certificate

Pasted to the inside of the front cover of the manuscript, an unexpected text has been preserved. It is a copy of a certificate issued by the Oxford theologian Thomas Gascoigne.[61] As it deals with the relics of St Bridget, the contents must have been of importance to the Syon brethren. But the reason

---

[60] Mortlake Manor belonged to the archbishops of Canterbury until the time of Henry VIII.
[61] Thomas Gascoigne (1403–1458), Chancellor of Oxford University, Syon benefactor. He is said to have translated a life of St Bridget of Sweden into English for the use of the sisters of Syon (Blunt, *The Myroure of our Ladye*, introduction; and cf. Gillespie, *The Book and the Brotherhood*, p. 185).

for placing this letter more or less as binding material is not clear. Neverthe-less, the story told by Gascoigne is worth reporting. He describes how Bridget's relics were brought to Sweden after her death in Rome, and proceeds to present some confusing facts as to the dating of the transport to Vadstena, setting the date to 7 October 1391 – the day of St Bridget's official canonisation.

The transferral of St Bridget's bones from Rome to Sweden is, in fact, a complicated affair to sort out. According to the Diarium Vadstenense, the first *translatio* took place at Vadstena on 4 July 1374, a year after her death, soon after her children had arrived from Rome bringing with them their mother's body. But some of her bones seem to have remained in Rome (or to have been transported back). They were displayed there during the festive arrangements following the canonisation. A solemn translation feast 'of *the whole* of her body' was then celebrated at Vadstena on 1 June 1393. Most probably, the relics still in Rome would have been transported to Vadstena after the cer-emonies in Rome, and this is what Gascoigne refers to.[62]

Let us return to the certificate, which goes on to report that one of the earliest confessor generals of Syon Abbey, Robert Bell, on a visit to Vadstena,[63] received, as a gift from the Swedish Bridgettines, a bone from Bridget's shrine that had its place in Vadstena Abbey.

> ... *Et dominus Robertus Belle, secundus confessor generalis monasterii Syone in Anglia, fuit in monasterio Wastenensi in regno Swecie. Et ibi recepit ex concensu [i.e. consensu] illius conuentus ordinis sancti nostri Saluatoris vnum os sancte Birgitte de scrinio, in quo requiescunt eius sancta ossa in Wastena in regno Swecie* ...

> '... And Sir Robert Bell, the second Confessor General of the monas-tery Syon in England, stayed in the monastery of Vadstena in the kingdom of Sweden. And here, with the consent of this convent of our order of Saint Saviour, he received a bone of Saint Bridget from the shrine where her bones rest in Vadstena, in the kingdom of Sweden ...'

---

62 Gejrot, *Diarium Vadstenense*, n. 31, 64, 77. The problems of Bridget's translation feasts and the various sources mentioning them are discussed in detail in A. M. Jönsson, 'Den heliga Birgittas skrinläggning', in *Kyrkohistorisk årsskrift 1987* (Uppsala, 1987), pp. 37–53. Seeking to find out why 28 May is the calendar day for Birgitta's translation, Jönsson arrives at the conclusion (p. 50) that there must have been yet another *translatio* in Vadstena on 28 May, 1381, not mentioned by the Diarium.

63 Robert Belle visited Vadstena (together with Thomas Sterington) in the spring of 1427 (arriving on 18 April: Gejrot, *Diarium Vadstenense*, n. 376). This visit to the Swedish monas-tery has already been mentioned above.

A 'large part' of this bone was then given by Bell to Gascoigne on 22 August 1454. Gascoigne presented the relic, enclosed in crystal, to the monastery of Osney:

> *Et ego predictus magister Thomas Gascoigne, filius et heres Ricardi Gascoigne in comitatu Eboracensi in Anglia, feci illud os sancte Birgitte sponse Cristi eterne includi in berillo incluso in capsa seu scrinio argenteo et deaurato. Et sic inclusum dedi monasterio beatissime semper virginis Marie de Osneye[64] iuxta vniuersitatem Oxoniensem, eo quod abbas et conuentus eiusdem loci anno Domini M° cccc° liiij° concesserunt, quod quolibet anno imperpetuum hoc mundo durante haberent missam de eadem sancta Birgitta vidua ...*

'And I, Master Thomas Gascoigne, the son and heir of Richard Gascoigne in the county of York in England, had this bone of St Bridget, Christ's eternal bride, enclosed in crystal in a box or reliquary of silver and gold. And I gave it enclosed in this way to the monastery of the most holy, perpetual Virgin Mary at Osney, close to Oxford university, since the abbot and the convent there in the year 1454 had consented to celebrate mass for the same saint, the widow Bridget, every year, eternally and as long as this world exists ...'

The Vows of Obedience

Between the historical texts and the obituary there is a section containing the formulaic versions of the vows of obedience that were to be taken by new members on the male side of Syon Abbey. These formulae[65] are interesting in several ways. From a linguistic point of view, we find here clear markers for the choice of language among the brothers. As is to be expected, the ordained priests were to read an oath in Latin, while the lay brothers were to speak English. It is tempting to compare this with the words of the Vadstena *Liber usuum*, in a passage on the consecration of new members: *et si nesciant Latinum, legant in lingua materna* ('and if they do not know Latin, they may read in the vernacular').[66]

At least a week after profession, these oaths were to be read aloud by every single new brother in the presence of the Confessor General and all the

---

[64] The monastery of Osney (Oxford) was founded in 1129 for Augustinian canons; see H. R. Luard (ed.), *Annales monastici*, Vol. 4, *Annales monasterii de Oseneia A.D. 1016–1347* (London, 1869).

[65] Fols 18v–20r.

[66] S. Risberg (ed.), *Liber usuum fratrum monasterii Vadstenensis. The Customary of the Vadstena Brothers*, Acta Universitatis Stockholmiensis, Studia Latina Stockholmiensia L (Stockholm, 2003), p. 132.

brethren, who had gathered in the chapter house. The original form included deacons – the phrase used is *frater professus in ordine et gradu sacerdotali vel diaconali* – but a later editing hand has for some reason crossed out the latter category. The newly professed priest was to give the Confessor General (and his successors) a formal promise to obey and accept the Bridgettine Rule and the Syon Additions, and indeed every kind of document or custom known in the monastery. Special emphasis is laid on the *Bulla reformatoria*, the papal bull issued for Syon in 1425. Based on the Bridgettine privilege of 1413, *Mare Magnum*, it is also known as the *Mare Anglicanum*.[67] At the end of the oath the priest declares that he has put his sign, or signature, in the official chapter house register (*signum meum manuale in communi registro domus nostre capitularis impressi*). The English texts – intended for lay brothers and focaries – are *mutatis mutandis* translations of the Latin version. It is worth mentioning that the scribe left empty spaces at the same places in both versions, after the words *omnia alia*, corresponding to 'al other ordynaunces' in the English variant. Perhaps the reason for this editorial detail is to make it possible to include future bulls and legislation also to be obeyed. Extracts of the first oath in both versions are quoted here side by side.

In nomine Patris et Filij et Spiritus sancti. Amen. <E>go N N ffrater professus in ordine et gradu sacerdotali vel diaconali (....) Quapropter reputans me fore contentum de omnibus et singulis premissis promitto tibi confessori generali huius monasterij et successoribus tuis me obedienciam seruaturum secundum regulam beati Augustini et constituciones beate Birgitte acceptando et approbando necnon et admittendo litteras apostolicas – et precipue illam, que inter nos vocatur Bulla reformatoria, cum alijs scriptis autenticis dicte bulle non dissonis aut discrepantibus – addiciones	In nomine Patris et Filij et Spiritus sancti. Amen. <I> N N brother professyd in the order *and* degre of a lay brother or focary (…) Therfor I, holdyng me fullyche contente of alle premysses, promytt to the generalle confessour of thys monasterij and to thy successours me to kepe obedyence after the rewle of Seynt Austyn and constitucions of seynt Birgitt acceptyng and allowyng and also admyttyng the popys lettres or bulles and namely that bulle, whiche amonge vs is clepyd Bulla reformatoria, whith other autentyk writynges not discrepaunt nor discordynge to the seyd bulle,

---

67 See Höjer, *Studier i Vadstena klosters och Birgittinordens historia*, p. 256; Cnattingius, *Studies in the Order of St. Bridget of Sweden*, pp. 150–5; and F. R. Johnston, 'Joan North, First Abbess of Syon', *Birgittiana*, 1 (1996), 52.

quoque et statuta localia,
consuetudines laudabiles,
iniuncciones ordinarias, decreta et
omnia alia per sorores et fratres
ante me professos pensatis
pensandis racionabiliter et
voluntarie acceptata, approbata
necnon et admissa ex eorum
communi consensu et assensu (...)
In quorum omnium et singulorum
testimonium signum meum
manuale in communi registro
domus nostre capitularis[68]
impressi.

acceptyng also allowyng *and*
admyttyng the addicions addyd to to the
seyd rewle, *pri*uileges, ordynary
iniunccions, loca*lle* statutes, laud-
able custons, decrees *and* al other
ordynaunces wylfully admytted
and resonably approuyd by the
comen consente of sustres and
brethren *pro*fessyd to fore me (…)
In to wytnes wherof I haue made
my signe manualle in the comen
register of *our* chapte*r*hous.

There is also a shorter text that could be chosen instead, a compressed version, as it were, of the first text, about half as long. But time is precious, and tediousness to be avoided: in the case of many men taking the oath at the same time, there is a further, very brief version to be used.

Si plures fuerint, singuli dicant
idem vel brevius sic:

Yf there be moo, eche of hem schal
say the same or els thus more breuely:

In nomine Patris etc. <E>go N N
promitto tibi confessori generali
huius monasterij me obedienciam
seruaturum iuxta formam
prenotatam.

In nomine Patris etc. I N N
*pro*mitte to the general*le*
confessour of this mo*n*astery me to
kepe obedience after the seyd
forme.

Are these formulae similar to preserved documents from Vadstena? I have found only one example that deserves mention here. We still have an original certificate written in 1492, before the introduction of the future Confessor General Sueno Tordonis (Sven Tordsson). The Vadstena text is written by the postulant himself, and it is probably the closest parallel to be found. Containing promises to take on the burdens of a priest brother, the certificate falls within the same category as the Syon vows, but it is in fact quite different from the variants used by the English Bridgettines, as we have seen.[69] There is

---

[68] The words *diem octauam professionis mee* have been crossed over in the ms (so also in the shorter version).

[69] *Ego Sweno Tordonis presbiter protestor et recognosco per hec proprie manus mee scripta, quod elegerim assumj inter fratres sacerdotes et ad eorum statum et gradum cum suis annexis*

a reason for this. The Syon vows of obedience are the result of regulations in the 1420s that concerned only the English house. The oaths themselves are mentioned in the Syon Additions for the brethren, and we get to know where they are to be found: 'in the comen register of the chapter house'.[70] We may assume that the texts in the Martiloge were copied from this common register, which must be the same as the source mentioned in the oaths, as quoted above.

* * *

The Syon Martiloge, which we have described and discussed in this essay, is a unique document. It is utilised and quoted by many historians and other scholars, it provides dates and facts on Syon and the people connected to the house, it mirrors both the stability of the first centuries and Syon's dramatic time in exile. To the philologist it offers further possibilities. Like few other sources it is a natural and rewarding witness to the gradual change of the traditional monastic idiom, in style as well as in orthography and vocabulary, as we have seen in the text excerpts from various periods. The Martiloge takes its modern readers on a long journey, starting in pre-Reformation England and landing in a new, uncertain world.

---

officiis et oneribus in monasterio Watzstenensi per fratres huiusmodi in tali gradu et statu exerceri solitis vsque ad finem vite mee sine murmure et reclamacione a me tenendis et peragendis de uera et libera mea voluntate electis, circa festum Petri advincula habitum suscepturus. In testimonium premissorum sigillum meum hic inferius est impressum ('I, Sven Tordsson, priest, who will receive my habit by the feast of Saint Peter ad Vincula, truly certify by this letter written by my own hand that I have chosen to be accepted among the priest brothers and to their place and rank with the offices and duties connected to them in Vadstena monastery, such duties that are usually performed by the brothers in that place and rank. I promise to do and fulfil these duties to the end of my life without complaining or disapproval as they are chosen by me by my own true and free will. As testimony of this, my seal has been impressed below'). Orig. on paper, [1492], National Archives, Stockholm.

[70] For an edition of the Syon Additions see James Hogg (ed.), *The Rewyll of Seynt Sauioure, 3. The Syon Additions for the Brethren and The Boke of Sygnes from the St. Paul's Cathedral Library Ms*, Salzburger Studien zur Anglistik und Amerikanistik Band 6 (Salzburg, 1980), esp. pp. 51–2. These were based on the Vadstena Additions (of Prior Petrus Olavi) but contained specific instructions for Syon; see Johnston, 'Joan North', pp. 50–2 (with further references). Cf. Gillespie, *The Book and the Brotherhood*, p. 203 (n. 3); and Gillespie, 'Hid diuinite', p. 195.

8

Syon Abbey Preserved: Some Historians of Syon[1]

ANN M. HUTCHISON

Early Accounts

> The 25th daie of November the howse of Sion was suppressed into the Kinges handes, and the ladies and brethren putt out, which was the vertues howse of religion that was in England, …[2]

This, by now familiar, entry for 1539 from Charles Wriothesley's *A Chronicle of England During the Reigns of the Tudors, from A.D. 1485 to 1559*, apparently announcing the end of a great religious house, is actually one of the earliest in a series of 'historical' glimpses of Syon Abbey.[3] The centuries of Syon's continuing existence have not passed uneventfully, and over the years interested men and women, both inside and outside of the Order, have, with various ends in mind, taken up the task of recording its story. A number of these histories, either originating within the Syon Abbey community or kept there, have recently been passed on to the custody of the University of Exeter, and to mark the transfer of the documents and manuscripts, it is perhaps pertinent to consider the authors of such histories and what aspects of Syon they 'preserve'.

Before Wriothesley's *Chronicle*, there are references to and some accounts of Syon indicating that from the early years of its foundation the abbey had

1 An earlier version of this essay was given as a paper at a conference at the University of Exeter designed to celebrate the deposit of manuscripts, books and research materials from Syon Abbey in the University's Old Library. As a long-time user of the notebooks of Canon John Rory Fletcher, I am greatly indebted to his work to which I wish to pay special tribute. I am also grateful to Lady Abbess and the community of Syon Abbey for drawing my attention to this material when I first visited in 1986, and for their continuing help with my research both in answering questions and in allowing me access to papers and archives still in their keeping.
2 The entry concludes: 'the landes and goodes to the Kinges use'.
3 Charles Wriothesley, *A Chronicle of England During the Reigns of the Tudors, from A.D. 1485 to 1559*, ed. W. D. Hamilton, Camden Society 1 (Westminster, 1875), p. 109.

acquired a reputation for strict observance and especially efficacious prayers. Two of these merit special mention because they indicate that from its foundation Syon's reputation for sanctity and spiritual power was widely known. The first is the 'Salutacio Sancte Brigitte', a poem seeking the intercession of St Bridget,[4] and composed by the Augustinian canon, John Awdelay, some time between 1422 and 1426 at around the time that Syon became an enclosed, functioning monastery.[5] Of particular interest is his detailed knowledge of Syon Abbey, or 'Bregitsion',[6] as he calls it throughout the 207-line poem. He knows its precise location, 'Beside þe Chene, soþly, seuen myle fro Lundun' (136) and is very much aware of the 'precious prayoure' (183) of that 'spiritual plas' (181) whose members 'han þat pouere' (185) to 'purches here our grace' (183). Awdelay may have actually gone to Syon for its famous Pardon, which he mentions several times (e.g. 59–61, 150–3) and describes at some length (139–44).[7] We know for certain from her *Book* that Margery Kempe about a decade later (c.1434) did go to Syon precisely for its Pardon. She arrived, her *Book* tells us, 'a iij days beforn Lammes Day, for to purchasyn hir pardon'; once in the Church she was moved to 'gret devocyon and ful hy contemplacyon' and, as a result, experienced one of her famous fits of tears.[8]

Writing about Syon Abbey in his *Chronicle* more than a century later, Wriothesley does not seem to have been so personally and urgently impelled. Yet, the entry on the closing of Syon stands out when compared to other suppressions noted in the *Chronicle*. More typically, for instance, the entry for Bury St Edmunds, immediately preceding that of Syon, merely states:

> Also this moneth [i.e. November] the Abbey of Burie, in Suffolke, was suppressed, and the monkes putt out and changed to secular priestes, and all the goodes and landes [confiscated] to the Kinges use.[9]

---

4   See Ella Keats Whiting (ed.), *The Poems of John Audelay*, EETS 184 (London, 1931), pp. 164–7.

5   Syon was founded in 1415, and was enclosed in 1420; the first professions were made in April of that year. The elections of the first Abbess and first Confessor General were ratified by the bishop of London in 1421; see, for example, John Rory Fletcher, *The Story of the English Bridgettines of Syon Abbey* (South Brent, Devon, 1933), pp. 20, 24–5.

6   'Bregitsion', or 'Bridget's Syon', also indicates the close association of the Swedish saint with the English house of her Order at this period.

7   See Michael Bennett, 'John Audelay: Some New Evidence on His Life and Work', *The Chaucer Review*, 16 (1982), 344–55. This was the *de vincula* Pardon, a special privilege given to Syon by the Pope, and it was offered in Lent and on Lammas Day, 1 August.

8   Barry Windeatt (ed.), *The Book of Margery Kempe* (London, 2000; repr. Cambridge, 2004); see Chronology, p. viii and book II, ch. 10, pp. 418–21.

9   Wriothesley, *Chronicle*, I, p. 108.

Such bare facts seem to be the general pattern; although when the recipient is other than the king, Wriothesley does give some detail about the disposition of the goods and lands; and he occasionally offers personal information, as, for example, at Barking where he notes that 'Sir Thomas Denis [the recipient of 'the howse with the demeanes'] hath to wife my ladie Murffen, some tyme wief to Mr. Murfen, late Major of London, and daughter to Mr. Angell Dunne, and sometime Mrs. to Alis my wife that now is.'[10] Concerning the *Chronicle*, Gordon Kipling notes in his *Oxford DNB* entry, Wriothesley, 'Always conscious of his position as a herald [in December 1534 he had been promoted to Windsor herald] and member of the king's household, ... strove to create a chronicle at once loyal and carefully observant', and he adds that 'Particularly in the earlier portions of his *Chronicle*, he endeavours to present a sympathetic account of Henry VIII's religious reforms.'[11] In this context, then, the remark about the virtuousness of the Syon community says a great deal about the reputation of Syon at the time of the Dissolution. Nowhere else does Wriothesley appear to react in any significant way to the events he is chronicling.[12]

Perspectives of Two Syon Nuns in the Late Sixteenth Century

From later in the century, during the 1580s, two fascinating accounts survive by and about two contemporary nuns who were forced by circumstances on the Continent to return to England. The first, entitled *The Life and Good End of Sister Marie*, was most likely written in 1580 by someone who attended Sister Mary Champney during the last weeks of her life; in describing her life, the author indicates her views on a number of issues and quotes her own words.[13] The second consists of two letters written by Sister Elizabeth Sander[14] from Syon Abbey after the community had settled in Rouen;[15] these can be dated with some certainty to 1587, the year Sister Elizabeth returned to her community. Concerning *The Life*, the only known contemporary manu-

---

[10] Wriothesley, *Chronicle*, I, p. 108.

[11] See 'Wriothesley, Charles', *ODNB*.

[12] Wriothesley's aunt, Agnes, had been a choir sister at Syon; her name appears, as 'Agnes Wrysley', on the election list of Constancia Browne in 1518. When she died on 30 October 1529, she was buried at Syon. Perhaps Wriothesley had actually visited her there and thus might have had firsthand experience of the monastery.

[13] For my edition, see *Birgittiana*, 13 (2002), 3–89. Hereafter cited as *The Life*.

[14] The name appears in various forms: Sanders, Saunder, Saunders, but the commonly accepted form today is Sander; see *ODNB*.

[15] Syon moved from Spanish Flanders to Rouen in 1580 since life had become intolerable for religious houses in Flanders at that period. At the same period, the English College moved from Douai to Rheims.

script is British Library, Additional 18,650, and the watermark suggests that it belongs to the last decade of the sixteenth century. From at least 1697, when it appears in the inventory of the Denbigh library at Newnham Paddox, Warwickshire, compiled by Edward Bernard, the manuscript remained with the Feilding family until it was purchased on 10 May 1851 by the British Museum from the seventh Earl of Denbigh in the sale of his manuscripts.[16] So far, I have not been able to discover how it came into the possession of the Feildings, but, a Catholic family, they were exactly the audience for which the work was intended. There is also a typescript with notes appended made by John Rory Fletcher when he was working on his history of Syon Abbey. This is now, along with the rest of Canon Fletcher's papers, at the University of Exeter.[17] *The Life* tells the story of Sister Mary Champney, who became a Bridgettine in 1569 when Katherine Palmer was the Abbess and the Syon community was at Mishagen in Spanish Flanders. She must have first been introduced to Abbess Palmer more than a year earlier, since there needed to be time for renewal of the request to join the Order (usually three months) and for probation (usually a year).[18] She was with Syon when they had to flee from Mishagen and seek refuge in Antwerp, and in Mechelen, or Malines, where they settled next. In the late summer or early autumn of 1578, however, she was one of a group of about eleven or more of the younger nuns who were sent back to England in disguise, both for their own safety – as it was becoming dangerous to be a Catholic in Flanders at this period – and, it was hoped, to collect alms for the impoverished and virtually starving community.[19] Her

[16] I am indebted to Professor T. A. Birrell for this information; see *The Life*, p. 30, nn. 66, 67.

[17] Autograph; vol. 32. Exeter University Library. This is no. 32 in the list drawn up by Tore Nyberg in his helpful catalogue, 'The Canon Fletcher Manuscripts in Syon Abbey', *Nordisk Tidskrift för Bok – och Biblioteksväsen*, 47 (1960), 56–69, at p. 68. Unaware of the earlier provenance of the manuscript, Nyberg suggested it had remained with the community until the return of Abbess Halford.

[18] By January 1568, the community had certainly come to Mishagen, and perhaps earlier. Mishagen is about three miles from Antwerp.

[19] Nancy Bradley Warren, in ch. 6, 'Dissolution, Diaspora, and Defining Englishness: Syon in Exile and Elizabethan Politics', of her recent book, *Women of God and Arms: Female Spirituality and Political Conflict, 1380–1600* (Philadelphia, 2005), presents an interesting discussion of the opposing Catholic and Protestant agendas at the time of Elizabeth. In claiming that the younger nuns were sent back to England for political purposes, however, she misconstrues the main motives for doing so and underestimates the danger of their situation in Spanish Flanders in the late 1570s (not to mention the Order's extreme poverty at this period which resulted in poor nourishment, one cause of the severe illness experienced by a number of the young women); see pp. 147–8. Moreover, it should be noted that this course of action was undertaken with reluctance and misgivings only after all other alternatives had been investigated, and even then it was not condoned by all (as indicated in a letter sent to Douai on 15 December 1578 and received on 15 February 1579: 'Many of the wisest sort hath found great fault with the sendinge

story is recorded in or near London during Lent of 1580 as she lay very ill with a wasting disease of the lungs.[20] The manuscript, clearly intended for circulation among, and the edification of, English Catholics – and thus devoid of names of living people and places – describes the life and last days of Sister Mary with a considerable degree of narrative skill. Most notably, in structuring the story of Mary Champney, the author exploits the flashback, primarily to provide necessary background information, but with the added effect of interrupting the story's present and whetting the reader's appetite to return to the gripping and sensitively told deathbed narrative. The anonymous author, definitely not a Bridgettine (since the pronoun 'their' is commonly used to refer to any aspect of the Order), was, judging by the respectful way in which both priests and nuns are referred to or addressed, most likely a lay person. From the very detailed observations of Sister Mary's physical appearance, I have mused that the writer may have been a woman, and if Canon Fletcher is correct in guessing that the Fulham house which afforded refuge to the young nuns was that of Thomas and Magdalen Heath,[21] it might even have been Mrs Heath herself.

Although this is certainly a very biased narrative – as Canon Fletcher comments, 'the highly coloured and imaginative style which is characteristic of the hagiography of the time in some parts requires correction' – it has much interesting information to offer. Indeed, the English officers, or the 'wolves', that is, the men who escorted the young sisters, or 'lambes', safely to ports of embarkation in Flanders, were not only protective of their countrywomen, but, in providing food and money to the obviously destitute young women,

---

over of the younge nuns …'; see T. F. Knox (ed.), *The First and Second Diaries of the English College, Douay* (London, 1878), p. 149.

[20] The text makes quite clear that the visitors who came to see Sister Mary came during the last months of her life when she was either in London or just outside in Fulham, where her story was being recorded, not, as Warren imagines, in Flanders between 1569 and 1578 (see *Women of God and Arms*, p. 148).

[21] See Fletcher, *Story*, p. 58, and the Syon Abbey periodical, *The Poor Souls' Friend*, 13.3 (May–June, 1965), 82, n. 28 (hereafter *PSF*). We learn about the house in Fulham from the letters of Sister Elizabeth Sander (see below), and since these were written after her return to Syon Abbey in Rouen, she could be more explicit than the author of *The Life*. Although we do not know for sure with whom Sister Mary stayed when she first arrived in England in 1578, from internal evidence we can deduce that when she died in April 1580 she was at the same house in Fulham where Sister Elizabeth stayed with the very ill Sister Anne Stapleton (Sister Anne's black beads were given as a gift to one of Sister Mary's visitors; see *The Life*, pp. 18–20). Canon Fletcher, however, had suggested that the house might have been that of Lord Vaux at Hackney (see *Story*, p. 59), but Lord Vaux rented this house at Hackney somewhat later when he was released from prison some time in 1583; see Godfrey Anstruther, *Vaux of Harrowden, A Recusant Family* (Newport, 1953), pp. 149, 117.

generous as well, showing that, in their minds at least, nationality took priority over religion. Such loyalty on the part of the English military was again evident almost two years later when the rest of the community was in peril and forced to seek safety in Antwerp before fleeing to France. Incidentally, in the course of the narrative, we learn much about the relatively 'relaxed' atmosphere in the Catholic community in and around London in the spring of 1580 before the arrival in June of the Jesuits, Persons and Campion, both of whom in one way or another touched the lives of the English Bridgettines. Priests, doctors and other visitors attending Sister Mary seem to have been able to come and go; two of her sisters were brought (probably from the country)[22] to be with her, as was the custom, at her death; and her funeral seems to have been carried out with due Bridgettine ceremony. Most relevant to our interest, however, is the light the narrative throws on aspects of the life of an enclosed, contemplative order and on those who had chosen to live that life.

Not unexpectedly of a community trying to maintain a continuing existence against all odds, the members of Syon seem to have been very conscious of the requirements of the Bridgettine Rule and tried to follow it as closely as possible, though the wise Katherine Palmer had in 1564 obtained a papal rescript granting Syon a *sanatio* dispensing 'all infringements of Canon Law or their Rule which might have occurred in the past, or might occur in the future', in view of the 'peculiar difficulties' of their exile.[23] One such change that affected Mary Champney was that her year of probation – for obvious reasons – was spent in the enclosure, or house, rather than away;[24] but most tenets, such as individual possession of property of any kind without permission of the Abbess, dietary rules, and especially adherence to the daily office and to devotional activities of reading, meditation and prayer, were upheld as far as possible. *The Scale of Perfection*, a book read by many sisters in the pre-Dissolution period, was, along with 'sayntes lyves' and 'histories of holie scriptures' (fol. 6v), well known to Sister Mary. Moreover, as Chantress, Mary found particular solace in the 'solempnytye' (fol. 6v) of their service which was strictly kept up at the urging of Abbess Palmer 'that they never lett

---

[22] They may have been part of the group staying at Lyford Grange, the home of Francis Yate, one of their chief benefactors.

[23] Katherine Palmer, one of the younger nuns when Syon Abbey was taken by the crown in 1539, had led a group of sisters and brothers to Antwerp, and on the death of Abbess Agnes Jordan in 1546, she had returned to England to collect those who had been with Abbess Jordan at Denham in Buckinghamshire. Although she had been the nominal head of the community since Abbess Jordan's death, when the community returned to England under Queen Mary in 1557, her position as Abbess was formalised on 1 March of that year (see Fletcher, *Story*, p. 41). For the *sanatio*, see *PSF* 12.1 (Jan.–Feb., 1964), 19–22.

[24] *PSF* 12.1 (Jan.–Feb., 1964), 21.

downe theire quier for any decaye of theire companye'. When, on 8 November 1576, the enclosure of their house in Mechelen was broken into and pillaged, 'the vse of the quier' was 'quite lefte of', leaving the sisters, and particularly Mary, like their namesakes described in the Psalm (136/137), 'vpon the fluddes of Babilon morninge and sobbinge'. From that time, though survival seemed to become the main concern, 'they continewed the same holy vse ... as the alteracion of their state might permit'. In coming to England, Sister Mary brought at least one service book with her, and during her last illness a new one was being copied for her, as we learn from the fact that it was eventually to be given to one of Syon's young benefactors, 'a virtuous youthe' (fol. 13v), who had promised substantial alms. This young benefactor had also offered funds to pay for the printing of their service books and the *Scale of Perfection*, described as 'another of their bookes as needefull to be renewed for the mendynge of the olde prynte' (fol. 14v), more likely a reference to the language, rather than the physical state of this book. From other sources,[25] we know that this enthusiastic benefactor was George Gilbert, a member of a group of young Catholics who would a few weeks later greet and assist Fathers Persons and Campion during their mission in England. Gilbert, in fact, visited Syon in Rouen some years later on his way to Rome, where he eventually became a Jesuit himself.

Sister Mary's death occurred on 27 April 1580, and *The Life* concludes with a closely detailed account of her last hours and a final request to readers for prayers. Some years later, after Syon was safely, as they then hoped, established in Rouen, the young nuns were recalled. Of those who survived, most did not return before May of 1587. Among these was Sister Elizabeth Sander, younger sister of Dr Nicholas Sander (a key writer and activist for the Catholic cause) and of Margaret, who had been the Prioress of Syon and had died at Mechelen in March of 1576.[26] Sister Elizabeth's letters describing her sometimes hair-raising adventures in England are the next source – and, once again, transcripts and documentation are amongst Canon Fletcher's papers.[27] The usual practice at Syon was, and is, for the Abbess to look after the

---

[25] See *PSF* 13.1 (March, 1905), 20; quoting from Henry Foley's *Records of the English Province of the Society of Jesus*, 7 vols in 8 (London, 1875–1883), a letter from Father Agazzarri, SJ, to Father General Acquaviva in the life of George Gilbert (iii. 689).

[26] Margaret Sander, Syon's eleventh Prioress, died in Mechelen on 4 March 1576; see *PSF* 14.3 (May–June, 1966), 79; also noted in *PSF* 12.2 (March–April, 1964), 51 n. 6, and 12.5 (Sep.–Oct., 1964), 147; and earlier mentioned in *PSF* 1.12 (Feb., 1894), 285.

[27] See Nyberg, 'The Canon Fletcher Manuscripts in Syon Abbey'; the E. Sander letters are listed under: '6. History of Syon Abbey. 1563–1580. Syon in Exile. II', pp. 62–3. Nyberg notes that the second letter is taken from the *PSF* (see n. 30 below).

correspondence, but Sister Elizabeth wrote at the request of Sir Francis Englefield, a devout Catholic who had left England at the succession of Elizabeth and who concerned himself both with the well-being of other English Catholic exiles (it was he who had helped Syon find a house when they first moved to Mechelen) and with assistance to the English mission.[28] Sir Francis was then in Spain, and from Sister Elizabeth he hoped to learn about conditions in England and especially the names of those who had assisted her. When it appeared that Sir Francis did not receive the first 'long letter', Sister Elizabeth wrote a second. The two letters eventually ended up in the Englefield Correspondence at Valladolid: the original of the second, lost early on, is available in a Spanish version,[29] while a copy of the first, once apparently lost, now survives in a sixteenth-century hand. The letters have been published in *The Poor Souls' Friend*: the second appeared in 1894 (and again in 1905) in a translation of the Spanish made by Dom Adam Hamilton, OSB (another preserver of Syon's past);[30] and both letters were printed in 1966.[31]

Sister Elizabeth writes at a brisk pace and, though the extraordinary experiences she describes happened some years earlier, she skilfully brings them to life. Her first letter, more detailed than the second, provides a useful key to some of the people and places mentioned in Sister Mary Champney's *Life*. Unlike a number of the other sisters, who were arrested on their arrival in England, Sister Elizabeth, having managed to satisfy the official who examined the group at Gravelines, arrived at Billingsgate and then Fulham without incident. She was surprised to find herself alone at Fulham, but after a week a

---

[28] Sir Francis Englefield was from a prominent Berkshire family with connections to the court. He himself became a courtier, and under Mary rose to become Master of the Court of Wards and Liveries in 1554. He left England in 1559, and as a result of former connections with Philip II, became an advisor to the Duke of Alva in 1568. After troubles arose in Spanish Flanders and the death of his wife in England in 1580, he moved to Madrid and eventually to St Alban's College in Valladolid, where he died in 1596; see 'Englefield, Sir Francis', *ODNB*.

[29] See Diego de Yepes, *Historia Particular de la Persecucion de Inglaterra* (Madrid, 1599); repr. with introduction by D. M. Rogers (Westmead, Farnborough, Hants, 1971), pp. 724–37. According to Rogers, this version had been published twice before being incorporated into Robert Persons's *Relacion de algunos martyrios* in 1590, the source for Yepes's version (Rogers, 'Introduction', p. viii).

[30] See *PSF* 1.12 (Feb., 1894), 285–6; 2.1 (March, 1894), 11–14 (here the ordering of paragraphs has become confused, p. 12); 2.2 (April, 1894), 30–1; 2.3 (May, 1894), 56–7; and *PSF* 12.11 (Jan., 1905), 299–300; 12.12 (Feb., 1905), 330–2; 13.1 (March, 1905), 19, 20–1, in this printing the second letter is cut short, and the account of Fathers Vivian and Marsh found in the first published version (*PSF* 2.3 [May, 1894], 56–7) is omitted; for Hamilton's history see below.

[31] For the first letter see *PSF* 14.1 (Jan.–Feb., 1966), 11–22; for the second translated letter see *PSF* 14.2 (March–April, 1966), 43–54; but, as in 1905, the second letter is missing the account of Fathers Vivian and Marsh.

very ill Sister Anne Stapleton arrived, and Sister Elizabeth tells us she stayed with her from 'St Symon & Jude day' (28 October) until 'St Thomas day [21 December] at which tyme I was sent away fro her (for some respects) much against myne owne mynde'.[32] Sister Elizabeth's unwillingness to leaving her dying sister reflects her wish to follow Bridgettine custom, but this desire must have been outweighed by fears for her safety (the 'some respects' mentioned obliquely), prompted, as Canon Fletcher suggests, by the risk of enquiries at the time of a death.[33] Sister Elizabeth thus spent Christmas with one of her blood sisters who lived at Abingdon, but afterwards, hearing that Sister Juliana Harman was staying nearby at Lyford Grange, she moved there.[34] Sister Elizabeth tells us she was there for a year and a half, that is, from January 1579 until about June or July of 1580, when, 'that place beyng in daunger of troubles' (p. 12), she went to stay with another of her sisters in Hampshire. Though, as we learn from Canon Fletcher, Elizabeth's brother-in-law, Henry Pitts, was a Protestant, the rest of the family were very staunch Catholics, and on arrival there Sister Elizabeth joined her nephew in distributing copies of Campion's *Challenge* and was eventually arrested. Thus began a long and continuous series of interrogations and imprisonments for Sister Elizabeth, not so much on account of what she had been doing, but more importantly because her name was Sander and it was thought that she had been sent as part of a delegation by her brother, Nicholas, 'in hope', as she reports, 'that our Relygion and Order should come upp agayne' (p. 13). Despite denials that she had not seen her brother 'in many years' (p. 13), and her repeated stating of the fact that driven out of their house abroad she had been forced to seek refuge among friends, she was not believed. Eventually she was sent to Winchester for further interrogation, but still refused to reveal any information about those who had been looking after her in England or who might have been visiting her brother-in-law's house. Finally she was put in Bridewell prison, 'a place indeed for Roogs' (p. 15), as she tells us, and deprived of her books and other possessions, and of food and light for periods of up to nine days (p. 16) – tactics that somehow resonate today. Continuing attempts by the warden and others to persuade her to attend church and harsh treatment at the Assizes, to which she was periodically summoned and fined for recusancy, failed to move her, and so she remained in Bridewell for three more years.

---

32 *PSF* 14.1 (Jan.–Feb., 1966), 11; the underlined letters indicate the expansion of an abbreviation in the original.
33 Fletcher, *Story*, p. 60.
34 It worth noting that Lyford Grange (the moated manor house of Syon benefactor Francis Yate) is where, on 17 July 1581, Campion was arrested, along with the two Syon nuns who were still staying there at the time, Sisters Juliana Harman and Catherine Kingsmill.

At this point in her first letter, Sister Elizabeth pauses, clearly feeling somewhat uncomfortable, to remind Sir Francis that this account has been written at his wish, on account of 'the prompt Dewty which I am always most ready to performe towards you', and, she continues, at the wish of 'my Lady and our ffather', otherwise 'I have byn very loathe to have done, the matter being of myself' (p. 17). If Sister Elizabeth has seemed 'heroic' so far, this was not all. Letters came from the Abbess and Confessor General recalling the nuns to France, and one was addressed to her in particular, in the hope that it might secure her release from prison. In her attempt to comply she was advised by priests whom she had consulted that unless she was set at liberty by Council or by Judges, she could not in all conscience go; the sense being, that though one could ignore the law of the established church, the law of the land was binding. Sister Elizabeth did not, however, give up. By virtue of an invitation to attend Mass in a house in Winchester and being apprehended there, Sister Elizabeth was placed in Winchester Castle, a much less severe prison where the wife of the Governor was sympathetic and twice helped her escape.[35] The first attempt took place at night: Sister Elizabeth was let down over the wall of the castle by rope and had to make her way across the fields to the appointed safe house, that of Mrs Tichbourne.[36] In her first letter, the whole episode is briefly described, but in the second she writes that, 'had it not been for the great desire I had to obey my superior, and find myself again with my Sisters, which gave me strength, I would not for a thousand worlds have put myself into such a dangerous position, and one that, considered in itself, was more than rash'.[37] Once again, however, the three priests who were then resident at the house of Mrs Shelley in Mapledurham to which she had moved for safety, after some debate with Sister Elizabeth and consultation amongst themselves, insisted that she return to prison, partly on account of concern that the wife of the Governor might come to harm and also for fear that the 'heretics', as the authorities were called, might impose harsher conditions on Catholics. Although humiliated, after her return to Winchester Castle on horseback, accompanied by a servant, and 'a crowne in mony' (p. 20), she was treated more leniently, and another escape with the tacit approval of the

---

[35] Warren suggests that Sister Elizabeth 'managed multiple escapes from prison' (*Women of God and Arms*, p. 147); but prisons were more porous then than now (i.e. one could leave temporarily), and only two actual escapes are mentioned, motivated, as she herself stated, by her desire to obey her superiors and return to her monastery.

[36] Her son, Nicholas, is among the prisoners Sister Elizabeth listed at Bridewell, and Mrs Tichbourne was a benefactor during the entire period of her imprisonment, and helped again when she eventually left prison (see Letter no. 1, *PSF* 14.1 (Jan.–Feb., 1966), 18, 21.

[37] Letter no. 2, *PSF* 14.2 (March–April, 1966), 48.

Governor was effected. Sister Elizabeth's trials did not end there, however, as it seems that the pursuivants had their eye on her. Eventually through the bribes of her cousin, Erasmus Sander, who was well known to the pursuivants, and through the alms of Francis Yate and William Hoorde, she managed to slip into France undetected and find her way to Syon Abbey in Rouen in the late spring of 1587.[38]

Besides a story of what to most people would be almost unimaginable hardship, Sister Elizabeth's letters provide a brief glimpse of a woman firmly dedicated to her religion and her community; these in turn, along with her habits of prayer and meditation, must have given her an identity powerful enough to allow her to carry on despite circumstances far removed from those of her convent. At the point when it seemed that she would never gain her freedom on account of being the sister of the 'dreaded' Nicholas Sander and of not having paid her fines (by now of hundreds of pounds), she resolved, she tells Sir Francis in her second letter, not to think more about it 'but ... to stay there all my life, and look upon my prison as my convent'.[39] Standing back, however, one can see some ground to the fear of the 'heretics' that Catholics indeed had 'hope' of re-establishing their religion, as we remember that Sister Elizabeth was initially apprehended for distributing the *Challenge*, or *Brag*, of Father Campion. In *The Life* too, Sister Mary Champney expresses the hope that Syon, referring, I think, both to the house and to its religious ethos, 'shalbe builded vp agayne more bewtifully ... then it ever was in our tyme'. On the same occasion, Sister Mary is asked, most likely by a priest, to offer her prayers for 'the speedie conversion of Englande' and 'also for Godes cheife prisoner', adding parenthetically, 'you knowe what good Ladye I meane' (fol. 8) – here covertly referring to Mary, Queen of Scots. The narrating author then adds that Sister Mary had also mentioned that Syon held the secret hope of being someday re-established in the north of England. There does not seem to be any question of treason, but given the early deaths of her siblings, from the perspective of the times, a long life for Elizabeth would not be predicted with any certainty. This view seems to have been shared by many of the exiles (and also by many of the former religious unable to travel abroad), and was indeed the impetus behind the founding of the English mission begun by William Allen in 1574.[40]

---

[38] A letter dated 22 May 1587, sent by Thomas Bayley, the Vice-President of Douaï College (then at Rheims), to John Gibbons, rector of the Jesuit College in Trier, notes her safe return: 'I hear that Sister Saunders is lately come out of England to Syon again'; see Foley (ed.), *Records of the English Province of the Society of Jesus*, iv. 483.

[39] Letter no. 2, *PSF* 14.2 (March–April, 1966), 47.

[40] See D. M. Rogers, who discusses the importance of Allen in the introduction to Yepes's *Historia*, p. [i]. I thus would agree with Warren's view that Syon did indeed envisage a Catholic

Robert Persons, SJ, 'The Wanderings of Syon', and Dom Adam Hamilton, OSB

We turn in the second half of this essay to an intertwined series of narratives that recount Syon's 'wanderings' during their years of exile, and the efforts of some of the abbey's modern historians to disentangle them. The author of the first of these histories was an extremely supportive friend of Syon Abbey and, at the same time, was deeply involved in English Catholic affairs. Although he cannot as readily be cleared of treason, or of treasonous efforts, as the Syon community, there have in recent years been a number of reassessments of him. I am referring to Father Robert Persons (Parsons), SJ (1546–1610).[41] From 1566, Persons had been at Balliol, first as a student, then from 1569 as a fellow. In 1571, he became a lecturer in rhetoric, and from that time until he resigned on 13 February 1574, he held various administrative positions in the college. On his way to Padua to study medicine in June of that year, he stopped in Louvain and under William Good performed the spiritual exercises of Loyola. The effect was such that on 4 July 1575, having left Padua, he became a postulant of the Society of Jesus and, in July of 1578, he was ordained priest. A short time later, Persons began a long collaboration with William Allen in work on the English mission,[42] and on 18 April 1580 left Rome for England where he arrived disguised as an army captain on 17 June 1580. Himself a brilliant writer (even Swift admired his style, as he wrote in *The Tatler* of 28 September 1710[43]), Persons also understood the importance of the printed word in the work of the mission, and so one of the first things he did on arrival in England was to set up a printing press.[44] Following the arrest

England quite different from that of Elizabeth, but the 'participation' of the nuns, as might be expected of an enclosed, contemplative order, was chiefly spiritual, through prayer – and out of the monastery in England, conversation – rather than covert activity; see *Women of God and Arms*, passim.

[41] See 'Persons [Parsons], Robert (1546–1610), Jesuit', *ODNB*; see also Victor Houliston's *Catholic Resistance in Elizabethan England. Robert Person's Jesuit Polemic, 1580–1610* (Aldershot, 2007).

[42] Allen had come to Rome in 1579 with plans to launch a missionary venture; see Houliston, *Catholic Resistance*, p. 24.

[43] ' "The writings of Hooker, who was a Country Clergyman, and of Parsons the Jesuit", wrote Jonathan Swift in The Tatler, 28 September 1710, "are in a style that, with very few Allowances, would not offend any present Reader; much more clear and intelligible than … several others who wrote later" (*Prose Writings*, 2.177).' Quoted in Houliston, 'Persons', *ODNB*.

[44] The press, initially used for intervention in the controversy that blew up over Campion's *Brag*, was forced to change location at least twice, and in the spring of 1581 was at Stonor Park and was being used to print Campion's *Decem rationes*, his apology for the Catholic faith; see 'Persons, Robert', in *ODNB*.

of Campion in July of 1581, he withdrew to Michaelgrove in Sussex[45] and in August arrived safely in Rouen, where he was secretly given shelter in the house of Michel de Monchy (de Monsi), one of the powerful clerical figures in the city.[46] No records, I think, survive to suggest that he encountered any of the Bridgettine sisters while he was in England, though he must certainly have known of their existence there. In Rouen, where Syon moved in mid-July of 1580, he must have visited them, or at the very least been in contact, since he spent time in Rouen until September of 1585 when he departed for Rome.[47] Some time in early 1589, in the wake of the Spanish Armada, he was sent to Spain, where he was instrumental in founding the English seminary at Valladolid, and where he stayed until September 1596, when he was recalled to Rome, and there remained for the rest of his life as rector of the English College. Obviously a very able administrator, Persons was even more noted as a writer; his *Christian Directory* is thought to have been 'one of the most widely dispersed and influential English books of spirituality of the post-Reformation period'.[48]

Our interest in Persons stems from the time he was in Spain. One of his roles there had been to assist displaced students from seminaries in France, a task for which he had obtained the support of Philip II.[49] He also realised that through the printed word, he could explain the plight and needs of the English students to their uneasy Spanish hosts – understandably after the defeat of the Armada.[50] As an extension of this, or a similar enterprise, Persons and Sir Francis Englefield solicited material concerning the 'wanderings' and

---

[45] Michaelgrove, or Michelgrove, was where the Catholic Shelley family lived; see *PSF* 8.5 (Sep.–Oct., 1960), 139.

[46] See John Bossy, 'The Heart of Robert Persons', in Thomas M. McCoog (ed.), *The Reckoned Expense. Edmund Campion and the Early English Jesuits* (Woodbridge, 1996; 2nd edn, Rome, 2007), pp. 187–207, at pp. 190–1. Bossy points out that de Monchy was involved in the Catholic 'semi-underground' which in 1585 became the Catholic League, and as a result of Persons's contact with him Persons became 'a Leaguer *avant la lettre*'. This alliance may in turn have influenced the Confessor General of Syon who also relied on the League.

[47] *The Wanderings of Syon* (see below n. 72) report that Father Foster, Syon's Confessor General, claimed that he knew Father Persons, 'a learned Jesuit', and reported that he had 'said Mass in our Church' and later on in Lisbon testified to the Archbishop on Syon's behalf (*PSF* 17.3 [May, 1909], 69–70).

[48] See 'Persons, Robert' in *ODNB*.

[49] Following the murder of the Duke of Guise and his brother the cardinal in 1589, and even a little before, France, where many English Catholics had moved on account of the deteriorating situation in the Spanish Netherlands, had become less safe and so many exiles looked to Spain to find refuge and places to study (see Rogers, 'Introduction', p. [i]).

[50] Persons first wrote a brief *Informacion* which he later incorporated in a book in Spanish published in 1590 in Madrid under the title *Relacion de algunos martyrios*. This account seems to have been a forerunner of Yepes's later *Historia*; see Rogers, 'Introduction', p. [ii].

hardships of the Syon community from Seth Foster, then Confessor General of Syon.[51] This most likely occurred some time in or shortly after 1594, when Syon moved from Rouen to Lisbon. In a Preface prepared for a detailed account of the move from Rouen to Lisbon, Persons constructed a brief overview of the entire history of Syon from its foundation to the arrival in Lisbon, giving particular emphasis to Syon's Lancastrian origins and connections so as to provide a strong rationale for their reception and safe sojourn in Portugal, whose royal house was of Lancastrian descent. In his conclusion to the 'history' of Syon, we see something of his rhetorical skill in the way he puts this political heritage to use:

> And now, considering the circumstances of these Religious, it certainly seems not to be without a mystery, that by the particular Providence of God they have been brought through so many travels and banishment to the kingdom of Portugal, there to repose themselves securely within the protection of the descendants of the House of Lancaster, and of the blood royal of their founder, King Henry the Fifth, who (as aforesaid) was the second king of that house: for the kings of Portugal descend in a right line from the royal house of Lancaster, Queen Philippa, daughter to John of Gaunt, Duke of Lancaster, and sister to Henry the Fourth, King of England, being wife to John the First, King of Portugal, and mother to Don Edward, his son and successor.[52]

In the course of his ongoing project of gathering material on the plight of English Catholics, Persons met Philip's confessor, Fra Diego de Yepes, a member of the influential Hermits of St Jerome, or Hieronymites (one of whose houses was the great monastery-palace of the Escorial, built near

---

[51] Persons's 'Preface' is reproduced as 'A Preface, Written by Father Robert Parsons, S.J., to the History of the Wanderings of Syon. From a Manuscript Preserved at Syon Abbey, Chudleigh' by Dom Adam Hamilton, OSB, in *The Angel of Syon. The Life and Martyrdom of Blessed Richard Reynolds, Bridgettine Monk of Syon, Martyred at Tyburn, May 4, 1535* (Edinburgh, 1905), pp. 97–113. Following the heading of the 'Preface' a rubric states: 'Preface collected by Father Parsons, from an information which the said Father Parsons and Sir Francis Inglefield sent for to our Father before the printing their Spanish Relation [*sic*]', p. 97.

[52] Quoted from Persons's 'A Preface' as reproduced in Hamilton's, *Angel of Syon*, p. 111. See also Warren, *Women of God and Arms*, for a discussion of how Persons's version of Syon's 'Lancastrianism' opposes that claimed by Elizabeth I and the reformers (pp. 152–4). I feel certain that the well-informed Persons would have been aware of the 'official' English claims, so that this may well have been a quite deliberate riposte. In addition, it appears, *pace* Warren (p. 154), that Henry VIII, for whom Henry V had been a role model in his piety and in his insistence on the state control of religion, left the closing down of Syon to Cromwell (who did so on the technical point of *praemunire*) and did not insist on receiving the keys or seal of Syon, so that Syon can justly claim a continuous existence.

Madrid, by Philip II). In a letter dated 3 October 1596, Yepes asked Persons for details about the recent history of Catholics in England, urging him to put down '*into writing*' every narrative available.[53] Book VI, the last book of Yepes's *Historia Particular de la Persecucion de Inglaterra*, includes a Spanish version of Persons's account of the foundation, institution and state of the monasteries of Syon and Sheen in England, and the fate of those who were subsequently forced to leave their native land.[54] The *Historia* was published in Madrid in 1599, and a comparison between Persons's 'Preface' and Book VI of Yepes's Spanish text, covering the period from Syon's foundation by Henry V in 1415 until their arrival in Lisbon on 20 May 1594, shows that the latter is almost a direct translation. In the Spanish edition, however, a number of small errors, usually involving numbers, have crept in.[55] In Yepes's *Historia*, the Syon material supplied by Persons served two main purposes: first, to urge support for the English religious refugees, and second, to serve as background to the Spanish translation of Sister Elizabeth Sander's second letter which follows.[56] It is not impossible that Persons exerted some 'editorial' influence on this letter, especially since he appears to have been its original translator;[57] it seems more 'literary' – and certainly more rhetorically forceful – than the first. Such intervention would indeed strengthen the case being made in Yepes's *Historia*.[58]

Before passing on to Persons's story of Syon's 'Wanderings' proper, I would like to mention the manuscript now in the library of the Duke of Norfolk at Arundel Castle which was compiled some time in the early 1620s, probably 1623, in Lisbon and dedicated to the 'Princess of Wales', who would be, it was hoped, the Infanta Maria of Spain, second daughter of King Philip III.[59] With the accession of James I in 1603, English-Spanish relations had

---

[53] Italics mine. Rogers points out that a great deal of the material was supplied by Joseph Creswell who stayed in Spain after Persons's departure for Rome in 1597 (actually Persons left Spain in September of 1596, see 'Persons, Robert', in *ODNB*; see Rogers, 'Introduction', pp. [iv–v].

[54] Yepes, *Historia*; the 'story' of Syon runs from p. 714 to p. 722; p. 723 is devoted to the Carthusians of Sheen (cf. the concluding part of Persons's 'Preface', pp. 112–13).

[55] The date of foundation has been mistakenly recorded as 1416 (Yepes, *Historia*, p. 715), while in Persons's English 'Preface' it is 1415, the correct date (p. 99); Henry VI is said to be nine years old on succession ('nueve años' –Yepes, *Historia*, p. 715), rather than 'nine months' (Persons, 'Preface', p. 98).

[56] Yepes, *Historia*, pp. 724–37. This is the complete second letter of Sister Elizabeth Sander which Hamilton translated back into English; it was printed in several issues of the *PSF* in 1894, as mentioned above (see p. 235 and n. 30).

[57] See above n. 29.

[58] This is a matter I plan to investigate further.

[59] See John Martin Robinson, 'Introduction', in de Hamel, *Syon Abbey*, pp. [3]–10, at p. [3].

begun to thaw, and somewhat later, during a period of particular rapproche-
ment, plans had been initiated for a marriage between the Infanta Maria and
Prince Charles. Syon, of course, had much interest in such a marriage since it
was expected it would pave the way for their return to England,[60] and so an
elaborate manuscript depicting in text and nine accompanying illuminations
the history of Syon had been prepared.[61] In this version of their story, the role
of Philip II in helping Syon over the years of their exile is highlighted, but the
narrative, though brief, seems very similar to the version of the foundation of
the Order by Henry V and the wanderings of the community following their
expulsion by Henry VIII in 1539 prepared by Persons from the material
supplied by Foster. The earlier version may once again have been adapted for
this new circumstance.[62] Unlike the earlier versions, however, this 'history',
whose purpose was never realised, remained, unseen by the outside world, in
the possession of Syon.[63]

In his 'Preface' Persons noted that in thirty-seven years, by which he must
have meant from 1559 to 1594 inclusive, the Syon community had 'changed
their habitation and country' eight times, 'all which time they have been in
exile and banishment from their so greatly beloved monastery of Sion'. He
concluded his recitation of the individual moves by noting: 'and at last from
Rouen to Lisbon, which last voyage is the subject of the following treatise'.[64]
The reference is clearly to a version of 'The Wanderings of Syon', and indeed

---

[60] One of the conditions stipulated by the Spanish (who had offered a very large dowry) had
been that Penal Laws be suspended and freedom of worship be granted to English Catholics
(see Robinson, 'Introduction', pp. 4–5).

[61] The actual history begins with the founding of the Order itself by St Bridget of Sweden
(mentioned in Persons's 'Preface', p. 99), who is the subject of the first illumination. The
founding of Syon, the subject of the second, is mistakenly dated 1413 in both the text accompanying the illumination and the 'Short Explanation of What the Following Pictures Show' (see
de Hamel, *Syon Abbey*, pp. 18, 30, 35, 37, 40).

[62] Persons had died in 1610, but Syon would undoubtedly have maintained strong connections
with the English College in Valladolid founded by Persons, and possibly also with the Spanish
court.

[63] The manuscript was brought back to England in 1809, when some members of Syon, fearing
an invasion of the Iberian peninsula by Napoleon, 'unofficially' returned. It was subsequently
bought from the nuns by the Earl of Shrewsbury, and on his death in 1856 passed to a descen-
dant, the Duke of Norfolk's third son, and has remained in the Arundel Castle library since that
time (see Robinson, 'Introduction', pp. 9–10). In 1991, the 600th anniversary of the canonisation of St Bridget, the manuscript was prepared for publication by the Roxburghe Club, and
appeared in 1993. Warren's suggestion that assertions concerning the English monarchy in this
text, which remained in the community of Syon, and Mary Champney's *Life*, which undoubtedly had some circulation but shows no evidence of ever being used politically, were a 'troubling
force' seems somewhat overstated; see *Women of God and Arms*, pp. 159–62, at p. 160.

[64] 'Preface', pp. 110, 111.

in his *Historia* Yepes alludes to a 'relacion' of this 'vltima peregrinacion' which indicates how God's providence preserved the community from their enemies.[65] In a note in *The Angel of Syon*, Dom Adam Hamilton stated that 'The Wanderings' were 'Never yet fully published in English', but that they survive in manuscript at Syon.[66] While this reference to 'The Wanderings' might seem confusing, [67] Hamilton's introductory remarks to his own edition make clear that he was referring to a longer version of the story written by someone in the community, since the original version (i.e. that given to Persons) was written in haste and was felt to be lacking completeness and 'defective in many things'.[68] The story in this 'revised' version of 'The Wanderings', to which Hamilton gave the title, *The Wanderings of Syon. A narrative of the vicissitudes of the Bridgettine community of Syon from 1559 to 1594. From a MS. at Syon Abbey*,[69] actually comprises a narrative describing events in Rouen in the 1580s, the subsequent hurried departure from Rouen, the incidents that occurred on the voyage to Lisbon, and the community's arrival there on 20 May 1594, and continues up to 1597.

Dom Adam Hamilton (1841–1908) had been educated at Stonyhurst and was ordained in England. He later went to Italy and in 1858 took his vows as a Benedictine at Subiaco near Rome. He spent a number of years in Italy, but

---

[65] Yepes, *Historia*, p. 722.

[66] Hamilton, 'Preface', p. 111n. The manuscript at Syon, as will, I hope, become clear, is not the one by Persons, but a longer, more extensive version of 'The Wanderings'.

[67] In his 'Preface', Persons is referring, not to the story published by Yepes in Spanish (which is, in effect, his 'Preface'), but to a separate narrative, undoubtedly the 'relacion' mentioned by Yepes (p. 722). This 'relacion' most likely was the one put together by Persons (from material supplied by Foster) and translated into Spanish by Carlos Dractan, a priest at Valladolid, which was published in Madrid in 1594 as the *Relacion que Embiaron las Religiosas del Monasterio de Sion de Inglaterra, que estaban en Roan de Francia, al Roberto Personio de la Compania de Iesus, de su salide de aquella cuidad, y llegada a Lisboa de Portugal. Traduizida de Ingles en Castellano, por Carlos Dractan, sacerdote Ingles del Colegio de Valladolid*. This account was quite likely taken from material that formed the first, 'defective' version of 'The Wanderings' (see below). There is a 'photographic' copy of the early printed edition of this *Relacion* at Valladolid; the actual edition (Madrid, 1594) is held in the Real Biblioteca del Monasterio de El Escorial in Madrid. I am grateful to Nancy Bradley Warren for drawing my attention to this work.

[68] See *PSF* 13.2 (April, 1905), 34. Hamilton also states that the nuns do not have a copy of the translation of the original version.

[69] Hamilton tells us in his 'Historical Preface' to *The Angel of Syon*, that he has faithfully transcribed the copy of the 'decayed' original made by one of the nuns in 1841 (p. 10). He, or an earlier copyist, must have adapted the title of Persons's 'Preface' since, as it is cited in *The Angel of Syon*, it appears to 'belong' to this longer version of 'The Wanderings', although the 'Preface' itself suggests otherwise (see above n. 51). This may result from proximity in the MS of 1841, for Hamilton notes that the 'Preface' follows the Life [of Reynolds] and has appended to it the note about the 'decayed' original (pp. 9–10).

then returned to England and taught theology at the college attached to the Benedictine monastery at Ramsgate. In 1881 he joined the community at Buckfast and was the only native English speaker at their refoundation in 1882. During the time he worked on their history, Syon Abbey was close by at Chudleigh. In editing *The Wanderings*, Hamilton kept the chapter divisions found in the manuscript, but, throughout, he modernised the spelling. He speculated, correctly as it first appears, that this version must have been written by one of the nuns,[70] and he suggested that the account was actually composed in about 1600.[71] All but twelve chapters were published in *The Poor Souls' Friend* from April 1905 until November 1909.[72] Preceding most of the monthly instalments of *The Wanderings of Syon*, Hamilton provided what he modestly termed 'a few notes ... to supplement the narrative'.[73] The notes or prefaces vary in length and consist of material gleaned from then available histories.[74] While the 'notes' fill in some of the events of the 1530s that form the background to the expulsion of the community from their house at Isleworth in 1539, they are quite comprehensive, even including details about some of the members of the Syon community.[75] Hamilton's edition begins with his notes on 'The Origin of the Wanderings', an account of the second closing of the house following the accession of Elizabeth and citing the entry from the *Diary* of Henry Machyn that describes the departure of the communities of Syon and Sheen on 4 July 1559.[76] Then, somewhat telescoping events,

---

[70] He bases this suggestion on a passage in chapter I in which the author seems to refer to the nuns as 'us': 'Of the nuns thus violently rejected some died in England, and others of us' (*PSF* 13.2 [April, 1905], 34; see p. 36 for the actual passage). There are other more compelling passages, however, such as 'we were but poor orphans, friendless and harmless women' (p. 36).

[71] *PSF* 13.2 (April, 1905), 34.

[72] Dom Adam Hamilton died on 12 December 1908, but the publication continued posthumously, completing what Hamilton had edited. With respect to the missing twelve chapters, Hamilton himself adds a note at the end of ch. 41: 'Some chapters previous to this one have been omitted, as being less suitable to this Magazine than to the publication of the *Wanderings* in book form' (*PSF* 15.5 [July, 1907], 128n). In the interest of brevity, this version of 'The Wanderings' edited by Hamilton and published in *PSF* from April 1905 to November 1909 will be referred to as *The Wanderings of Syon*.

[73] From the outset, it seems, Hamilton envisioned a future book, as indicated by his prefatory remarks: 'To each monthly section of the "Wanderings" I propose to prefix a few notes by way of preface, which will serve to supplement the narrative, and can be revised when the work appears in permanent form'; see *PSF* 13.2 (April, 1905), 34.

[74] A number of these histories are listed by Hamilton in the 'Historical Preface' to *The Angel of Syon*, pp. 1–10, especially pp. 8–9.

[75] Some of these latter notes may have formed the basis of Fletcher's very useful 'Syon's Who's Who'; see Nyberg, 'The Canon Fletcher Manuscripts', #12, p. 64.

[76] J. G. Nichols (ed.), *The Diary of Henry Machyn, Citizen and Merchant-Taylor of London, from A.D. 1550 to A.D. 1563*, Camden Society 42 (London, 1848), p. 204. The entry reads:

Hamilton moves forward to the request by Francis Englefield and Father Parsons for a narrative of the community's peregrinations, a request that did not, as we know, come for some time after Syon's arrival in Lisbon.

Hamilton's keen interest in Syon's history may have arisen during the period he had been Syon's spiritual advisor. When he died almost a year before the publication of *The Wanderings of Syon* in *The Poor Souls' Friend* was complete, he was called 'Syon's greatest friend', and though he served other communities, it was said that his 'work of predilection' was for the 'Daughters of St Bridget'.[77] Researching Syon's history and poring over its documents were clearly tasks he enjoyed,[78] and indeed in the 'Historical Preface' to *The Angel of Syon* composed on the Feast of St Bridget 1904, aware of the wealth of material available, he had written: 'At some future date the "History of the Wanderings of Syon" will no doubt be carefully edited.'[79]

John Rory Fletcher, Indefatigable Researcher

Despite having accomplished a great deal, during the last months when he was seriously ill, but aware that much was left to be done in recording the history of this remarkable community, Dom Adam Hamilton hoped to be able to continue his work, and one cannot help feeling that he would have been delighted had he known that another careful editor did take up the task. This was John Rory Fletcher (1861–1944), a Catholic convert, whose second – or even third – career became the work of collecting and documenting all possible material concerning Syon in both its pre- and post-Dissolution manifestations. His papers, now mainly held at the University of Exeter, form a magnificent resource for those interested in Syon Abbey and its history. Fletcher began his professional life in the medical field. He trained at Charing Cross Hospital, came first in his class at completion in 1886 and was immediately appointed House Surgeon at the same hospital. In 1887, at the age of twenty-six, he was received into the Catholic Church, but continued his medical practice until the death of his mother in 1899, when he began studying for the priesthood. He was ordained in 1902, and until 1931 he

---

'The iiij day of July, the Thursday, the prests and nuns of Syon whent a-way, and the Charter-howsse [referring to Sheen]'. In 1559, 4 July actually fell on a Tuesday, but the dates for June and July 1559 in the diary are not entirely in order.

[77] See *PSF* 16.12 (Feb., 1909), 320–5, at pp. 322, 321.

[78] Before he began editing *The Wanderings*, he had contributed a number of articles to the early volumes of *PSF* (beginning at vol. 1, no. 5 and continuing intermittently until he began his edition), under the title, 'Chapters from the Chronicles of Syon Abbey'.

[79] 'Historical Preface', p. 8.

carried out pastoral work and kept up his medical interests. From 1921 until 1939, he was a member of the Council of the Catholic Record Society as a result of a long-time fascination with Recusant matters.

I have not been able to determine exactly when his contact with Syon Abbey began, but on his patronal feast, 24 June, in 1923, he was admitted into the fraternity of the abbey as a brother of the chapter, or *frater ab extra*, as such members are referred to at Vadstena, the Order's mother house.[80] The illuminations on his certificate of fraternity were done by Sister M. Veronica, at the time the youngest member of the Syon community. Sister M. Veronica was Canon Fletcher's cousin; and in a note on the day of his admission as a brother of the chapter, he mentions that he clothed her and took her temporary vows.[81] At about this time, or perhaps earlier, Canon Fletcher began what became extensive research on Syon Abbey.[82] In 1933, he published *The Story of the English Bridgettines of Syon Abbey*,[83] an indispensable guide, but since it was intended as a popular book, its scant documentation belies the knowledge and scholarship that lay behind it, material that is readily available in his numerous notebooks. Tore Nyberg, himself a major historian of the Bridgettine Order, in 1960 published a catalogue of Fletcher's notebooks and drew attention to their importance: 'Canon Fletcher was no mere dilettante. ... The main importance of [his] work lies in the careful and necessary investigations on Syon Abbey history in many public libraries and archives in England.'[84] It was not until the mid-1930s when he was in his mid-seventies that Fletcher began recording his findings and writing his 'serious' history in the dated notebooks now on deposit at the University of Exeter.[85] *The History of Syon Abbey* can be found in volumes 3 to 9 of Nyberg's list, and in September of 1957, just over thirteen years after his death, it began to be

---

[80] As E. A. Jones noted on hearing the first version of this paper, J. R. Fletcher's career path was to some extent similar to those of a number of the pre-Dissolution brethren, especially of the late fifteenth and early sixteenth centuries, who left successful professional careers in ecclesiastical office, or at Oxford and Cambridge, to join the Order.

[81] Sister M. Veronica, herself a preserver of memories of twentieth-century Syon, died on 22 April 2008, just one week short of her ninety-fourth birthday; some of her fine illuminated work can be found in Syon's archives.

[82] Material on Canon Fletcher was generously provided by Lady Abbess from the archives at Syon Abbey; some of the details of his early life were included in an appreciation, 'From the Archives: a distinguished priest of the diocese – Canon Rory Fletcher', by Father Michael Clifton, the diocesan archivist of Southwark, where Fletcher was a canon of St George's Cathedral (clipping from an undated publication of the diocese, Syon archives).

[83] It was published by Syon Abbey, see above n. 5.

[84] Nyberg, 'The Canon Fletcher Manuscripts', p. 58; for full details, see above n. 16.

[85] Fletcher noted his starting date: 'I begin this history on the feast of St Bernard, 20th August 1935, in the seventy-fifth year of my age' (*PSF* 5.5 [Sep.–Oct., 1957], 139.

printed in *The Poor Souls' Friend*.[86] As before, the printed version fails to do justice to Fletcher's detailed research, and again Professor Nyberg cautions: 'The printed passages, however, only contain a few of the original notes and references to authorities. For research the material ought to be studied in the abbey itself [where the notebooks then were].'[87]

Having introduced John Rory Fletcher as another 'careful editor', I would like to turn again to the account of *The Wanderings of Syon* edited by Hamilton. The matter of the author – or presenter – of this story of Syon during their time in Rouen and their 'escape' to Lisbon seems to be more complicated than at first glance. During the course of publication, Hamilton seems to have changed his mind, since in his view the narrative voice appears to shift as the story proceeds; ultimately the work of Fletcher is helpful here. At the outset, as we have seen, the writer certainly seemed to have been one of the nuns,[88] but at the end of chapter 61 the description of preparations for a potential conflict with another ship creates some doubt: 'We all put red caps on our heads, and pikes in our hands like mariners, to make a show that we were many to affright them, or else to die for our company, viz. the Sisters.'[89] Yet a note states: 'From this chapter it is quite clear that the Narrative was written by one of the Monks, but not by Fr. Foster.'[90] Unlike Hamilton, however, I do not think the matter is entirely clear, especially considering the earlier very distinct references indicating a female voice.[91] Instead, I think

---

[86] Printed under the title, *The History of Syon Abbey*, the work is described by the editor of *PSF* as 'a fully documented manuscript history of our monastery and community' (*PSF* 5.5 [Sep.–Oct., 1957], 139); its publication continues on and off up to the last number of *PSF* 16.3 (May–June, 1968), 75–86; it continues into the new journal, *Syon*, but only for one or two issues – this journal produced only a few numbers.

[87] Nyberg, 'The Canon Fletcher Manuscripts', p. 59.

[88] See above, n. 70. Hamilton actually suggested that it might have been either Ann or Barbara Wiseman, whose names appear on a list of the community dated 1607, since from other evidence the Wiseman sisters were known to have had 'literary training'; see *PSF* 13.2 (April, 1905), 34.

[89] See *PSF* 16.7 (Sep., 1908), 190.

[90] *PSF* 16.7 (Sep., 1908), 190n. The voice in chapter 61, however, resembles that of an omniscient narrator, and the only person who could have known all that was taking place in the various parts of the ship was Father Foster himself. Earlier, in his prefatory remarks to ch. 29, Hamilton had noted: 'From the language used in the ensuing chapter it is clear that Fr. Foster was not the writer of the "Wanderings," as the writer addresses the nuns, it looks as it [*sic*] the writer were one of the monks' (*PSF* 13.11 [Jan., 1906], 305). The voice is indeed confusing in this chapter concerning the accomplishments and death of Abbess Bridget Rooke; but one can observe that the pronouns 'you' and 'your' are used when events that occurred before Foster joined the community are being mentioned; then in lamenting the loss of Abbess Rooke in 1594 (well after Foster had come to Syon), the pronouns become 'we', 'us', 'ours' (*PSF* 13.11 [Jan., 1906], 305–6).

[91] See above p. 245 and n. 70.

that Fletcher found the most probable solution: 'I have no doubt that it was written by Father Foster or at his dictation.'[92] Fletcher noted that Hamilton eventually thought the 'author' was one of the three brothers who came from Rouen to Lisbon. Listing their names, Fathers Vivian, Marsh and Kemp, Fletcher suggested the likelihood of Kemp, a Calvinist convert, on account of the wealth of Old Testament illustration. From internal evidence, Fletcher also suggested a later date for the account, and, linking the timing to 'authorship', provided his rationale. Hamilton had suggested a date of about 1600,[93] but Fletcher noticed a reference in the manuscript to George Birket 'afterwards Archpriest in England'; Birket succeeded the deposed Archpriest Blackwell in 1608 and served in this position until his death in 1614.[94] In addition, Fletcher speculated that *The Wanderings of Syon* (in this rendering) had been written as a response by Foster to scandalous accusations made against him by Thomas Robinson, who had been at the community in Lisbon in 1616–17, and who in 1622 had published an inflammatory, anti-Catholic pamphlet, *The Anatomie of the English nunnery at Lisbon in Portugall Dissected and laid open by one that was sometime a younger brother of the conuent, 1622.*[95] Fletcher therefore suggested a date of composition between 1622 and 1628, the date of Foster's death.[96] Tellingly he added: 'I think one cannot read the present account without recognizing that it is the Apologia of Fr Foster – Dom Hamilton admitted this – and one might add, a panegyric of "our Father".'[97] Any reader of the account quickly becomes aware of the repeated use of 'our Father'; as Fletcher pointed out, it 'dominates every page'. Moreover, the account itself begins, not when Syon arrives in Rouen in 1580, but with the arrival of Father Foster in early 1584.[98] At that time Syon was without a Confessor General, since the last, Thomas Willan, had died on

---

[92] Fletcher devoted several pages to the topic; see 'The Syon Manuscript "The Wanderings of Syon" ', *PSF* 14.3 (May–June, 1966), 81–4, at p. 83.

[93] See above, p. 245, n. 71.

[94] Birket (1549–1614) had been one of Blackwell's assistants; he was made Archpriest because in 1607 Blackwell had taken the oath of allegiance to the crown; see 'Birket [Birkhead], George', in *ODNB*.

[95] STC 21123–6. For a response to the actual pamphlet, see BL, MS Add. 21203 fols 42v–55 (16 Dec. 1622). Robinson seems to have 'infiltrated' the monastery at a time when male postulants were needed, but from what we know of his history he does not seem to have had any genuine intention of becoming a Catholic priest, as he may have led Foster to believe; see 'Robinson, Thomas', in *ODNB*. The timing of the pamphlet also seems to have coincided with the marriage negotiations between Prince Charles and the Spanish Infanta, something the English Protestants were very much against.

[96] Seth Foster died in Lisbon on 24 May 1628.

[97] *PSF* 14.3 (May–June, 1966), 83.

[98] In fact, in ch. 2 Foster is actually quoted as saying: 'In this work, I ... will ... only relate ... that which I have heard with my ears, seen with my eyes, and have passed through mine own

22 February 1583, and the only brother was an elderly Marian priest, Father John Johnson, who had become a Bridgettine.

During this period, Foster, as we learn, had been preparing for the English mission at Douai (then in Rheims), and on his way to Paris to complete his training he broke his journey at Rouen where he met the Bridgettines and learned of their plight. In response to the urging of some of Syon's English supporters, and of the community itself, he obtained permission from Cardinal Allen to relinquish his training and enter the Bridgettine Order, which he did on 8 March 1584. Owing to the circumstances of Syon, after a relatively short time he became professed as a brother and on the same day, 15 August 1584, he was elected the twelfth Confessor General. Much of this story is included in *The Wanderings of Syon*,[99] as are accounts of the sufferings his mother, a Catholic, endured in England, of his own dreams, of his narrow escapes from death, and so forth. This version of Syon's history ends in early 1597, just as Syon is about to receive a brief from Pope Clement VIII putting the community under his protection rather than that of the ordinary of Lisbon, as would have been Syon's customary practice.[100] Removal from the jurisdiction of Portuguese ecclesiastical authorities, as Fletcher astutely observed, was exceedingly fortunate for Syon, for among other things, it allowed the community to remain English; thus they were not, like other religious houses in Portugal, suppressed by lay power.[101] While *The Wanderings of Syon* does provide interesting detail about Rouen at the time of the League and the two sieges (1589 and 1591–2), the account mainly centres upon Father Foster himself and, concerning the Syon community, aims to show 'that our preservation was rather divine than human'.[102] It seems virtually certain, as Fletcher suggested, that the narrative was composed under the firm guidance of Father Seth Foster. I myself wonder if the occasional confusion of voice may be attributed to the strong possibility that the person actually recording the story and ultimately responsible for its final form was indeed one of the nuns.[103]

---

hands'; he claimed St John as his source (*PSF* 13.3 [May, 1905], 68). Perhaps he was thinking of John 3:32: 'And what he hath seen and heard, that he testifieth ....'

[99] Fletcher, however, corrected one or two of the details in his 'Who's Who', vol. III; this is reproduced in *PSF* 15.4 (July–Aug., 1967), 109–14.

[100] Bridgettine Rule stipulated that the ordinary of the place in which the monastery was situated was the superior; this had been the case in Flanders and in France, but troubles in Portugal had required that a different arrangement be made while the community was in Lisbon; see Fletcher, *Story*, p. 117.

[101] Fletcher, *Story*, p. 118.

[102] See *PSF* 13.2 (April, 1905), 35, also 36.

[103] We also know that over the years it was the sisters who made new copies as the old ones wore out; see Fletcher, *PSF* 14.3 (May–June, 1966), 82.

Unlike *The Wanderings of Syon*,[104] Canon Fletcher's *History* and the scholarly research involved in its production have much to reveal. His spade work in locating, transcribing, and annotating documents, letters, manuscripts, and so forth, which, as he tells us, took place in his spare time over a period of twelve years, affords a rich resource for scholars and others interested in many aspects of Syon Abbey and its community from events in 1405 that lay behind its foundation in 1415 and continuing up to the last years of Canon Fletcher's life which ended during the war in 1944.[105] Research since that time, the discovery of previously unknown material, new editions of letters, manuscripts, and so forth, now make it necessary to update Fletcher's research; nevertheless, his numerous volumes of notes and transcriptions, including a 'Who's Who' of Syon, a work begun on 5 August 1942, completed on 5 March 1943, and then sent out of London to the safety of Syon Abbey in Devon, offer an abundant legacy for future labourers in the Syon vineyard. Even so, Fletcher's *History* still remains what was once described as 'one of the most precious possessions of the Library of Syon'[106] – only now, in the safe-keeping of the Old Library of the University of Exeter it is easily accessible for the increasing number of scholars who seek to learn more about the unique history of Syon Abbey and the English Bridgettine Order.[107]

[104] The actual text, that is. Fletcher very often acknowledges and includes the work of Hamilton in his own, as does the later compiler of Fletcher's *History* (e.g. *PSF* 6.6 (Nov.–Dec., 1958), 176–82).

[105] Archbishop Richard Scrope was executed on 8 June 1405, and Henry IV's part in this lay behind the original impetus to found religious houses, a task taken up by his son, Henry V. Fletcher began to write in August 1935 and continued working more or less until the time of his death on 27 February 1944. While his twelve years of research would have been those prior to 1935, he must have continued some research while writing – especially in the years before the outbreak of war – as corrections in his notebooks and elsewhere seem to indicate.

[106] *PSF* 5.5 (Sep.–Oct., 1957), 139.

[107] This survey of historians has necessarily been selective, with the chief focus on those associated with the Syon community. The pioneering work of G. J. Aungier in *The History and Antiquities of Syon Monastery, the Parish of Isleworth, and the Chapelry of Hounslow* (London, 1840) was an important source for Hamilton and Fletcher, and Fletcher's annotated copy is in the Rare Books Room of St Michael's College, University of Toronto.

APPENDIX

Syon Abbey's Books at the University of Exeter

Since 1989, when the Syon community decided to relocate from Marley House itself to new accommodation created from a courtyard of former farm buildings on the estate, the nuns have been entrusting their manuscript and printed books to the keeping of the University of Exeter, where they are held in Special Collections. Further details may be found at: http://library.exeter. ac.uk/special.

In 1989–90, as part of the preparations for that move, the community's collection of printed books was catalogued by Marion Glasscoe and Claire Johnson. The books were arranged in sixteen classes, as follows: A Early books, B Bibles, C Liturgy, D Saints' lives, E Theology, F History, G Swedish, H Fiction, J Poetry, K Drama, L Non-fiction, M Reference, N Marian literature, O Art, P Periodicals, R Children's literature. Among the materials associated with this catalogue is a file listing the books kept by each sister in her cell for personal use during the year 1989–90. The catalogue and its associated papers are now EUL MS 265.

In September 1990, more than 1,100 books printed before 1850 (classmark A in the classification described above) were deposited with the University. The earliest dated volume is a 1513 edition of Jerome's letters printed by Nicolaus de Benedictis at Lyon (Syon Abbey 1513/JER/X). All but a few of the books post-date Syon's exile, and they are a rich resource for the study of counter-reformation and later Catholic print culture. Many volumes, like the Borromeo testament noted in our introduction, have been inscribed or anno-tated, and in some cases supplemented with handwritten material, by their Bridgettine readers. These books are included in the Exeter University Library catalogue with the classmark Syon Abbey.

At the same time, the University received thirty-five notebooks containing the handwritten notes of John Rory Fletcher, whose work on Syon's history is discussed in the essay in this volume by Ann Hutchison. Some consist of lists and brief notes on Syon gathered from a wide range of published and unpub-lished sources; others are chapters of the detailed history of Syon that Fletcher wrote during the 1930s and 1940s, but which is available in print in the form only of the popular history he produced early in his work on the abbey in

1933, and in the partial serialisation published in the *Poor Souls' Friend* from 1957 (see above pp. 247–8). There is an account of the Fletcher manuscripts by Tore Nyberg, 'The Canon Fletcher Manuscripts in Syon Abbey', *Nordisk Tidskrift för Bok- och Biblioteksväsen*, 47 (1960), 56–69. They were still at Syon when Nyberg described them, but are now EUL MSS 95/1–35.

The present volume arises from a symposium that was conceived to celebrate the arrival at Exeter in 2004 of Syon's medieval and early-modern manuscripts. They are now grouped under the shelfmark EUL MS 262, as follows:

262/1	Processionale, mid-15th century
262/2	Horae S. Trinitatis, mid-15th century
262/3	Breviarium, 14th or 15th century
262/4	Horae, 15th century, first half
262/5	Horae, early 15th century
262/6	Breviarium, 15th century, first half
262/7	Sermo de Sancta Anna et alia, 15th century, second half
262/8	Missale Hollandicum, 16th century
262/9	Officium parvum Beate Mariae, 15th century
262/10	Breviary, 17th century
262/11	Antiphonale, 17th century
262/18	A looking glace for the religious, 16th century or 17th century

MSS 262/1, 2, 4 and 6 were part of the library of the medieval Syon, though none has been in the abbey's continuous possession: they were all reacquired in the twentieth century (see the list of manuscripts in de Hamel, *Syon Abbey*, pp. 122–3, nos, 68, 78, 77, 79). MSS 262/1–7 are described in N. R. Ker and A. J. Piper, *Medieval Manuscripts in British Libraries, Vol. IV: Paisley – York* (Oxford, 1992), pp. 335–48 (from which the datings given above are taken), and also by James Hogg, 'Brigittine Manuscripts Preserved at Syon Abbey', *Studies in St. Birgitta and the Brigittine Order*, 2 vols (Salzburg, 1993), pp. 228–42 (pp. 228–32).

A further collection of manuscript fragments that were discovered in one of the attics of Marley House during preparations for the move of 1990 do seem to have been in Syon's possession since the Middle Ages. They are now EUL MSS 262/fragments 1–8. The leaves are taken from liturgical manuscripts and had been used as wrappers for other material, even though (as James Hogg noted) 'several of the folios display the remnants of very fine illuminated initials and other decorations' ('Brigittine Manuscripts', p. 232). There is an account of them in Hogg ('Brigittine Manuscripts', pp. 232–3), and a detailed list in Ker and Piper (*Medieval Manuscripts*, pp. 348–9), though their descriptions do not correspond to the fragments' present numbering. The eight fragments are listed as follows by de Hamel (nos. 81–5, *Syon Abbey*, pp. 123–4):

fragments 1–2, 4	from the Rule of St Saviour
fragment 3	from the Additions to the Rule
fragments 5, 6, part of 7	from lectionaries
part of fragment 7	from a breviary
fragment 8	from a gradual

Finally, in 2009, a further 180 manuscripts in two sequences were deposited with the University; they are catalogued as MSS 262/add. 1 mss 1–157 and 262/add. 2 mss 1–24 They date between the sixteenth and the twentieth century, and are mostly devotional in character – copies and translations into English of prayers, meditations, saints' lives and the like – plus some liturgical material and notes on the history of the abbey. There is a typescript handlist of add. 1 mss 1–157 and a bound manuscript register of add. 2 mss 1–24. The latter was printed by Hogg, 'Brigittine Manuscripts', pp. 233–42.

Syon Abbey still retains its collection of modern printed books, its archive, and some manuscript treasures, including the Marian deed of restoration.

INDEX

The index includes individual authors and works in manuscript or printed before 1700 if they are of Syon authorship, or if there is some discussion of their contents or ownership; texts mentioned only in lists of books and catalogue entries are not included. Works by Syon brothers appear under their authors' names.